4

Springer Series in Electrophysics
Volume 1

Edited by King Sun Fu

Springer Series in Electrophysics

Editors: Günter Ecker Walter Engl Leopold B. Felsen

Volume 1 **Structural Pattern Recognition**
By T. Pavlidis

Volume 2 **Noise in Physical Systems**
Editor: D. Wolf

Volume 3 **The Boundary-Layer Method in Diffraction Problems**
By V. M. Babič, N. Y. Kirpičnikova

Volume 4 **Cavitation and Inhomogeneities in Underwater Acoustics**
Editor: W. Lauterborn

T. Pavlidis

Structural Pattern Recognition

With 173 Figures

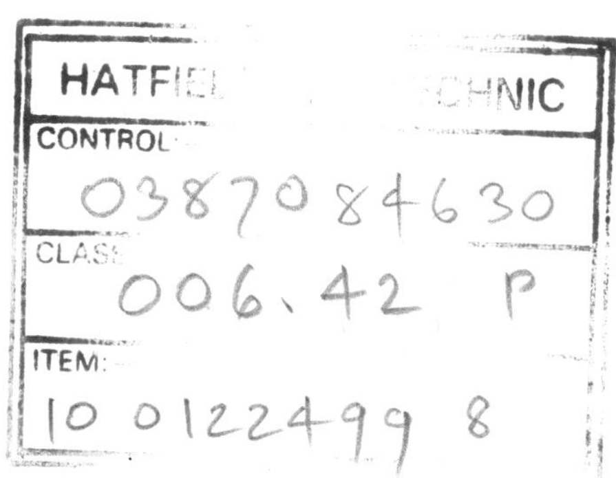

Springer-Verlag
Berlin Heidelberg New York 1977

Theodosios Pavlidis, PhD

Department of Electrical Engineering and Computer Science, Princeton University
Princeton, NJ 08540, USA

Volume Editor:

Professor King Sun Fu, PhD

School of Electrical Engineering, Purdue University,
West Lafayette, IN 47907, USA

Series Editors:

Professor Dr. Günter Ecker

Ruhr-Universität Bochum, Theoretische Physik, Lehrstuhl I,
Universitätsstrasse 150, D-4630 Bochum-Querenburg, Fed. Rep. of Germany

Professor Dr. Walter Engl

Institut für Theoretische Elektrotechnik, Rhein.-Westf. Technische Hochschule,
Templergraben 55, D-5100 Aachen, Fed. Rep. of Germany

Professor Leopold B. Felsen, PhD

Polytechnic Institute of New York, 333 Jay Street, Brooklyn, NY 11201, USA

Second Printing 1980

ISBN 3-540-08463-0 Springer-Verlag Berlin Heidelberg New York
ISBN 0-387-08463-0 Springer-Verlag New York Heidelberg Berlin

Library of Congress Cataloging in Publication Data. Pavlidis, Theodosios. Structural pattern recognition. (Springer series in electrophysics; v. 1). Bibliography: p. Includes index. 1. Pattern perception. I. Title. II. Series. Q327.P39 001.53'4 77-21105

Offset printing and bookbinding: Zechnersche Buchdruckerei, Speyer
2153/3130-54321

To Marion

Preface

This book originated from the classnotes of a one-semester course which I have been teaching and which has been attended by both graduate students and undergraduate seniors in Computer Science and Electrical Engineering at Princeton University. During the lectures I have been emphasizing the process by which pictorial data are transformed into mathematical structures suitable for further processing by statistical or syntactic techniques. This emphasis is reflected in the choice of material for this book. I have endeavored to show that what is commonly referred to as "feature generation" can be performed in a systematic way without excessive reliance on heuristics and intuition.

Since pattern recognition is a fledgling field with a great deal of flux in methodology, it is difficult to select specific subjects to include in a one-semester course or a book of limited size. I discuss statistical pattern recognition only briefly because it seems to have reached maturity and is treated by many good texts and monographs. On the other hand, I have tried to cover thoroughly the various approaches to shape analysis, including the medial axis transformation, the method of moments, Fourier descriptors, the chain code, polygonal approximations, decompositions, integral projections, etc. There exists a significant literature on all these topics but they are not usually included in texts or monographs. Here, picture segmentation is discussed in a general way stressing data structures: region adjacency graphs, the "pyramid", etc. The related algorithms are described in terms of logical predicates allowing their adaptation to segmetation according to a variety of criteria. This can be useful in areas such as texture analysis where there are no generally acceptable criteria and one might want to experiment with different techniques. I have also tried, as much as possible, to give detailed listings of the various algorithms so that they can be implemented in most high level languages without too much difficulty. I hope that this will make the book useful to both students and researchers.

During the writing I was fortunate to receive the aid of many people: I would like to thank the editor of this volume, Professor K.S. Fu, for our many discussions, both in my previous research on structural pattern recognition and during the writing of this book. C.M. Bjorklund and T. Bock were very helpful with their careful reading of the manuscript at various stages. Their suggestions led to many improvements in form and substance. My treatment of the relaxation methods benefitted from discussions with S.W. Zucker and S.L. Davis. Many of the examples have utilized software written by S.L. Horowitz or F. Ali. Special thanks are due to A.W. Evans for his excellent artwork. The cooperation of Dr. H. Lotsch of Springer-Verlag in various editorial matters is very much appreciated. The original manuscript was prepared with the help of the Unix software on the PDP11/45 machine of the Department of Electrical Engineering and Computer Science, and when this was not available, on the machine of the Statistics Department. The support of the National Science Foundation, and in particular the Bioengineering and Automation program headed by N. Caplan, is gratefully acknowledged. And last, but not least, I want to thank my wife Marion and my children Paul, Karen and Harry for their patience and support while I was preoccupied with my writing.

Princeton, New Jersey, September 1977 *T. Pavlidis*

Addition to the Second Printing

I want to thank K. Abend and C. Arcelli for pointing out a number of errors in the first printing.

Berkeley, California, June 1979 *T. Pavlidis*

Picture Acknowledgements

Thanks are due to the following individuals and organizations for permission to reproduce figures from their publications:

Association for Computing Machinery, Inc., for Fig. 4.15, 4.16, 5.1, 5.7-5.16, 7.27, 8.14-8.16, 10.14.
S.L. Horowitz for Fig. 8.14 and 8.15.
M.H. Hueckel for Fig. 4.15 and 4.16.
Institute of Electrical and Electronic Engineers, Inc., for Figs. 2.3, 5.2, 7.9, 7.10, 7.21, 7.22, 7.23, 7.29, 7.30, 9.12, 9.28, and 10.7.
International Business Machines Corporation for Figs. 9.1 and 9.2.
R. James for Fig. 1.1.
L. Kanal for Fig. 8.16.
I. Tomek for Figs. 7.21-7.23.
Figures 4.2, 4.5, 5.7, 5.8 and 5.9 were originally produced by using an overprinting program developed by P. Henderson and S.L. Tanimoto.

Contents

1. Introduction

"Seeing is deceiving" M. LUCKIESH [1.9]

1.1 What We Mean by Pattern Recognition

The word *pattern* is derived from the same root as the word patron and, in its original use, means something which is set up as a perfect example to be imitated. Thus *Pattern Recognition* means the identification of the ideal which a given object was made after. This is a rather loaded definition and it touches on a number of deep questions. For one, it reminds us of Plato's ideas, the perfect forms which the objects of the real world are imperfect replicas of. In psychology, Pattern Recognition is defined as the process by which "external signals arriving at the sense organs are converted into meaningful perceptual experiences" [1.1]. This is also a rather complex definition, since it is difficult to define precisely what a "meaningful perceptual experience" is.

One major question is how the concept of the ideal, or pattern, is formed. This might be done either by a deductive or an inductive process. In the first instance, we asssume that the concept of the ideal is innate to the observer, in the other, that he *abstracts* the concept through the observation of many imperfect examples. This process may also be called *learning: With a teacher,* if the examples shown are labeled as representing one or more given ideals. *Without a teacher,* if no such labeling is available.

The mental processes, by which these tasks are achieved, are obviously complex and not too well-known. Pattern recognition is a process performed not only by humans, but also by animals, and has a definite survival value in an evolutionary sense. Indeed, "abstraction" or "idealization" allows an organism to cope with new situations in a similar manner as was proven necessary by previous experience with situations of the same type. For lower (in the biological sense) organisms, "abstract concepts" may be limited to *Danger, Food, Mate*. Higher organisms obviously have richer repertories. The biological importance of pattern recognition points out the possibility that the nervous systems of humans and animals have developed very efficient circuitry. We may generalize this observation by saying that the nervous system is far more efficient in handling tasks which have survival value than tasks which do not. Thus is not surprising that humans perform very complex pattern recognition tasks quite easily, but have great difficulty with, for instance, multidigit multiplication.

The advent of the digital computer about thirty years ago made available a machine which far exceeds the human capacity for complicated numerical operations. The natural question was, then, whether this machine would prove as capable for nonnumerical operations, in particular mental functions like pattern recognition. Problems of the latter category were generally lumped under the term *Artificial Intelligence*, although a more appropriate name might be *Machine Intelligence*.

Today we may say that the early optimism was not justified. In retrospect, that is not at all surprising, especially in view of the biological argument. The human brain possesses a far higher degree of complex organization than the most advanced computers. The fact that the "human computer" is not well-suited for numerical operations is to be expected, since the ability to perform such operations had no adaptive advantage (in the biological sense) until the last century. The existence of a machine outperforming humans in those tasks does not imply at all that the general "computing" power of the machine exceeds that of humans. It would have been an amazing coincidence if this had been the case.

The above discussion might have been of purely intellectual interest if it were not for the fact that Mechanical Pattern Recognition is of great practical interest. There are many "tedious" jobs whose automation involves pattern recognition: Mail sorting and inputing data to computers both require recognition of typed or handwritten letters. Blood cell counting, inspection for quality control, and assembly of mechanical parts require general shape recognition. Similar requirements are found in the analysis of aerial and satellite pictures, bubble chamber photographs in nuclear physics, automated radiograph scanning, etc. At the time of this writing, some of these problems have been solved. There are commercially available machines which read by optical means printed or typed text of a limited variety of fonts. Blood cell counters are currently field tested. However, many other problems still remain open.

Before going on, we state here a few useful definitions. Pattern recognition is obviously related to *Classification*, where an object must be assigned to one of many classes. The two processes are not equivalent since we may have one without the other. In this discussion we will use the term "classification" to mean assignment to classes, each one of which corresponds to a pattern. We should also distinguish between pattern and *property*.

The latter term is broader, and might be taken to include pattern as a special case. The term pattern has traditionally been used to describe aggregates of complex properties. A systematic discussion of the psychological aspects of pattern recognition is outside the scope of this work. For that the reader is referred to the excellent introductory text by LINDSAY and NORMAN [1.1].

1.2 Various Approaches to Pattern Recognition

Because of its practical importance, pattern recognition has been a very active field. A short historical review is in order. Many of the earlier attempts have used in essence a "Gestalt" approach. Whatever the input object was, it was represented by an array of numbers which were the results of various measurements performed on the raw data. These numbers could be interpreted as coordinates of points in a vector space which is why the term *geometrical* is often used to describe this approach. *If* the proper measurements have been made, then it may happen that points corresponding to objects coming from the same pattern are close to each other in terms of geometrical distance. Then the pattern recognition problem becomes one of finding the regions in space where points from a single pattern lie. According to our earlier discussion, this would also be called classification. The term *statistical pattern recognition* is also used, since the methodology for solving such problems is based on the theory of probability and statistics.

There is a considerable literature in this area, and for this reason we shall touch upon it only briefly, in Section 10.2, mostly to give pointers to appropriate references. At this moment we may point out some of the major strengths and weakness of the geometrical approach. On the positive side, one has available a large variety of algorithms, well-documented and analyzed, which can be used successfully, if the "right" measurements have been made. However, this is a very big "if". In general the method provides no guidance about what measurements to make. There are ways for finding the most appropriate ones from among a large candidate set (the process is often called *feature selection*), but one must first find such a set. This *feature generation* must be performed on the basis of other considerations, perhaps physical models of the objects.

This difficulty was recognized as early as 1960, leading a number of investigators onto a different approach. The basic idea was that *a complex pattern could be described recursively in terms of simpler patterns*. For example, letters of the alphabet can be described in terms of strokes [1.2,3]. This recursive description is quite similar to the way a phrase of text is described in terms of its words and, for this reason, much of the methodology of formal languages was found to be applicable. Therefore, the terms *linguistic pattern recognition* and *syntactic pattern recognition* were used to describe the methodologies based on this idea. NARASIMHAN [1.4] and LEDLEY [1.5] were among the first to develop grammatical parsers for pattern recognition. Later, SHAW developed a picture description language and applied it to the analysis of bubble chamber photographs [1.6]. The subsequent years saw great activity along these lines. The reader is referred to the text by FU [1.7] for a thorough treatment of the topic.

The application of the theory of formal languages was only one aspect of the methodology. The major reason for its promise was probably the fact that the intuitive or physical definitions of patterns could be used to generate descriptions appropriate for processing by computer. In essence, the *structure* of the objects was used for their description. The use of syntactic techniques was important but it was not really the defining point. Thus, in the late sixties, the term *structural pattern recognition* came into use [1.8].

Structural pattern recognition has as its goal the derivation of descriptions of objects using mathematical models suitable for further processing. Such processing should be relatively simple. If syntactic tools are to be used, the corresponding grammars should be easily parsable. If the geometric description is to be used, the points corresponding to objects of the same class should be tightly clustered according to a simple metric. Note that the last statement implies that structural descriptions need not be recursive. However, most of the interesting methodology is concerned with the recursive case.

1.3 Structural Representation of Objects

In order to process any type of information by computer, one must first quantize it, i.e., express it in terms of numbers. This generally results in large volumes of data. For example: A picture can be divided by a grid into sufficiently small regions where the brightness and color are uniform as far as our measuring instruments are concerned. Then it can be represented by two matrices. The elements of the first could be code numbers corresponding to the color of the respective grid squares while the elements of the second could be measures of light intensity. An electrocardiogram can be sampled at discrete time intervals and represented as an array of the amplitudes of the waveform at those times. Such an array is a quantized waveform. The condition of some mechanical equipment can be expressed by a collection of quantized waveforms describing temperature, oil pressure, etc., as functions of time, plus other individual measurements. The condition of a patient can also be described by a collection of waveforms (electrocardiogram, electroencephalogram, etc.), numbers (temperature, blood counts, etc.), and logical variables (describing the presence or absence of symptoms). Though such descriptions preserve all the available information, they are too detailed to be of any direct use.

The effort involved in handling this *raw information* without preprocessing is very great. Therefore it is necessary to express the objects under consideration in a more compact way, yet without any loss of information, if possible. In a sense this is an encoding problem and it is the first step in any pattern recognition algorithm. Obviously, the representation depends strongly on the type of data. For example, a waveform can be expressed through the coefficients of a series expansion. The same is possible for a picture (hologram), though other possibilities exist. One would be to divide the picture into the largest possible regions of constant color and light intensity and then describe it in terms of the boundaries of such regions. Either of these two types of representations does not necessarily involve any loss of information, and any loss which may occur is controlled. For example, a waveform consisting of 512 sample points can be expressed in terms of 512 Fourier coefficients (256 sine and cosine terms). Low amplitude harmonics can be ignored, further reducing the size of the representation. In this case, the error introduced can be kept under strict limits. Also, in a piecewise constant approximation of the brightness function on a picture, one can enlarge the regions by allowing greater brightness variations from the average over each region.

Such representations should be distinguished from other reduction schemes, such as optical page readers which represent letters by binary vectors indicating the incidence or absence of certain configurations from the character image. The same representation could be obtained from images with very diverse visual shapes. It is only when such measurements are restricted to typed English characters that they become meaningful shape descriptors. Pattern recognition problems where the objects come from a great variety of sources cannot be treated in such a way.

There is another reason for avoiding representations which result in an "uncontrolled" loss of information. A machine designed to read English text in this way would be at a complete loss when faced with text in the Slavic or Greek alphabet even though the few new characters are formed in ways not very different from those of the English alphabet (e.g., И and N or T and П. Many additional new measurements may be necessary to represent the new symbols. Consider, on the other hand, an information preserving scheme, based on stroke representation. One would need to add only as many more descriptors as new characters. These would be essentially class definitions rather than preprocessing functions, and therefore the modification of the machine would be trivial. Besides the direct economics of the situation, the use of general descriptors has the advantage of allowing the development of a general theory of description for a wide class of objects. Instead of having to solve many variations of the same problem from scratch, one solves a sequence of problems from the general to the specific. Variations of the goal would necessitate new solutions only for some of the subproblems. The price that one must pay is that such general representations may be more difficult to implement than ad hoc measurements. This can be circumvented by solving each problem theoretically in general and then devising special implementations. Illustrations of this point will be given later in the text.

1.4 Pictorial Pattern Recognition

Some of the most challenging pattern recognition problems occur when the data are in the form of pictures. The subject presents a special challenge to structural pattern recognition because the physical basis of human visual perception is not well-known. The existence of *optical illusions* suggests that we are dealing with a highly complex process and that a mechanistic treatment of visual information would be inadequate without taking into account higher level mental process [1.1,9]. In general, pictorial pattern recognition involves the following steps:

a) *Picture Sampling and Quantization:* A scene or a photograph is transformed to an array of numbers, suitable for processing by computer.

b) *Picture Segmentation:* Regions of the picture with uniform brightness, color, or texture are identified.

c) *Scene Analysis:* The regions obtained from the segmentation are merged or modified so that they can be identified with objects.

d) *Shape Description:* The objects are encoded into a quantitative structure reflecting their shape.

e) *Object Description:* This may be simple classification (e.g., the object seen is classified as the letter "A") or verbal description (e.g., the object seen consists of two discs joined by a horizontal line).

The first step definitely belongs in the area of signal processing in general and picture processing in particular. Thus we will not discuss it at all in the sequel because it lies outside our scope. Whenever we discuss pictures we will assume that we are given a function of two variables $f_c(x,y)$ describing the brightness of the color, or spectral band, c at the point (x,y). For monochromatic pictures, the subscript c will be omitted. In practice, the variables x and y are discrete, but sometimes we will assume them to be continuous for the sake of mathematical convenience. The domain of this function will be denoted by R, and will always be assumed to be finite and bounded. Usually it will be a rectangular array. Picture segmentation lies on the boundary between Image Processing and pattern recognition. Thus it will be the first problem which we will discuss in detail. Then we will proceed with scene analysis, shape description and object description. It is probably obvious that, at least in the process of human pattern recognition, these steps are interacting. If an initial segmentation produces results which yield "strange" shapes, a new segmentation may be performed. A good illustration of the phenomenon is provided by Fig.1.1. In technical terms one may speak of a *bottom up* approach if no prior knowledge of the subject is used during segmentation. If such knowledge is used

Fig. 1.1 Most observers perceive this picture as a more or less random black and white pattern. The mention of the word "Dalmatian" introduces immediately organization into the perceived scene (photograph by Ron James)

then the term *top down* is commonly used. We will discuss both techniques in the sequel.

In addition to bottom up and top down approaches, we will classify the various proposed methodologies for each of the above steps according to the mathematical techniques used. On the other hand, we will not structure our discussion according to the origin of the data, i.e., whether they are biomedical pictures, alphanumeric characters, satellite photographs of the earth, etc. Many of these applications can be handled by common routines and it is our goal to provide a set of methodologies from which the most appropriate ones for each application might be chosen. In this treatise we will stretch the term "pictorial" to include waveforms which must be treated according to their shape.

1.5 Future Prospects for Pattern Recognition

The variety of areas of applications may cause one to wonder whether a general approach to Pattern Recognition is at all possible. This book is based on the assumption that an affirmative answer exists. The problem can be expressed in general terms and a general methodology can be developed. Of course, the engineer or scientist must exercise his judgment for choosing the right tools to use in each particular case. General methodologies cannot substitute for poor judgment or lack of imagination. But they can help one to avoid reinventing the wheel. In the previous section we distinguished five major steps. These are necessary for all pattern recognition problems, although their relative importance varies. Thus high contrast, noise-free pictures simplify the segmentation problem. Highly stylized data simplify the classification problem, etc. Much of the past research has been application oriented and work in character recognition, for example, proceeded independently from work in automated cytology, or work in the interpretation of natural scenes. A careful reading of the literature reveals many common methodologies and approaches, often hidden under different terminology. Curve and surface fitting, graph theory, theory of formal languages, have all been used in addition to the standard statistical and signal processing techniques.

In many earlier studies simplicity of the algorithms used has been emphasized. This certainly simplifies the design procedure but does little else. As a rule the simplicity of the algorithm has little to do with its speed of execution. The Fast Fourier Transform is a prime example of this.

It is far more difficult to program than the classical transform but much faster. Another example can be found among the sorting algorithms where there is an almost inverse relation between program length and speed of execution. Of course, complexity in itself is not a virtue, but we should not be surprised if some of our pattern recognition algorithms turn out to be quite complex (given the ambitious goal) nor expect them to be necessarily slow in execution time. Even if a complex algorithm has significant computational requirements, it may still be useful. We are in the midst of rapid technological developments in the areas of computer hardware and architecture, accompanied by substantial decreases in the cost of computing equipment. It will probably not be too long before parallel computation becomes an everyday reality. Such prospects should encourage us not to shy away from complex algorithms, especially if the following two requirements are met: they can be implemented by parallel computers and their computational complexity is either a linear or, at most, a low order polynomial function of the size of data. The latter is particularly important for the following reason. During research and development algorithms are often tested on relatively simple or small size pictures. They may be found to have *prohibitive* costs on more complex or larger pictures. If the increase in the cost is linear, then an advance in technology which results in a tenfold increase for given costs will also increase the practical power of the algorithm by a power of ten. On the other hand, if growth of the requirements is exponential, the same technological advance will have hardly any effect. As an extreme example let us consider a chess playing program. There is an exponential growth of computing time as a function of the number of moves the program looks ahead. Let us assume that with each extra move the time increases by a factor of ten. Then a tenfold increase in the speed of the hardware will result only in one move increase in the look ahead tree.

1.6 A Note on the Format of Algorithms

The algorithms in this book are described in a structured format based on blocks. In the main text, or within the algorithms themselves, statements are referenced through their block number and their number within the block. The basic control structures are:

```
While (condition) do block xx.
   Begin block xx;
      .........
      Statements
      .........
   End block xx;

x. If (condition) do block xx.
   Begin block xx;
      .........
      Statements
      .........
   End block xx;

_. Else do block yy.
   Begin block yy;
      .........
      Statements
      .........
   End block yy;
```

x, xx, and yy stand for statement and block numbers. Such structures can be translated easily into those of any high level languages. Readers familiar with ALGOL, PL/I, or C can ignore the reference numbers and implement directly the block structures. For example, in C all statements "Begin block ..." are mapped into the symbol "{", and all "End block ..." into "}". Those using FORTRAN will have to rely on the numbers.

The block structure has not been followed in the case of some very long algorithms, like 2.1.

2. Mathematical Techniques for Curve Fitting

2.1 On the Mathematical Representation of Pictorial Data

As we pointed out in the previous chapter, the brightness matrix of a picture must be transformed into a more compact mathematical structure before we can proceed with any pattern recognition analysis. Curve and surface fitting is a popular technique in many branches of engineering and computer science when large volumes of data must be described in a compact way. We describe a number of such techniques in this chapter. Sections 2.2-4 deal primarily with least integral square error approximations of functions of a single variable over their whole domain. Section 2.5 discusses uniform approximations (i.e., those minimizing the maximum pointwise error). Splines and piecewise approximations are introduced in Section 2.7 and their properties are investigated in Sections 2.8-12. Readers may prefer to skip this chapter, except possibly Section 2.6, on first reading and refer to it whenever its material is used in the sequel. Section 2.6 discusses some of the problems associated with the application of curve fitting techniques to pattern recognition and their relation to transforms.

It is probably worthwhile to discuss here a question of a general nature before proceeding any further. In many cases, one comes across mathematical methods which claim to solve a problem provided that the data have a certain regularity. For example, a minimization algorithm may converge only if the cost function is continuous. Although the mathematical definition of continuity is precise, its practical interpretation is not always so. In applications one always deals with discrete data of the form $\{t_i, f_i\}_1^N$ for functions of a single variable or $\{x_i, y_j, f_{ij}\}_{11}^{MN}$ for functions of two variables. Such data can be always embedded into a continuous function f(t) so that

$$f(t_i) = f_i$$

where f(t) is not only continuous but also has continuous derivatives. We shall describe methods for doing so in Section 2.7. On the other hand, there exist properties (such as convexity) for which no such embedding is possible. In general, it is easy to decide whether our data can fit the required regularity conditions. A more difficult question is whether a method is amenable to implementation in a discrete form. Consider, for example, the following problem: Let $f(t)$ be a positive (i.e., $f(x)>0$), continuous, increasing function on the interval $[a,b]$. We want to find a point x such that

$$\int_a^x f(t)dt = \int_x^b f(t)dt \quad . \tag{2.1}$$

This problem always has a unique solution, and the reader can think of a number of ways for finding it. Let us now consider its discrete version. We assume that $\{t_i,f_i\}_1^N$ is such that

$$f_i > f_{i-1} > 0 \quad \text{for all } i \quad , \tag{2.2}$$

and search for an index j such that

$$\sum_{i=1}^{j} f_i = \sum_{i=j+1}^{N} f_i \quad . \tag{2.3}$$

Usually no such solution exists. If the problem is modified to require that the difference between the two sums is less than some constant δ, it may still have no solution (if δ is chosen to small) or it may have more than one (if δ is chosen too large). The correct modification is to search for a j such that

$$\left(\sum_{i=1}^{j} f_i - \sum_{i=j+1}^{N} f_i\right)\left(\sum_{i=1}^{j+1} f_i - \sum_{i=j+2}^{N} f_i\right) \le 0 \quad . \tag{2.4}$$

Difficulties of this nature tend to occur quite often in the implementation of iterative schemes. Even if they converge in the continuous case, many of their discrete versions will tend to cycle. With proper care though, these difficulties can be avoided. In the sequel we will use continuous and discrete formalism interchangeably, depending on which one is more convenient. A special type of problems occurs in translating concepts from continuous geometry into discrete. These questions will be discussed in Chapter 3.

2.2 The Basics of Curve Fitting

For most of this chapter, we assume that we are given a set of discrete points

$$\{t_i, f_i\} \quad i = 1,2,\ldots N \quad , \tag{2.5}$$

and that we are looking for a "smooth" function g(t) of the form

$$g(t) = \sum_{j=1}^{m} a_j b_j(t) \quad , \tag{2.6}$$

approximating the discrete data. As a rule, m is taken to be significantly less than N. The functions $b_1(t), b_2(t), \ldots b_m(t)$ can be powers of t, polynomials, exponentials, trigonometric functions, etc. They must be *linearly independent*, i.e., there must exist no set of coefficients $v_1, v_2, \ldots v_m$, not all of them zero, such that

$$\sum_{j=1}^{m} v_j b_j(t_i) = 0 \quad \text{for} \quad i = 1,2,\ldots N \geq m \quad . \tag{2.7}$$

It will also be necessary to define measures of the quality of approximation. The following are two of the most commonly used.

a) Integral square error E_2 given by:

$$E_2 = \sum_{i=1}^{N} [f_i - g(t_i)]^2 \quad . \tag{2.8}$$

b) Maximum error E_∞ given by:

$$E_\infty = \max_i |f_i - g(t_i)| \quad . \tag{2.9}$$

Approximations minimizing E_∞ are called *uniform*, and they show a closer fit to the individual points. Those minimizing E_2 have a better "average" fit. The difference between the two can be seen in the case of approximation by a constant, i.e., when m = 1 and $b_1(t) = 1$ for all t. Substituting (2.6) into (2.8) and differentiating with respect to a_1 then yields as a necessary condition for E_2 to be a minimum:

$$2\sum_{i=1}^{N}[f_i - a_1] = 0 \quad ,$$

or

$$a_1 = \frac{1}{N}\sum_{i=1}^{N} f_i \quad . \tag{2.10}$$

On the other hand, the quantity $\max_i \{|f_i - a_1|\}$ is minimized when a_1 is half-way between the maximum and the minimum of f_i, i.e.,

$$a_1 = \frac{1}{2}[\max_i\{f_i\} + \min_i\{f_i\}] \quad . \tag{2.11}$$

Thus the value of f_i at a single point can significantly affect the approximation under the E_∞ norm. This may or may not be desirable, depending on the application. For many types of data, though, the two criteria give very similar results. For example, if $f_1, f_2, \ldots f_N$ are normally distributed and N is sufficiently large, the values of a_1 given by (2.10) and (2.11) should be very close. It is easier computationally to find the approximation when E_2 is minimized, than when E_∞ is. There exist closed form expressions for the first problem but only iterative methods for the second. We shall describe both techniques in subsequent sections.

Equations (2.8) and (2.9) evaluate the pointwise error along one of the coordinate axes and therefore are more appropriate for waveforms than for curves of arbitrary orientation. In the latter case it is more natural to measure the error along the normal to the curve or to g(t). However, this creates a number of analytical difficulties. The treatment of such schemes will be postponed until Section 7.9.

In order to avoid cumbersome expressions, we introduce some vector notation to be used in the rest of the chapter. Overlined expressions represent column vectors of N components, and underlined ones column vectors of m components. In particular, we define:

$$\bar{f} = \mathrm{col}[f_1, f_2, \ldots f_N)] \quad . \tag{2.12a}$$

$$\bar{g} = \mathrm{col}[g(t_1), g(t_2), \ldots g(t_N)] \quad . \tag{2.12b}$$

$$\bar{b}_j = \mathrm{col}[b_j(t_1), b_j(t_2), \ldots b_j(t_N)] \quad j = 1,2\ldots m \quad . \tag{2.12c}$$

$$\underline{a} = \mathrm{col}[a_1, a_2, \ldots a_m] \quad . \tag{2.12d}$$

We also define an $m \times N$ matrix B whose rows are the transposes of the vectors $\bar{b}_j$, i.e.,

$$B_{ij} = b_j(t_i) \quad . \tag{2.12e}$$

Under this notation (2.6) becomes

$$\bar{g} = B'\underline{a} \quad , \tag{2.13}$$

where the prime (') denotes the transpose of a matrix. Also, (2.8) can be written as

$$E_2 = (\bar{f}-\bar{g})'(\bar{f}-\bar{g}) \quad . \tag{2.14}$$

When $N \to \infty$, the vector space of the overlined vectors becomes a Hilbert space. This is the usual framework in most advanced texts dealing with approximation theory [2.1-5].

2.3 Integral Square Error Approximation

In order to find the optimal approximation we must first differentiate (2.14) with respect to the vector $\underline{a}$. It is best to do this in two steps. First we evaluate δE_2, the difference in E_2, caused by a change δg in $\bar{g}$.

$$\begin{aligned} \delta E_2 &= [\bar{f} - (\bar{g}+\delta\bar{g})]'[\bar{f} - (\bar{g}+\delta\bar{g})] - (\bar{f}-\bar{g})'(\bar{f}-\bar{g}) \\ &= -2(\bar{f}-\bar{g})'\delta\bar{g} + \delta\bar{g}'\delta\bar{g} \quad . \end{aligned} \tag{2.15}$$

Then we observe that the change caused in $\bar{g}$ by a change in the vector $\underline{a}$ is

$$\delta g = B'\delta\underline{a} \quad . \tag{2.16}$$

We may now substitute (2.16) into (2.15) and let the difference $\delta\underline{a}$ go to zero. Then we find that the gradient of E_2 with respect to $\underline{a}$ is

$$\operatorname*{grad}_{\underline{a}} E_2 = -2(\bar{f}-\bar{g})'B' \quad . \tag{2.17}$$

Setting this quantity equal to zero and substituting $\bar{g}$ from (2.13), we find the defining equation for the coefficient vector $\underline{a}$ to be

$$BB'\underline{a} = B\bar{f} \quad . \tag{2.18}$$

We show now that the matrix BB' is positive definite. Indeed, (2.7) implies that, for any nonzero vector $\underline{v}$

$$\underline{v}'B \neq \underline{0}' \quad . \tag{2.19}$$

This means that the norm of the vector $B'\underline{v}$ (the transpose of the above) will always be positive, or

$$(B'\underline{v})'(B'\underline{v}) = \underline{v}'BB'\underline{v} > 0 \quad \text{if } \underline{v} \neq 0 \quad . \tag{2.20}$$

The last inequality shows that the $m \times m$ matrix BB' is indeed positive definite. Therefore (2.18) can be solved with respect to $\underline{a}$ to yield

$$\underline{a} = (BB')^{-1}B\bar{f} \quad , \tag{2.21}$$

and

$$\bar{g} = B'(BB')^{-1}B\bar{f} \quad . \tag{2.22}$$

If $N = m$, then the matrix B is square (and also nonsingular) so that $(BB')^{-1} = B'^{-1}B^{-1}$. Equation (2.22) then yields $\bar{g} = \bar{f}$, implying $E_2 = 0$. In this case, $\underline{a}$ can be thought of as the *transform* of $\bar{f}$ under (2.21), with (2.13) giving the *inverse transform*. We should point out that the preceding results are valid when N goes to infinity, i.e., for the continuous case. Indeed, N appears only as a summation index in (2.21) and (2.22). If $N \to \infty$ we need only replace the sums by integrals and work in a *Hilbert space* rather than a finite dimensional space. To be specific, the jk^{th} element of the matrix BB' will be given in each case by:

$$(BB')_{jk} = \sum_{i=1}^{N} b_j(t_i)b_k(t_i) \quad , \tag{2.23a}$$

$$(BB')_{jk} = \int_0^T b_j(t)b_k(t)dt \quad , \tag{2.23b}$$

where we have set $t_1 = 0$ and $t_\infty = T$. Although the matrix BB' is positive definite, it has a very small determinant for many choices of the basis vectors. For example, if

$$b_j(t) = t^{j-1} \quad \text{(powers of t)} \quad , \tag{2.24}$$

then we find that, in the interval [0,1], the matrix BB' has the form

$$(BB')_{jk} = \frac{1}{j + k - 1} \quad . \tag{2.25}$$

Its determinant equals 1/12 for m = 2, 1/2160 for m = 3, and $1/(6\times10^6)$ for m = 4, making its inversion problematic. This difficulty can be bypassed by choosing *orthonormal* basis vectors. Eqs. (2.23) then show that the matrix BB' equals the identity matrix, so that (2.21) and (2.22) are simplified into

$$\underline{a} = B\bar{f} \quad , \tag{2.21'}$$

$$\bar{g} = B'B\bar{f} \quad . \tag{2.22'}$$

Notice that, in this case, the transpose of B equals its inverse. When N = m as well, the equations for the transform and its inverse are symmetric. The Fourier transform is a well-known special instance of those expressions. Fourier series also fit into this formalism by taking $m < N$ $(= \infty)$. Then the above discussion contains the well-known result that the coefficients of such a series are chosen in such a way as to minimize the integral square error of the remainder of the expansion. We shall discuss the overall question of transforms in Section 2.6. We conclude this section by giving the value of E_2 when $\underline{a}$ is chosen optimally, first for the general case, and then for an orthonormal basis:

$$E_2 = \bar{f}'\bar{f} - \underline{a}'BB'\underline{a} \quad , \tag{2.26}$$

$$E_2 = \bar{f}'\bar{f} - \underline{a}'\underline{a} \quad . \tag{2.26'}$$

Surface fitting can be treated in a similar way. If the data points are given as a matrix, then we can still present them as a vector $\bar{f}$ by concatenating the rows (or columns) of the matrix.

2.4 The Karhounen-Loeve Expansion and its Variants

It is natural to expect that the basis functions adapted to the problem lead to accurate approximations with fewer terms. The Karhounen-Loeve expansion [2.6,7] offers a means of doing just that. It derives the basis functions on the basis of a *statistical sample* of the data of interest. Using the notation of Section 2.2, we assume that we are given M such samples $\bar{f}_i$, $i = 1,2,\ldots M$. The $N \times N$ matrix

$$R = \frac{1}{M}\sum_{i=1}^{M} \bar{f}_i \bar{f}_i{}' \tag{2.27}$$

is an estimate of the *autocorrelation matrix* of the process generating $\bar{f}_i$. Let $\bar{e}$ be an *eigenvector* of R, so that

$$R\bar{e} = r\bar{e} \tag{2.28}$$

for an eigenvalue r of R. In general, R will have N such eigenvectors which can be chosen to be orthonormal. Any sample $\bar{f}_i$ can then be approximated by a sum of such eigenvectors. The relevance of this approach to our problem can be seen by the following example. Let

$$\bar{f}_i = \sum_{j=1}^{K} x_j^i \bar{v}_j + \bar{n}_i \quad , \tag{2.29}$$

where $\bar{v}_i, \bar{v}_2, \ldots \bar{v}_k$ are unknown but fixed orthonormal vectors, x_j^i independent random variables with zero mean, and $\bar{n}_i$ white noise with zero mean and unit variance. Then

$$R = \frac{1}{M}\sum_{i=1}^{M} \left(\sum_{j=1}^{K} x_j^i \bar{v}_j + \bar{n}_i\right)\left(\sum_{k=1}^{K} x_k^i \bar{v}_k + \bar{n}_i\right)' \quad . \tag{2.30}$$

If M is sufficiently large, then R is very close to the autocorrelation matrix. Elementary probability theory can be used to show that the above assumptions imply that (2.30) can be written as

$$R = \sum_{j=1}^{K} \sigma_j^2 \bar{v}_j \bar{v}_j{}' + I \quad , \tag{2.31}$$

where σ_j^2 is the variance of the random variable x_j and I the $N \times N$ identity matrix. It can be verified by direct substitution that $\bar{v}_j$ $(j=1,\ldots K)$ is an eigenvector of R with eigenvalue $\sigma_j^2 + 1$. Furthermore, R has only K (linearly independent) eigenvectors with eigenvalues greater than one. The eigenvectors corresponding to unit eigenvalues are all orthogonal to the set $\bar{v}_1, \bar{v}_2, \overline{\ldots v}_K$. Thus the Karhounen-Loeve expansion allows the retrieval of the information about the structure of the process generating the observed data.

Although the assumptions of this example are quite strict, they are not unrealistic for a number of practical problems. They basically mean that the data are generated as a mixture from the output of K sources. Even if the assumptions do not hold exactly this approach still gives useful results. However, one should be aware of a possible pitfall. If the eventual goal is separation of two classes, then finding the best basis for *representation* is not necessarily a good idea. Instead one should search for the best basis for *separation*. In other words we must look for functions which are likely to appear in the expansion of a signal from only one of two classes. Formally this can be handled as follows:

Let R_1 and R_2 be the autocorrelation matrices computed separately for each class. Then the autocorrelation matrix for both classes taken together will be

$$R = R_1 + R_2 \quad . \tag{2.32}$$

Now define an $N \times N$ matrix Q such that

$$QQ = R \quad . \tag{2.33}$$

It can be shown that R is semipositive definite (in a similar manner to the method used in Sec.2.3 for BB'), so that Q always exists. It can be found in a number of ways [2.8]. After Q is determined, we define two new matrices

$$S_1 = Q^{-1}R_1Q^{-1} \quad , \tag{2.34a}$$

$$S_2 = Q^{-1}R_2Q^{-1} \quad . \tag{2.34b}$$

These are normalized autocorrelation matrices and have the properties that

a) $S_1 + S_2 = I$ (the identity matrix)

b) They have the same eigenvectors $\bar{e}_1, \bar{e}_2 \ldots, \bar{e}_n$ which form an orthonormal set.

c) If $s_1, s_2, \ldots s_n$ are the eigenvalues of S_1, then the eigenvalues of S_2 are $1 - s_1$, $1 - s_2$, ... $1 - s_n$.

d) The above eigenvalues are all between zero and one.

Let s_1 be the smallest eigenvalue. Then the corresponding eigenvector $\bar{e}_1$ will offer a good possibility for discrimination. Indeed, let

$$\bar{w}_1 = (Q^{-1})'\bar{e}_1$$

be a basis function. Then its coefficient in the expansion of a signal $\bar{f}$ will be

$$c_1 = \bar{f}'\bar{w}_1 \quad ,$$

and one can show that, if $\bar{f}$ belongs to the first class, the expected value of c_1^2 is s_1, while if $\bar{f}$ belongs to the second class, its value is $1 - s_1$. Eigenvectors corresponding to eigenvalues near 1/2 will result in coefficients whose expected values are similar regardless of the class of $\bar{f}$. A "good" basis can be chosen from among the eigenvectors corresponding to eigenvalues near 0 or 1. If no such eigenvalues exist, then a different method for classifying the signals is necessary. The method has been used successfully in a number of applications, including the classification of biomedical data, engine signatures, pictorial data, etc. [2.9-15]. In addition, it is widely used in feature selection under the name of principal component analysis [2.6,7,16,17]. The major obstacle for its use in practice is the size ($N \times N$) of the matrix R. In a typical problem N can be up to 1000 and finding the eigenvectors and eigenvalues of such matrices is a very challenging computational problem. Large values of N are particularly common when the method is used for pictorial data. Certain approximate techniques have been suggested but they also require considerable computation [2.14].

2.5 Uniform Approximations

Approximations using the integral square error as a norm have the disadvantage that they may miss such details of the data as a "spike" of short duration. Uniform approximations do not suffer from that problem, but require more computational effort. This additional cost may be justified, depending on the application. The problem is that of finding a set of coefficients $a_1, a_2, \ldots a_m$ minimizing the error

$$e = \max_{1 \le i \le N} \left\{ \left| f_i - \sum_{j=1}^{m} a_j b_j(t_i) \right| \right\} \quad . \tag{2.35}$$

This can be expressed as a *linear programming* problem in the following manner [2.18,19].

Find an (m+1)-dimensional vector $\underline{v} = \mathrm{col}(e, a_1, a_2, \ldots, a_m)$ to minimize e, subject to the 2N constraints

$$\left.\begin{aligned} e + \sum_{j=1}^{m} a_j b_j(t_i) &\ge f_i \\ e - \sum_{j=1}^{m} a_j b_j(t_i) &\ge -f_i \end{aligned}\right\} \quad i = 1,2,\ldots,N \quad . \tag{2.36}$$

Since N is usually much greater than m, it is more efficient to solve the *dual* problem with 2N unknowns and only m + 1 constraints: Finding a 2N dimensional vector

$$x = \mathrm{col}(u_1, v_1, u_2, v_2, \ldots, u_N, v_N)$$

to minimize

$$F = \sum_{i=1}^{N} (u_i - v_i) f_i \quad , \tag{2.37}$$

subject to the m + 1 constraints

$$\sum_{i=1}^{N} (u_i + v_i) = -1 \quad , \tag{2.38a}$$

$$\sum_{i=1}^{N} (u_i - v_i)\, b_j\, (t_i) = 0 \quad j = 1,2,\ldots,m \quad . \tag{2.38b}$$

and the requirement that u_i and v_i are nonnegative for all i. In this case

$$e = -F \quad . \tag{2.39}$$

Note that the above formulation is what is often referred as the primal problem and the original is in the form of the dual [2.20]. Either way the solution of one of the problems can be used to find that of the other. From the theory of linear programming we know that all the coefficients u_i, v_i will be zero except for at most m + 1 of them [2.20]. These will correspond to locations where the local error equals the error norm (if $u_i \neq 0$) or the negative of the error norm (if $v_i \neq 0$). In this way, the simplex method of solving the linear programming problem corresponds closely to the exchange algorithm [2.21]. However, a detailed discussion of this point lies outside the scope of this work.

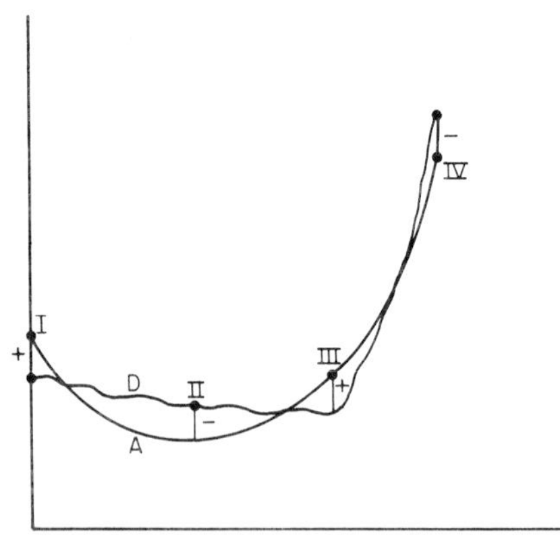

Fig. 2.1 Illustration of the equioscillation property of uniform approximations. The error at points I and III has the same magnitude as the error at II and IV, but opposite sign. A is an approximating parabola (m=3) for the data of the curve D

A fundamental property of uniform approximation is *equioscillation*, i.e., the maximum error is achieved at m + 1 points (at least) with alternating signs (see Fig.2.1) [2.1-5,21]. Thus, if $k_1, k_2, \ldots, k_r$ are the values of indices i for which u_i is nonzero, and $\ell_1, \ell_2, \ldots, \ell_p$ those for which v_i is nonzero, then either

$$k_1 < \ell_1 < k_2 < \ell_2 \ldots \quad , \tag{2.40a}$$

or

$$\ell_1 < k_1 < \ell_2 < k_2 \ldots \quad , \tag{2.40b}$$

with

$$r + p = m + 1 \quad . \tag{2.41}$$

We assume now that the basis functions have the so-called *Chebyshev property*, i.e., they are linearly independent for any choice of m + 1 points. (This is true for polynomials and trigonometric functions). Then the choice of a *basic feasible solution* for the linear programming problem corresponds to the choice of indices satisfying (2.41) and either (2.40a) or (2.40b). Because of the usual relative size of m and N, it is efficient to use the *revised simplex method* [2.19,20] for the solution of the problem. This leads to Algorithm 2.1.

Algorithm 2.1: Uniform approximation through linear programming

Input: Data points f_i, $i = 1,2,\ldots,N$. Basis functions $b_j(t)$, $j = 1,2,\ldots,m$.

Output: Coefficients of approximation a_j, $j = 1,2,\ldots,m$, maximum absolute error e (all as components of the vector $\underline{y}$), and locations where e occurs. (See text.)

Steps:

1: Set flag = 1 and choose a set of indices $k_1,k_2,\ldots,k_r$ and $\ell_1,\ell_2,\ldots,\ell_p$ satisfying (2.40a) and (2.41) (This determines uniquely the values of r and p).

2: If flag = 1, then define an $(m+1) \times (m+1)$ matrix

$$C = \begin{bmatrix} 1 & 1 & 1 & \\ b_1(t_{k_1}) & -b_1(t_{\ell_1}) & b_1(t_{k_2}) & \cdots\cdots \\ \cdot & \cdot & \cdot & \cdots\cdots \\ \cdot & \cdot & \cdot & \cdots\cdots \\ b_m(t_{k_1}) & -b_m(t_{\ell_1}) & b_m(t_{k_2}) & \cdots\cdots \end{bmatrix} . \tag{2.42a}$$

If flag = -1, then define

$$C = \begin{bmatrix} 1 & 1 & 1 & \cdots\cdots \\ -b_1(t_{\ell_1}) & b_1(t_{k_1}) & -b_1(t_{\ell_2}) & \cdots\cdots \\ \cdot & \cdot & \cdot & \cdots\cdots \\ \cdot & \cdot & \cdot & \cdots\cdots \\ -b_m(t_{\ell_1}) & b_m(t_{k_1}) & -b_m(t_{\ell_2}) & \cdots\cdots \end{bmatrix} . \tag{2.42b}$$

3: Invert the matrix C. Let d_{ij} be the elements of its inverse.

4: Define the (m+1)-dimensional vector $\underline{c}$ as having components $f_{k_1},-f_{\ell_1},f_{k_2},-f_{\ell_2}$, etc. if flag = 1; or $-f_{\ell_1},f_{k_1},-f_{\ell_2},f_{k_2}$, etc., if flag = -1.

Then compute the (m+1) dimensional vector $\underline{z}$ having components

$$z_i = \sum_{j=1}^{m+1} d_{ij}c_j \quad . \tag{2.43}$$

5: Find the maximum V of the terms

$$z_1 + \sum_{k=1}^{m} z_{k+1}b_k(t_i) + f_i \quad (i=1,2,\ldots,N) \quad , \tag{2.44a}$$

and let J be a value of i where it occurs. Also find the maximum W of the terms

$$z_1 - \sum_{k=1}^{m} z_{k+1}b_k(t_i) - f_i \quad (i=1,2,\ldots,N) \quad , \tag{2.44b}$$

and let K be a value of i where it occurs. If both V and W are nonpositive then *exit* by going to 11.

6: If $V \geq W$ set $P = 1$ and $i_0 = J$
If $V < W$ set $P = -1$ and $i_0 = K$.

7: If i_0 equals one of the indices $k_1,k_2,\ldots,k_r$ or $\ell_1,\ell_2,\ldots,\ell_p$ then set flag = -flag and *restart the algorithm* by going to 2. (Wrong guess of the sign of the errors at the points where the maximum value is reached).

8: Set $a_1 = 1$ and

$$a_{j+1} = Pb_j(t_{i_0}) \quad j = 1,2,\ldots,m \quad . \tag{2.45}$$

Then compute the vector

$$h = C^{-1}\underline{a} \quad . \tag{2.46}$$

9: Find the minimum of the ratios of the elements of the first column of C^{-1} divided by the corresponding element of $\underline{h}$ if positive (ignore terms for which h_i is nonpositive). Let j_0 be its location $(1 \leq j_0 \leq m+1)$.

10: Replace the j_0^{th} index of the sequence $k_1,\ell_1,k_2\ldots$ (or $\ell_1,k_1,\ell_2\ldots\ldots$) by i_0 and do the corresponding updating of the elements of the matrix C and the vector $\underline{c}$. Reorder the indices to satisfy (2.40a) (or(2.40b)) and *start a new iteration* by going to 3.

11: Optimal solution is found:

$$\underline{y} = -\underline{z} \quad . \tag{2.47}$$

The following remarks are pertinent. The variable "flag" denotes whether the error is positive at the first location where it is observed (if flag = 1) or negative (if flag = -1). If our initial guess is wrong, step 7 will cause a quick rectification. In view of (2.47), step 5 checks all points to verify that the maximum error is indeed less than its assumed value. If it is not, the point where it occurs is added to the basis, replacing one determined in step 9. It is not necessary to invert explicitly the matrix C. Instead, steps 3 and 4 may be combined to find the vector z by the Gauss elimination method. This requires $(m+1)^3$ operations, while in step 5, we must perform m multiplications, 2m additions (or subtractions) and 2N comparisons. It is well-known that the number of iterations in linear programming problems is usually of the same order as the number of constraints, i.e., m + 1 [2.20]. Thus the total computational effort is of order

$$T = A_1 m^4 + A_2 mN + A_3 \tag{2.48}$$

for some constants A_1,A_2, and A_3. The second term is usually the dominant one. Typically $m \leq 4$, while N could easily be 500. Furthermore, for a given m, the matrix C can be inverted explicitly in advance, so that the first term is even less significant. For example, for a linear approximation with $b_1(t) = 1$ and $b_2(t) = t$, we have

$$C^{-1} = \begin{bmatrix} r_2 - r_3 & -(r_2+r_3)\text{flag} & r_4\text{flag} \\ 1/2 & -1/2 & 0 \\ r_1 - r_2 & (r_1+r_2)\text{flag} & -r_4\text{flag} \end{bmatrix} , \tag{2.49a}$$

where if i_1,i_2,i_3 are the indices k_1,ℓ_1,k_2 or ℓ_1,k_1,ℓ_2, then

$$r_j = \frac{t_{i_j}}{2(t_{i_1} - t_{i_3})} \quad j = 1,2,3 \quad , \tag{2.49b}$$

$$r_4 = \frac{1}{t_{i_1} - t_{i_3}} \quad . \tag{2.49c}$$

This requires only 4 divisions and 4 additions or subtractions. Overall, the computational effort seems comparable to that of L_2 approximation where m sums over N points must be evaluated. However, there is a big difference. If the interval of approximation is modified slightly, it is easy to update the sums by looking only at the deleted and added points. In an L_∞ approximation it is necessary to reexamine all N points, unless the deleted points do not contain one where the maximum error occurs or the added points have pointwise errors less than e for the existing approximation. In such cases no updating is required. Unfortunately, these tend to be rare, since the maximum error often occurs at the endpoints of an interval (Fig.2.1).

2.6 Transforms and Space Domain Techniques

One of the major dichotomies in pictorial pattern recognition methodology involves the distinction between *transform* and *space domain* techniques. Because of the large size of the brightness matrix f(x,y) (usually over 256 × 256), an alternative representation of the data must be found before anything else can be done. One approach is to find a *transform* matrix g(k,ℓ) given by a relation of the form

$$g(k,\ell) = \sum_{x=1}^{N} \sum_{y=1}^{N} K(k,\ell,x,y)f(x,y) \qquad k,\ell = 1,2\ldots N \quad , \tag{2.50}$$

for some appropriate kernel K. If

$$K(k,\ell,x,y) = e^{\frac{-2\pi jkx}{N}} e^{\frac{-2\pi j\ell y}{N}} \quad , \tag{2.51}$$

we have the *Fourier Transform*. The hope is that g(k,ℓ) will be a sparse matrix and that the small number of its significant elements can be used as a *feature vector*. The discussions of the previous sections allow us to express the conditions when such an economy can be expected. Although our derivations were only for functions of a single variable, they can be extended to the two variable cases without any difficulty except for some more cumbersome notation. We refrain from doing this and instead present our fundamental argument in terms of the single variable case.

For an orthonormal basis, the value of a_j is independent of the values of $a_1,\ldots a_{j-1}$ as can be seen from (2.21'). Therefore, if we start with m = N and find that most of the a_i's are near zero, we can reorder the vectors of the basis so that all the small coefficients come at the end. Let m_0 be the index of the last significant coefficient. Then if we choose $m = m_0$ and repeat the process we will obtain the same result. Furthermore, $\bar{g}$ will be very close to $\bar{f}$. Equation (2.13) then implies that the input function is the sum of a smaller number of the basis functions. Transform representations are economical if and only if the input signal has that property.

Such an expectation is justified if the natural process generating the picture can be thought of as superposition of other processes. The transform methods became popular for the processing of one-dimensional signals because their fundamental assumption is satisfied in both electronic circuits and speech. It is not at all clear whether this is a realistic assumption for any other nontrivial cases. The human ear has specific frequency receptors, but there is no such evidence for the eye. Although the eye can discriminate spatial frequencies, that does not seem to be a primary operation. The lack of a rigorous justification for the universal application of transform techniques is further demonstrated by the fact that the behavior of most of the basis functions (polynomials, real and complex exponentials, etc.) in one part of their domain is related to that in other parts. As a matter of fact, they can be defined over the whole domain by their values in an arbitrarily small connected subintervals (in the continuous case) [2.1]. Since f(x,y) is a sum of only a few of them, it will also have the property that its behavior in one part of its domain is related to that of the others [2.1]. This is obviously not true for pictures which contain a number of physically unrelated objects.

It is, of course, well-known that this is the case, and considerable work has been done in *edge detection* and related topics, which attempts to divide a picture into parts where f(x,y) behaves in a more or less uniform way, perhaps dark versus light areas. Such approaches can be grouped under the heading of *space domain techniques*. A general theory for their treatment can be developed within the framework of a functional approximation. The problem of separating dark from light areas can be expressed as follows: If D is the picture domain, find a minimal partition of D into regions $D_1, D_2, \ldots D_n$. Such a partition can be found in one of two ways: By searching for the boundaries of the regions as curves where f(x,y) changes significantly (*edge detection*) or looking directly for the regions (*region analysis*). It seems that the first technique is preferable for high-contrast, low noise pictures, while the second is preferable for more "difficult" pictures. We will discuss these points in detail in Chapters 4-6. A general mathematical formalism for space domain techniques is possible under the theory of *splines*, which is described in Sections 2.7-12.

2.7 Piecewise Approximations and Splines

The previous sections have demonstrated the limitations of approximations by sums of "simple" functions. These limitations are often undesirable, not only in the context of pattern recognition, but also in many other areas of applied mathematics and computer science. A suitable extension is to divide the domain of the input data into a finite number of intervals and use a different approximation on each one of them. There are many special problems associated with such approximations, including the choice of the subintervals of the domain. We shall discuss these problems in the rest of this chapter, using the continuous formalism, i.e., assuming that the data are in the form f(t), rather than $\{t_i, f_i\}$. This results in a simpler notation, and it does not affect the results in any way.

Definition 2.1: For an interval of interest [a,b], we define a *partition* $\underline{x}$ to be a sequence of points $x_i (i=0,1,\ldots n)$ such that

$$a = x_0 < x_1 < x_2 < \ldots < x_n = b \quad . \tag{2.52}$$

The points with coordinates x_i are referred to in the literature by a number of names, including *knots, joints,* and *breakpoints.*

Definition 2.2: A *spline* $S_{\underline{x},m,r}(t)$ is defined as a function

$$S_{\underline{x},m,r}(t) = h_k(t) = \sum_{j=1}^{m} a_{kj} b_j(t) \quad \text{for} \quad x_{k-1} < t \leq x_k \quad , \quad k = 1,2,\ldots,n \quad , \tag{2.53}$$

such that

$$h_k^{(p-1)}(x_k) = h_{k+1}^{(p-1)}(x_k) \quad , \quad k = 1,2,\ldots, n-1 \quad , \quad p = 1,2,\ldots,r \quad , \tag{2.54}$$

where $h^{(q)}(t)$ denotes the qth derivative of h(t) with $h^{(0)} = h(t)$. If $r = 0$, there are no constraints at all. The above definition is broader than some of the definitions seen in the literature [2.5] and narrower than some others [2.22]. (It also assumes that the partition $\underline{x}$ is given).

There has been a variety of representations used for splines since they were formally introduced by SCHOENBERG in 1946 [2.23]. They have become a popular subject of mathematical research, and the reader is referred to the book by RICE [2.1] for an extensive discussion, as well as to the numerous literature on the subject [2.22-28]. They have found applications in a wide variety of fields, including the solution of differential and integral equations, statistical estimation, graphics, and computer controlled machine tools.

In general, the term *polynomial spline* is used when the basic functions are powers of t (like those given by (2.24)) or linear combinations of them. In this chapter, we deal only with such splines. The popular *cubic spline* is the special case with m = 4, r = 3. Piecewise constant approximations are also a (trivial) special case, with m = 1 and r = 0. We shall use the term "$(m-1)^{th}$ order spline" for one where the basis functions are polynomials with up to m - 1 powers of t. Note that Definition 2.2 provides r(n-1) constraints for mn unknowns. Even for the maximum meaningful value of r, which is m - 1, there are n + m - 1 degrees of freedom. A more economical description of splines will use only this number of parameters. This can be achieved by using the auxiliary function

$$x_+^j = \begin{cases} x^j & \text{if} \quad x > 0 \\ 0 & \text{otherwise} \end{cases} \quad . \tag{2.55}$$

Then we can write the spline equation as

$$S_{\underline{x},m,r}(t) = g(t) + \sum_{k=1}^{n-1} \sum_{j=r}^{m-1} s_{kj}(t-x_k)_+^j \quad , \tag{2.56}$$

where g(t) is defined in Section 2.2 and s_{kj} are coefficients reflecting the discontinuities at the knots. A more explicit, but far more complicated, expression for the spline can be given if we use the functional J(x,f) defined as the discontinuity of f(t) at t = x. Then

$$\begin{aligned} S_{\underline{x},m,r}(t) = & \sum_{j=0}^{m-1} S_{\underline{x},m,r}^{(j)}(x_0)\frac{(t-x_0)^j}{j!} \\ & + \sum_{k=1}^{n-1} \sum_{j=r}^{m-1} J[x_k, S_{\underline{x},m,r}^{(j)}(t)]\frac{(t-x_k)_+^j}{j!} \quad . \end{aligned} \tag{2.57}$$

This equation has as parameters the m values of the spline and its first m - 1 derivates at x_0 plus the (n-1)(m-r) values of discontinuities at the joints. For $r = m - 1$ this leaves exactly $n + m - 1$ degrees of freedom, and the second summation with respect to j does not appear since the only discontinuities are in the $(m-1)^{th}$ derivative. However, this economy has the disadvantage that the value of the spline at a point involves many more than the $m - 1$ coefficients required by (2.53).

Given a set of data $\{t_i,f_i\}$ for $i = 1,2...,N$, we may want to represent them by a spline in a number of ways. The simplest one is the *interpolating spline*, where we choose the knots to coincide with the data points, setting $n = N - 1$, and use as many continuity constraints as possible, so that $r = m - 1$. This fixes the value of the spline at $n + 1$ points, leaving only $m - 2$ constraints. If $m = 2$ this specifies completely a not very interesting first-order spline. For a cubic interpolating spline, we must specify two parameters, which are usually taken to be the directions of the tangents at the two extreme points. Interpolating splines are useful for display purposes where a "nice" curve can be shown in the place of discrete data points. They also allow us to map discrete data into continuous curves with continuous derivatives (of any desired order if we use high enough m). This, in turn, makes possible the application of results from the theory of continuous functions to discrete data. If the data are noisy, the interpolating splines usually show strong oscillations, and are not appropriate for further analysis. It is then best to use an *approximating spline*. The first problem then is the choice of the partition. It is a common experience among workers in the field that the "key to the successful use of splines is to have the location of the knots as variables" [2.1]. Ideally, one would like to leave them as free parameters to be chosen during an optimization procedure, but this turns out to be a very nasty mathematical and computational problem. One may chose a partition empirically and then proceed to choose the remaining parameters in order to minimize a certain error criterion. We will discuss such techniques in the next section. Later, we will attack the problem of the choice of a partition. This is a central problem when functional approximation is used in the context of pattern recognition.

2.8 Approximating Splines with Fixed Knots

We observe that (2.53) is linear with respect to the coefficients a_{jk}, and therefore the problem can be treated in a similar fashion as that of Section 2.3, if we choose to minimize the integral square error. The same is true when (2.56) and (2.57) are used. Using the last formalism, we may rewrite either one of them in vector form as follows:

$$\bar{g} = B'\underline{a} + \sum_{k=1}^{n-1} s_k \bar{b}_m^{+k} \quad , \tag{2.58}$$

where we have assumed $r = m - 1$ and we have simplified the notation accordingly. The vector $\bar{b}_m^{+k}$ is defined as having all its components zero up to K, which corresponds to the largest index such that t_K is less than x_k. The remaining ones are given by

$$b_m^{+k}(t_i) = b_m(t_{i-K}) \quad i > K \quad . \tag{2.59}$$

Here s_k is a scalar denoting the discontinuity in the last derivative, properly scaled. We observe now that the vectors $\bar{b}_m^{+k}$ are linearly independent from each other and from the $\bar{b}_1, \bar{b}_2, \ldots \bar{b}_m$ defined in Section 2.2. Therefore, we may form a new matrix C whose first m rows are those of B and whose remaining ones consist of the transposes of the $\bar{b}_m^{+k}$. We may also form a new coefficient vector $\underline{c}$, whose first m components are those of $\underline{a}$ while the remaining ones are the s_k's used in (2.58). Then (2.58) can be rewritten as

$$\bar{g} = C'\underline{c} \quad . \tag{2.60}$$

But this has exactly the same form as (2.13), and therefore all the results of Section 2.3 are applicable. Thus, at least in principle, finding an approximating spline for given knots is a straightforward process. In particular, we may find an orthonormal basis from the given vectors $\bar{b}_i$ and $\bar{b}_m^{+k}$ (i=1,2,...m and k=1,2,...n-1). Although this is the most obvious, it is not necessarily the most satisfactory approach from a numerical viewpoint [2.1]. An alternative way for finding approximating splines involves the use of B-splines as a basis [2.28]. Surface approximation by splines is a significantly more difficult problem than surface approximation by polynomials, unless there are no constraints. [2.29-32].

2.9 Piecewise Approximations with Variable Joints

I. General Properties

It is obvious that the choice of the location of the joints has a significant effect on the way a spline fits a set of data points or a given function (Fig.2.2). This point is particularly important for the subject of this book. The optimal location of the joints may indicate certain *features* of the input. Or, conversely, the features of the input determine the location of the joints. Thus a piecewise constant approximation can be thought of as an *edge detector*, where procedures determining points of discontinuity can be used to locate optimally the "joints" of a piecewise constant approximation. This is illustrated in Fig.2.3, which displays a raster scan from an electron microscope picture. One is interested in the location and size of the jumps in the concentration of sulphur. The large amount of high-frequency noise prohibits the use of simple differentiation. The noise may be eliminated by a linear low-pass filter, but this will also smooth out the jumps, with a resulting loss of information. The figure shows a piecewise constant approximation which overcomes these problems.

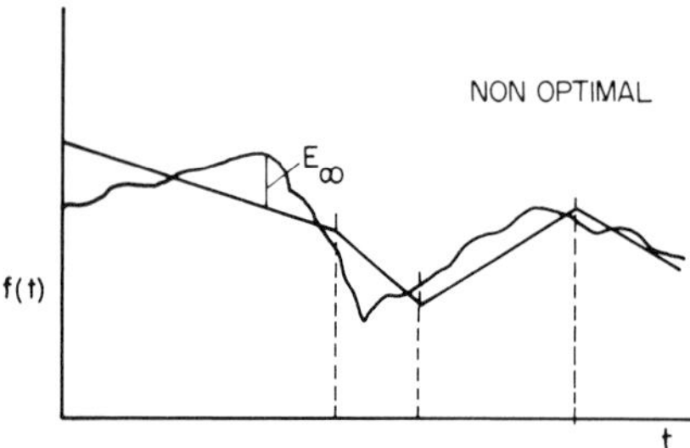

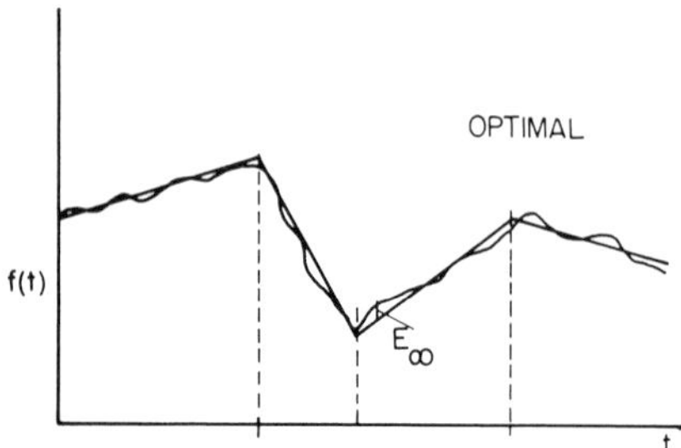

Fig. 2.2 Illustration of the importance of knot location in approximations by a piecewise linear function

It would be nice if there were a simple algorithm for locating the joints optimally, but this is definitely not the case. While the curve fitting problem for fixed joints is a *linear* one (since the coefficients can be obtained by solving a system of linear equations or linear inequalities) the present problem is *nonlinear*. Thus the only available methods are iterative. One well-known technique for finding such a curve is to use a *descent* algorithm: An initial partition $\underline{x}$ is chosen. Then variations of it, $\underline{x} + \delta\underline{x}$, are considered, and the one resulting in the smallest error norm is taken as the next estimate. The process is repeated until no further improvement can be achieved. Unfortunately, there are a number of things wrong with such an

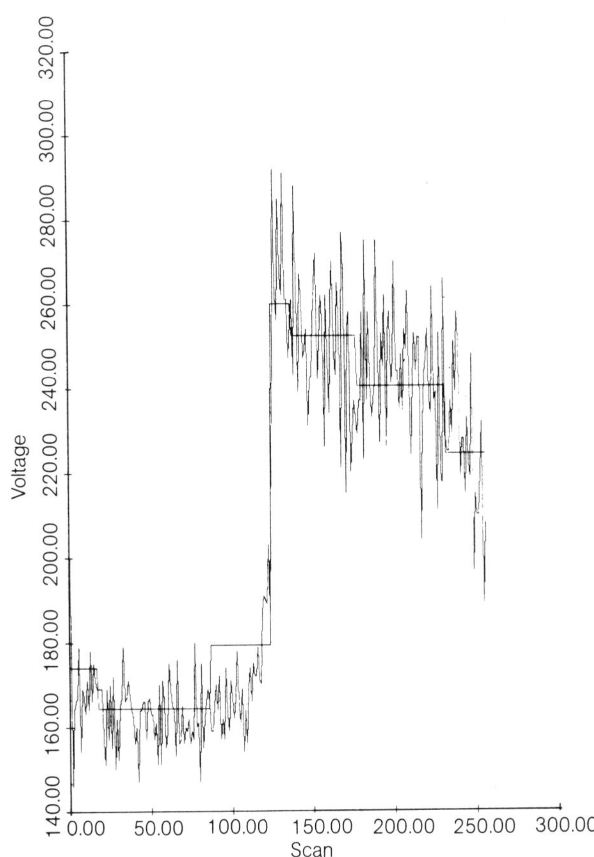

Fig. 2.3 A scan by an electron microscope of an aluminum/cadmium-sulphite junction, plotted together with its piecewise constant approximation. The variables in the plot are sulphur concentration (measured as voltage) versus distance expressed in number of discrete sampled points (CALCOMP plot). (From [2.33])

approach. One is that a *local* rather than a *global* optimum may be reached. Another is the need to estimate too many splines $S_{\underline{x}+\delta\underline{x},m,r}(t)$. Therefore, it is necessary to look for more efficient methods or improved descent schemes.

In this treatise, we emphasize first-order splines, i.e., piecewise linear approximations, and quite often we will ignore the continuity constraints. The reasons for this preference will be explained fully in Chapter 7. Here we point out some of them: a) linear approximations (i.e., by line segments) seem to be particularly relevant in shape perception; b) for them, continuity can be obtained as a "bonus" of the optimal location of the breakpoints (see Sec.2.10); c) the theoretical problems are much more complex when $m > 2$ and $r > 0$; d) the substantial computational effort required for high order approximations can be prohibitive for online applications; e) finally, in most pattern recognition problems, continuity conditions are not pertinent, as illustrated by the edge detection problem. There are a number of relevant results for unconstrained approximations. We present next one of the simplest, and continue with more in the rest of this chapter.

Theorem 2.1: Let the error norm of the approximation be a nondecreasing function of the length of the interval of approximation. (Both L_2 and L_∞ have this property). Let $e_j(\underline{x})$ be that error norm over $(x_{j-1}, x_j]$ for the partition $\underline{x}$. Then, if

$$e_1 = e_2 = \dots = e_n \quad , \tag{2.61}$$

the partition $\underline{x}^*$, for which this is achieved, has the property that

$$\max_j\{e_j(\underline{x}^*)\} \le \max_j\{e_j(\underline{x})\} \quad , \tag{2.62}$$

for any other partition $\underline{x}$.

A partition satisfying (2.61) is said to have the *balanced error* property.

Corollary 2.1: A balanced error partition is optimal for uniform approximations.

Proof of Theorem 2.1: Let x_i^* denote the joints of the partition $\underline{x}^*$, and x_i those of $\underline{x}$. It is easy to show that there must be at least one interval $(x_{i-1}, x_i]$ containing one of the intervals $(x_{j-1}^*, x_j^*]$. Then

$$e_i(\underline{x}) \ge e_j(\underline{x}^*)$$

and furthermore, because of (2.61)

$$e_i(\underline{x}) \ge \max_j e_j(\underline{x}^*) \quad . \qquad \text{Q.E.D.}$$

In the case of L_∞ approximations, the pointwise errors at the endpoints of an interval are often equal to the error norm. When this happens, a balanced error solution will produce approximations, which at each joint will be either continuous or symmetric with respect to f(t). Therefore continuity can be expected in a number of joints, even though it was not imposed during the approximation.

2.10 Piecewise Approximations with Variable Joints

II. The L_2 Case

In unconstrained (r=0) L_2 approximations, we want to minimize

$$E = \sum_{k=1}^{n} e_k(\underline{x}) \quad . \tag{2.63}$$

The balanced error property cannot be used. Instead, we proceed with a direct differentiation. Let e(k,t) denote the pointwise error at t when the approximation on the kth interval is used. (The subsequent discussion is independent of whether the error is defined as "function minus approximation" or "approximation minus function"). Strictly speaking e(k,t) depends also on the coefficient vector $\underline{a}_k$ shown in (2.53), but we suppress explicit notation of this dependence in order to avoid cumbersome expressions. Furthermore $\underline{a}_k$ will be chosen optimally whenever a best approximation is computed. The total error of the approximation is given by

$$E = \sum_{k=1}^{n} \int_{x_{k-1}}^{x_k} e(k,t)^2 \, dt \quad . \tag{2.64}$$

We can state the following result:

Theorem 2.2: The partial derivatives of E with respect to the breakpoints are given by

$$\frac{\partial E}{\partial x_k} = e(k,x_k)^2 - e(k+1,x_k)^2 \qquad k = 1,2,\ldots n-1 \quad , \tag{2.65}$$

i.e., a necessary condition for a breakpoint distribution to be optimal is that the squares of the pointwise errors on either side of each breakpoint be equal. This means that at the breakpoints the approximation will be either continuous or symmetric with respect to the original curve.

Proof of Theorem 2.2: The partial derivative of an interval with respect to its upper limit equals the value of the integrand at the point, while the partial derivative with respect to the lower limit equals minus the value of the integrand there. Any given breakpoint occurs explicitly only as the upper limit of the kth interval and as the lower limit of the integral at the $k+1^{th}$ interval. Applying these results on (2.64), we obtain (2.65). Note that, although $\underline{a}_k$ also depends on the breakpoints, it does not appear in the above expression because we take only partial derivatives. One can show that if $\underline{a}_k$ is chosen optimally, its partial derivatives with respect to the breakpoints are indeed zero [2.34]. Q.E.D.

It turns out that a related result can be obtained in the general case ($r>0$). The minimization of E subject to the constraints of (2.54) can be achieved with the help of Lagrange multipliers L_{kp} by minimizing the following quantity (instead of E)

$$F = E + \sum_{k=1}^{n-1} \sum_{p=1}^{r} L_{kp}[e^{(p-1)}(k,x_k) - e^{(p-1)}(k+1,x_k)] \quad . \tag{2.66}$$

Then the partial derivatives of F with respect to the breakpoints are

$$\frac{\partial F}{\partial x_j} = e(j,x_j)^2 - e(j+1,x_j)^2 + \sum_{p=1}^{r} L_{jp} [e^{(p)}(j,x_j) - e^{(p)}(j+1,x_j)] \tag{2.67}$$

$$j = 1,2,\ldots,n-1 \quad ,$$

where we have used the fact that the partial derivative of $e^{(p-1)}(k,x_k)$ with respect to x_j is zero if $j \neq k$ and $e^{(p)}(j,x_j)$ if $j = k$. A necessary condition for optimality is that all these partial derivatives be zero. The first two terms, as well as the differences of the error derivatives from $p = 1$ to r, are zero because of (2.54). Therefore (2.67) is simplified into

$$\frac{\partial F}{\partial x_j} = L_{jr} [e^{(r)}(j,x_j) - e^{(r)}(j+1,x_j)] \quad . \tag{2.68}$$

In order that the right hand side be zero, it is necessary that either L_{jr} be zero or that the rth derivative be continuous at x_j. In general we have no way of knowing which will be the case. However, if $r = m - 1$, then the difference of the error derivatives cannot be zero because this would imply an inactive breakpoint. Indeed, equality of the approximation plus its first $m - 1$ derivatives at a breakpoint would imply no breakpoint at all. According to a theorem proven by DeBOOR and RICE, this would contradict the optimality of the solution unless E were zero [Ref.2.1, p.143]. Therefore in order to have zero partial derivatives we must have

$$L_{jr} = 0. \tag{2.69}$$

The fact that the Lagrange multipliers for the last constraint vanish means that only those for the first r - 1 constraints will appear in the equations for $\partial F/\partial \underline{a}_k$. Therefore, the last constraints may be ignored when the $\underline{a}_k$'s are chosen. This is a rather remarkable result, and it can be summarized as follows:

Theorem 2.3: A necessary condition for the optimal location of the breakpoints in a spline approximation with the maximum number of continuity constraints is that the continuity of the highest derivative may be ignored during the approximation for that particular partition, and it will still be achieved.

The following special case will be of particular interest in the sequel.

Corollary 2.2: A necessary condition for the optimal location of the breakpoints in a continuous piecewise linear approximation (m=2) is that the unconstrained optimal approximations on each subinterval result in a continuous approximation over the whole interval.

The result may seem counterintuitive, and requires some explanation. In particular, it does not claim that we must ignore the constraints during the optimization. It only states that, after a solution is found, the constraints may be ignored. The next section shows a simple example of its application. In order to derive sufficient conditions, we must evaluate the matrix of the second derivatives of E with respect to the breakpoints. To do this correctly, the explicit forms for the pointwise errors, describing their dependence on the breakpoints, must be replaced in (2.65). Their calculation is quite lengthy and we present here only their final form. Their derivation can be found in the literature [2.34]. We define first the auxiliary expression

$$r(i,j) = e(i,x_j)/(x_i-x_{i-1}) \quad . \tag{2.70}$$

We will use a prime (') to denote a first derivative. Then the second derivatives are given by

$$\begin{aligned} \partial^2 E/\partial^2 x_i &= 2e(i,x_i)\, e'(i,x_i) - 2e(i+1,x_i)\, e'(i+1,x_i) \\ &\quad - 2m^2 e(i,x_i) r(i,i) - 2m^2 e(i+1,x_i) r(i+1,i) \quad , \end{aligned} \tag{2.71a}$$

$$\partial^2 E/\partial x_i\ \partial x_{i+1} = 2(-1)^{m-1}\ me(i+1,x_i)\ r(i+1,i) \quad . \tag{2.71b}$$

Both terms are defined for $i = 1,2,\ldots,n - 1$. All the other derivatives are zero. The matrix J of the second derivatives takes the following form:

$$J(i,i) = \partial^2 E/\partial x_i^2 \qquad i = 1,2,\ldots,n \quad , \tag{2.72a}$$

$$J(i,i-1) = \partial^2 E/\partial x_{i-1}\ \partial x_i \qquad i = 2,3,\ldots,n \quad , \tag{2.72b}$$

$$J(i,i+1) = \partial^2 E/\partial x_i\ \partial x_{i+1} \qquad i = 1,2,\ldots,n - 1 \quad , \tag{2.72c}$$

$$J(i,k) = 0 \quad \text{otherwise} \quad . \tag{2.72d}$$

We note that, at the optimal location, where the pointwise errors are equal, the first two terms in (2.71a) reflect the change of the slope at a breakpoint and therefore should be larger than all the remaining ones, which are proportional to ratios of a pointwise error over the length of an interval. Therefore, the matrix of the second derivatives is expected to have diagonal dominance for any "reasonable" approximation. When this is true we will say that the approximation satisfies condition R. By inspection of (2.71), we can see when J will be positive definite and hence when a sufficient condition for a local minimum of the error will hold. In this case we can state the following result.

Theorem 2.4: A choice of breakpoints satisfying the condition of Corollary 2.2 as well as condition R will be locally optimal if the change (along increasing t) in the slope of the approximation at a breakpoint has the same sign as the pointwise error there.

Its proof is straightforward, observing that in this case the first two terms in (2.71a) will be positive and all the others will be negligible because of the assumption about R. We shall show later on how this result can be used for the construction of algorithms for finding an optimal partition. For the time being we point out an illustration of a situation where condition R holds, shown in Fig.2.4.

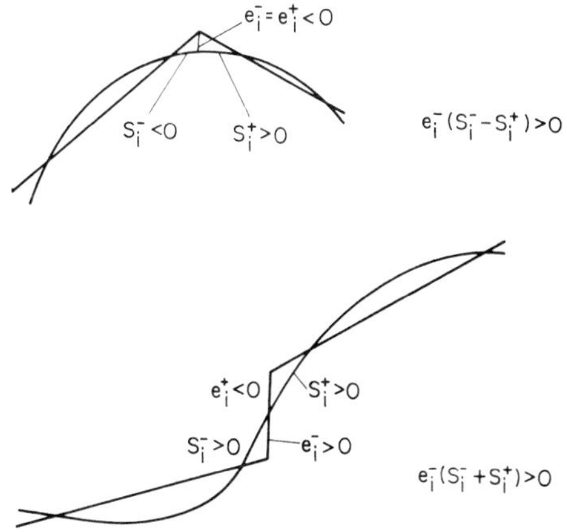

Fig. 2.4 Examples where the quantities of (2.71) are positive. The figure is plotted with the pointwise error defined a "function minus approximation"

2.11 Piecewise Approximation with Variable Joints

III. A Simple Example

Because some of the results of the previous section are counterintuitive, we present here a brief illustration of their application for an optimal first order spline approximation to the function sgn(t) (sign of t) over the interval [-1,1]. First we obtain the approximation by a single straight line $a_1 t + a_0$ over the interval [-1,x] for x nonnegative. A straightforward calculation yields

$$a_0 = - \frac{(1-x)(1-4x+x^2)}{(1+x)^3} \quad , \tag{2.73}$$

$$a_1 = \frac{12x}{(1+x)^3} \quad , \tag{2.74}$$

$$E = a_1^2 \frac{x^3+1}{3} + (a_0+1)^2 + (a_0-1)^2 x - (a_0+1)a_1 + (a_0-1)a_1 x^2 \quad . \tag{2.75}$$

If we have just one breakpoint and we attempt to place it in the interval (0,1) then, according to Corollary 2.2, its location x must satisfy

$$a_1 x + a_0 = 1 \quad . \tag{2.76}$$

Substituting (2.73) and (2.74) into (2.76) and simplifying yields the following quadratic equation:

$$4x^2 + 2x - 2 = 0 \quad , \tag{2.77}$$

which is satisfied for $x = 1/2$. (The other root is -1, which violates the assumption of nonnegative x). Substituting this value into (2.73-75) yields

$$a_1 = 16/9 \quad a_0 = 1/9 \quad E = 4/9 \quad . \tag{2.78}$$

A solution symmetric to the above ($x = -1/2$) can be obtained if we require the breakpoint to be nonpositive. The value of E above gives the integral square error for the whole interval since E equals 0 on [1/2,1].

Let us consider, on the other hand, the "intuitive" solution obtained by deciding that on the basis of symmetry the breakpoint must be placed at 0. The symmetry argument suggests in this case that the breakpoint is going to be inactive (a direct calculation of the first order spline for that location yields the same result) and this seems to contradict Corollary 2.2. However, in this case, (2.73-75) must be evaluated for $x = 1$ to yield

$$a_1 = 3/2 \quad a_0 = 0 \quad E = 1/2 \quad , \tag{2.79}$$

with the latter exceeding the value of E found for a solution satisfying Corollary 2.2. The second derivative of E with respect to x at the optimal solution is zero because the pointwise errors are zero, and therefore we cannot verify the sufficient conditions for optimality. (We would have to check whether the fourth derivative is positive). We may notice though that the slope of the approximation is decreasing in the manner shown in Fig.2.4.

The simplicity of the example allows a rigorous solution by using (2.58) with an orthonormal basis. Indeed, the first two members of the basis are Legendre polynomials [2.2,3], and are given by

$$b_0(t) = \frac{1}{\sqrt{2}} \quad b_1(t) = \sqrt{\frac{3}{2}}\, t \quad . \tag{2.80}$$

By using the Gram-Schmidt orthonormalization procedure [2.2] we find that $(t-x)_+$ gives rise to

$$b_2(t) = 0 \quad \text{if } t < x \quad , \tag{2.81a}$$

$$b_2(t) = \frac{\sqrt{24}[(t-x) - K - Lt]}{\sqrt{(1-x)^3\,(1+x)^3}} \quad \text{if } t \geq x \quad , \tag{2.81b}$$

where

$$K = \frac{(1-x)^2}{4} \qquad L = \frac{3}{2}\left[\frac{1}{2} - \frac{x}{2} - \frac{x^3}{6}\right] \quad . \tag{2.81c}$$

Eq. (2.21') can now be applied to sgn(x) for this basis. The result is

$$a_0 = 0 \quad , \quad a_1 = \sqrt{\frac{3}{2}} \quad ,$$

$$a_2 = \sqrt{\frac{3}{2}}\frac{x(1-x)}{\sqrt{(1-x)(1+x)^3}} \quad .$$

Substituting the above expressions in (2.26') we obtain

$$E_2 = \frac{1}{2} - \frac{3}{2}\frac{x^2(1-x)}{(1+x)^3} \quad .$$

Differentiating this equation with respect to x we find that

$$\frac{dE}{dx} = -3\,\frac{x(1-2x)}{(1+x)^4} \quad ,$$

which is zero for $x = 0$ and $x = 1/2$. The second derivative is found now to be

$$\frac{d^2E}{dx^2} = -3\,\frac{1 - 7x + 4x^2}{(1+x)^5} \quad ,$$

which is negative for $x = 0$ and positive for $x = 1/2$. Therefore, the second point is indeed a minimum. Substituting this value in (2.80) and (2.81) we can simplify the resulting expressions and then verify the values given by (2.78).

2.12 Algorithms for Piecewise Approximations with Variable Joints

In this section we will briefly review certain of these algorithms. We postpone treatment of others for later chapters, when the algorithms will be used for feature extraction. The results of Sections 2.8 and 2.9 suggest that the optimal partition can be found as the zero of a vector valued function, for both the L_2 and L_∞ approximations. Indeed, let $\underline{F}(\underline{x})$ be a vector whose i^{th} component $(i=1,2,\ldots,n)$ is given by

$$F_i(\underline{x}) = e_i(\underline{x}) - e_{i+1}(\underline{x}) \quad , \tag{2.82}$$

where

$$e_i(\underline{x}) = \max_{x_{i-1} < t \leq x_i} \{|f(t) - g_i(t)|\} \quad . \tag{2.83}$$

Algorithm 2.2: Optimal joint location for uniform approximation

1. Choose an initial partition $\underline{x}$ and evaluate $\underline{F}(\underline{x})$.
2. If $||\underline{F}(\underline{x})|| < \delta$ then exit.
3. Update $\underline{x}$:

$$\underline{x} = \underline{x} - c\underline{F}(\underline{x}) \quad . \tag{2.84}$$

4. Go to step 2.

Algorithm 2.2 implements a first-order iteration method for finding a zero of $F_i(\underline{x})$. δ is the tolerance for deciding whether a balanced error solution was reached, c is a constant whose size must be chosen sufficiently small to guarantee convergence. In particular,

$$c < 1/|e_{ij}| \quad \text{for all} \quad i,j \quad , \tag{2.85}$$

where e_{ij} denotes the ratio of a change in the error norm of the ith interval for a change in x_j. Since there are no explicit formulas for such changes, c must be estimated during the iteration. It can be shown that this algorithm converges to a solution [2.35], although it may be rather slow because of the small step size in adjusting $\underline{x}$. However, there is a compensating factor. At each iteration of the algorithm, the approximations on all the segments must be reexamined. If two segments have a significant overlap, then they may share all or most of the points where the maximum error occurs. In the first case, there is no need to calculate a new approximation, while in the second many fewer iterations of the linear programming algorithm may be needed than for a new interval (see Sec.2.5).

In the case of L_2 approximation, we search for the zero of $\underline{F}(\underline{x})$, where

$$F_i(\underline{x}) = \frac{\partial E}{\partial x_i} \quad , \tag{2.86}$$

as given by (2.65). In this case, the matrix J of the first derivatives of $\underline{F}(\underline{x})$ coincides with the matrix of the second derivatives of E (see Sec.2.10). Newton's method is then applicable and it is implemented by Algorithm 2.3.

Algorithm 2.3: Optimal joint location for L_2 approximation

1. Choose an initial partition $\underline{x}$ and evaluate $\underline{F}(\underline{x})$.
2. If $||\underline{F}(\underline{x})|| < \delta$ then exit.
3. Update $\underline{x}$:

$$\underline{x} = \underline{x} - J^{-1}\underline{F}(\underline{x}) \quad . \tag{2.87}$$

4. Go to step 2.

The inversion of J is easy because it is tridiagonal and furthermore, as shown in the previous section, it is likely to have strong diagonal dominance. In this case the Gauss elimination method can be used to solve the system

$$J\delta\underline{x} = \underline{F}(\underline{x}) \quad , \tag{2.88}$$

in time linearly proportional to n - 1.

For uniform approximations a limited descent technique can be used as follows: Let $y_{i1}, y_{i2}, \ldots y_{ir}$ be the locations where the maximum error occurs on the interval $(x_{i-1}, x_i]$, i.e.,

$$e(y_{ij}) = \pm e_i \quad j = 1,2,\ldots,r \quad r \geq m + 1$$

where m is the number of degrees of freedom of the approximating function. During a breakpoint adjustment, it is necessary to move past one of these locations in order to see any change in the error norm. This suggests Algorithm 2.4. It is easy to show that this algorithm is correct and indeed terminates in a finite number of steps. The strict inequality in step 5 guarantees that no partition $\{x_1, x_2, \ldots, x_n\}$ will repeat itself. In order to study its computational requirements we proceed as follows:

Algorithm 2.4: Optimal joint location for uniform approximation *by descent*

1. For k = 1,2 do block 11.

    Begin block 11;

    1. For i = k, k + 2, k + 4,...,n do block 12.

        Begin block 12;

        1. $D = e_i - e_{i+1}$.
        2. If $D > 0$ set $z = y_{i,m+1} - 1$,

            If $D < 0$ set $z = y_{i,r-m} + 1$,

            If $D = 0$ go to step 4.

        3. Let Z_i and Z_{i+1} be the error norms on $(x_{i-1},z]$ and $(z,x_{i+1}]$. If $\max(Z_i,Z_{i+1}) < \max(e_i,e_{i+1})$ then $x_i = z$. Else leave x_i as it stands.
        4. Continue

        End block 12;

    End block 11;

2. If any breakpoint changes have been made go to step 1. Else terminate.

Let $(x_i,x_{i+1}]$ be the interval where the maximum error norm occurs at a given step (if more than one such interval exists then arbitrary choice is made). In subsequent steps the endpoints will be moved only if a decrease in the error norm (and hence a decrease in the interval length) is possible. Thus the situation

$$(x'_i,x'_{i+1}] \supset (x_i,x_{i+1}]$$

cannot occur. (The primes denote the values of the breakpoints at a subsequent iteration). Thus the present value of at least one of the endpoints will bound all subsequent ones, i.e.,

$$x'_i \geq x_i$$

or

$$x'_{i+1} \leq x_{i+1}$$

(possibly both inequalities can hold).

At each iteration, at least one of these points will be moved, unless such moves cause both of the adjacent intervals to have an error norm in excess of the original maximum. In that case the norms of these three intervals will be "balanced" and no further moves will be made until at least one of the adjacent intervals is reduced in length. Thus at each step at least one of the breakpoints will be moving in the "right" direction. Therefore, the total number of steps is bounded from above by nN. This is a very conservative bound, for it assumes that all breakpoints are originally clustered at the wrong end of the interval and at each step only one is moved towards its final position while the rest oscillate. At each iteration, curves are fitted to a total number of N points and all known algorithms are also of order N. Thus the total effort can be of order nN^2. There is no guarantee that this algorithm will lead to a global optimum. This is so because of the restriction in the directions of descent used. If e_{max} and e_{min} denote the maximum and minimum error norms on the n intervals and e_{opt} the value of the error norm in a globally optimal solution, then

$$e_{max} \leq \frac{e_{max}}{e_{min}} e_{opt} \quad .$$

Thus the degree of "imbalance" gives a bound on how far from the global optimum a given solution is. A comparative study of various versions of this algorithm as well as some others was made by VANDEWALLE [2.36]. It turned out that for an electrocardiogram the maximum error resulting from this algorithm could be reduced by up to a factor between 1.5 and 2 if more descent directions were used. At the same time, the computational time could be increased by a factor ranging from 3.5 to 10. It is a good idea to use this method in conjunction with Algorithm 2.2. The discrete nature of the data may cause the latter to oscillate near a solution (see Sec.2.1), so that it may be desirable to switch to a descent scheme. It is easy to devise a similar algorithm for the L_2 norm, and again it can be used in conjunction with Algorithm 2.3.

Surface approximation by piecewise polynomial functions, where the region boundaries are variable, is almost intractable [2.4]. There are numerous difficulties which have to do with the proper definition of the region boundaries. Some suboptimal solutions will be discussed in Chapters 4 and 5.

3. Graphs and Grids

3.1 Introduction

In this chapter we shall review some concepts from graph theory and discrete geometry which are useful in picture processing. The description of pictures in terms of graphs is quite natural and it has been done, explicitly or implicitly, in most of the literature on pictorial pattern recognition and scene analysis. Unfortunately there is wide variability in graph terminology among various users and part of the purpose of the review is to give the definitions for the terms which we will be using later on.

Discrete geometry is a rather "esoteric" subject and it is not emphasized often in the picture processing literature. However, it is quite important in the implementation of various algorithms where one must decide, for example, which are the neighbors of a point, where two curves cross, etc. Since the domain of the picture is a discrete grid we are faced with the need to define a number of geometrical operations in such an environment, a problem which is by no means trivial. An alternative is to map the discrete grid into a continuous space. This approach, which has been proposed by SKLANSKY and his associates [3.1-3], emphasizes the translation of a "mosaic" into a continuous curve. Thus in Fig.3.1 one must define a curve passing through all the shaded squares. Once such a curve is found, the processing can continue within the framework of continuous geometry. The choice of the continuous curve is, in essence, an approximation problem. Indeed each square can be thought of as representing a single discrete point, and we may then require that a set of such points be approximated by a continuous curve passing within a certain distance from them. If the desired curve is a polynomial, then the problem can be solved easily by the techniques discussed in the previous chapter. If a piecewise approximation is desired, as it is usually the case, then special techniques come into play. We shall review some of them in Chapter 7.

Performing geometrical operations on a discrete grid has a number of advantages, including the possibility of using simple logical operations

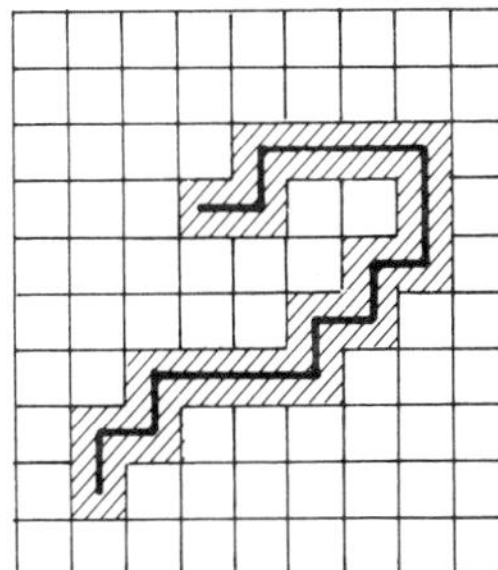

Fig. 3.1 Definition of a continuous curve on a discrete grid. The shaded cells represent pixels marked as belonging to, say, the boundary of a region during a quantization process. Then a continuous boundary might be defined as the curve joining their centers

rather than real arithmetic. It requires, though, the definition of discrete counterparts for concepts like "connectivity", "boundary of a set", etc. Such a study was first made by ROSENFELD [3.4] and a systematic theory within the framework of abstract algebra was developed by MYLOPOULOS [3.5,6]. We shall devote the last three sections of this chapter to this approach.

3.2 Fundamentals of Graph Theory

We give here a brief review of the fundamental properties of graphs and list the definitions of the most common terms used in a graph theory. For more details the reader is referred to the many books on the subject, for example [3.7-9]. We emphasize only those terms and concepts which are particularly relevant to pattern recognition.

Definition 3.1: A *graph* G consists of a set of nodes V together with a set B, whose members are unordered pairs of nodes, the *branches* of G. A *directed graph* is one where the pairs in the set B are ordered. A *subgraph* of G is a graph whose nodes and branches are also those of G. Two nodes of a graph are said to be *adjacent* if there is a branch between them.

For the examples of Figs.3.2a,b we have

V = {1,2,3,4,5,6} and B = {(1,2), (2,3), (3,4), (2,4), (3,5), (4,6), (6,5)}.

V = {1,2,3,4} and B = {(1,2), (2,1), (2,3), (4,2)}.

The heavy lines mark a subgraph. Note that this formal definition provides us with a way of describing a graph without drawing a picture. This can be quite useful when we want to process graphs by computer, since all one has to do is to input the set B, the *branch list* of G. Another way of describing graphs is through a *node adjacency list* where for each node a list of the

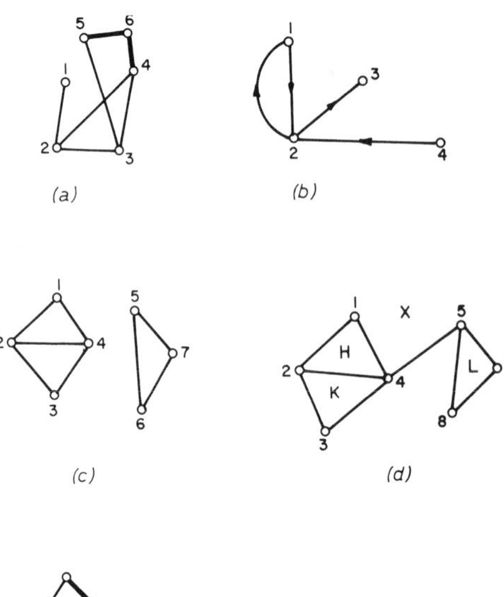

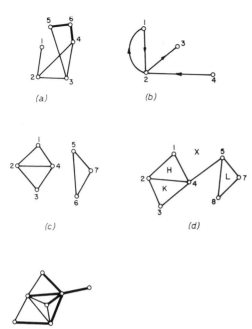

Fig. 3.2a-e Illustration of the definitions of graph theory terms: a) An undirected graph. b) A directed graph. c) A disconnected graph with two components. d) A graph with a bridge, two cutnodes, and four faces. e) A spanning tree of a graph marked by heavy lines

nodes adjacent to it is given. If the graph is directed, then one needs two lists: nodes connected by "*in*" and "*out*" branches. For the examples of Fig. 3.2a,b we have

a) 1[2], 2[1,3,4], 3[2,4,5], 4[2,3,6], 5[3,6], 6[4,5]

b) 1 + [2] - [2], 2 + [1,3] - [1,4], 3 + [] - [2], 4 + [2] - []

where + denotes an "out" and - an "in" list. A third method for graph description is by an *adjacency matrix*, whose rows and columns correspond to nodes, and whose elements are zero if the corresponding nodes are not connected and one if they are. For a directed graph the i,j^{th} element of the matrix is set to one if there is branch *from* node i *to* node j. The adjacency matrix is always symmetric for an undirected graph, but not always for a directed graph. For the graphs of Fig.3.2a,b we have:

$$\text{a)}\quad \begin{array}{cccccc} 0&1&0&0&0&0\\ 1&0&1&1&0&0\\ 0&1&0&1&1&0\\ 0&1&1&0&0&1\\ 0&0&1&0&0&1\\ 0&0&0&1&1&0 \end{array} \qquad\qquad \text{b)}\quad \begin{array}{cccc} 0&1&0&0\\ 1&0&1&0\\ 0&0&0&0\\ 0&1&0&0 \end{array}$$

There are a number of synonymous terms for nodes and for branches. In particular the terms *point*, *junction*, and *vertex* are used instead of node and the terms *arc*, *line*, and *edge* are used instead of branch. Some authors reserve the use of the term arc for branches of directed graphs only.

Definition 3.2: The *degree* of a node equals the number of branches incident upon it. For directed graphs we distinguish in- and out-degrees, equal to the number of branches whose direction is respectively toward and away from the node.

Definition 3.3: A *path* is a sequence of distinct nodes (except possibly for the last, which may be the same as the first), such that any two adjacent members of the sequence are connected by a branch (e.g., 1246 in Fig.3.2a and 123 in Fig.3.2b). A path is called a *cycle* if its first and last points coincide (e.g., 246532 in Fig.3.2a). (The term circuit is sometimes used as a synonym for cycle. Most authors reserve this term for a different use.)

Definition 3.4: A graph is *connected* if there is a path between all pairs of its nodes. It is *complete* if there is a branch between all pairs of its nodes. The symbol K_n denotes the complete graph with n nodes. A *component* of G is a connected subgraph of G which is not a subgraph of any other connected subgraph of G. (Thus the graph of Fig.3.2c has two components with node sets {1,2,3,4} and {5,6,7} respectively.) The (*node*) *connectivity* of a graph is the minimum number of nodes which must be removed to make it disconnected or empty. The *branch connectivity* of a graph is the minimum number of branches which must be removed to make it disconnected.

Definition 3.5: A *bridge* (or *cutbranch*) of G is a branch whose removal from G increases the number of its components by one (e.g., (4,5) in Fig.3.2d). A *cutnode* (or *articulation point*) C of G is a node such that there exist two other nodes, A and B, with all paths between A and B passing through C (e.g., 4 and 5 in Fig.3.2d). A graph without cutnodes is said to be *biconnected*. A *block* of a graph G is a maximal biconnected subgraph of G.

Definition 3.6: A *tree* is a graph without circuits. A *spanning tree* of a graph G is a subgraph of G which contains all its nodes and which is a tree (shown by heavy lines in the example of Fig.3.2e).

A tree can always be *ordered* in the following fashion. A node is selected to be the *root* of the tree. All nodes adjacent to the root are said to be the *children* of the root. (We also say that the root is their parent). We define the rest of the order recursively: If a node j has already become the child of another node, all the other nodes attached to j are called the children of j. Then a partial ordering has been established by the relation parent-child. The terms *ancestor* and *descendant* of a node have the obvious meaning. Usually trees are drawn with the root uppermost and all the nodes which are *siblings* at the same level as shown in Fig.3.3. There the ancestors of 5 are 1 and 2, while its descendants are 9, 10, 11, and 14. This terminology is in part due to the fact that a tree denoting the blood relations in a family among relatives of a single sex looks exactly that way. The partial ordering may become total by ordering siblings in some arbitrary fashion, and plotting them from left to right. This order is expressed in Fig.3.3 by the numerical labels. See [3.10] for further discussion of tree orders. For such a tree, nodes of degree one which are not the root are called *leaves*. (Note that all other nodes are cutnodes, except for the case when the root has less than two children).

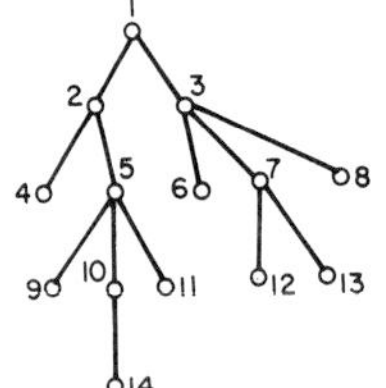

Fig. 3.3 An ordered tree

Definition 3.7: A *planar* graph is one which can be drawn on the plane without having any of its branches intersect. A *plane* graph is one already drawn that way (e.g., the graph of Fig.3.2a is planar but not plane). A plane graph divides the plane into regions which are called its *faces* (marked by capital letters in Fig.3.2d) with the unbounded region called the *exterior face*, (X in Fig.3.2d).

Definition 3.8: A planar graph is *outerplanar* if it can be drawn on the plane with all its nodes lying on the same face. (The graph of Fig.3.2d has this property; that of Fig.3.2e does not).

Definition 3.9: The (geometric) *dual* of a plane graph G is a graph H constructed as follows: For each face of G create a node for H. For each branch of G create a branch in H, connecting the nodes corresponding to the two faces adjacent to that branch (Fig.3.4a).

If one is given a map, then it is possible to construct a "map" graph by assigning a node to each country and connecting two nodes if the

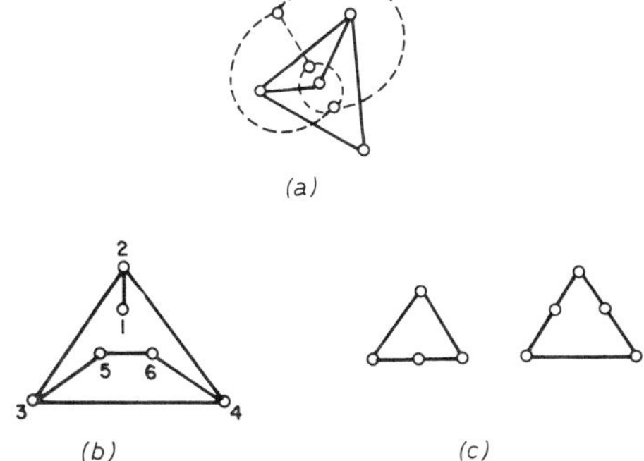

Fig. 3.4a-c Illustration of the definitions of graph theory terms: a) The geometric dual of a graph. The original graph has solid lines for branches and the dual broken lines. b) This graph is isomorphic to the graph of Fig.3.2a. The numbers at the nodes denote their correspondence under the isomorphism. c) Two homeomorphic graphs

respective countries share a border. This graph is obviously plane. Such graphs are quite important in Picture Processing and Pattern Recognition, and we shall review them in detail in Chapters 4-6. The connection between maps and graphs is best known because of the "Four Color Problem", namely the search for a proof that every map can be colored with four colors without any two adjacent countries having the same color. (Such a proof has been found recently [3.11]).

Definition 3.10: A *coloring* of a graph is an assignment of colors to its nodes, such that no two nodes connected by a branch have the same color. The *chromatic number* of a graph is the minimum number of colors required for a legal coloring. (it is 3 for the graph of Fig.3.2a and 4 for that of Fig.3.2e). A *bipartite* graph is one whose chromatic number is 2.

Definition 3.11: Two graphs are *isomorphic* if there is an one-to-one correspondence between their nodes which preserves adjacency. (The graph of Fig.3.4b is isomorphic to that of Fig.3.2a). Two graphs are *homeomorphic* if both can be obtained from the same graph by inserting nodes into branches. (Fig.3.4c shows two such graphs). A graph G is *contractible* to a graph H if H can be obtained from G by a sequence of the following operations: If i and j are two adjacent nodes of G, they are replaced by a single node k and all other nodes which were connected to i and j are connected to k.

3.3 Basic Algorithms for Graphs

In this section we describe a number of algorithms which are commonly used on graphs in the context of a variety of applications. The first problem we are faced with is that of *graph traversal*. In many cases it is necessary to *traverse* a graph, i.e., visit all its nodes. If 1 is the starting node and it is connected to more than one other node, then we may choose one of them and proceed. In this way we may reach a node from which no further advance is possible (e.g., a leaf in a tree) and there may still exist unvisited nodes in the graph (e.g. some of the other nodes adjacent to 1). Thus when we leave a node we must keep track of those adjacent to it, so that we can return to them eventually. We can perform a traversal in an orderly fashion by placing the indices of all the nodes connected to the starting node in a *stack* S and choosing as the next node to be visited one from the stack. Then we can place the nodes adjacent to it in the stack and so forth. We may mark nodes already placed on S so that they will not be placed twice. The policy of selection of a node from S determines the kind of traversal. One possibility is *First In First Out* (FIFO). For the graph of Fig.3.5a the sequence will be 1237456 if the nodes adjacent to the *current node* are placed in S in numerical order. Note that in this case S should be called a *queue* rather than a stack. A *Last In First Out* (LIFO) policy will traverse the graph of Fig.3.5a in the sequence 1365427. Each traversal generates a spanning tree for the graph that contains all the branches visited during the traversal. Fig.3.5b shows the spanning tree for the FIFO traversal and Fig.3.5c for the LIFO. A traversal policy of special interest is known as *depth first* and it can be described informally as follows. For

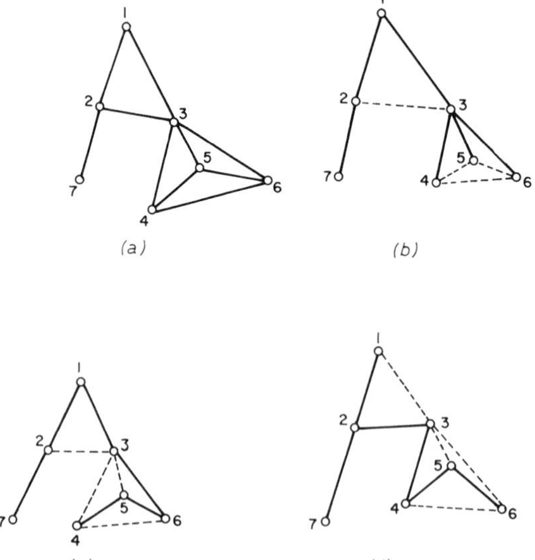

Fig. 3.5a-d Different spanning trees of the graph shown in a): b) FIFO. c) LIFO. d) Depth first

each node pick up an adjacent node (if an unvisited one exists) and make that the current node. Proceed in this way as far as possible. When no further advance can be made, backtrack until an unvisited node is found. Then use that as the current node and repeat the process. For the graph of Fig.3.5a we may proceed initially through 1, 2 and 7. From 7 we backtrack to 2 and there we take the first unvisited node 3, etc. Formally the strategy is given by Algorithm 3.1.

Algorithm 3.1: Depth first traversal of a graph

Input: Graph in the form of a node adjacency list nn(i,j) with the array d(i) containing the degrees of the nodes (note that $1 \le j \le d(i)$). N is the number of nodes.

Output: List of nodes.

Note: S is a stack whose elements are pairs of nodes. It is initially empty.

Steps:

1. Mark all nodes with 0. Set k = 0, i = 1, j = 1.
2. Do block 11 while k is less than N.

    Begin block 11;

    1. If j > d(i) remove from S a pair of nodes and set i and j equal to its first and second members. (All the nodes adjacent to i have been visited and we replace the current node from the stack S).

    _. Else do block 12.

        Begin block 12;

        1. If node nn(i,j) is marked, then increment j. (Proceed along the list of nodes adjacent to the current one until an unmarked one is found or the list is exhausted).

        _. Else do block 13.

            Begin block 13;

            1. Mark nn(i,j), increment k and output i.
            2. Place on the stack the pair (i,j+1). (Mark the place where we came from).
            3. Set i = nn(i,j) and j = 1.

            End block 13;

        End block 12;

    End block 11;

The depth first traversal of the graph of Fig.3.5a is 1234567, and the respective spanning tree is shown in Fig.3.5d. Depth first spanning trees (DFST) have the following important property. (For a proof see [3.12]).

Theorem 3.1: Let (i,j) be a branch of a graph G not belonging to its DFST. Then i is an ancestor of j (according to the tree order) or vice versa.

An examination of Fig.3.5 illustrates not only that this property is true for the DFST, but also that it is not (necessarily) true for the others. This property can be used to derive a very efficient algorithm for finding the cutnodes and cutbranches of a graph. Let us label each node with the order in the tree of the senior ancestor, which is the end of a branch closing a circuit containing the current node. In Fig.3.5d we have 4, 5 and 6 labeled by 3, 3 by 1, and all other nodes labeled by their own order in the tree. (Note that in this example the order in the tree is the same as the number marking the node in the figure). This is always true for the root and also nodes which are not part of any circuit [3.12]. Then we observe that a node V will be a cutnode if one of the following two things happens: a) V is the root of the DFST and has more than one child *in the tree*; b) V's order in the tree is less than or equal to the label of at least one of its children, i.e., there is no bypass between a child of V and an ancestor of V. In Fig.3.5d we see that the order of 3 in the tree is 3 and it has children whose labels are 3. Therefore 3 is a cutnode. Node 2 has a child with label 7, greater than 2; therfore 2 is a cutnode. But 4 has order 4 which exceeds the label of its child 5 (which is 3). We also observe that the node at the end of a cutbranch is connected to no other ancestor than its own parent. Therefore, for such a node, its label will equal its order in the tree. The only other node with this property is the root of the tree and this allows to find cutbranches easily. In Fig.3.5 (2,7) is a cutbranch because 7 is labeled by its own order in the tree and it is not the root. Blocks are readily found because all their nodes have the same label. It is possible to modify Algorithm 3.1 so that it labels the nodes appropriately. Then it is a simple matter to go over the graph once more comparing labels of nodes. This process is implemented in Algorithm 3.2.

A more detailed discussion of this algorithm and related topics can be found in [3.12]. Probably its most important feature is that it requires time proportional to the number of the branches of the graph. Any algorithm dealing with this question must examine all the branches; therefore Algorithm 3.1 is optimal in the sense that if there exists a faster algorithm it will be faster only by a constant factor.

Algorithm 3.2: Graph labeling for finding cutnodes and cutbranches

Input: Graph in the form of a node adjacency list as in Algorithm 3.1.

Output: Labels of nodes in arrays 01(i) (order of node i in the DFST) and 02(i) (value of 01 for the senior ancestor completing a circuit containing node i).

Note: S is a stack as defined in Algorithm 3.1. p(i) is an array containing the parent of i in the DFST.

Steps:

```
1. Mark all nodes with 0. Set k = 0, i = 1, j = 1.
2. Do block 11 while k is less than N or S is not empty.
    Begin block 11;
    1. If j > d(i) then do block 115.
        Begin block 115;
        1. Set i_old = i.
        2. Remove from S a pair of nodes and set i and j equal to its
           first and second members. [All the nodes adjacent to i have
           been visited and we replace the current node from the stack
           S].
        3. If 02(i_old) is less than 02(i) set 02(i) = 02(i_old).
        End block 115;
    _. Else do block 12.
        Begin block 12;
        1. If node nn(i,j) is marked then do block 125. [Proceed along
           the list of nodes adjacent to the current one until an un-
           marked one is found or the list is exhausted].
            Begin block 125;
            1. If nn(i,j) is not p(i) and 01(nn(i,j)) is less than 02(i)
               then set 02(i) = 01(nn(i,j)).
            2. Increment j.
            End block 125;
        _. Else do block 13.
            Begin block 13;
            1. Mark nn(i,j), increment k and set p(nn(i,j)) = i.
            2. Set 01(nn(i,j)) and 02(nn(i,j)) equal to k. [Initially all
               the labels are equal to the order in which a node is added
               to the DFST].
            3. Place in the stack S the pair (i,j+1). [Mark
               the place where we came from].
            4. Set i = nn(i,j) and j = 1.
            End block 13;
        End block 12;
    End block 11;
```

In some cases it is necessary to find what is called a minimum weight spanning tree. One is given a graph whose branches are labeled with non-negative numbers and is required to find a spanning tree where the sum of labels of its branches is minimum. Such trees have found numerous applications in pattern recognition [3.13-15]. Algorithm 3.3 achieves this goal [3.12,16]. It is more efficient than other algorithms [3.12,16] if the graph is dense.

Algorithm 3.3: Minimum weight spanning tree

Input: Graph G in a node adjacency list as in Algorithm 3.1. Array $\ell(i,j)$ contains the branch weights.

Output: List of spanning tree branches.

Notes: The multidimensional array A holds intermediate information. v(i) is initially zero and is set to 1 when a node is added to the spanning tree.

Steps:

1. Set m = 1 and v(1) = 1.
2. For i = 2 to N set A(1,i) = 1 and A(2,i) = $\ell(1,i)$
3. While m < N-1 do block 11.

   Begin block 11;

   1. Find the minimum of A(2,*) and let j be its position.
   2. Set v(j) = 1 and increment m. Also set q=A(1,j) and output branch (q,j).
   3. Do block 12 for i = 1,N.

      Begin block 12;

      1. If v(i) = 0 and $\ell(i,j)$ < A(2,i) then set A(2,i) = $\ell(i,j)$ and A(i,1) = j.

      End block 12;

   End block 11;

Block 11 is executed N-1 times and contains two steps (1 and 3) which require time proportional to N. Therefore the algorithm requires, at most, time proportional to N^2. The complexity of algorithms looking for paths between two nodes of a graph, or looking for the shortest path, is also of the same order as the above [3.12,16]. Therefore, such algorithms tend to be rather fast and can be used easily within a picture processing environment. The existence of fast algorithms for some problems should not obscure the fact that there exist problems, and the time required for their solution is apparently an exponential function of the size of the graph (number of nodes plus number of branches). One such problem is to check whether two given graphs are isomorphic or homeomorphic [3.7]. The same is true about the problem of subgraph isomorphism, i.e., verifying whether a given graph is isomorphic to a subgraph of another. The latter problem requires exponential time, even if both graphs are planar [3.17]. We shall discuss some of the implications of these requirements in the context of Scene Analysis in Chapter 6.

3.4 Fundamentals of Discrete Geometry

A host of (often hidden) troubles in picture analysis is caused by the discrete nature of the data. A simple example is offered by the difficulty in defining connectivity in the example of Fig.3.6. If we decide to define connectivity only along "rook" moves then the figure contains four separate components. If we allow connectivity along "bishop" moves as well as "rook" moves then there only two sets. In the last case both sets contain paths entirely within themselves, but which also intersect! In the first case the diagonals from A to B and C to D intersect at a point belonging to neither set.

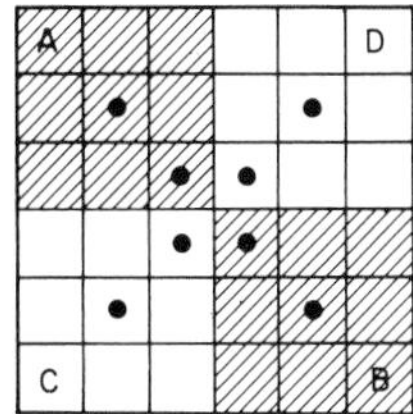

Fig. 3.6 Connectivity paradox on a discrete grid. If we assume that sets can be connected along diagonals, then the paths AB and CD (represented by solid circles) cross each other, even though each lies entirely within a different set. If we assume that sets cannot be connected along diagonals, then we have a situation where the black squares form two sets, each simply connected, with the same being true for their complement, the white squares

In a more "esoteric" view, the contradictions carry to the definition of topological equivalence, or *homeomorphism*. Two sets A and B are called homeomorphic if there is a one-to-one mapping from A to B which is continuous and whose inverse is also continuous [3.18]. On the basis of this definition it can be shown that size is not a topological invariant, i.e., sets of different size can be homeomorphic. On the other hand, in the discrete case the one-to-one requirement imposes size invariance. Thus, the sets A and B in Fig.3.7 cannot be called topologically equivalent under the standard definition. A third difficulty is illustrated by an effort to define a *straight line* in a discrete space [3.19]. In the Euclidean plane, the shortest path between two points is unique. But in Fig.3.7, the shortest distance between 1 and 2 is 12 steps and there is definitely more than one path with that length (924 to be precise!). The difficulties caused by such problems are not only "esthetic" but quite real in the implementation of algorithms as we shall see later on. It is therefore worthwhile to focus our attention for a while on the development of discrete geometry.

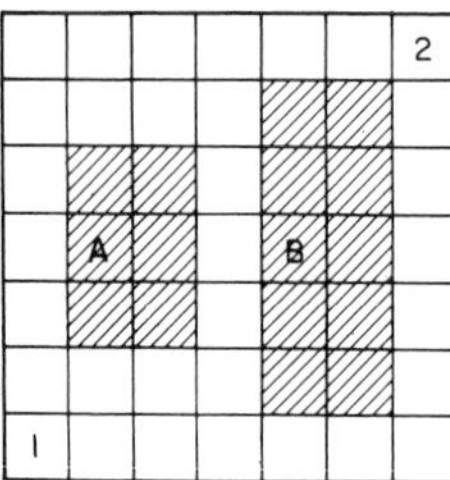

Fig. 3.7 A direct extension of the classical definition of topological equivalence characterizes sets A and B as being topologically different. Another paradox is that there is no unique shortest path between points 1 and 2

We shall follow the methodology developed by MYLOPOULOS [3.5,6,21] which is a generalization of the earlier work of ROSENFELD [3.4]. For other examples of work on such problems see [3.19,22]. We start by defining a set of fundamental directional vectors on the plane $\underline{e}_1$, $\underline{e}_2$, ...$\underline{e}_n$ of unit length. Then we create a discrete grid as follows:

Definition 3.12: The direct neighbors of a point P of the plane pointed at by a vector from the origin $\underline{x}$ are the 2s points pointed by the vectors $\underline{x} + \underline{e}_1$, $\underline{x} - \underline{e}_1$,...$\underline{x} + \underline{e}_s$, $\underline{x} - \underline{e}_s$. The direct neighborhood of P is defined as the set consisting of P and its direct neighbors and it will be denoted by ND(P).

Readers familiar with abstract algebra will recognize the above as the definition of a finite Abelian group with s generators. If the s vectors are linearly independent (which in the plane means s = 2) then the group is free. The grid may also be considered as a graph, where each node is connected to 2s others, its direct neighbors.

Definition 3.13: A direct path from a point P to a point Q is an ordered sequence of points $P_1, P_2, \dots P_n$ such that

$$P_1 = P, \; P_n = Q$$

$$P_{i+1} \neq P_i \quad \text{and} \quad P_{i+1} \in ND(P_i) \quad i = 1,2,\dots n-1 \quad .$$

We may extend the definition of neighborhood as follows:

Definition 3.14: The neighbors of a point P of the plane are its direct neighbors plus all points Q (with vectors from the origin $\underline{y}$) such that the shortest direct path between a pair of direct neighbors of P, not passing through P, passes through Q. An indirect neighbor is a neighbor that is not a direct neighbor.

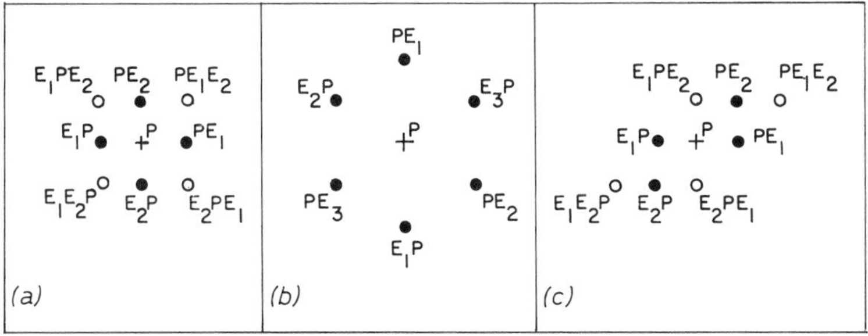

Fig. 3.8a-c Three different types of neighborhoods of a point on discrete grids. Solid circles mark direct neighbors and open circles indirect neighbors of points marked by +

The effect of this definition is that a point is "surrounded" by its neighbors. Fig.3.8 shows the neighbors and direct neighbors in the following three cases:

a) $\underline{e}_1 = (1,0) \quad , \quad \underline{e}_2 = (0,1)$

b) $\underline{e}_1 = (0,1) \quad , \quad \underline{e}_2 = (\frac{\sqrt{3}}{2}, \frac{-1}{2}) \quad , \quad \underline{e}_3 = (-\frac{\sqrt{3}}{2}, \frac{-1}{2})$

c) $\underline{e}_1 = (1,0) \quad , \quad \underline{e}_2 = (\frac{1}{\sqrt{2}}, \frac{1}{\sqrt{2}}) \quad .$

Case a) represents the common rectangular grid, while b) describes a hexagonal grid. There all neighbors are also direct neighbors. We will use N(P) to denote the neighborhood of P, i.e., the set of all neighbors plus P itself and the notations PE_i and E_iP to denote the points pointed at by the vectors $\underline{x} + \underline{e}_i$ and $\underline{x} - \underline{e}_i$, respectively. If $N(P_i)$ replaces $ND(P_i)$ in Definition 3.13 above, we simply have the definition of a path. We should also mention that many authors use the names 4-point and 8-point neighborhood, respectively, for ND(P) and N(P).

3.5 Connectivity and Topological Equivalence for Binary Pictures

We can state now the main definition:

Definition 3.15: A set F of points on a discrete grid is d-connected if any two points P', P" ∈ F can be joined by a direct path. A set F is connected if any two such points can be joined by a path.

We have two types of connectivity, removing some of the paradoxes mentioned earlier. Indeed, the paradox of Fig. 3.6 vanishes if we used d-connectivity for the black points and connectivity for the white ones. Note that if we use the directions specified in b), the paradox disappears without the necessity of dual definitions. The resulting grid is triangular or hexagonal. Examples of picture processing involving such grids can be found in the literature [3.23,24]. It can be shown also that a hexagonal grid minimizes the quantization error when a finite area of a picture is replaced by a single picture element whose brightness is the average of that area [3.25]. However, a grid of this type has also a number of disadvantages: 1) it yields awkward data structures in implementation. A rectangular grid can be represented easily by a two-dimensional array, while a hexagonal grid requires a rather complex linked list; 2) it makes digitization somewhat complicated, since the vertical spacing among points has a ratio of 0.866 to the horizontal spacing; 3) it still leaves unresolved the paradox of topological equivalence; 4) its improvement in quantization error over the square grid is only marginal [3.25]; 5) and finally, it does not avoid some of the problems occurring in multicolored pictures. We discuss the latter point in more detail in the Section 3.6. We present next certain results related to the degree of connectivity, and then introduce the notion of topological equivalence for discrete grids.

Definition 3.16: A subset F' of F is a d-component (component) of F if and only if F' is not empty and whenever $P \in F'$ and $Q \in ND(P) \cap F$ ($Q \in N(P) \cap F$) then $Q \in F'$. A hole (d-hole) in F is defined as a component (d-component) of the complement of F, $\bar{F}$, i.e., the set of all points of the grid not belonging in F.

Note that in order to be consistent, we must refer to d-components with holes, and components with d-holes. Let now #F and *F denote the number of d-components and components of F. We may consider points P whose removal from or addition to F does not change the number of d-components of F *in the neighborhood of P, and* also points which have the same property with respect to components of F and $\bar{F}$ in their neighborhood. Formally these are defined as:

Definition 3.17: A point P is d-inessential to F if

1) $\#[N(P) \cap (F \cup \{P\})] = \#\{[N(P) - P] \cap F\}$
   (number of d-components of F is not affected).
2) $*[N(P) \cap (\bar{F} \cup \{P\})] = *\{[N(P) - P] \cap \bar{F}\}$
   (number of components of $\bar{F}$ is not affected).

The point P is inessential to F if

1') $*[N(P) \cap (F \cup \{P\})] = *\{[N(P) - P] \cap F\}$
   (number of components of F is not affected).
2') $\#[N(P) \cap (\bar{F} \cup \{P\})] = \#(N(P) - P) \cap \bar{F}$
   (number of d-components of $\bar{F}$ is not affected).

P_1	P_2	P_3
P_4	P_5	P_6
P_7	P_8	P_9

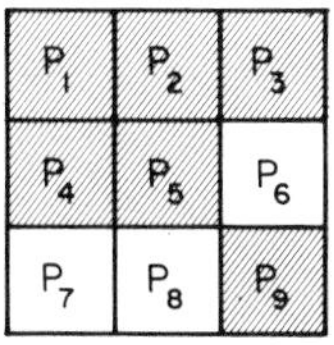

Fig. 3.9 Illustration of Definition 3.17. The point P_5 is d-inessential but not inessential for the set F, which consists of the shaded points

We see that "inessential" means that adding or deleting such a point does not change the number of components. Fig.3.9 shows a case where P_5 is d-inessential, but not inessential. Notice that

$N(P_5) \cap (F \cup \{P_5\}) = \{P_1,P_2,P_3,P_4,P_5,P_9\}$ with 2 d-components and 1 component,
$[N(P_5) - \{P_5\}] \cap F = \{P_1,P_2,P_3,P_4,P_9\}$ with 2 d-components and 2 components,
$N(P_5) \cap (\bar{F} \cup \{P_5\}) = \{P_5,P_6,P_7,P_8\}$ with 1 component and 1 d-component,
$[N(P_5) - \{P_5\}] \cap \bar{F} = \{P_6,P_7,P_8\}$ with 1 component and 2 d-components,

i.e., removing P_5 from F changes neither the d-connectivity of F or the connectivity of $\bar{F}$ but it changes both the connectivity of F and d-connectivity of $\bar{F}$. Note that if $P_5 \notin F$ then the same conclusions hold. The following theorem is due to MYLOPOULOS [3.6,20] and it states that we can check the number of components and holes of a set by local operations only.

Theorem 3.2: If a set F can be transformed into a set G by the addition or removal of d-inessential points from F, then the two sets have the same number of d-components and holes, and only then.

This is the closest that we can come to topological equivalence in discrete spaces. An abstract treatment of these questions in the context of computational topology can be found in the paper by TOURLAKIS and MYLOPOULOS [3.26]. The following is a natural definition of the boundary of a set, which we shall use in later sections, after considering the question of multicolored pictures.

Definition 3.18: The inside boundary of a set F, IB(F), is the set of all points P such that $P \in F$ and $N(P) \cap \bar{F} \neq \emptyset$. The outside boundary of F, OB(F), is similarly defined as the set of all points P such that $P \in \bar{F}$ and $N(P) \cap F \neq \emptyset$.

3.6 Discrete Geometry in Multicolored Pictures

The definitions and results of the two previous sections can be used easily for binary pictures, where we may be interested only in the boundaries of, say, the black areas. We are still left with problems in the case of non-binary or multicolored pictures.[1] There we deal with at least three types of regions and cannot escape with the dual definitions. One would like to define two regions to be adjacent if their boundaries intersect. In the two-color case this will work well if we use the inside boundary for one color and the outside for another. If a third color is present and we decide to use either of the two boundaries defined above we will be immediately faced with the old contradictions. The following two definitions provide one way around this difficulty [3.27].

[1] In this section and the rest of the book we will often use the word color in a loose sense. It may also denote different shades of grey, as is the case in a "black and white" photograph.

Definition 3.19: The *extended boundary* of a set F, EB(F) is the union of the following four sets for $\underline{e}_1$ and $\underline{e}_2$ as given in Fig.3.8a:

Top Boundary TB(F) $= \{P \mid P\in F \text{ and } PE_2\notin F\}$

Bottom Boundary BB(F) $= \{P \mid P\notin F \text{ and } PE_2\in F\}$

Left Boundary LB(F) $= \{P \mid P\in F \text{ and } [(E_1P\notin F) \text{ or } (P\notin TB(F) \text{ and } E_1PE_2\notin F)]\}$

Right Boundary RB(F) $= \{P \mid P\notin F \text{ and } [(E_1P\in F) \text{ or } (P\notin BB(F) \text{ and } E_1PE_2\in F)]\}$

Definition 3.20: Two regions are said to be *adjacent* if the extended boundary of at least one of them intersects the other region.

							1		
							2		
F_1							3		F_2
			8	7	6	5	4		
			9						

Fig. 3.10 The shaded squares represent the extended boundary between F_1 and F_2. (The two sets are separated by the heavy solid line). We have
$LB(F_2) = RB(F_1) = \{\text{squares } 1,2,3,4,8,9\}$
$TB(F_2) = BB(F_1) = \{\text{squares } 5,6,7,8\}$

Figure 3.10 illustrates the four boundary sets and shows that the extended boundaries of sets F_1 and F_2 are each intersecting the other set. These asymmetric definitions allow us to escape a number of paradoxes for multicolored pictures. The asymmetry is now not with respect to color but with respect to a *direction*. In particular we can show now that parts A and B in Fig.3.6 are adjacent, i.e., they "touch each other", while C and D are not. Fig.3.11a depicts the extended boundaries of A and B and Fig.3.11b those of C and D. Point 1, which belongs to B, is also a point of the right boundary of A. The same point belongs to neither of the set C and D. The set of points of a grid belonging to the extended boundaries of all the regions present in the grid forms a line drawing in the sense that no point in it has more than two neighbors, except where more than two regions meet. This example suggests how the definitions for connectivity and topological equivalence can be extended to multicolor pictures.

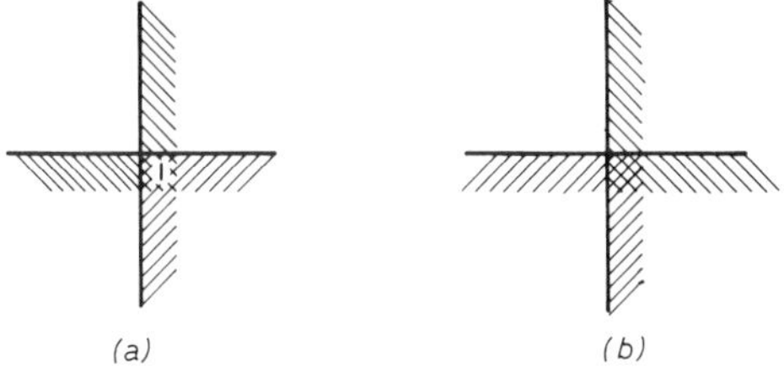

Fig. 3.11a,b Resolution of the paradox of Fig.3.6 through the definition of extended boundaries. a) Shading at -45 degrees marks the EB of A, while shading at 45 degrees marks the EB of B. b) Shading at -45 degrees marks the EB of D, while shading at 45 degrees marks the EB of C

Definition 3.21: A region is connected if any subset of it is adjacent to the set containing the remaining points.

It is probably worthwhile to point out some fundamental reasons for the need of asymmetric definitions in discrete geometry. When we examine regions of different color in the plane under the usual topology, we have to consider whether the sets are closed (i.e., include all their boundaries), open (i.e., include none of their boundaries) or "mixed" (i.e., include some boundary points but not all). The paradox of Fig.3.6 disappears if we state that all the black regions are closed and all the white ones are open. Then A is connected to B, but C is not connected to D. Requiring regions of one color to be closed is equivalent to allowing connectivity in the discrete case, while requiring them to be open is the equivalent of direct connectivity. In the multicolor case, it is not feasible to have only closed and open sets. We have to allow "mixed" sets. The two definitions of this section imply, in effect, that the sets contain their right and lower boundaries if viewed under the continuous topology.

4. Fundamentals of Picture Segmentation

4.1 Introduction

Picture segmentation is a term which has been used with various meanings by different people. In this treatise it will refer to the operation of looking at a scene and picking up objects from the background. In such an effort we divide the picture into different parts which have some meaning for the viewer. Thus in Fig.4.1 we lump all black parts together and thus produce a segmentation of the picture into 6 regions. A similar operation can be done on Fig.4.2, although the distinction there is not as clear. Nevertheless, we group together all points which are darker than some average value. Segmentation by brightness level is not the only way to analyze a picture. Figs.4.3 and 4.4 show examples of segmentation by texture or context. An automatic picture processor which is going to simulate human response must be able to perform these operations. This can be a formidable task if we want our system to handle cases like that of Fig.4.4. It can be very easy if we limit our attention to simple examples like that of Fig.4.1, where a simple *thresholding* operation suffices: Points are assigned to one of two regions depending on whether or not their brightness exceeds a threshold value. Our goal in this chapter and the next two chapters is to describe segmentation techniques which are applicable to a variety of pictures. The present state of the art is such that we cannot hope to handle examples as difficult as that of Fig.4.4. On the other hand, there exist methods for handling cases more difficult than those shown in Figs. 4.1-3.

The problem is basically one of psychophysical perception, and therefore not susceptible to a purely analytical solution. Any mathematical algorithms must be supplemented by *heuristics*, usually involving *semantics* about the class of pictures under consideration. Figs.4.5 and 4.6 illustrate a simple example. Because of the noise, a thresholding of the original (Fig.4.5) will produce a segmentation with a "Swiss cheese" appearance (Fig.4.6). We may add now a heuristic saying that: "Regions with area less than a value A must be merged into other regions". The value of A can be chosen on the basis

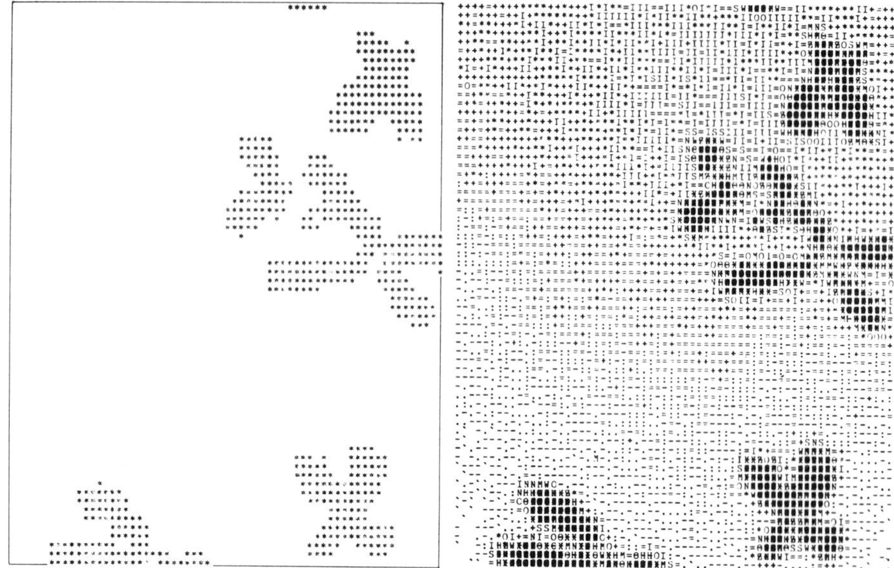

Fig. 4.1

Fig. 4.2

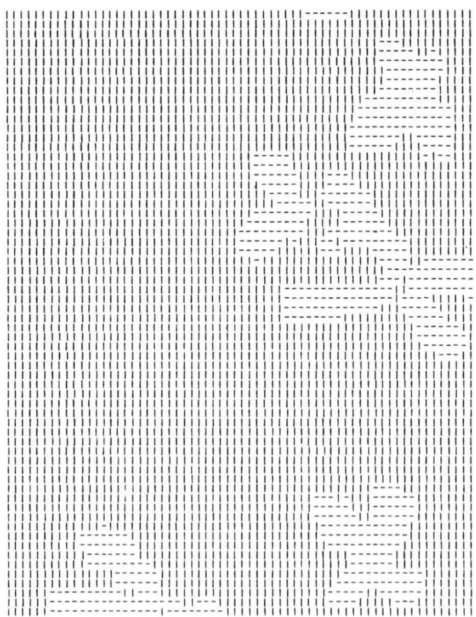

Fig. 4.3

Fig. 4.1 A binary picture of chromosomes. Here the segmentation problem is trivial

Fig. 4.2 A gray scale picture of chromosomes (7 bits per pixel). Here segmentation is nontrivial, but not very difficult either. Fig. 4.1 was obtained from this one by a simple thresholding operation (see Sec. 4.5)

Fig. 4.3 This is a picture where the objects are obvious to a human observer, but it is difficult to segment with a general purpose program (i.e., without specifying that the background consists of vertical lines and the foreground of horizontal). The average brightness is about the same over both types of regions, which differ primarily by *texture*

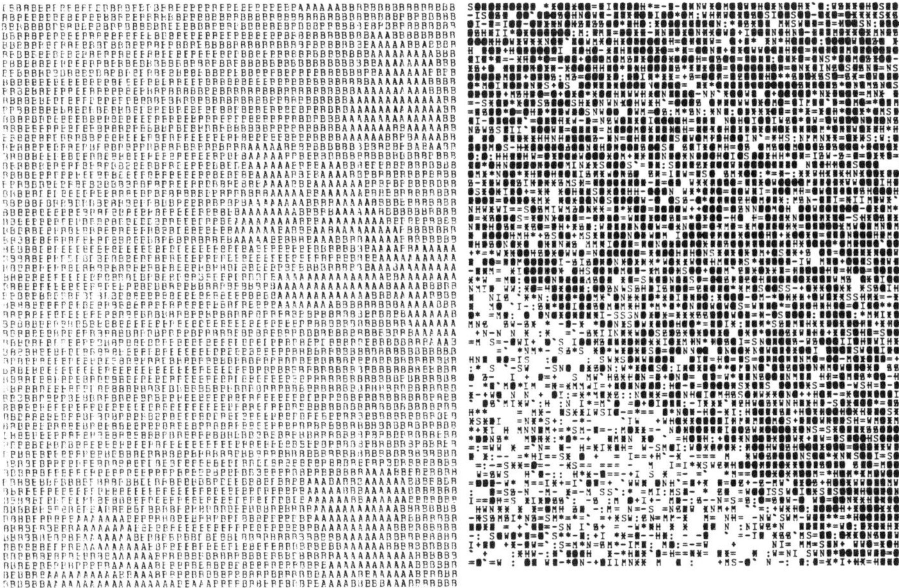

Fig. 4.4

Fig. 4.5

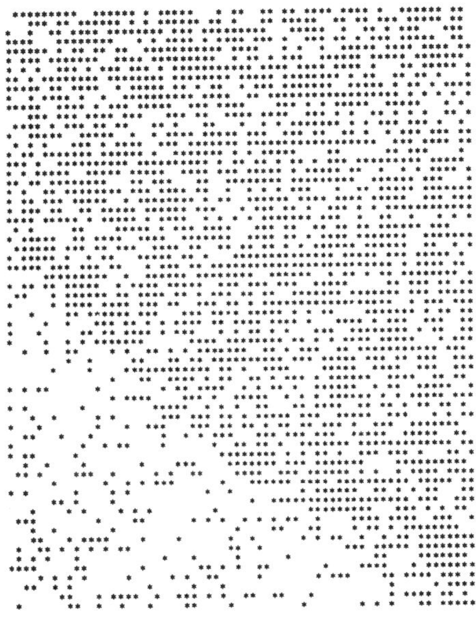

Fig. 4.6

Fig. 4.4 A human observer can identify the chromosomes here, although with some difficulty. Automatic segmentation is hopeless

Fig. 4.5 In spite of the large amount of noise, a human observer detects easily the boundary between the dark and the light region

Fig. 4.6 A simple thresholding operation on Fig.4.5 produces a rather unsatisfactory result, as shown here

of the expected size of regions for the class of pictures at which we are looking. Of course this is not the only method of processing the picture of Fig.4.5 and we will see in the sequence additional techniques. Quite often, one must go beyond such simple heuristics, and the introduction of a priori knowledge about the picture is essential. The well-known example of the dalmatian dog picture (Fig.1.1) is a good illustration of the use of such knowledge by humans. In such cases picture segmentation proceeds simultaneously with picture *understanding*. The term *Scene Analysis* is frequently used to describe studies of this type. In this chapter we discuss segmentation techniques which do not involve semantics or interpretation, i.e., we emphasize the "mechanics" of the process and we will give complete descriptions only for some simple schemes.

We are going to use the following notation and assumptions: The picture is given as an $N \times M$ matrix $f(i,j)$ resulting from sampling the original analog input. Usually $M = N$ and their values are between 64 and 1024. The term *pixel* is used to refer to a single element of the matrix $f(i,j)$ (a picture element). The values $f(i,j)$ correspond to (quantized) brightness. The choice of the proper sampling rates and quantization levels is in itself an interesting problem but lies outside the scope of this treatise. We also assume without any loss of generality that $f(i,j)$ never takes negative values. The result of the processing, i.e., the segmented picture, is another $N \times M$ matrix $s(i,j)$ whose values are region names or labels.

4.2 A Formal Definition of Segmentation

Intuitively, we want to subdivide a picture into regions which have a certain uniformity. In order to keep our analysis as general as possible we assume that we are given a *uniformity predicate* defined as follows.

Definition 4.1: Let X denote the grid of sample points of a picture, i.e., the set of pairs

$$\{i,j\} \quad i = 1,2\ldots,N \quad , \quad j = 1,2\ldots,M \quad .$$

Let Y be a subset of X containing at least two points. Then a uniformity predicate P(Y) is one which assigns the value *true* or *false* to Y, depending only on properties of the brightness matrix $f(i,j)$ for the points of Y. Furthermore, P has the property that if Z is a nonempty subset of Y then P(Y) = true implies always P(Z) = true.

We may extend this definition to the case when Y is a single pixel by assigning the value true to any uniformity predicate evaluated over a single pixel.

The following are a few simple examples of uniformity predicates:

$P_1(Y)$ = true if the brightness value at any two points of Y is the same.

$P_2(Y)$ = true if the brightness values at any two points of Y do not differ by more than a given amount e.

$P_3(Y)$ = true if the brightness value at any point of Y does not differ by more than a given amount from the average value of f(i,j) taken over a set S containing Y.

$P_4(Y)$ = true if the maximum of the brightness value over Y does not exceed a given value.

The following are examples of predicates not satisfying the definition:

P(Y) = true if Y has less than ten points. (P should depend only on the values of f(i,j) on Y).

P(Y) = true if the maximum of f(i,j) on Y exceeds a given value. (This might not be true on subsets of Y).

We are now ready to introduce a formal definition for segmentation.

Definition 4.2: A *segmentation* of the grid X for a uniformity predicate P is a partition of X into disjoint nonempty subsets $X_1, X_2 \ldots X_n$ such that:

1) $\bigcup_{i=1}^{n} X_i = X$.

2) X_i is directly connected or connected for i = 1,2,...,n. (See Secs.3.5 and 3.6 for the definition of these terms).

3) On each X_i the uniformity predicate $P(X_1)$ is true.

4) P is false on the union of any number of adjacent members of the partition.

The above definition does not imply that the segmentation is unique, or that n is the smallest possible value for a legal partition. Fig.4.7 illustrates this point in a one-dimensional situation which can be extended trivially to two dimensions by assuming no brightness variation along a direction perpendicular to the page. Let us assume that $P((x_i, x_{i+1}])$ is true if f(t) can be approximated on $(x_i, x_{i+1}]$ by a line segment with error less than a given constant e, according to any of the methods discussed in Chapter 2. The reader can verify that it is possible to have P true on the intervals $(a,x_1]$, $(x_1,x_2]$, $(x_2,b]$, $(a,y_1]$, and $(y_1,b]$ and false on $(a,x_2]$, $(x_1,b]$ and (a,b]. Then both segmentations shown on Fig.4.7 satisfy the definition.

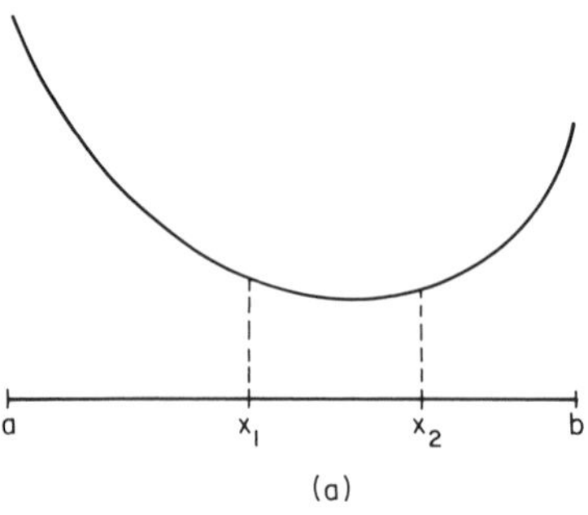

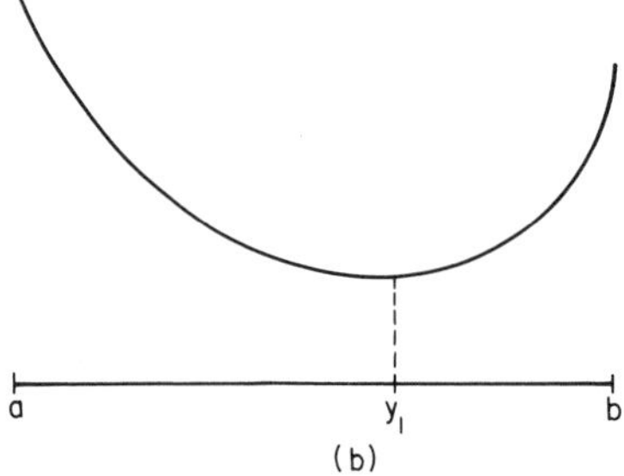

Fig. 4.7 Illustration of the nonuniqueness of segmentations satisfying Definition 4.2

Furthermore there can be situations where not even the minimal segmentation is unique. This will be the case if P is true on $(a,x_1]$, $(x_1,b]$, as well as $(a,y_1]$, $(y_1,b]$ but not on $(a,b]$. (Sec.2.11 provides one such case).

This example points out the conditions under which we may expect to have a minimal segmentation, or even only one segmentation satisfying the definition for a given picture. The lack of uniqueness in this case occurred because the chosen predicate did not really "fit" the data. The function f(t) looks more like a quadratic and we were attempting to perform a piecewise linear approximation on it. If f(t) was piecewise linear, possibly with the addition of small amplitude noise, and if e was chosen in such a way as to reflect the characteristics of the noise, then it is likely that there would be only one segmentation satisfying the definition. Or if there were more than one, they would all have breakpoints close to those of the original data. Indeed, let us consider a picture produced from an original having only two grey levels, say G_1 and G_2, corrupted by noise of maximum amplitude G_n. If

$$\frac{1}{2}G_n < e < |G_1 - G_2| \quad ,$$

then the predicate P_2 above will yield only one legal segmentation.

4.3 Data Structures for Segmentation

With the exemption of simple techniques like thresholding, segmentation algorithms require the examination of each point in comparison to its neighbors. Thus it is necessary to specify ways of "moving around" in a picture. This can be accomplished by defining appropriate *data structures*. A number of them are used in the implementation of segmentation algorithms, and pictorial pattern recognition in general. We give brief descriptions in this section and more extensive ones later.

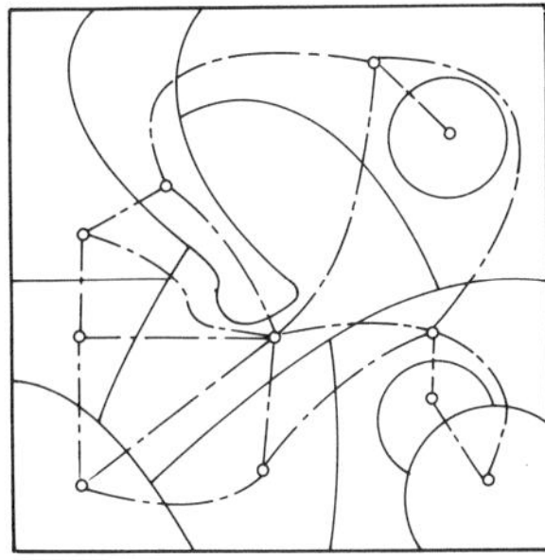

Fig. 4.8 A RAG superimposed over a segmentation. Solid lines denote region boundaries and mixed lines the branches of the RAG

a) The Region Adjacency Graph (RAG): This is a classical map graph with each node corresponding to a region (or country), and branches joining nodes representing adjacent regions (countries). Fig.4.8 shows a typical RAG on top of the corresponding regions. There is no restriction as to the type of the regions for which a RAG may be constructed. In particular, there may be single pixels which are connected to their neighbors or direct neighbors. We shall refer to this very simple RAG as the *grid*, since it coincides with the picture grid. The RAG has been used, at least implicitly, in various forms in most picture segmentation algorithms. Explicit use has been relatively recent [4.2-5]. It is quite useful even after the final segmentation, because there are many properties of the picture which can be deduced from it [4.2-5]. For example, nodes of degree one correspond to holes (i.e., regions completely surrounded by another) or regions adjacent to the frame of the picture. If we assign a node to the picture frame then all nodes of degree one correspond to holes. We shall discuss this and other properties in Section 5.3.

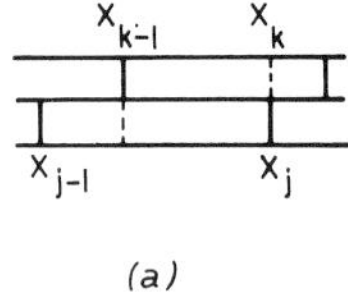

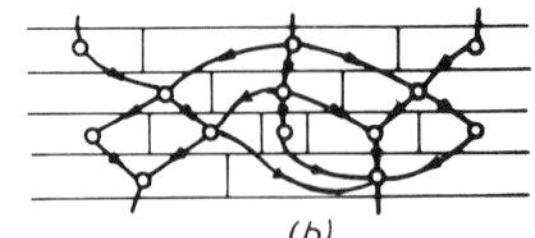

Fig. 4.9 a) Overlapping segments in adjacent raster lines. b) A LAG superimposed over a segmentation along raster lines

b) The Line Adjacency Graph (LAG): In many cases, a picture may be processed line by line, with each line segmented into a number of intervals. A graph then can be constructed by mapping line intervals into nodes and connecting nodes if the following conditions are met: the corresponding intervals lie on adjacent lines and their projections on a single line overlap [4.6,7]. This is illustrated in Fig.4.9a. The nodes corresponding to (x_{k-1},x_k) and (x_{j-1},x_j) will be connected if one of the following sets of inequalities holds.

1) $x_{j-1} < x_{k-1} < x_j$, 2) $x_{k-1} < x_j < x_k$,

3) $x_{j-1} < x_{k-1}$ and $x_k < x_j$, 4) $x_{j-1} > x_{k-1}$ and $x_k > x$.

Figure 4.9b shows such a graph. Note that intervals on the same line are not joined under this construction. However, we may link them if it is desirable, although it will be a good idea to label such branches differently from those connecting across lines. If such branches are included, then the LAG becomes a special case of the RAG. We shall discuss various uses and properties of the LAG later.

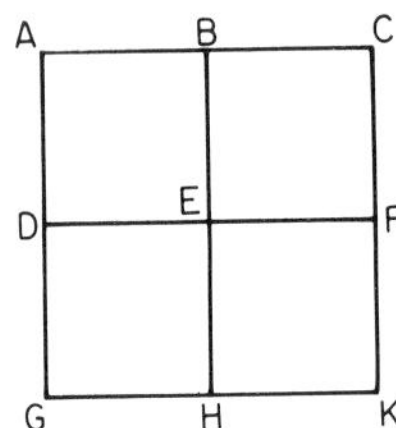

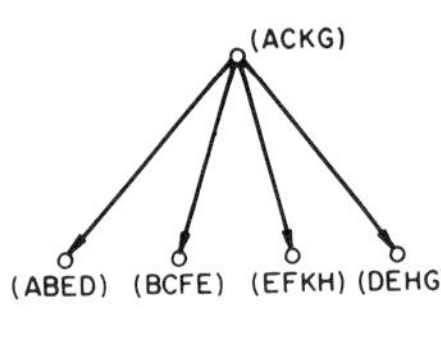

Fig. 4.10 Illustration of the definition of a picture tree

c) The Picture Tree (PT): This is a graph which emphasizes inclusion rather than adjacency relations. Its root corresponds to the whole picture and its leaves to single pixels. The children of each node A represent regions which form a partition of the region corresponding to A. Quite often, it is constructed by dividing each region into four equal parts in the manner shown in Fig.4.10. If the original grid has dimensions $N \times N$, where $N = 2^L$, then the picture tree has L levels. Nodes at distance j from the root correspond to squares of size 2^{L-j}. We shall call this a *Quartic Picture Tree (QPT)*. The picture tree has been used for segmentation as well as picture paging and picture processing [4.4,8-17]. It is often called the pyramid but we will reserve this term for a slightly different concept, which we discuss after noticing the following important property of the QPT.

Definition 4.3: A *cut* of a tree is a subset of its nodes with the following two properties: I) no two nodes in it belong to the same path from the root to a leaf, and II) no more nodes can be added to it without its losing property I.

Theorem 4.1: A segmentation of a picture always corresponds to a cut of the QPT.

Proof: Starting with the lowest level of the QPT, label all leaves with the number of the region to which they belong and place them in a set S. Then proceed recursively as follows. At any instance, replace in S four nodes of the same label by their parent, if this is possible. If no more replacements are possible, then exit. In this way, any path from the root to any leaf must contain at least one node in S, since all leaves were placed originally in S and were removed from there only when they were replaced by a parent. By this construction no node in S has any children in S, or any parents. Therefore all shortest paths from the root to the leaves contain exactly one element of S and S has no elements which do not belong to such paths (they may be possibly ends of such paths). Q.E.D.

Figure 4.11 illustrates this result.

1	2	3	4
5	6	7	8
9	10	11	12
13	14	15	16

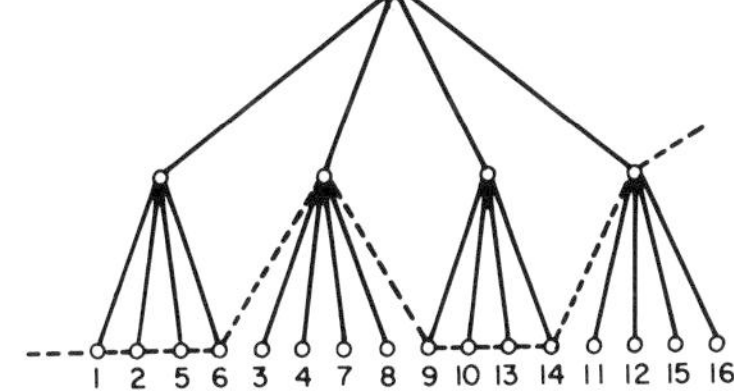

Fig. 4.11a and b Segmentation as a tree cut. a) The segmentation is defined by the solid lines. b) Broken lines join the nodes belonging to the cut

d) The Pyramid: This is a sequence of L pictures of increasing size from 1×1 to $N \times N$. The jth picture has size $2^j \times 2^j$, and its pixels correspond to regions represented by the nodes of the jth level of the Quartic Picture Tree. The brightness of each pixel is the average of the brightness of its children in the PT. A simple calculation can show that the total space required for it is only

$$S_P = \sum_{j=0}^{L} 4^j = \frac{4^{L+1} - 1}{3} = \frac{4}{3} N^2 \quad ,$$

i.e., we may store the whole pyramid by using only about 30 percent additional space over that of the original picture. A major advantage of the pyramid is that one may perform certain operations on a coarse resolution copy of the picture and then, on the basis of their results, may decide to proceed at parts of higher resolution. This can save considerable computing time and the pyramid has found wide use during the last five years. KELLY [4.8] seems to be the first one to have used it in a picture processing context. KLINGER [4.9] and UHR [4.10] also developed the concept independently. Systematic studies of its properties have been performed by TANIMOTO [4.13,14], RISEMAN and HANSON [4.12,16] and KLINGER and DYER [4.15], among others.

4.4 Approaches to Segmentation

An overview of the literature suggests that we should distinguish between those methods which consider regions directly and those which attempt first to identify region boundaries or *edges*. This distinction is not as clear-cut as it may seem. Indeed, we may define an *edge predicate* as follows:

Definition 4.4: Let X denote the grid of sample points of a picture (defined in Sec.4.2). An edge predicate Q(Y) is defined to be *true* on a nonempty subset Y of X if the following conditions are met: I) Each point of Y has at least one direct neighbor outside Y. II) A uniformity predicate P is false over the union of Y and the (direct) neighbors of the points of Y.

For example, we may have

Q(Y) = true if each point of Y has at least one direct neighbor outside Y and the difference between its brightness value and that of at least one of its neighbors exceeds a given value e.

In this case the uniformity predicate P_2 (defined in Sec.4.2) is used. More elaborate predicates can be found by considering edge detection operators of the type described in Section 4.6. We proceed now to give another formal definition.

Definition 4.5: An edge is a connected subset Y of X, such that an edge predicate Q(Y) is true, and there is no other subset Z of X, which contains Y and for which Q(Z) = true, i.e., an edge is a maximal subset where Q(Y) is true.

Fig. 4.12 When edges are detected as areas of high contrast they do not necessarily create a segmentation of the picture

Note that finding edges does not necessarily result in a segmentation, except in a trivial way, i.e., by having the partition of X consist of the edges and the connected components of the complement of their union. This is illustrated in Fig.4.12. There is no region there which is "surrounded" by edges, as it would be desirable intuitively. Therefore, one must perform some *edge tracing* in order to bridge gaps and obtain well-defined regions. The choice of the methodology depends significantly on the application. If we want to analyze a line drawing, like a cartoon, then there is little need to close up gaps in the edges, since the edges found by an edge predicate should be exactly the lines we are looking for. On the other hand, if our pictures contain well-defined regions, then we should look for a segmentation satisfying the formal definition in a nontrivial way. Algorithms for finding edges or other regions may be classified according to the data structure used, and the way it is used.

a) Local Schemes: These use only the grid, and label each point according to value of brightness there or at a fixed neighborhood of it. Thresholding is a prime example of the methodology. Most of the simple edge detection techniques are local. In either case, points with the same label need not belong to a single connected region. A segmentation satisfying Definition 4.2 or 4.5 can be obtained by identifying regions with the connected components of the sets which have the same label. These can be found easily by a number of algorithms.

b) Merging Schemes: These are schemes which start at the single pixel level or at an initial segmentation which is below the segmentation cutset in the QPT. Therefore, they proceed *bottom up* in terms of the QPT. P(Y) is always true over all the regions, but property 4) of Definition 4.2 is not satisfied until the end. Not all of them use the QPT explicitly, although they all must use a RAG. In their simplest form they can be thought of as graph labeling algorithms operated over the grid. They are quite often called *region growing* algorithms, but we prefer the present term in order to include "edge growing" schemes as well. Also the term "region growing" has been used in a broader sense to denote all algorithms which attempt to determine regions as distinct from those which look for edges [4.18]. The first part of the method by BRICE and FENNEMA [4.19] is a typical example of a merging algorithm. More complex versions have been described by BAJCSY [4.20], by FELDMAN and YAKIMOVSKY [4.21] and by GUPTA and WINTZ [4.22]. Merging schemes based on piecewise planar approximations have been investigated by HOLDERMANN and KAZMIERCZAK [4.23], PAVLIDIS [4.24], FENG and PAVLIDIS [4.25], ERNST and HOLDERMANN [4.26] and SOMERVILLE and MUNDY [4.27], among others. The edge growing approach is exemplified by the work of RAMER [4.28], BAIRD [4.29], VAMOS [4.30], and PERKINS [4.31]. Related to these techniques is the spatial clustering procedure developed by HARALICK and DINSTEIN [4.32].

c) Splitting Schemes: These start at the root of the PT or at a level higher than the segmentation cutset. They proceed *top down* by subdividing regions where P(Y) is false. They all used the QPT and they must always be followed by a merging scheme using the RAG because points which are very close geometrically on the picture may lie quite far apart on the PT. As a rule splitting schemes have been less popular than merging schemes. They tend to require more processing time but they have the advantage of allowing reliable estimates of predicates defined over a large number of pixels, e.g., variance of the brightness over a region. This property makes them less sensitive to noise than merging schemes which start from single pixels. The method of ROBERTSON, SWAIN and FU [4.33] belongs to this category.

d) Split-and-Merge Schemes: These combine the above operations in an effort to take advantage of the good points of both and also to reduce the overall computation time. They were first proposed by PAVLIDIS and HOROWITZ for curve fitting [4.34] and later extended to pictures [4.4,35]. Since pure merge or pure split schemes can be considered as special cases of the combined schemes we will describe only the latter in detail.

We should point out that at the end of the application of any of the above schemes, the results are usually "unfit for human consumption", i.e., the resulting segmentation does not correspond to human intuition, except in rather simple cases. It is almost always necessary to use some editing scheme which exploits additional features of the picture. Semantic information is particularly appropriate. We shall discuss such schemes in the next two chapters.

4.5 Thresholding and Segmentation Through Histograms

This, the simplest segmentation technique, does not strictly satisfy the formal definition. However, one which does can be obtained easily by finding the connected components for each value of the entries of the picture represented by the matrix s(i,j). The matrix s is binary and can be formed quickly by the simple rule:

$$s(i,j) = \begin{matrix} 1 & \text{if} & f(i,j) \geq T \\ 0 & \text{if} & f(i,j) < T \end{matrix} \quad ,$$

for some threshold value T. Each point of the picture is examined only once, and therefore the time requirements are exactly

$$T_1 = MN \quad .$$

The new matrix can be stored in place of the old one, so that the space requirements are

$$S_1 = MN \quad .$$

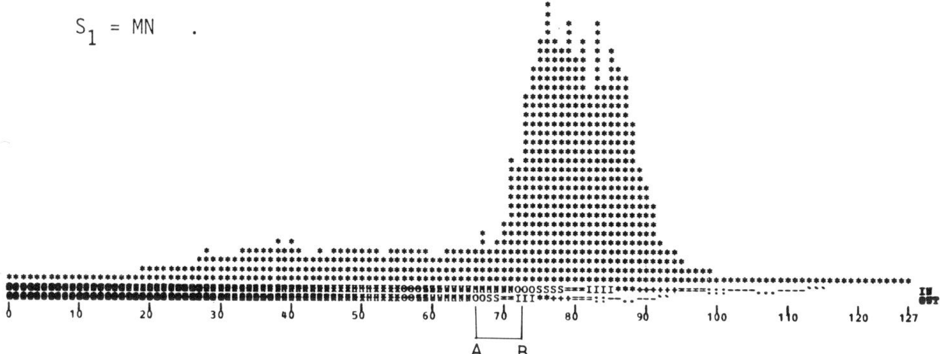

Fig. 4.13 Brightness histogram of Fig.4.2. The peak represents the background (bright area) and the zone AB denotes likely values for a threshold. The two lines at the bottom illustrate the code used for the reproduction of the particular intensity. The first corresponds to the code under the default parameters, and the second to the code actually used for printing Fig.4.2

A potential difficulty is the choice of the value of the threshold. A simple way of finding it is by constructing a *brightness histogram* of the picture. Fig.4.13 shows such a histogram for the original of Fig.4.2. There is one distinct peak, and any brightness value in the zone AB can serve as the threshold. If the histogram does not have such a form it will be necessary to use some other criterion. A relatively simple extension, proposed by ROSENFELD and NAGEL [4.36], is obtained by Algorithm 4.1.

Algorithm 4.1: Thresholding using gradient

Input: Picture matrix f(i,j).
Output: Binary matrix s(i,j).
Steps:
1: For each (i,j) compute the gradient norm by taking the average g(i,j) of the absolute values of the differences between f(i,j) and f(i+1,j), f(i-1,j), f(i,j+1), f(i,j-1) respectively. If g(i,j) exceeds a threshold H set h(i,j) = 1 else h(i,j) = 0
2: Form the histogram of h(i,j)*f(i,j) and choose a threshold T at a valley of the histogram. (If no such valley exists the method fails).
3: Perform a threshold operation on f(i,j) with T to obtain s(i,j).

The auxiliary matrix h(i,j) contains the points of significant change in brightness. It is usually easier to choose H rather than T. This search may be made only once for a class of typical pictures. On the other hand, it may be necessary for each sample (adaptive threshold choice) and in this case its computational requirements are non-trivial. In particular we have

$$T_2 = 12MN + MN + (\log_2 L)MN + 2L + MN = (14+\log_2 L)MN + 2L$$

where the terms correspond to the gradient operation (one subtraction, one absolute value and one addition for each of four neighbors), the comparisons with H, the formation of the histogram ($\log_2 L$ comparisons for L grey levels and one addition), the search for a minimum on the histogram and the final thresholding. The total space required is

$$S_2 = 2MN \quad .$$

A simple adaptive threshold scheme which has been used in commercial devices involves averaging the brightness values over the area of interest and then finding the threshold as a function of brightness with an empirical formula [4.37].

A direct generalization of thresholding can be made for the case of multilevel pictures. The output matrix can be defined as:

$$s(i,j) = k \quad \text{if} \quad T_{k-1} \le f(i,j) < T_k \quad k = 0,1,\dots,m \quad ,$$

where $T_0, T_1 \dots T_m$ are threshold values with T_0 equal to the minimum and T_m the maximum of expected brightness values. The computational complexity of this scheme is of the same order as that of simple thresholding, since each point of the picture is examined only once. We will use the term *multi-thresholding* for the method. The choice of the delimiters T_i and the value of m can once again be made on the basis of a brightness histogram. Segmentation by histograms has been used by a number of researchers. NAGAO et al. [4.38] used it for the recognition of geometric solids. Such objects have distinct surfaces and, if illuminated from the proper angle, each surface has a distinct brightness. Even for this limited class of pictures the segmentation had to be supplemented by semantic information in order to achieve reasonable results. The source of the difficulties is that often histogram peaks need not correspond to perceptually distinct areas. This can be the case when linear gradients are present. Conversely small regions may not be detected because their contribution to the histogram may be literally overshadowed by the noise from other regions.

OHLANDER [4.39] has proposed a segmentation scheme based on multithresholding utilizing nine histograms: color intensity for red, green and blue (this can be measured easily through filters), overall intensity (the average of the three colors at each pixel), hue, etc. The procedure is recursive and thresholds the picture repeatedly until all regions have a sharply peaked histogram in at least one of the parameters. BAIRD and KELLY [4.40] have used a sequence of threshold values for segmentation in the context of a human face recognition program.

4.6 Edge Detection Techniques

The simplest edge detector is a counterpart to thresholding. It evaluates a gradient of the picture and assigns to edges all points where the gradient exceeds a given value. In particular, we may define

$$g(i,j) = |f(i,j) - f(i-1,j)| + |f(i,j) - f(i,j-1)| \quad . \tag{4.1}$$

In general, points where g(i,j) has a value greater than zero may have no direct neighbor where g(i,j) is zero, so that the resulting edges will not satisfy Definition 4.5. For example, f(i,j) may be a linear function of j in which case g(i,j) is a constant over the whole picture. Therefore, the choice of the nonuniformity predicate is important. (This is not really a defect in the method. Choosing P_2 as a uniformity predicate for such a picture and attempting a segmentation will result in a series of parallel stripes, not a particularly informative result). A somewhat more complex gradient formula has been attributed to SOBEL [4.41]. This formula compares the brightness of a point with that of both the direct and indirect neighbors. Using the notation of Fig. 4.14 we have:

$$\begin{aligned} g(e) = &\left|[f(a) + 2f(b) + f(c)] - [f(g) + 2f(h) + f(i)]\right| \\ &+ \left|[f(a) + 2f(d) + f(g)] - f(c) + 2f(f) + f(i)]\right| \quad . \end{aligned} \tag{4.2}$$

a	b	c
d	e	f
g	h	i

Fig. 4.14 Notation of the neighborhood of a point used in the Sobel edge detector

For a binary picture the maximum value of this gradient is 6 and it is achieved at a corner or diagonal edge. For vertical or horizontal edges its value is 4. A number of edge detectors use more complicated gradient schemes than that given above. They are all of the form

$$g_h(i,j) = \sum_k \sum_\ell h(k,\ell) f(i+k,j+\ell) \quad , \tag{4.3}$$

where $h(k,\ell)$ is a weighting function. A set of such functions might be used, and one could define

$$g(i,j) = \max_h \{g_h(i,j)\} \quad . \tag{4.4}$$

The last expression represents a search for an optimal matching between the pictorial data and some edge. In addition to the value of g(i,j) we obtain information about the edge which best matches the data. Such information may include both its direction and its size. Then g(i,j) will be only a confidence level. Edge detection can be considered an approximation problem in the following sense. After a direction is chosen at a point, one may look for optimal approximations of parts of the picture on either side by some kind of smooth functions. If the approximations differ significantly, then one may decide in favor of an edge. In the simplest case the approximations can be piecewise constant. Such techniques have been proposed by HUECKEL [4.42,43] and YAKIMOVSKY [4.44] among others.

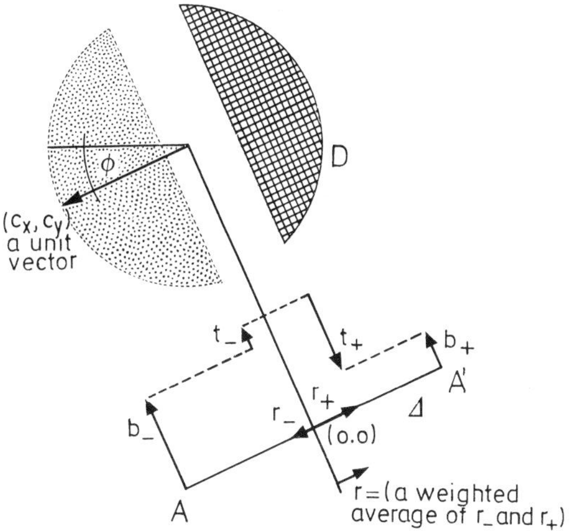

Fig. 4.15 Definition of the neighborhood used by HUECKEL [4.42,43] for the line and edge detector. (Reproduced from [4.43])

We proceed to describe these two in some detail.

a) The Hueckel operator: This is one of the most general operators which has been described in the literature and it is actually both an edge and a line operator. Its kernel $h(k,\ell)$ depends actually on six parameters shown in Fig.4.15 plus the size of a circular domain D centered at (0,0). The first parameter is an angle ϕ, formed with the x-axis by the normal AA' to the (hypothesized) direction of the edge. If u denotes the signed distance from the center along AA', then we have $u = \cos\phi k + \sin\phi\ell$ and

$$
\begin{aligned}
h(k,\ell) &= b- \quad \text{if} \quad u \le r- \ , \\
h(k,\ell) &= b- + t- \quad \text{if} \quad r- < u \le r+ \ , \\
h(k,\ell) &= b- + t- - t+ \quad \text{if} \quad r+ < u \ .
\end{aligned}
\tag{4.5}
$$

In other words $h(k,\ell)$ is a piecewise constant function. Edge and line detection is achieved by determining for each position (i,j) the values of the six parameters which minimize the integral square error between $f(i+k,j+\ell)$ and $h(k,\ell)$ over the disc D. The problem reduces to a series of minimization (for each value of ϕ) of zero order splines with variable breakpoints. Since this must be repeated at every point of the picture, the computational requirements of the method seem forbidding. A simplification occurs by observing that the set of all real functions over D is a Hilbert space, and therefore it is possible to find an appropriate basis on D to simplify the computation. If r denotes the distance from the center of the disc, then the following functions are the first nine members of such a basis:

$$
\begin{aligned}
H_0(p,q) &= Q(1-r^2+3r^4) & H_4(p,q) &= 18^{1/2}Q(p^2-q^2) \\
H_1(p,q) &= Q(5r^2-2) & H_5(p,q) &= 18^{1/2}Q2pq \\
H_2(p,q) &= 3Qp & H_6(p,q) &= 45^{1/2}Q(2r^2-1)p \\
H_3(p,q) &= 3Qq & H_7(p,q) &= 45^{1/2}Q(2r^2-1)q \\
& & H_8(p,q) &= Q(-2+17r^2-21r^4)
\end{aligned}
\tag{4.6}
$$

where $r^2 = p^2 + q^2$ and

$$
Q = 2\sqrt{\frac{1-r^2}{3\pi}} \quad . \tag{4.7}
$$

These functions are orthonormal and also orthogonal to the constant, except for H_0 which forms a scalar product with 1 equal to $4(3\pi)^{1/2}/7$. Fig.4.16 shows their sign over the disc D and their zero crossing lines. For these functions it is possible to derive explicit expressions giving the error of approximation in terms of integrals of the basis functions and the angle ϕ.

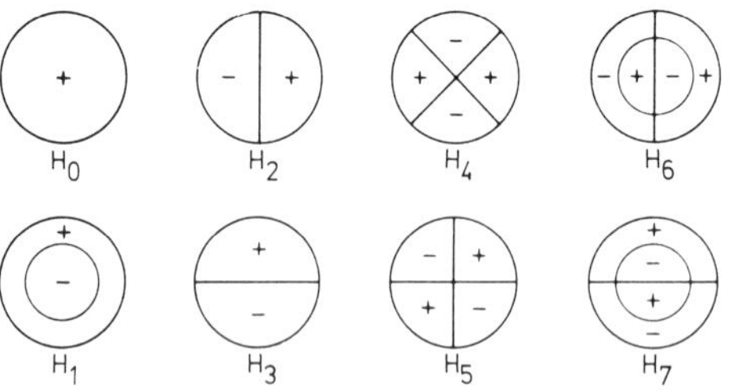

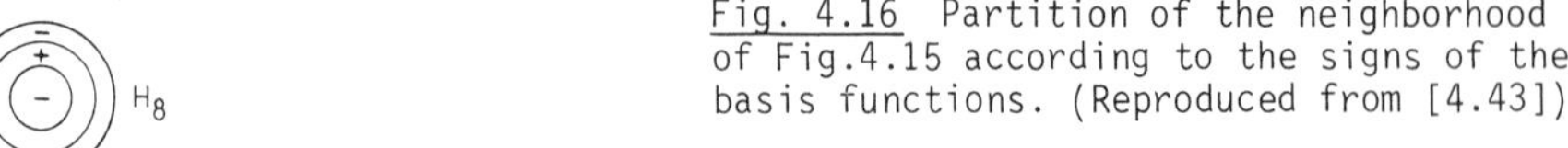

Fig. 4.16 Partition of the neighborhood of Fig.4.15 according to the signs of the basis functions. (Reproduced from [4.43])

Let

$$a_i = \sum_{p,q} H_i(p,q)f(p,q) \quad . \tag{4.8}$$

Then the error norm equals

$$E = (\tfrac{4}{3}a_1^2+a_2^2+a_3^2+2a_4^2+2a_5^2+a_6^2+a_7^2)/2 - M(C_p,C_q) \quad , \tag{4.9}$$

where the last quantity is given by

$$M(C_p,C_q) = (e_2C_p+e_3C_q)^2 + e_4C_p + e_5C_q \quad , \tag{4.10}$$

with

$$C_p = \cos(2\phi) \quad \text{and} \quad C_q = \sin(2\phi) \quad , \tag{4.11}$$

$$e_2 = \sqrt{\tfrac{2}{3}}a_4 \quad \text{and} \quad e_3 = \sqrt{\tfrac{2}{3}}a_5 \quad , \tag{4.12a}$$

$$e_4 = 2\sqrt{\tfrac{1}{3}}a_1e_2 + (a_2^2+a_6^2-a_3^2-a_7^2)/2 \quad , \tag{4.12b}$$

$$e_5 = 2\sqrt{\tfrac{1}{3}}a_1e_3 + a_2a_3 + a_6a_7 \quad . \tag{4.12c}$$

Therefore, the error norm will be minimum where $M(C_p,C_q)$ is maximum. The parameters b-, t-, t+, r-, r+ can also be found in terms of the above quantities. Using a disc of 69 points, the method requires 521 arithmetic operations per pixel. If the matching is not performed everywhere but only at a sufficient density to have each pixel covered by only three discs (rather than 69), then only 23 arithmetic operations per pixel are required. Although this is far more than the computation required by either (4.1) or (4.2), the application of the method yields better results than the simpler techniques [4.45].

b) Statistical edge detection: This has been used by YAKIMOVSKY as part of his scene analysis program [4.44]. Let N_1 and N_2 be two disjoint but adjacent subsets of the picture grid. Then we may test the hypothesis H_0, that both N_1 and N_2 belong to the same "object" versus the hypothesis H_1, that they come from different "objects". One possible implementation of this idea is achieved by assuming that the brightness of each region obeys a Gaussian distribution with both the mean and variance different among regions. If n independent samples $x_1,\dots x_n$ are taken from a Gaussian distribution with mean m and variance σ^2, then it can be shown that the joint probability density of generating the combined reading is given by

$$P = \frac{1}{2\pi^n} e^{n/2} \frac{1}{\sigma^n} \quad . \tag{4.13}$$

Let m_i, σ_i denote the mean and variance for the following three distributions: the one of a single object under the hypothesis H_0 (i=0); that of the object from where N_1 was taken (i=1); and that of the object where N_2 was taken (i=2). If N_1 contains n_1 points and N_2 n_2, we find that the likelihood ratio for the two hypotheses is:

$$L_{01} = \frac{P_1 P_2}{P_0} = \frac{\sigma_0^{n_1+n_2}}{\sigma_1^{n_1}\sigma_2^{n_2}} \quad . \tag{4.14}$$

One may choose to evaluate this ratio at all points of a picture for appropriately chosen neighborhoods. Typical examples of the latter can be halves of a disc with the diameter at different orientations. Then the gradient may be set equal to the maximum of the ratio taken over all possible directions. At an "ideal" edge the two variances at the denominator will be zero, while inside a uniform region all of them will be zero. Therefore L_{01} will vary between 1 and ∞. In general the values of the variances will not be known a priori, but they can be estimated, together with the means, according to the following formulas:

$$m_i = \frac{1}{n_i}\sum_{j=1}^{n_i} x_j \qquad \sigma_i^2 = \frac{1}{n_i}\sum_{j=1}^{n_i} (x_j - m_i)^2 \qquad i = 0,1,2 \quad . \tag{4.15}$$

In the above $n_0 = n_1 + n_2$. Note that the quantities for i = 0 can be evaluated in terms of the other two, without having to recalculate the sums. In terms of approximation theory the comparison involves that of the mean square error of the union of N_1 and N_2 with the product of the corresponding errors on each segment.

We conclude this section by pointing out that in the case of binary images, it is possible to find the boundary of regions by a direct application of Definition 3.18. This is advisable if one is interested in knowing which points belong to the boundary, but not in their particular order. In general this does not save much effort because one must trace the boundary in any case in order to avoid spending time proportional to the area of the picture. However, if most of the regions are very "thin" and one is concerned more with programming simplicity than with efficiency he can implement directly the operations of definitions of boundaries discussed in Chapter 3. In many cases the segmentation can be quite easy except for the presence of high frequency noise. A simple operation like thresholding may produce regions with many small holes as well as small protrusions like the example of Fig.4.6. If the noise level is not too high, then it is possible to eliminate its effect by a combination of a sequence of expansion and shrinking processes. These are defined formally as follows:

Expansion $E(R) = R \cup OB(R)$
Shrinking $S(R) = R - IB(R)$

where OB and IB denote the outside and inside boundary as given by Definition 3.18. Algorithm 4.2 combines them for the purpose of filtering.

Algorithm 4.2: Smoothing of boundary

Input: Region R.
Output: Region Q.
Notation: $C(P)$ = Points in $IB(P)$ whose only neighbors are in $IB(P)$ or the complement of P.
Steps:
1. $Q = E(R)$. (Expansion)
2. $Q = S(Q)$. (Q is now R with some of its holes filled)
3. $Q = Q - C(Q)$. (Eliminate some protrusions)

Figure 4.17 shows an example of the application of this algorithm. Note that repeated applications can fill bigger and bigger holes and remove bigger and bigger protrusions. At the same time the boundary is obtained trivially.

We have not exhausted here the subject of edge detectors because it belongs more properly in picture processing and such algorithms are used primarily as early preprocessors for pattern recognition. For more details the reader is referred to the review paper by DAVIS [4.46]. Also, the recent papers by ENOMOTO and KATAYAMA [4.47] and by PERSOON [4.48] describe effective edge detectors based on some very interesting mathematical ideas.

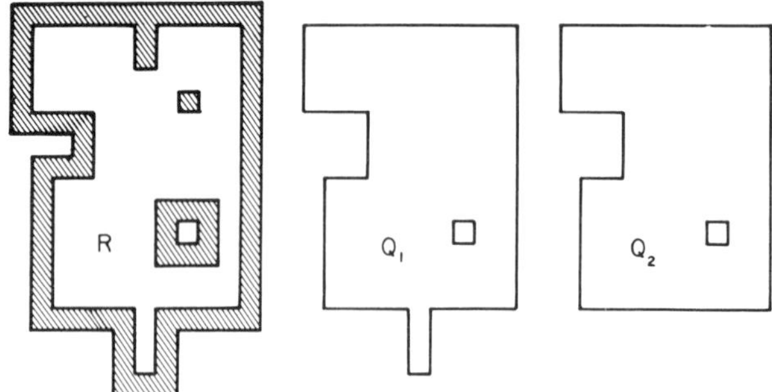

Fig. 4.17 Filtering of noise by expansion and shrinking. The shaded region is the OB(R). Set Q_1 is obtained after one application of these operations and set Q_2 after step 3 of Algorithm 4.2 has been applied

4.7 Segmentation as Functional Approximation

An interesting class of uniformity predicates P can be obtained by approximating f(i,j) with some mathematical function. Let $b_k(i,j)$ $k = 1,2,\dots,m$ be a finite family of linearly independent functions defined on X. Then we may define

$P_5(Y)$ = true if, at all points of Y, f(i,j) differs by less than h from the sum

$\sum_{k=1}^{m} a_k b_k(i,j)$, and false otherwise.

The coefficients $a_1,\dots a_m$ are chosen to minimize the maximum pointwise error over Y by a method similar to those discussed in Chapter 2. In other words, $P_5(Y)$ is true if the error norm of the best uniform approximation of f(i,j) by a linear combination of $b_k(i,j)$ $k = 1,2\dots m$ is less than or equal to h within Y. Instead of the uniform approximation, one may choose approximation by least integral square error and define

$P_6(Y)$ = true if, E_2 defined by

$$E_2 = \sum_{Y} [f(i,j) - \sum_{k=1}^{m} a_k b_k(i,j)]^2$$

is less or equal to a quantity H. It is false otherwise. The coefficients $a_1,\dots,a_m$ are chosen to minimize E_2.

A very simple special case occurs when $m = 1$ and $b_1(i,j) = 1$. Then segmentation is reduced to piecewise constant approximation and one can verify that, using P_4,

$$a_1 = \frac{1}{2}\,[\max_Y\{f(i,j)\} + \min_Y\{f(i,j)\}] \quad , \tag{4.16}$$

in order to minimize the maximum pointwise error e, which then is given by

$$h_1 = \frac{1}{2}\,[\max_Y\{f(i,j)\} - \min_Y\{f(i,j)\}] \quad . \tag{4.17}$$

If $e = 2h$, then P_5 becomes equivalent to P_2 (Sec.4.2)

E_2 is minimized if a_1 equals the mean or average value $f(i,j)$ in Y (see Sec.2.10). In this case it is given by

$$E_2 = \sum_Y [f(i,j) - a_1]^2 \quad . \tag{4.18}$$

Then

$$P_{60}(Y) = \text{true} \quad \text{if} \quad \sum_Y [f(i,j) - a_1]^2 < H, \quad \text{false otherwise.}$$

A segmentation using P_2 is closely related to multi-thresholding if

$$T_k = T_{k-1} + 2h \quad , \tag{4.19}$$

which in turn is equivalent to segmentation by *contours*. However, there is an essential difference, which is illustrated by Fig.4.18. The one using P_2 adjusts itself to produce fewer regions. In addition the choice of the parameter h is much easier than that of the thresholds. In particular, h depends only on the noise level and the number of bits we want to ignore from the brightness function. Thus it can be fixed a priori for a large class of pictures.

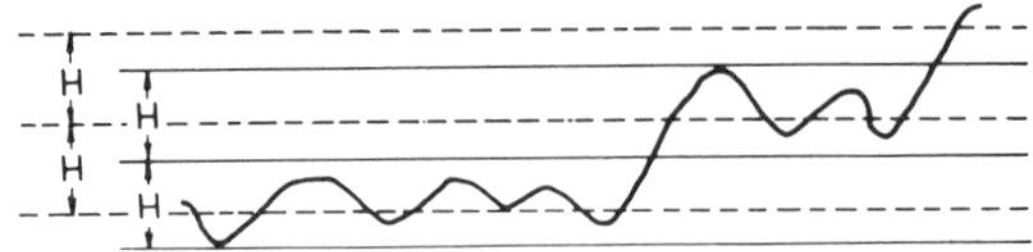

Fig. 4.18 The segmentation produced by multi-thresholding depends on the choice of the origin in the brightness scale. Note that the segmentation produced by the solid lines results in far fewer regions than that produced by the broken lines. On the other hand, a segmentation according to P_2 will always follow the solid lines for the same choice of tolerance

There exist many variants of this approach in the literature. YAKIMOVSKY [4.44] calculates for each region R the mean square error with respect to the brightness mean according to the formula:

$$V(R) = \frac{1}{N}\sum_{k=1}^{N} [f(i_k,j_k) - f_m]^2 \quad , \tag{4.20}$$

where N is the number of points of the region, f_m is the mean brightness (optimal constant approximation) and the index k denotes a scanning of the region according to some rule. Two regions R_i and R_j are merged if the ratio $V(R_i \cup R_j)/(V(R_i)V(R_j))$, is less than a given threshold and the boundary between the two is "weak".

The new formalisms can handle easily pictures with linear variation by simply using linear approximations to f(i,j) in the definitions of P_5 and P_6. Such approaches have been used by a number of authors [4.23-27]. It can also handle cases like the one shown in Fig.4.3 in the following manner: Let Z be the smallest rectangle (of dimension $N_1 \times M_1$) containing Y as shown in Fig.4.19. Define $f_1(i,k)$ as equal to f(i,k) within Y and zero at other points of z. Let F*(u,v) be the Fourier transform of $f_1(i,k)$, i.e.,

$$F^*(u,v) = \sum_{i=0}^{N_\ell-1}\sum_{k=0}^{M_\ell-1} f_1(i,k)\exp\left(-j\frac{2\pi ui}{N_1}-j\frac{2\pi vk}{M_1}\right) \quad . \tag{4.21}$$

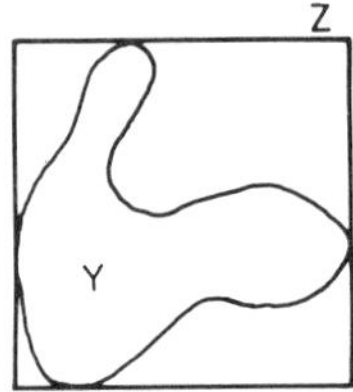

Fig. 4.19 If f(i,j) is defined as zero over Z-Y, then it is possible to evaluate a Fourier transform over Z and obtain some information about the spectrum of f(i,j) over Y. However, this transform will also reflect the shape of Y

Then over Y

$$f(i,k) = \sum_{u=0}^{N_\ell -1} \sum_{v=0}^{M_\ell -1} F^*(u,v) \exp\left(j\frac{2\pi ui}{N_1}+j\frac{2\pi vk}{M_1}\right) \quad . \tag{4.22}$$

Let p(i,k) be a sum of the terms in the above expression with, say, the five largest coefficients (in modulus) of F*(u,v). Then let

$$E = \sum_{Y} [f(i,k) - p(i,k)]^2 \quad .$$

We may now define a predicate

$P_7(Y)$ = true if E as defined above is less or equal to H, false otherwise.

The effect of such a definition will be a segmentation where in each region f(i,j) will be approximated closely by a few components of its Fourier transform. We should point out, though, that in this case F*(u,v) reflects not only the form of f(i,j) but also the shape of the region Y. If the latter is of a "smooth" form, a windowing function is used, and the spectrum of f(i,k) is of relatively high frequency; then F*(u,v) will reflect primarily the form of f(i,k). Alternatively we may evaluate the transform in rectangles *inscribed* in Y. Then no distortions due to the shape of Y are introduced, but low frequency information is lost. Fourier transforms have been used for segmentation by texture [4.20,49], but although they seem promising, they require very large computation time and this limits their applicability. We shall return briefly to the subject of texture in the next chapter.

5. Advanced Segmentation Techniques

5.1 Introduction

Simple techniques like thresholding are adequate for high contrast pictures, but they fail whenever the picture has gradual variations in brightness and color or when the different regions are characterized by texture rather than color. In this chapter we describe a general split-and-merge algorithm using the QPT (or pyramid) as its basic data structure. In addition, we outline certain simple editing techniques and how to obtain ordered lists of the boundary points from the output of such an algorithm. The description is in terms of predicates defined over regions rather than specific brightness or color criteria. Therefore, the algorithm is a frame which can be "dressed" according to the problem at hand. Segmentation according to brightness or color is relatively easy and a specific example of the algorithm for this case has been reported by HOROWITZ and PAVLIDIS [5.1]. In this form the algorithm is closely related to the various region growing algorithms described in the previous chapter. However, it can also be used for segmentation according to texture by keeping the same data structure and defining different predicates. At the time of this writing the characterization of texture is very much an open problem. There is, probably, general agreement that the second order statistics of the brightness function describe texture but the computation of many of them is quite time consuming. Furthermore, there is evidence that local shape recognition may be involved as well [5.2]. Interesting comparisons of various types of texture algorithms have been published recently by WESZKA et al. [5.3] and by CONNERS and HARLOW [5.4]. The adaptability of the general algorithm to segmentation by texture has been demonstrated in a preliminary study using the Fourier power spectrum [5.5].

All of the algorithms mentioned up to this point search for regions on the basis of properties of the brightness function $f(i,j)$ only. Another class of popular techniques has been the "interpretation guided segmentation" where semantic information is introduced quite early and a picture is searched for objects, e.g., [5.6-8]. It turns out that this approach requires the solution of a set of subgraph isomorphism problems, which can be very time consuming if the graphs involved are of any significant size. The early introduction of semantics can be attributed, at least partly, to unsatisfactory results obtained by simple algorithms like multi-thresholding. Pure merging algorithms are often quite sensitive to noise, and, in view of their popularity, this may have been a factor which contributed to the overuse of semantics. Experience with the more sophisticated segmentation algorithms shows that "reasonable" segmentations can be achieved without the use of semantics. These may be introduced only after a set of initial regions has been found and thus have "interpretation guided editing". This can be less time consuming because of the reduction in the size of the graphs involved. Another problem with the use of semantics is that there may be little a priori information about the nature of the picture. Therefore, it is worthwhile to look for high quality segmentations on the basis of the intrinsic properties of the pictorial data. We shall discuss such algorithms in the next chapter under the title of Scene Analysis.

5.2 An Overview of Split-and-Merge Algorithms

In many cases we may be able to guess a segmentation, and we would like to have an algorithm to improve the initial guess. For a given data structure we may give a set of initial labels to the nodes of the graph and then proceed to change the labels until a legal segmentation is achieved. The merging and the splitting schemes discussed in Section 4.4 are limiting cases of this approach. However, schemes which perform both operations are of greater interest. A split-and-merge scheme starts with a set of regions and merges them or splits them, until the properties of a formal segmentation are satisfied. Such an approach is, in general, more efficient than either a pure merge or a pure split scheme for a number of reasons:

I) The cost of the segmentation consists of two terms, the calculation of quantities necessary for the evaluation of the uniformity predicate and the evaluation of the predicate itself. For example, if P_2 is used, the first part represents the effort for finding the maxima and minima of brightness over a region while the second part is the comparison of their difference with the tolerance e. In a pure merge operation (starting from pixels), the number of comparisons equals approximately the number of pixels, since the predicate must be tested before a pixel is added to a region. In a pure split operation, the number of such comparisons is approximately equal to the number of regions (which can be much less than the number of pixels). However, calculations of the first part may have to be repeated more than once for a given region. It is not difficult to show that if A is the picture area, effort proportional to AlogA may be necessary. There is an obvious trade-off, and by starting at the proper partition, we should be able to minimize the effort. Fig.5.1 illustrates this in terms of the QPT. The area between the starting level and the final cut reflects the computational effort. This is smallest for a split-and-merge scheme starting near the cut. Note that in the worst case the asymptotic efficiency of split-and-merge can be worse than that of pure merge procedure. On the average, though, split-and-merge is better by a constant factor.

II) In many cases an initial guess of the segmentation may be available, and it is more efficient to attempt to modify it than to start from scratch. This is typically the case in moving scenes where the segmentation of a previous frame may be used as an initialization for the current frame, and also in the processing of pictures of identical objects which are examined for flaws, a frequent occurrence in industrial automation.

III) More reliable information can be obtained about certain properties of regions by examining a number of pixels together. This is typically the case with texture [5.2-5,9-21].

Algorithm 5.1 implements split-and-merge segmentation in a general way. A concrete algorithm will be given in Section 5.4.

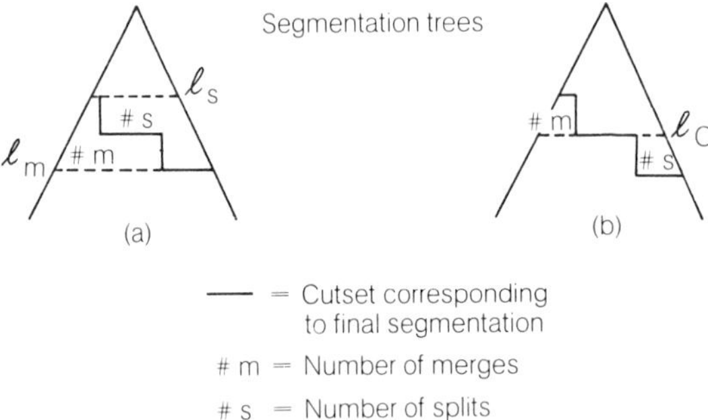

Fig. 5.1a,b Illustration of the computational economy achieved by the split-and-merge method. (Reproduced from [5.1])

Algorithm 5.1: General split-and-merge scheme

Input: A RAG representing an initial segmentation satisfying conditions [1] and [2] of definition 4.2.

Output: A legal segmentation.

Steps:

1. Set s = true
2. While (s=true) do block 22.
   Begin block 22;
   1. Set s = false
   2. For each node j of the RAG evaluate $P(X_j)$. If false, set s = true and split X_j into M regions according to some pre-assigned rule and given M. Also update the RAG. If true do nothing.

   End block 22;
3. Set m = true.
4. While (m=true) do block 44.
   Begin block 44;
   1. Set m = false.
   2. For each node j of the RAG and for each one of the nodes adjacent to it, say k, do block 45.
      Begin block 45;
      1. If $P(X_j \cup X_k)$ is true, merge the two regions, set m = true and update the RAG. If it is false, do nothing.

      End block 45;

   End block 44;

A large variety of specific split-and-merge algorithms can be derived by choosing the criteria for splitting, the number M and the order of visitation of the nodes of the RAG. It includes as special cases pure merge algorithms (if the initial regions are single pixels) and pure split algorithms (if there is only one initial region, the whole picture). Note that all the splitting occurs before any merges and therefore there is no possibility of cycling. Section 5.4 describes an algorithm where M = 4, the split is performed along the QPT and the merge along both the QPT and the RAG.

5.3 Picture Editing and Properties of the RAG

Segmentation algorithms using predicates based on the brightness matrix only rarely produce results in agreement with human intuition. Typically,

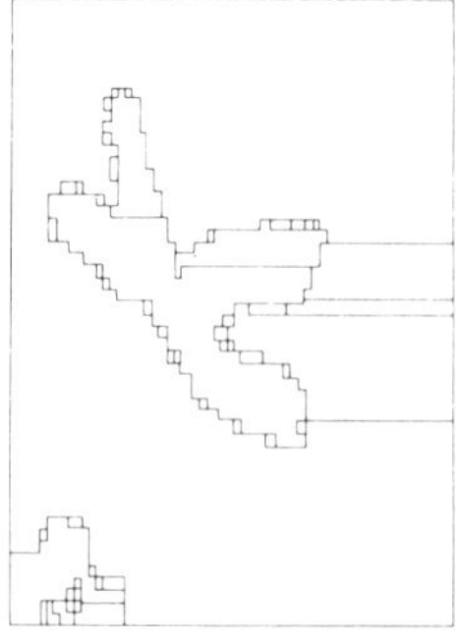

Fig. 5.2 Results of segmentation before small region elimination. (Reproduced from [5.27])

the number of regions is far too large. Fig.5.2 shows a segmentation of Fig.4.2 using the predicate P_2 (see Sec.4.2) and a merging algorithm on the LAG. (The raster segmentations were obtained by a one-dimensional split-and-merge algorithm). We observe a few large regions and a large number of small ones. A histogram of the region size is shown in Fig.5.3.

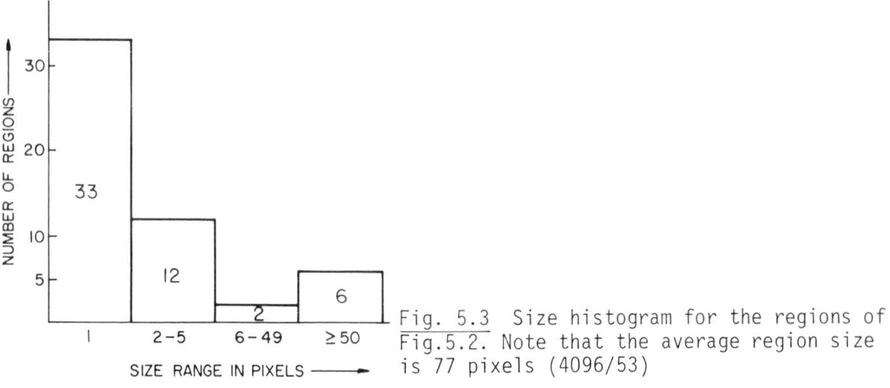

Fig. 5.3 Size histogram for the regions of Fig.5.2. Note that the average region size is 77 pixels (4096/53)

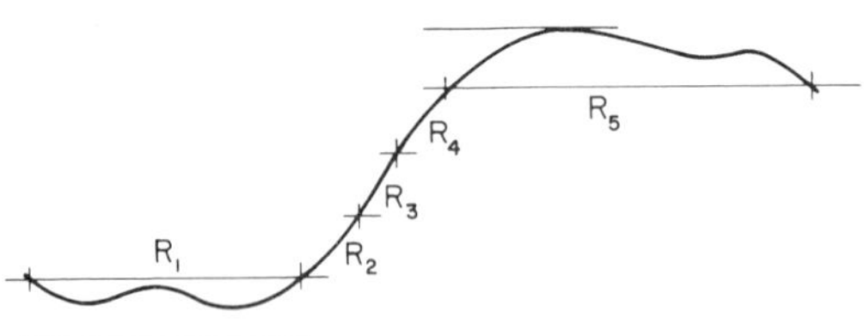

Fig. 5.4 The small regions R_2, R_3 and R_4 are created by the requirement that the brightness be approximately constant within each region. Human perception may lump them all as an "edge" and it is desirable to eliminate them during a picture editing process

Such results are typical for all segmentation schemes based only on local brightness information. They are basically due to three causes: one can be described as high frequency noise, resulting in many small regions scattered throughout the picture as seen in Fig.4.6; another is due to "smooth" transitions between regions of more or less uniform features (this is illustrated in Fig.5.4) where the application of the predicate P_2 produces the additional regions R_2, R_3 and R_4. Most of the small regions in Fig.5.2 are due to this factor; a third cause is that the human eye often ignores slow variations in brightness and perceives regions of different brightness as one, provided such changes occur smoothly (this problem is also apparent in Fig.5.2 because of a general gradient in brightness from the top to the bottom of the original picture (see Fig.4.2)). It is therefore necessary to perform a certain editing of the picture in order to obtain results conforming with human intuition to some degree. This can be done by one or a combination of some of the following techniques:

I) Examination of the size of individual regions and the difference between their features and those of their neighbors. This is in effect a merging algorithm using a different uniformity predicate and the condition that one of the regions be "small" before it is merged. The new predicate is typically a more "relaxed" version of the original. In the case of P_2 this corresponds to increasing the tolerance e. This process can result in the elimination of many of the extra regions caused by the first two causes.

II) Examination of edges and removal of questionable ones. This requires the use of an edge predicate to verify boundaries of regions. It can be very effective for eliminating the effects of the third cause of excessive regions.

III) Examination of certain topological properties of the RAG. It turns out that many features of the picture are reflected in the structure of the RAG. As a matter of fact, such properties are valuable not only for editing, but also for picture description and recognition. We summarize here some of the more salient ones. First we note that the use of Definition 3.20 for region adjacency guarantees that the RAG is always planar. Figs. 5.5,6 show a set of segmentations and the corresponding RAGs, where the 0 node corresponds to the frame. It is easy to show that a region surrounding holes corresponds to a *cutnode* of the graph. Also, nodes of *degree 1* always correspond to holes. Thus one can find which regions have holes by finding the cutnodes of the region adjacency graph. This is a relatively straightforward process, by using, for example, Algorithm 3.2. Regions with many holes are likely to correspond to subjective major regions and therefore such information can be used for editing. Actually a more general state-

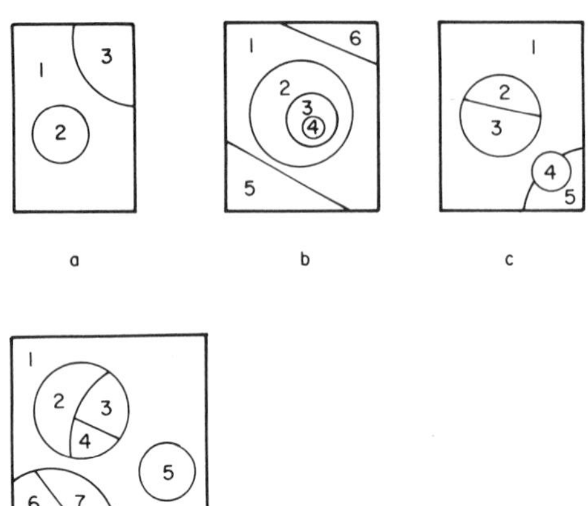

Fig. 5.5a-d Some simple configurations of multiply connected regions

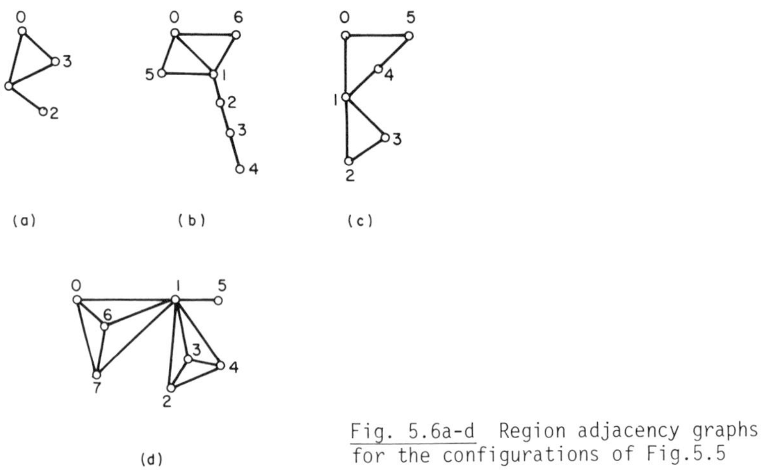

Fig. 5.6a-d Region adjacency graphs for the configurations of Fig.5.5

Fig. 5.7 Digitized photograph of a face reproduced by a line printer. The resolution is 64 × 64 with 7 bits per pixel. There is some distortion in the reproduction because there are 10 lines per inch horizontally, but only 8 in the vertical direction. (Reproduced from [5.1])

Fig. 5.8 Digitized chest radiograph reproduced in the same manner as Fig.5.8. The resolution is too low for distinguishing most of the details and the picture can be used only for the detection of gross features, like the lung outlines. (Reproduced from [5.1])

Fig.5.7

Figure caption see opposite page

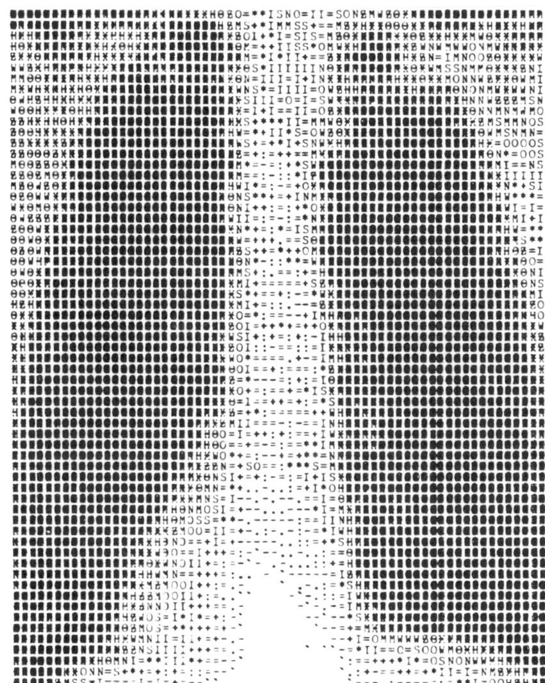

Fig.5.8

Figure caption see opposite page

Fig. 5.9 Digitized picture of a landscape reproduced in the same manner as Fig.5.7. (Reproduced from [5.1])

ment can be made. "Major" regions should correspond to nodes of the RAG with high degree while "transition" regions are likely to correspond to nodes of small degree and be connected to two nodes of very high degree. For example, it can be verified in Fig.5.2 that all regions adjacent to not more than two other regions should be eliminated.

IV) Use of information about the shape of the regions. For example, we may expect most regions to be convex.

V) Semantic information.

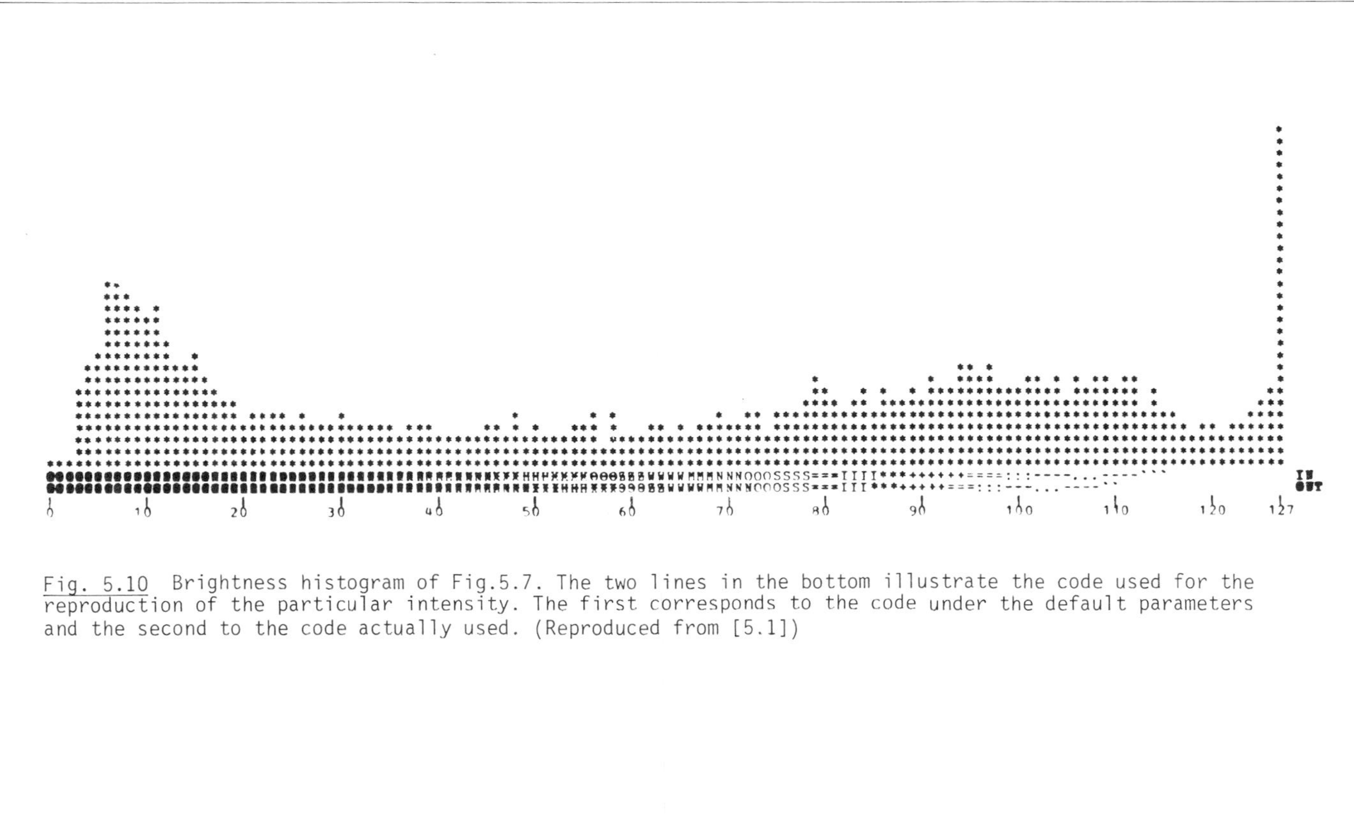

Fig. 5.10 Brightness histogram of Fig.5.7. The two lines in the bottom illustrate the code used for the reproduction of the particular intensity. The first corresponds to the code under the default parameters and the second to the code actually used. (Reproduced from [5.1])

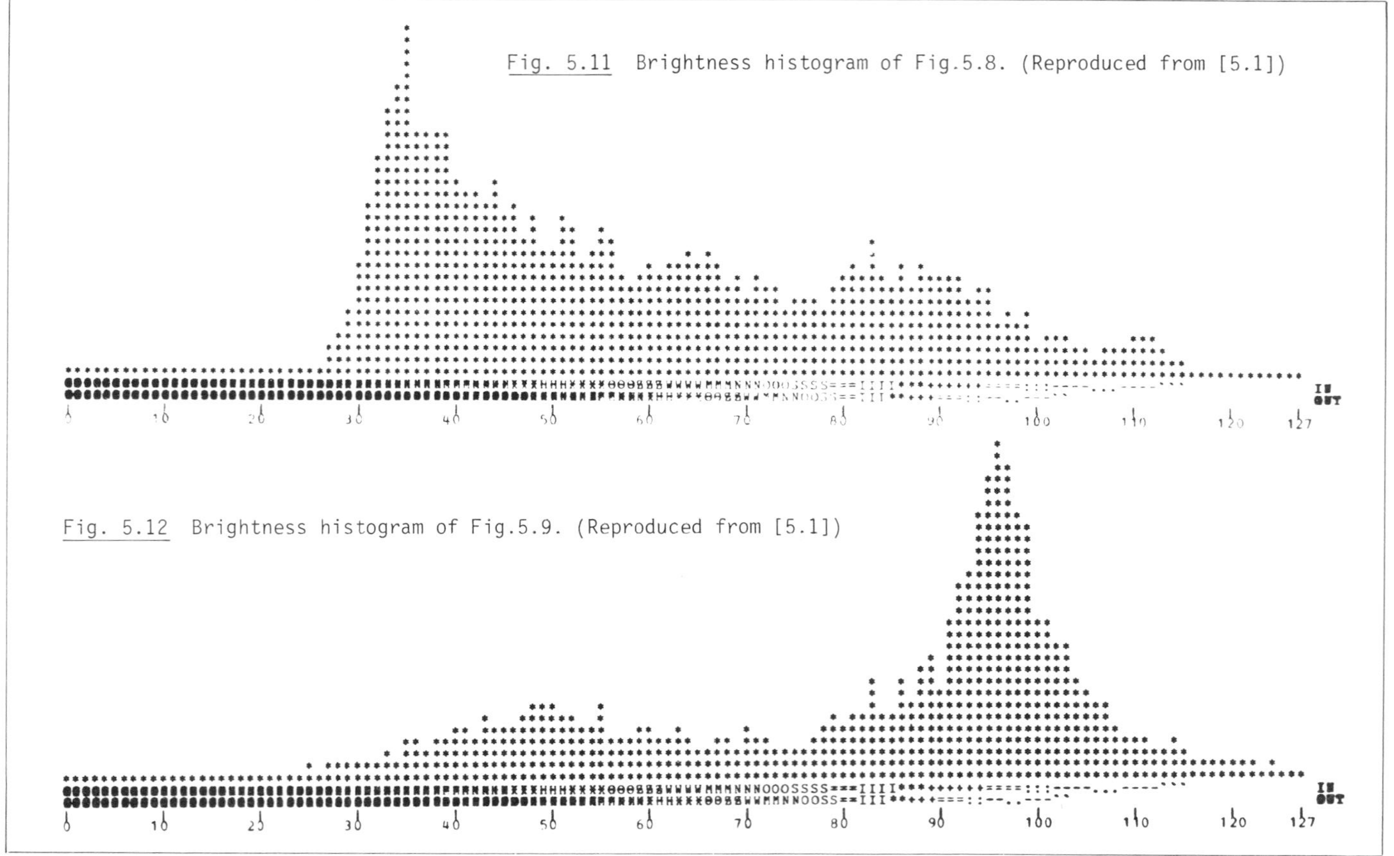

Fig. 5.11 Brightness histogram of Fig.5.8. (Reproduced from [5.1])

Fig. 5.12 Brightness histogram of Fig.5.9. (Reproduced from [5.1])

Fig. 5.13 Region boundaries plotted by a CALCOMP plotter for the original of Fig.5.7. The ordered list necessary for the plotting was found by Algorithm 5.3. (Reproduced from [5.1])

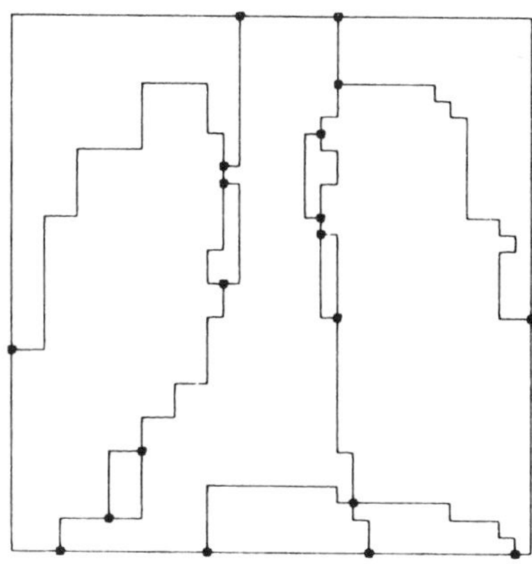

Fig. 5.14 Region boundaries for Fig.5.8. (Reproduced from [5.1])

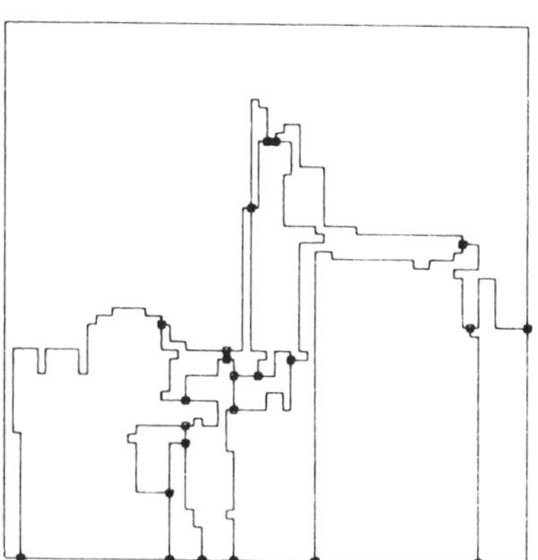

Fig. 5.15 Region boundaries for Fig.5.9. (Reproduced from [5.1])

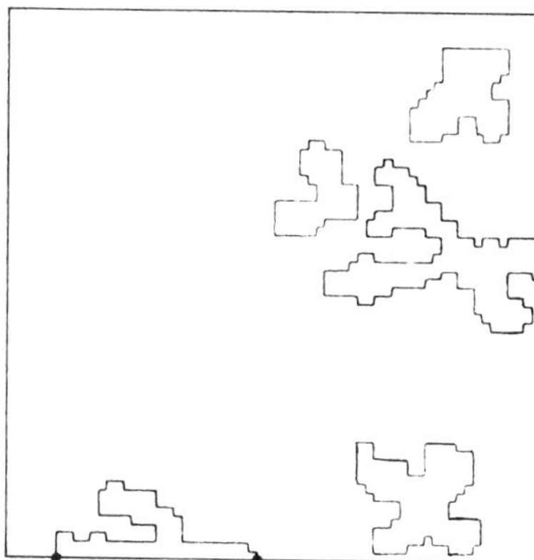

Fig. 5.16 Region boundaries for Fig.4.2. (Reproduced from [5.1])

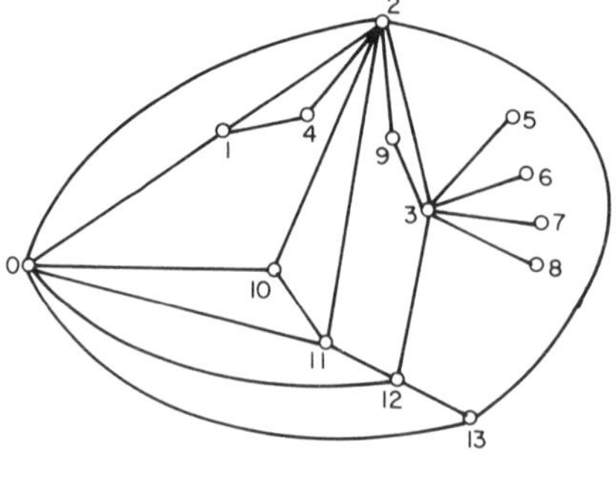

Fig. 5.17 Region adjacency graph for Fig.5.13

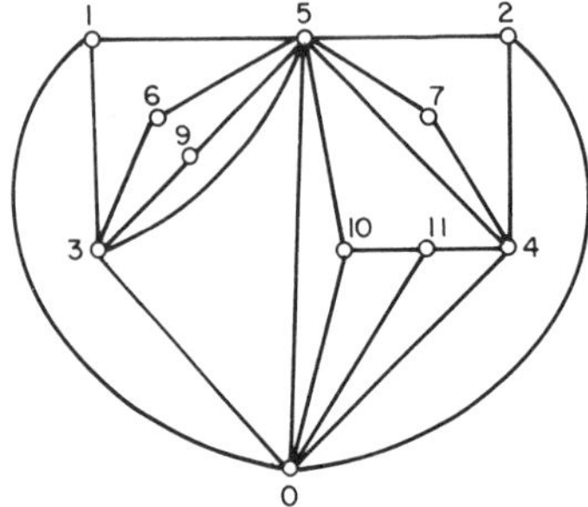

Fig. 5.18 Region adjacency graph for Fig.5.14

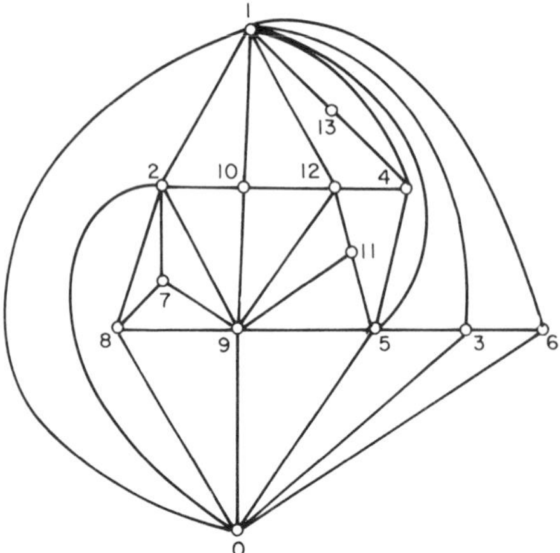

Fig. 5.19 Region adjacency graph for Fig.5.15

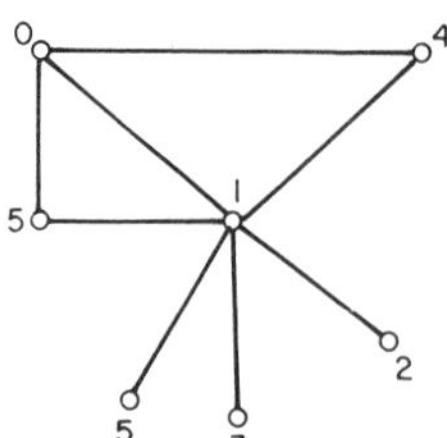

Fig. 5.20 Region adjacency graph for Fig.5.16

The last two techniques are more appropriately part of *scene analysis* rather than segmentation and we will return to them in Chapter 6. It turns out that quite powerful editing can be performed by nonsemantic techniques [5.1,22]. We shall demonstrate this by a sequence of examples taken from [5.1]. Figs.5.7-9 show digitized pictures with a 64×64 grid and 7 bits per pixel. Figs.5.10-12 show the respective grey level histograms. The "flatness" of the latter suggests that simple thresholding is neither advisable nor feasible. Also, the figures are noisy enough to discourage simple edge detection techniques. Figs.5.13-15 show the corresponding outlines obtained by applying a split-and-merge algorithm followed by an elimination of the small regions using a criterion of type I) above. Initialization was done in a uniform manner, i.e., a level of the pyramid was chosen as an initial segmentation. The complete algorithm is described in detail in the next section. Fig.5.16 shows the outlines for the chromosomes of Fig.4.2 obtained in the same manner. The actual drawing of the region boundaries was done by the algorithm discussed in Section 5.5. In all pictures, points where 3 or 4 regions "meet" were marked by squares. These are often useful for subsequent processing (see Sec.5.6). Figs.5.17-20 show the region adjacency graphs for the segmentation of Figs.5.13-16. These graphs may be processed by a number of available techniques. For example, information about the topology of the picture can be extracted by locating the cutnodes, bridges and blocks of the RAG by Algorithm 3.2 (a slight modification is necessary for finding the blocks).

5.4 A Two-Dimensional Split-and-Merge Algorithm

We describe now in detail a split-and-merge algorithm (Algorithm 5.2) for picture segmentation. The description is given in general terms so that the algorithm can serve as a frame for a wide range of specific segmentation algorithms, including according to texture. It uses somewhat arbitrary rules for splitting and merging in order to speed-up the overall computational effort. We assume that the picture grid has dimension N x N, where N is a power of 2:

$$N = 2^L \quad .$$

This is a realistic assumption for most computer implementations. L is usually between 5 (e.g., for alphabetic characters) and 10 (e.g., for radiographs).

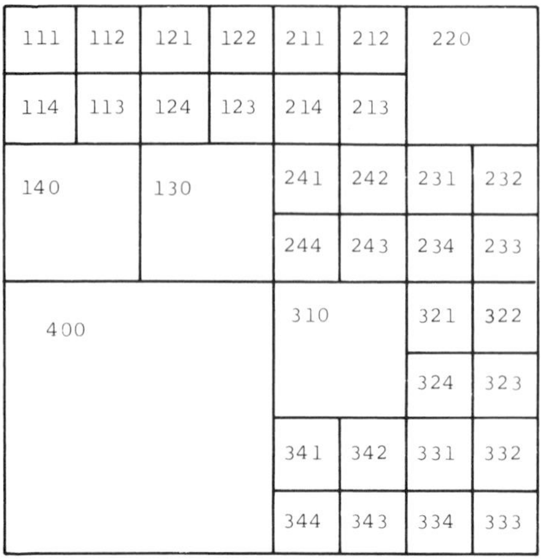

111 112 121 122 211 212 220
114 113 124 123 214 213
140 130 241 242 231 232
244 243 234 233
400 310 321 322
324 323
341 342 331 332
344 343 334 333

Fig. 5.21 First region numbering system. Trailing zeros are omitted if the are common to all regions. Thus for L = 7, N = 128 region 400 should be 4000000

The data structures used are both a quartic picture tree (QPT) and a region adjacency graph (RAG). The nodes of the QPT can be numbered in one of the following two ways:

I) At level 1, starting from the left corner, the four squares are assigned indices 1, 2, 3, 4 clockwise. Then each of their subsets is indexed in the same way, so that we have the notation of Fig.5.21. In this way, an increasing order of indices is established with each digit having a range 0-4. There will be at most L digits required or 3L bits. A binary numbering system would have required 2L bits, so that there is not much increase in space. (For a 512 × 512 picture L = 9 and, in a 32-bit machine, both indices would require a full word).

II) Each square is marked by its upper left corner and the size of its side so that the configuration of Fig.5.21 would look as it does in Fig.5.22. Then we have for each square 3 entries of L bits each; thus the storage requirements are again 3L. We will use the latter system in the sequel.

The operations of split or merge will be performed along the tree, i.e., quadruples of regions will be merged to their common parent, and regions will be split into their four children. In this way, the square shape of the regions will be preserved until the grouping step. In order to avoid confusion, we will call such regions *blocks*. Merging will be performed first by examining every fourth, sixteenth, etc., block from the initial

<table>
<tr><td>1,1,16</td><td>1,17,16</td><td>1,33,16</td><td>1,49,16</td><td>1,65,16</td><td>1,81,16</td><td colspan="2" rowspan="2">1,97,32</td></tr>
<tr><td>17,1,16</td><td>17,17,16</td><td>17,33,16</td><td>17,49,16</td><td>17,65,16</td><td>17,81,16</td></tr>
<tr><td colspan="2" rowspan="2">33,1,32</td><td colspan="2" rowspan="2">33,33,32</td><td>33,65,
16</td><td>33,81,
16</td><td>33,97,
16</td><td>33,113,
16</td></tr>
<tr><td>49,65,
16</td><td>49,81,
16</td><td>49,97,
16</td><td>49,113,
16</td></tr>
<tr><td colspan="4" rowspan="4">65,1,64</td><td colspan="2" rowspan="2">65,65,32</td><td>65,97,
16</td><td>65,113,
16</td></tr>
<tr><td>81,97,
16</td><td>81,113,
16</td></tr>
<tr><td>97,65,
16</td><td>97,81,
16</td><td>97,97,
16</td><td>97,118
16</td></tr>
<tr><td>113,65,
16</td><td>113,81,
16</td><td>113,97,
16</td><td>113,113,
16</td></tr>
</table>

Fig. 5.22 Second region numbering system assuming L = 7, N = 128

segmentation. Merged blocks will be flagged appropriately. During splitting, all new blocks will be placed at the end of the list of the originals. The resulting value of n (the number of blocks) will actually be higher than their real number. Fig.5.23a shows an initial segmentation and Fig.5.23b the results after one merge and five split operations. (We have used direct numbering for simplicity).

These operations are followed by a grouping using the RAG. A simple way of doing this is to form an $N \times N$ matrix A whose entries are the block numbers of the corresponding pixels. Given a block, one can search for the neighboring pixels of its boundary and can find from A the identifying numbers of the adjacent blocks. Because of the square shape of the blocks such a search is very easy. For this reason, the actual grouping (in step 6 of the algorithm) is postponed until all the blocks have been examined.

During that operation a region adjacency matrix T is prepared which is used subsequently during the small region elimination step. It is also part of the output of the algorithm, which uses, in addition, the following arrays, functions and predicates.

1) The brightness matrix $f(k,j)$ and the matrices A and T as explained above.

2) The array size (i) contains the size of the side of the square block X_k while it is set to zero to indicate a merged region (in step 2). During

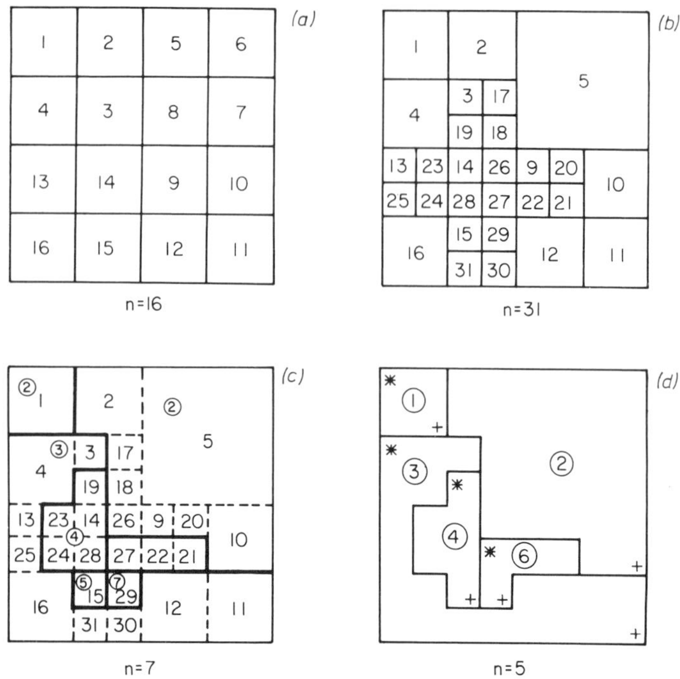

Fig. 5.23 Illustration of the application of Algorithm 5.2

grouping (step 6) it is used to flag regions which have been examined.

3) The array V(i) contains the region number where the block X_i belongs, while d(i) contains the number of usable elements of the array T(i,*).

4) q(i) is an array *structure* containing the information for evaluating the predicate $P(X_i)$. For example: If P_2 is used, then q(i) contains two elements: The maximum and minimum of f over X_i. If a polynomial approximation under the E_2 norm is used then q(i) will contain the values of the various integrals over X_i (see Sec.2.3). On the other hand, if an E_∞ norm is used with high order polynomial approximations, then q(i) must contain information about the boundary of X_i. For segmentation according to texture q(i) should contain the various second order statistics of f(k,j) over X_i, or the spectrum or any of the other features which are used by the various methods described in the literature [5.2-5,9-21].

5) The function F (with an arbitrary number of arguments) is used to update q(i) from q(i), $q(i_1)\dots q(i_r)$ when $X_{i_1},\dots X_{i_r}$ are merged into X_i. (The arbitrary number of arguments does not present any problem since F can be computed by the recursive application of a two argument function).

For example, if P_2 is used, then the new maximum (minimum) will be the maximum (minimum) of the maxima (minima) of f over the regions $S_i, X_{i_1}, \ldots X_{i_r}$. When the E_2 norm is used the updating corresponds to summation of integrals. Because the actual merging of the regions does not occur until the end of the algorithm, we shall use the notation Q(i) to denote q(i) under the tentative merges into the region i.

6) The stack S is a temporary location of the regions to be grouped.

7) The function G(i,j) measures the distance between two adjacent regions X_i and X_j and is used during the small region elimination to find regions with "similar" features. For example, if P_2 is used, then

$$G(i,j) = \max_{X_i}\{f\} - \max_{X_j}\{f\} + \min_{X_i}\{f\} - \min_{X_j}\{f\}$$

8) $P'(X_i, X_j)$ is the predicate used during small region elimination and it depends (in general) not only on the values of f over X_i and X_j but also on their areas.

The *input* to the algorithm consists of:

1) The brightness matrix f

2) The initial segmentation level l_0 (which can be used to evaluate the other features of the regions, e.g., q(i)).

3) The necessary parameters for P and P'.

4) The constant D which allows a quick screening of regions to be eliminated.

The *output* of the algorithm consists of:

1) The matrix A which gives the region number for each pixel. (Thus, A serves as the matrix s defined in Sec.4.1).

2) The region adjacency matrix T.

3) Certain coordinates of the boundary of each region. Their choice is discussed at the end of this section.

The algorithm uses three major procedures (or subroutines): TREE-MERGE (merge using the QPT), listed as Algorithm 5.2a, SPLIT, listed as Algorithm 5.2b, and RAG-MERGE (merge using the RAG), listed as Algorithm 5.2c. Fig.5.23c shows the region assignment after step 6 for the example of Figs.5.23a,b. For illustration we note in Table 5.1 the contents of the stack S and the changes in the arrays V and T(2,*) during the formation of the second region. Note that d(2) = 8. After step 81.1 the array T(2,*) will take the form

1,3,4,6,6,3,4,6,

Algorithm 5.2: Basic picture segmentation by split-and-merge

Input-Output: See text.

Note: The algorithm uses three procedures listed as Algorithm 5.2a-c.

Steps:

```
1. Set j = ℓ0, s = s0 = 2^(L-ℓ0), k = 1.
2. Execute TREE-MERGE.
3. Set j = ℓ0
4. Execute SPLIT.
5. Set m = 0.
6. Execute RAG-MERGE.
7. Examine all entries of A(i,j) and set
      A(i,j) = V(A(i,j)).
   [This assigns final region numbers]
8. For i = 1 to m by 1 do block 81.
     Begin block 81;
     1. For j = 1 to d(i) by 1 set T(i,j) = V(T(i,j)).
     2. Sort (lexicographically) the elements of the i^th row of T
        while eliminating duplicates and adjust d(i).
     End block 81;
   [Small Region elimination]
9. For i = 1 to m by 1 set V(i) = i.
10. For i = 1 to m by 1 do block 101.
     Begin block 101;
     1. If (area of X_i) < D then do block 102.
          Begin block 102;
          1. Use T(i,*) to find neighbors of X_i, say, j_1,j_2,...j_d(i).
          2. Find minimum of G(i,j) for, say, j = k over j = j_1,j_2,...j_d(i).
          3. If P'(X_i U X_k) is true then do block 103; else do nothing.
               Begin block 103; [merge X_i into X_k]
               1. V(i) = k.
               2. d(i) = -d(i)
               3. q(k) = F[q(k),q(i)]
               4. Update A
               End block 103;
          End block 102;
     End block 101;
11. n = m
```

12. For i = 1 to m by 1 do block 121.

Begin block 121;

1. If d(i) < 0 then do block 122.

Begin block 122;

1. For j = $j_1, j_2, \ldots j_{|d(i)|}$ [the elements of T(i,*)] and j $\neq$ V(i) in T(j,*) replace i by V(i), avoiding repetitions and modifying d(j).

2. In T(V(i),*) add j_1, j sub 2,...$j_{|d(i)|}$ and set d[V(i)] = d[V(i)] + |d(i)| - (number of repetitions)

3. n = n - 1

End block 122;

End block 121;

Algorithm 5.2a: Procedure TREE-MERGE

Steps:

1. Do block 21 while j > 0.

Begin block 21;

1. For i = 1 to n by $4^{\ell_0 - j + 1}$ do block 22.

Begin block 22;

1. If size (i) = size (i+k) = size (i+2k) = size (i+3k) = s then do block 23.

Begin block 23;

1. If $P(X_i \cup X_{i+k} \cup X_{i+2k} \cup X_{i+3k})$ is true then do block 24.

Begin block 24;

(Merge the four blocks as following:)

1. size (i) = 2s.

2. size (i+k), size (i+2k), size (i+3k) = 0.

3. q(i) = F[q(i), q(i+k), q(i+2k), q(i+3k)].

4. Update A.

End block 24;

End block 23;

End block 22;

2. j = j - 1.

3. s = 2s; k = 4k.

End block 21;

End of TREE-MERGE.

Algorithm 5.2b: Procedure SPLIT

Steps:

1. For i = 1 to n by 1 do block 41.
    - Begin block 41;
    - 1. If 0 < size (i) < = s_0 then do block 42.
        - Begin block 42;
        - 1. Do block 43 while $P(X_i)$ is false.
            - Begin block 43;
            - [Split X_i into four blocks, until $P(X_i)$ = true]
            - 1. size (i) = size (i)/2.
            - 2. size (n+1), size (n+2), size (n+3) = size (i)
            - 3. Evaluate q(i), q(n+1), q(n+2), q(n+3)
            - 4. n = n + 3
            - 5. Update A
            - End block 43;
        - End block 42;
    - End block 41;

End of SPLIT.

Algorithm 5.2c: Procedure RAG-MERGE

Steps:

1. For i = 1 to n by 1 do block 61.
    - Begin block 61;
    - 1. If size (i) > 0 then do block 62.
        - Begin block 62;
        - 1. size (i) = -size (i) [flag X_i as having been examined].
        - 2. m = m + 1.
        - 3. d(m) = 0.
        - 4. Place i in stack S and set Q(m) = q(i).
        - 5. Do block 63 while S is not empty.
            - Begin block 63;
            - 1. Remove the bottom element j from S [at first j = i].
            - 2. V(j) = m.
            - 3. Using the matrix A find all blocks adjacent to X_j, say, $X\{k_1\}, X\{k_2\}, \ldots X\{k_r\}$.

```
4. For k = k1,k2,...kr do block 64.
     Begin block 64;
     1. If size (k) > 0 do block 65.
          Begin block 65;
          1. If P(Xj U Xk) is true then do block 66. [Use Q(m)
             rather than q(j) in the evaluation of the predi-
             cate.]
               Begin block 66;
               1. size (k) = -size (k)
               2. Place k in stack S.
               3. Q(m) = F(Q(m),q(k)).
                  End block 66;
            _. Else do block 67.
                    Begin block 67;
                 1. d(m) = d(m) + 1.
                 2. T(m),d(m)) = k
                 End block 67;
            End block 65;
        End block 64;
    End block 63;
  End block 62;
End block 61;
End of RAG-MERGE.
```

Table 5.1 Illustration of the operation of Algorithm 5.2

S	V	T
2	no change	no change
5,17	V(2) = 2	1,3
17,18,9,20,10	V(5) = 2	1,3
18,9,20,10	V(17) = 2	1,3
9,20,10,26	V(18) = 2	1,3,19
20,10,26	V(9) = 2	1,3,19,22
10,26	V(20) = 2	1,3,19,22,21
26	V(10) = 2	1,3,19,22,21,11
0	V(26) = 2	1,3,19,22,21,11,14,27.

i	d	T
1	2	2,4
2	4	1,3,4,6
3	6	1,2,4,5,6,7
4	4	2,3,5,6
5	3	3,4,7
6	4	2,3,4,7
7	3	3,5,6

Table 5.2 Illustration of the operation of Algorithm 5.2

while after step 81.2 it will be

1,3,4,6,

with d(2) = 4. In the same example the form of T after the 8th step is given in Table 5.2.
If region 5 is merged into 4 and 7 into 6 then step 12 will proceed as follows:

For i = 5:
In T(3,*) 5 must be replaced by V(5) = 4. Since 4 is already present 5 is erased and d(3) = 5.
In T(7,*) 5 is simply replaced by 4.
T(4,*) = 2,3,5,6,7 and d(4) = 5.

For i = 7:
In T(3,*) 7 must be replaced by V(7) = 6. Since 6 is already present 7 is erased and d(4) = 4.
T(6,*) = 2,3,4,6 and d(4) = 6.
Fig.5.23d shows the final segmentation.

In general, the computationally most expensive operation of the algorithm is the evaluation of q(i) (initialization and step 43.3), since this requires effort proportional to the area of the picture. The same is true about the updating of A, although the operations there are much simpler. The operations in steps 6,8,10 and 12 are essentially proportional to the number of branches of the region adjacency graph. The merging step requires effort proportional to the initial number of regions.

It may be desirable for subsequent operations to obtain certain "key points" of the region boundary, e.g., the leftmost among the upper points. (These are marked by * in Fig.5.23d) or the rightmost among the lower points (marked by + in the same figure). Such points are trivially defined for blocks, and can be found for regions by successive updating during grouping (in block 66) and small region elimination (in block 103). We will discuss this point in the next section.

5.5 Construction of a Region Boundary List from the Segmentation Matrix and the Region Adjacency Graph

In the previous sections we described methods for segmentation, which form regions, either by growing them from single pixels, or by reduction of the original picture, or by combination of these methods. Their results are usually a matrix A with entries the region number for each pixel, a list of "key points" of the region boundary and a region adjacency matrix T (equivalent to a node list of a region adjacency graph). Such algorithms can be modified easily to include in the region adjacency list the "frame" of the picture (e.g., step 63.3 and block 65 are the places to do this for the split-and-merge algorithm). From such a description we can readily obtain an ordered list of the external boundary points of a region (clockwise or counterclockwise). However, the boundaries of holes can be obtained only indirectly. If a hole is itself a single region, then that boundary will be found as an external one for that region. The same is true if the hole contains a set of nested regions (Fig.5.5b). The boundaries of holes consisting of many regions can be found by an examination of the RAG: they correspond to certain of its biconnected components. Algorithm 5.3 can be used to obtain an ordered boundary point list BL from the segmentation matrix and the RAG. Two special symbols '##' and '#' will be used to denote the start of the external boundary and that of a hole, respectively, while n denotes the number of regions. It has been used in connection with Algorithm 5.2 to produce Figs.5.13-16 [5.1].

It is easy to verify that the time required by the algorithm is proportional to the length of the region boundaries, while it requires space proportional to the area of the picture. (We assume that the number of regions is small enough to be negligible in comparison to the area). Note that saving the region adjacency graph and the keypoints has allowed the construction of an algorithm with time requirements proportional to the boundary length. One can easily think of simple algorithms using only the segmentation matrix but which require time proportional to the area of the picture. The difference between the two can be substantial.

Algorithm 5.3: Derivation of list of external boundary points
[Find the outside boundaries]

Input: Pixel labeling matrix A, region adjacency matrix T, list of key-points.

Output: Boundary List BL.

Notation: (See text).

Steps:

```
1. For i = 1 to n by 1 do block 11.
     Begin block 11;
     1. Place '##' in BL followed by i.
     2. Let P be the key point of the i^th region. Place it in BL.
     3. Find the four direct neighbors of P and determine their regions from
        the matrix A. At least one of them must be different than X_i.
     4. If not all four points belong to regions other than X_i, then do
        block 12. [X_i is not a single pixel].
          Begin block 12;
          1. Trace the boundary of X_i by finding neighbors of successive
             points, their region numbers from A and determining a search
             direction
          End block 12;
     End block 11;
   [Find holes consisting of a single region or a series of nested regions]
2. Set D = false
3. Do block 31 while D = false.
     Begin block 31;
     1. Set D = true.
     2. For i = 1 to n by 1 do block 32.
          Begin block 32;
          1. If d(i) = 1 then do block 33.
               Begin block 33;
               1. Set D = false
               2. d(i) = 0
               3. k = T(i,1).
               4. Insert in BL before '##(k+1)' the part of BL between
                  '##i' and '##(i+1)', preceded by '#'.
               5. Drop i from T(k,*) and decrement d(k).
               End block 33;
          End block 32;
     End block 31;
4. Proceed to find the cutnodes of the adjacency graph by using Algorithm 3.2.
   Update BL by a method similar to that of step 3.
```

5.6 Where Three Regions Meet

It is often desirable to approximate the region boundaries by some other curves. If such an approximation is done independently for each region, it is possible to have conflicts in the sense that the common boundary between two regions may end up having two different approximations. If one region surrounds another completely, this problem can be avoided by performing only one approximation. The conflict in other cases can be resolved if boundary points common to three or more regions are determined and then boundary areas between pairs of such points are approximated [5.23]. These have been marked by squares in Figs.5.13-16. We will call such points *vertices*.

If the classical definition of boundaries is used on a discrete grid, then a number of problems arise. If extended boundaries are used, then vertices are characterized by the fact that they belong to the extended boundaries of three or four regions. A fast algorithm (though expensive in terms of space) for finding vertices can be formulated as follows. Set up a $M \times N$ matrix V initialized to zero. When a point is added to BL with coordinates (i,j) then increment the respective value of V, i.e.,

$$V(i,j) = V(i,j) + 1 .$$

After the construction of BL has been completed, the list is scanned and points with $V(i,j) > 2$ are marked as vertices.

An algorithm with smaller space requirements can be developed if the segmentation matrix is available during the construction of BL. Then when a point is added in BL, its neighbors are examined to determine whether it can belong to three or more regions. It can be verified that a point is a vertex if one of the following three conditions is met (see Fig.3.8 for notation).

I) P, E_1P and PE_2 belong pairwise to different regions.
II) P, E_1P and E_1PE_2 belong pairwise to different regions.
III) P, PE_2 and E_1PE_2 belong pairwise to different regions.

Such a check can be incorporated in block 12 of Algorithm 5.2.

5.7 Raster-by-Raster Analysis and the Line Adjacency Graph

A common form of processing pictorial data involves "raster-by-raster" analysis, in which each row of the brightness matrix f(i,j) is examined separately.

This has an advantage, especially for large pictures, in that one never has to store the whole picture in memory (an $N \times N$ array where N might be as large as 1024) but instead must store only a set of "important" points on each row. Such points can be found easily either by software or hardware. In the simplest case, a thresholding operation is performed, and the line is encoded by a sequence of *breakpoints* $x_1, x_2, \ldots x_n$ denoting the places where the threshold is crossed, i.e., if T is its value, we have

$$[f(x_i,j) - T]\,[f(x_{i+1},j) - T] < 0 \quad \text{or}$$

$$f(x_i,j) = T \quad .$$

The description will be complete if the sign of $f(i,j) - T$ for i less than x_1 is given. The major disadvantage of the method is that thresholding of single raster lines may not be advisable for noisy pictures. However, similar results can be achieved by examining the lines above and below the current one while determining the breakpoints. This approach has been used successfully by MOAYER and FU in the segmentation of fingerprint pictures [5.24]. In either case, the resultant data structure will be the LAG described in Section 4.3.

It is possible to make the LAG directed by establishing a node ordering in terms of their row index, say j (Fig.4.9). Note that there is no need to connect nodes corresponding to segments on the same line because they must belong to different regions. Furthermore, for a given j, the nodes may be ordered according to their index of segmentation k. Thus the LAG becomes a directed and ordered graph and if the nodes are labeled by the pair (j,k) then the ranking of any pair of nodes is readily available. Without loss of generality we assume that the ordering is in top-to-bottom, left-to-right fashion. The LAG may be described either through a node list constructed after the segment overlaps described in Section 4.3 have been checked or by the coordinates of the endpoints which contain the graph description implicitly. In the first case, it is necessary to use additional storage, while in the second, it is necessary to check segment overlaps repeatedly.

Algorithm 5.4 obtains the boundaries of regions from the LAG for "two color" pictures. In this case we look for the boundaries of regions of only one color, e.g., "black". Both external and internal boundaries are found. Boundaries belonging to the same region are marked by its number. The algorithm is essentially one which maps a directed and ordered plane graph into a string. Similar algorithms for binary trees are given as exercises in [5.25].

The only assumption needed for their extension to directed plane graphs is that all paths between a pair of nodes have the same length. This is certainly true for line adjacency graphs. This type of algorithm was first used in the context of picture segmentation by PAVLIDIS [5.26]. A related algorithm used later by FENG is described briefly in a paper dealing with the

---

Algorithm 5.4: Derivation of list of boundary points from the LAG

Input: Node adjacency list of the LAG with each node labeled by its left and right endpoints $i\ell$ and ir. (Nodes correspond to the "black" segments). The array $i\ell$ is also used to mark nodes which have been visited by changing its sign.

Output: Boundary list BL containing the x-y coordinates of points of the boundary in a list ordered counterclockwise for external boundaries and clockwise for internal ones. The special symbols ## and # denote the start of a region and a hole, respectively.

Note: This algorithm uses two procedures, UP and DOWN, listed as Algorithms 5.4a,b.

Steps:

```
1. Search the LAG, top to bottom and left to right. If iℓ(j,i) > 0 then do
   block 11;
     Begin block 11;
     1. Place (j,i) in a stack S and # in BL. [New region].
     2. While S is not empty do block 21;
          Begin block 21;
          1. Remove the top element of S: (j,i). Set new = 1.
          2. While iℓ(j,i) > 0 do block 22;
               Begin block 22;
               1. If (new=1) add # to BL followed by the left endpoint of
                  node (j,i); also set new = 0. [New contour: either external
                  boundary or a hole].
               2. Set down = 1.
               3. While down = 1 do procedure DOWN.
               4. Add the right endpoint of (j,i) to BL.
               5. While down = 0 do procedure UP.
               6. If iℓ(j,i) > 0 add the left endpoint of (j,i) to BL.
               End block 22;
          End block 21;
     End block 11;
```

Algorithm 5.4a: Procedure DOWN

Steps:

```
1. If node (j,i) has no children set down = 0; else do block 32.
     Begin block 32;
     1. Find its leftmost child (j+1,k).
     2. Place all other children in S.
     3. If (j+1,k) has a parent to the left of (j,i) then do block 33.
          Begin block 33;
          1. Set i = i - 1.
          2. Set down = 0.
          End block 33;
     _. Else do block 34.
          Begin block 34;
          1. Set j = j + 1 and i = k.
          2. Add the left endpoint of (j,i) to BL.
          3. Mark (j,i) by setting iℓ(j,i) = -iℓ(j,i)
          End block 34;
     End block 32;
End DOWN.
```

Algorithm 5.4b: Procedure UP

Steps:

```
1. If node (j,i) has no parents set down = 1; else do block 52.
     Begin block 52;
     1. Find its rightmost parent (j-1,k).
     2. If (j-1,k) has a descendant to the right of (j,i) then do block 53.
          Begin block 53;
          1. Set i = i + 1.
          2. Set down = 1.
          End block 53;
     _. Else do block 54.
          Begin block 54;
          1. Set j = j - 1 and i = k.
          2. Add the right endpoint of (j,i) to BL.
          End block 54;
     End block 52;
End UP.
```

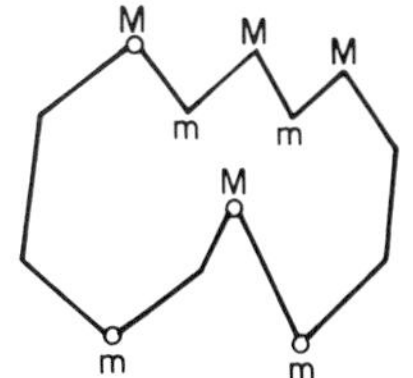

Fig. 5.24 Definition of the extrema of the face of a graph. M stands for maximum and m for minimum

generation of polygonal outlines from gray level pictures [5.27]. The algorithm uses two procedures (or subroutines), UP and DOWN, which are listed as Algorithms 5.4a and 5.4b.

Although this is a rather simple algorithm, its correctness is not obvious, and we proceed to prove it formally.

Lemma 5.1: Block 22 of the algorithm visits all the nodes of a face of the LAG at least once and at most twice.

Proof: Let F be a face of the LAG. Because the graph is directed, we can identify (locally) highest and lowest nodes in it. (See Fig.5.24). Let X be the starting node. If the exterior face is traversed in a counterclockwise manner the following is true: If a branch connects a maximum to a minimum, then one goes from a node to its leftmost child. If a branch connects a minimum to a maximum then, one goes to the rightmost parent. A similar strategy is valid when an interior face is traversed in a clockwise manner. If X is a maximum then the nodes before and after it during the traversal of a face must be children of X in sequence (e.g., the third and the fourth) while for a minimum they are parents in sequence. This is exactly what the algorithm is doing. In particular, block 33 and statement 22-4 handle minima while block 53 and statement 22-6 handle maxima. The algorithm does not drop out of block 22 until a node already marked is seen, so that it visits all the nodes. Note that the possibility remains that a node may be visited more than once because the sign of $i\ell$ is checked only at maxima (statement 21-2). A maximum will be seen after at most a complete traversal of the boundary and therefore a node can be visited at most twice.

Corollary 5.1: The algorithm always terminates.

Proof: Each face can be traversed at most twice and if its starting node is already marked it is not traversed at all. When a face is not traversed no more nodes are placed in the stack and therefore the stack will eventually be empty.

Lemma 5.2: The starting node on a face is always either a maximum (for an external face) or the child of a maximum (for an internal face).

Proof: The top-to-bottom and left-to-right scan guarantees that the first node to be visited is a maximum of the external face. Children nodes of this one are placed in the stack to be used as starting nodes of internal faces. Therefore we must show that no other nodes are placed in the stack. Suppose they are. Using the notation of Fig.5.25 we have four possibilities for a starting node which is not a maximum, or the child of a maximum:

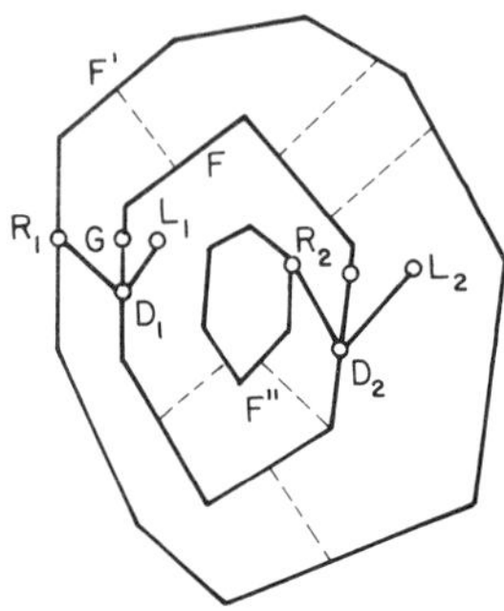

Fig. 5.25 Diagram for the proof to Lemma 5.2

D_1 was placed in S as a child of R_1 or L_1, or
D_2 was placed in S as a child of R_2 or L_2.

Neither L_1, nor R_2 can have any children to the left of D_1 or D_2, respectively, because this would violate the structure of the LAG. But leftmost children are never placed in S and therefore none of these two possibilities can exist. The structure of the LAG also requires that D_1 must be the rightmost child of of R_1 and D_2 the rightmost child of L_2. Because faces cannot "cross" we can have only the configuration shown in heavy lines on Fig.5.25, i.e., the faces must be nested. In this case face G will be traversed before F and therefore D_1 will be marked and could not serve as a starting node. Face F" cannot be traversed before F and therefore D_2 cannot be in the stack until after F has been traversed. We have reached a contradiction in all cases. Note that if D_1 or D_2 were children of a maximum, then they would need be rightmost children and there would be no contradiction. This completes the proof of the lemma.

Theorem 5.1: The boundary tracing algorithm is correct.

Proof: The maximum node of each internal face must belong to at least another face. Therefore its children will be placed in the stack and because of Lemma 5.2 only those will be in S. This implies that all faces will be visited and there will be no duplication since nodes in the stack which have been already marked are ignored (step 21-2). For such starting nodes

Lemma 5.1 implies that all the nodes of each face will be visited exactly once, since the only case where this happened was when the starting node was not the child of maximum.

Corollary 5.2: The algorithm traverses each edge twice only, and therefore its time complexity is linearly proportional to the size of the graph.

5.8. Extension of Raster-by-Raster Analysis

The algorithm of the previous section assumes well-defined region features and is primarily applicable to high contrast black and white pictures. In this section, we shall discuss some direct extensions of the raster-by-raster analysis. Arbitrary grey scale pictures can also be processed in this manner by a number of techniques. For example *run length encoding* processes the picture raster-by-raster and produces a sequence of intervals for each line. This term usually refers to piecewise constant approximations where a raster line is encoded as a sequence

$$(x_k, c_k) \quad k = 1,\ldots,n \quad . \tag{5.1a}$$

Then

$$|f(i,j) - c_k| < H \quad \text{for } x_{k-1} < i \le x_k \quad k = 1,2\ldots,n \tag{5.1b}$$

(x_0 stands for the left hand frame). H is a given constant (see Sec.4.7). The most general representation of this kind can be thought of as resulting from the use of a one-dimensional segmentation algorithm followed by optimization of the breakpoint location by one of the algorithms described in Section 2.10. Then the "profile" of the brightness function will be encoded as

$$(x_k, A_k) \quad k = 1,2,\ldots,n \quad , \tag{5.2}$$

where each A_k is a set of descriptors for the interval (x_{k-1}, x_k). For example, A_k may be an array of coefficients of a polynomial approximation. For simple run length encoding $A_k = c_k$. If thresholding has been used, then A_k contains only a binary variable a_k denoting above or below threshold (note that in this case we need only A_1). In the sequel we will avoid specifying

A_k any more, except to assume that we can tell whether two descriptors are alike and in particular that there exists a predicate

$$P(A_k,A_j) = \text{true} \quad \text{if} \quad A_k \text{ is like } A_j \quad . \tag{5.3a}$$

If A contains only a binary variable then

$$P(A_k,A_j) = \text{true} \quad \text{if} \quad a_k = a_j \quad . \tag{5.3b}$$

If A contains only a constant then we may choose to have

$$P(A_k,A_j) = \text{true} \quad \text{if} \quad |c_k - c_j| < h \tag{5.3c}$$

for some tolerance h.

If A_k contains the maximum M_f^k and minimum m_f^k of f(i,j) over (x_{k-1},x_k) then we may have

$$P(A_k,A_j) = \text{true} \quad \text{if} \quad \max(M_f^k,M_f^j) - \min(m_f^k,m_f^j) < h \quad . \tag{5.3d}$$

If A_k denotes a polynomial approximation then we may have

$$P(A_k,A_j) = \text{true} \quad \text{if error norm between the two approximations is small.} \tag{5.3e}$$

Note that A_k and A_j are generally not from the same line. In the last example (x_{k-1},x_k) will be different from (x_{j-1},x_i), and the comparison of the two norms should be made over a common subinterval, e.g., (x_{k-1},x_j) in Fig. 4.9. In general, P will be evaluated over two adjacent nodes of the line adjacency graph (LAG) described in Section 4.3. In such cases one must trace a boundary not only by examination of the segment overlap criteria but by evaluation of the predicate $p(A_k,A_j)$.

If one considers only the properties of adjacent nodes in the LAG then the evaluation of this predicate will be sufficient for creating a boundary list. It can be incorporated in the process of finding the successors or ancestors of a node in the algorithm of the previous section. However, this type of merging may result in *drifting*, i.e., the properties of the region may change gradually from one part to another. This may cause problems in the creation of boundary lists, as seen in Fig.5.26. There we may have

$P(A_1,A_2)$, $P(A_2,A_3)$ and $P(A_3,A_4)$ all true but $P(A_1,A_4)$ false. This can be avoided by testing the similarity of each segment with some global features of the region. This will make the shape of the regions dependent on the order of grouping and this may again cause problems with an algorithm like 5.4. One way out is to label the LAG by region numbers before finding the boundaries. Any type of graph traversal algorithm will be appropriate (e.g., depth first).

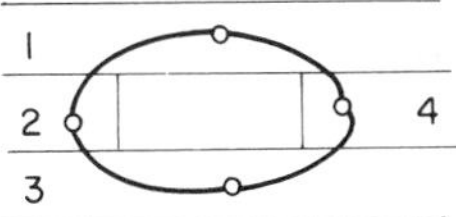

Fig. 5.26 Illustration of conflicts which may arise in the extended raster-by-raster analysis (see text)

6. Scene Analysis

6.1 Introduction

We shall use the term "scene analysis" to denote the assignment of labels or interpretations to the results of a segmentation algorithm. For example, we may decide to call a region the "right lung" in a chest x-ray picture, or a set of regions a "highway" in a satellite photograph. Furthermore, we may assign a group of regions to a single solid object. The early work of GUZMAN [6.1] is a typical example of a solution to this problem using some simple semantic rules. Scene analysis is a central problem in both pattern recognition and artificial intelligence and there is a rich literature on it. We could have postponed our treatment of the subject until the end of this book but we choose to discuss it here because of its traditional connection with picture segmentation. Such "interpretation guided segmentation" has been emphasized in the research of the Artificial Intelligence Laboratories and it is exemplified by the work of BAJCSY, BARROW, BINFORD, GARVEY, NAGAO, TENENBAUM, YAKIMOVSKY, and SAKAI, among others [6.2-13]. It has been also used in the context of medical image analysis by HARLOW and his colleagues [6.14,15]. We take advantage of this opportunity to discuss some important questions in "computer vision", which extend beyond segmentation.

In order to illustrate the major problems in scene analysis, we use a simple, everyday analogy, that of solving a crossword puzzle. There we are given a list of "definitions" which guide the selection of words to fill the space of the puzzle. These definitions correspond to the color or other local features of regions which have been found by an initial "local" algorithm of the type described in Chapters 4 and 5. Such "atomic" regions could correspond to single pixels, could be parts of a waveform, arcs of the boundary of an object, etc. (see Chaps.7 and 8). Sometimes the definition of a word in the puzzle is quite clear and one could fill it in without question. The same may be true in scene analysis. The features of the region may be such that we can decide about its interpretation on the basis of them only. For example, we may want to decide whether a region in a picture is black or white. If the brightness range is, say, 0-127 (7 bits of grey scale), then a region with maximum brightness 11 and minimum brightness 2 can be classified as black. Or, if we are interested in shape, a region which is convex and has a ratio of maximum width over minimum width equal to 10 can be classified as elongated. In the case of most puzzles, such local decisions are rare. There we may guess a number of possible alternatives and then attempt to see how they fit together. Thus the constraints of compatibility can be used to remove ambiguity. The same is possible in scene analysis. We have already seen in Section 5.3 the use of comparison between the features of adjacent regions for picture editing. This is probably the simplest possible form of scene analysis. Additional constraints may be provided by various type of semantics. In the case of the crossword puzzle one can follow a number of strategies and this provides simple analogs for the scene analysis methodology.

One possibility is to avoid making any "commitments" and keep tentative entries for each item until the whole puzzle is completed in this way. This is certainly a "safe" but impractical way to do the job. A counterpart in scene analysis is to start with a model of the whole scene and then try to match the individual interpretations to the model. This is certainly a very reliable strategy, but can be quite expensive computationally. In mathematical terms such a matching can be expressed as a problem of graph isomorphism (explicitly or implicitly). This approach has been popular in the context of Artificial Intelligence and we discuss it in Section 6.2. Not surprisingly, it runs into certain computational difficulties. The time required for the analysis of a scene may be an exponential function of the number of objects in it (see Sec.6.2). Therefore, people have looked for alternative methods, which may not be optimal in an absolute sense but which have reasonable requirements.

In the case of the puzzle, one fills small parts of it after checking the compatibility of a few words. We may think of a mathematical model of this process. Assignments are made final as soon as the joint probability of a set of interpretations exceeds a given threshold. Local interpretations have also been tried in scene analysis and are described in Section 6.3. Of course it is always possible to make mistakes, as anyone who has worked with a puzzle knows. Therefore, it is desirable to go over parts of the puzzle more than once. In the case of scene analysis it is desirable to iterate over assignments of interpretations. This can be done through a *filtering* or *relaxation* procedure. Such methods increase the reliability of an initial tentative labeling of the picture and were first proposed by WALTZ [6.16] and further developed by ROSENFELD and ZUCKER [6.17-19]. We discuss such techniques in Sections 6.4-6.

An interesting and promising method for checking compatibility of constraints is offered by *syntactic analysis*. This has been used widely for "one-dimensional" data and its original use has been the interpretation or translation of human language. Words are not assigned a meaning without examining some of their neighbors. In a rough way, the size of the neighborhood determines the complexity of the syntactical analysis or parsing [6.20]. Thus one has a trade-off between reliability of interpretation and speed. (Formally this is done by assuming models for the process generating a language. Once the model is specified, then the complexity of the parsing process is also specified). We shall discuss the use of such techniques for the analysis of boundaries and waveforms in Chapter 8. Their use in "two-dimensional" situations has been rather limited. The main reason is that "two-dimensional" grammars are rather difficult to analyze and have been studied only to a limited extent. (We shall review this topic in Chap.10.). However, a number of simplifications are possible and the approach seems quite promising. Certain encouraging results have been reported by BRAYER, SWAIN and FU [6.21] and more recently by KENG and FU [6.22].

The relation of the various techniques with each other is an open question. A discussion of this topic can be found in [6.23]. Within the framework of picture segmentation, an interesting recent development has been the use of reflectance and range data [6.24]. The choice of a particular technique is to a large extent a question of a trade-off between the quality of the results and the computational requirements involved. In principle it is possible to introduce semantics during the initial segmentation and examine each pixel in this context. Most of the algorithms to be discussed can be used in this way, although one pays a rather stiff price in terms of computational costs.

6.2 Scene Analysis as a Graph Matching Problem

In Section 5.3 we discussed the use of graphs for picture editing and showed that by examining the degree of the nodes of the RAG one can go fairly far in the editing process. The complete description of a picture requires a more detailed analysis of the RAG. After the completion of the segmentation and the initial editing, the nodes and branches may be labeled with information about the regions and boundaries they represent. Some of that can be the result of a shape analysis by the methods discussed in Chapters 8 and 9. Such labels will be called *intrinsic labels*. The area of a region, its (average) brightness, information about its shape, etc., are such possible labels. Semantic information about the kind of expected content of the pictures can also be given in terms of a labeled graph. Such labels will be called *external* or *interpretations*. In the case of a landscape, possible labels are "sky", "tree", "house", etc. Or in a simpler case an interpretation may be shadow or face of a solid. Certain constraints can be placed on the interpretations by stating that a window cannot be connected to the sky but only to a house or a tree. In the latter case some additional connections will be necessary as shown in the graph of Fig.6.1. The connection to a tree corresponds of course to partial occlusion. Under these conditions one is faced with the problem of reconciling two sets of labeled graph structures: those present in the RAG and those which form the semantic description. We define formally as SR a set consisting of all possible labeled RAGs (LRAGs) and as ST a set consisting of all labeled semantic graphs (LSGs). Then an *interpretation* is a mapping from SR into ST. Note that it is possible that different subgraphs of the LRAG will be mapped onto the same LSG. For example the configuration of Fig.6.1 may occur in many parts of a given picture. Therefore, in its full generality the scene analysis problem is equivalent to the *subgraph isomorphism* problem [6.2, 11,14].

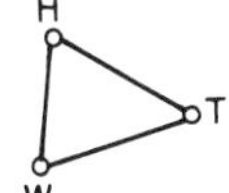

Fig. 6.1 Simple constraints on the labeling of an outdoor scene expressed as subgraphs

It can be shown that subgraph isomorphism is an NP-complete problem even when all the graphs involved are planar [6.25]. What this means in practical terms is that any algorithm for solving the general problem, most likely, will require time proportional to an exponential of the size of the graphs. In particular, one may have algorithms which work quite well on the analysis of simple scenes but they overwhelm the available computing power for more complex scenes. There are a number of examples in the literature where subgraph isomorphism has been used in the analysis of simple scenes [6.2,11,14] but none for highly complex scenes. The stated result on the NP-completeness of the problem implies that the lack of fast algorithms is due to the inherent difficulty of the problem. A recent algorithm for subgraph isomorphism proposed by ULLMANN [6.26] is not accompanied by any study of its complexity but the results of its tests on pseudorandomly generated graphs are certainly compatible with the exponential growth [Ref.6.26,Fig.2]. For an additional discussion of such "theoretical impediments to artificial intelligence" see the paper by RABIN [6.27]. These results suggest that: a) It is important to perform scene analysis after as "complete" an initial segmentation as possible, since this will reduce the number of regions and, therefore, the number of nodes of the graphs involved; b) We may have to be satisfied with suboptimal techniques. In particular, we may choose to assign interpretations to certain regions without examining their neighbors and thus simplify the labeling of the remaining ones.

The simplest possible approach is to examine each region individually and assign an interpretation to it without considering anything more than its intrinsic labels and, possibly, those of its neighbors. Such a matching can be done in time linearly proportional to the size of the RAG but it is usually impossible to decide on unique labels in this way. Therefore some intermediate method is desirable. We shall discuss such techniques after an illustration of the two "extreme" approaches for the example of Fig.5.7. We assume that we have nine possible labels: Background (B), hair (H), face (F), left eye (LE), right eye (RE), nose (N), mouth (M), neck (K), and shadow (S). For the 13 regions shown in Fig.5.13 we can assign the following labels:

1 = B 2 = H 3 = F 4 = H 5 = RE 6 = LE 7 = N
8 = M 9 = F 10 = S 11 = S 12 = K 13 = S

Or we may assign:

1 = F 2 = S 3 = F 4 = B 5 = M 6 = N 7 = RE
8 = LE 9 = B 10 = F 11 = K 12 = H 13 = H

The second interpretation is obviously absurd, but for automatic labeling we must formalize the reasons why this is so. We will do that first by introducing local constraints. Thus we may state that the labels N, M, RE and LE can only be assigned to regions with area below a certain threshold, while B, F and H can be given only to regions with large area. The labels H, M, RE, LE and S can be assigned only to regions with average brightness below a threshold T_1 while the label F can be assigned only to a region with average brightness above a threshold T_2. ($T_2 > T_1$). In this way we have formed a table of compatibilities between regions and interpretations. For example, the label F can be assigned only to 1 or 3, etc. The interpretation problem is then one of assigning the maximum number of external labels to regions.

This is a typical assignment problem and it is well-known that such problems can be solved by reducing them to maximum flow problems by forming a graph with the following structure. There are two sets of nodes: R (corresponding to regions) and S (corresponding to semantic labels) and two additional nodes A and B. A is connected to all the nodes in R and B to all the nodes in S. Each node in R is connected to a node in S if and only if the interpretations are compatible with the intrinsic labels. Fig.6.2 shows a simple example for a subset of the face labels. If A is interpreted as a source and B as a sink, and all branches of the graph are assumed to have capacity 1, then the number of assignments is maximized if the flow from the source to the sink is maximized. The latter problem can be solved efficiently by the Ford-Fulkerson algorithm [6.28]. Examples of labeling using a similar approach can be found in the recent work of TANIMOTO [6.29,30].

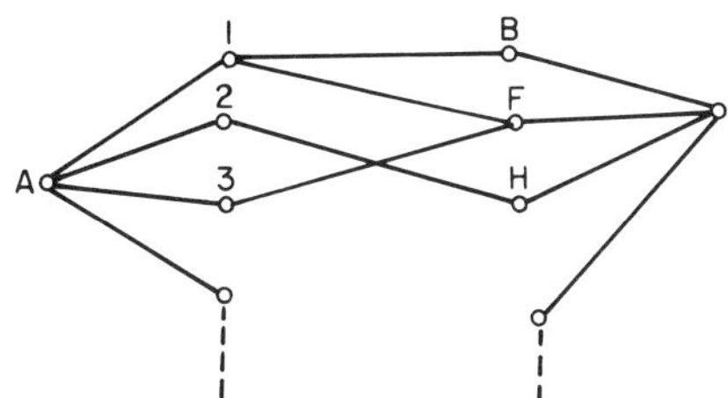

Fig. 6.2 Expression of the labeling problem as one of flow maximization. A region node (1,2,3...) is connected to a label node (B,F,H...) only if the label is applicable to that region on the basis of local constraints

Such local restrictions leave still too many interpretations possible. Additional constraints can be imposed by examining the structure of the graphs. For example, we may state that all regions with the same label must be adjacent. Or that the merge of all regions labeled F must result in a cutnode of the RAG (since the face must surround the eye, nose and mouth regions). In other words, we may replace the set of labels by a set of labeled graphs as shown in Fig.6.3. There the solid lines represent the

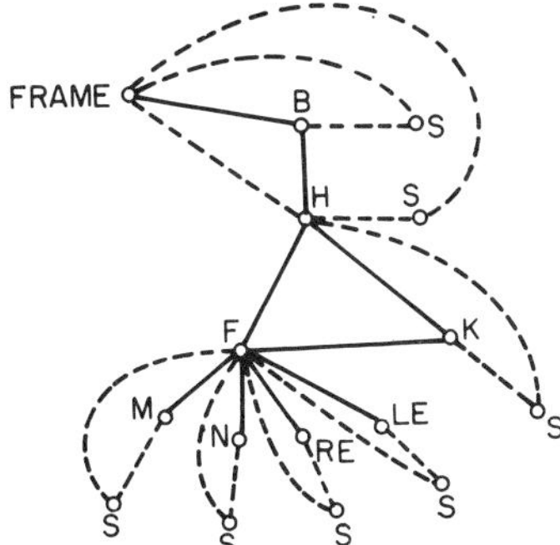

Fig. 6.3 Complete set of constraints for the face labeling problem of Figs.5.7,17

branches common to all the graphs of the set, while the broken lines represent branches which may or may not be present. Nodes connected to the common subgraph by broken lines only can be considered also as not always present. Combining the restrictions imposed by that graph to those stated above we see that both the graph of Fig.6.3 and the RAG of Fig.5.17 have only one cutnode, and therefore we may assign the label F to 3. Nodes 5-8 may be assigned any of the labels M, N, RE and LE for 6 possibilities. B must be connected to the frame (node 0 in the RAG); therefore one of the nodes 1, 2, and 10-13 must be B. 10-13 can be excluded on the basis of area restrictions. F must be connected to H; therefore one of the nodes 2, 9 and 12 must be H. The area constraint eliminates 9 and 12. In this way, we conclude that 1 must be B and 2 must be H. 4 can be either S, B or H. We are left with the five nodes 9-13 of the RAG which can be assigned any of the two labels K and S as well as H, since they are connected to a node already assigned the label H. Additional interpretations require the consideration of the location and the shape of the resulting regions. Location information can be used to assign unambiguously labels to regions 5-8. Shape information might be used to sever the lobe between regions 9 and 10 from region 2 and then assign the label S to the new region and to 9. We see that we have a rather messy problem, even for a picture with very few

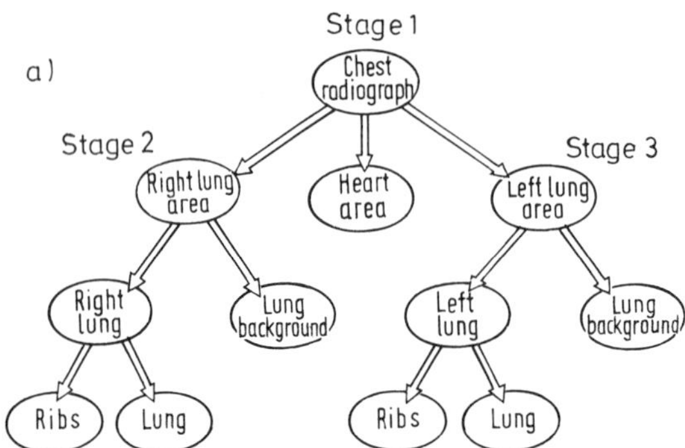

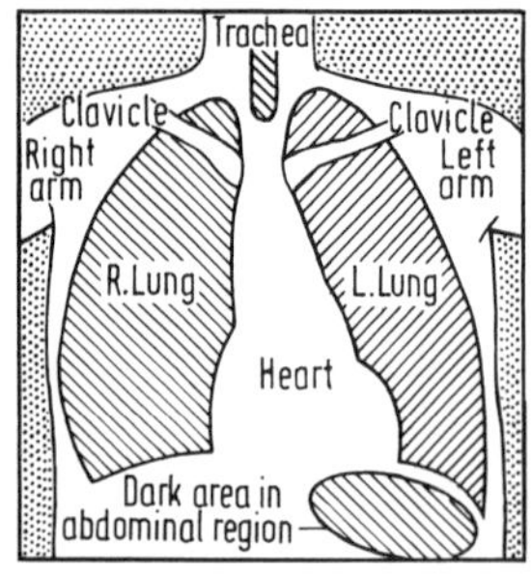

Fig. 6.4a,b Semantic constraints for a chest radiograph. a) Hierarchical structure of the constraints. b) Regions appearing in such a radiograph. (Reproduced from [6.15])

regions. Lengthy and elaborate computations are required to solve an almost trivial problem. We also see that strictly local techniques can be quite inadequate. A hierarchical approach can simplify the problem significantly, even if it misses some possible interpretations.

HARLOW and his colleagues [6.14,15] have used successfully this approach for the analysis of radiographs. In the case of a chest radiograph, the semantic graph and its relation to the picture are shown in Fig.6.4. Of special interest is the use of models for the analysis of scenes involving motion [6.31-33]. These examples suggest an important fact about the use of semantics. The scenes viewed must be from a rather narrow class of objects. This is certainly true in the case of radiographs, and in the case of moving scenes, where successive frames are fairly similar.

6.3 Local Techniques for Scene Analysis

In addition to their complexity, general interpretation schemes have the disadvantage that quite often there is no complete description of the scene but only some general knowledge of the kind of objects present. Thus, although local matchings are not always adequate by themselves, they can be used to simplify the original RAG either by region merge or by definite assignment of interpretations in some of the regions.

Many of the earlier attempts at scene analysis dealt with pictures of geometric solids, most often cubes. The faces of such objects are convex surfaces except when they are partially occluded and are therefore expected to have relatively small perimeters. BRICE and FENNEMA [6.34] used the following semantic rule to merge regions: A branch of the RAG is labeled by the length W of the parts of the boundary which are adjacent to pixels whose brightness does not differ by more than a given threshold. A node of the RAG is labeled by the perimeter P of the corresponding region. Nodes i and j are merged and branch ij is removed if $W_{ij}/\min(P_i,P_j)$ exceeds a certain threshold. In this case the LRAG is the output of the initial segmentation and the LSG the RAG where all possible mergers according to the above criterion have been made.

A more general approach, used by YAKIMOVSKY [6.3,35], is to formulate the problem in the following way. Let $R_1,R_2,\ldots,R_n$ be the regions resulting from an initial segmentation, and B_{ij} be the boundary between regions R_i and R_j. A *local interpretation* (LINT) is a function which maps the regions and boundaries into a system of labels, corresponding to semantic information.

Without loss of generality we may assume that the semantic labels are integers and we proceed to define:

$$P_{im} = \text{Prob}[\text{LINT}(R_i) = m | \text{intr. label of } R_i] \tag{6.1}$$

$$P_{ij,\ell} = \text{Prob}[\text{LINT}(B_{ij}) = \ell | \text{intr. labels of } R_i, R_j, B_{ij}] \quad . \tag{6.2}$$

These probabilities may be calculated by going through the regions in a linear order $R_1, \ldots, R_n$ and at each region examining the boundaries B_{ij}. The object of the analysis is then to maximize the probability (with respect to the choice of labels) of the overall interpretation

$$P_I = \prod_i P_{im} \times \prod_{ij} P_{ij,\ell} \quad . \tag{6.3}$$

In order to do this we form a tree with the following structure. Its root is R_1. The children of each node corresponding to a region are nodes with all possible semantic labels for that region labeled in turn with the respective probabilities. The children of each node corresponding to a semantic label of R_i are nodes corresponding to boundaries of that region which have been labeled as B_{ij} (rather than B_{ji}). The children of these nodes are boundary labels, labeled in turn with the appropriate probabilities. Then the products of (6.3) can be calculated along the paths from the root to each one of the leaves. Computational savings can be achieved by using a branch and bound method for traversing the tree.

We can illustrate this method in terms of the example of the previous section by introducing probabilities like the following: The probability that a region is H or B is an increasing function of its area while the probability that it is K or S is decreasing. Also the probability that it is B is an increasing function of the length of its common boundary with the frame (node 0 in the RAG). Then 1 and 2 are the only candidates for B and H with 1 the more likely to be B. Because of the adjacency requirement 4 must be only B or H. The labels K and S are left for any of the regions 9-13, etc. In this case we obtain the same result except that more flexible decisions were allowed.

The examination of each region separately is quite often inadequate as can be seen from the example of Section 6.2. It is possible to extend the model of (6.1-3) by introducing conditional probabilities with respect to the labels of other regions in computing 6.3 [6.3,35]. If A_i denotes the interpretation of the ith region, then we may write for n regions the following equation:

$$\mathrm{Prob}[A_1\&A_2\&\ldots\&A_n] = \mathrm{Prob}[A_n|A_1\&A_2\&\ldots\&A_{n-1}] \times \mathrm{Prob}[A_{n-1}|A_1\&\ldots A_{n-2}]\ldots \times \mathrm{Prob}[A_2|A_1] \times \mathrm{Prob}[A_1] \quad . \tag{6.4}$$

Note that the conditional probabilities do not depend on the intrinsic labels any more. This is a simplification which may have serious consequences. In particular it makes the assignment of labels depend on the order in which the regions are examined. It is theoretically correct only if the labels are independent of the features of the regions, an unlikely possibility. In terms of the crossword puzzle example of Section 6.1 it is equivalent to assigning words vertically so that they fit with those which are horizontal, while ignoring the given vertical definitions. In such a case, the value of the left-hand side of (6.4) is independent of the order in which the regions are labeled as can be seen from the elementary equation

$$\mathrm{Prob}(AB) = \mathrm{Prob}(A|B)\mathrm{Prob}(B) = \mathrm{Prob}(B|A)\mathrm{Prob}(A) \quad . \tag{6.5}$$

In general, we may not evaluate $\mathrm{Prob}[A_1]$ without knowing the other labels. YAKIMOVSKY [6.3,35] suggests the evaluation of probabilities in all possible sequences followed by a geometric averaging. This need not require excessive computation if the interpretation of each region depends only on few others, e.g., those adjacent to it. Sequential classification [6.36] can also be very helpful in this process. Examples of the use of local constraints can be found in the work of MARR, FREUDER and BULLOCK [6.37-39].

6.4 Filtering and Relaxation Techniques for Scene Analysis

These techniques were first used by WALTZ [6.16] for the description of solids and were later expanded by ZUCKER and ROSENFELD [6.17-19] for a variety of applications. They attempt to overcome the limitations imposed on the interpretation by the omission of the intrinsic labels in (6.4), and they succeed to a certain extent, as we shall see in the sequel. The basic idea is the following: If a set of external labels has been assigned to all the regions, then the probabilities P_{im}, as defined by (6.1), can be computed. If there is any contextual information, then one can evaluate various conditional probabilities of the type discussed in the previous section and use them to recalculate the values of P_{im} for some of the regions in terms of others, very much in the way of (6.4). If the labeling is *consistent* then the new values will be the same as the old ones. For example, assume that we have only two regions, A and B, which can have one of two colors, red and green. Let

$$\text{Prob(A is green}|\text{B is red)} = \text{Prob(B is red}|\text{A is green)} = 0.8 \quad ,$$

i.e., it is very likely that the two regions have different colors. The a priori probability for each color for either region is 0.5. Then

$$\text{Prob(A is green \& B is green)} = 0.1$$

and

$$\text{Prob(A is green \& B is red)} = 0.4 \quad ,$$

etc. Suppose now that we assign to both of them red with probability 0.5 for each one (computed on the basis of the intrinsic labels). We find that

$$\text{Prob(B is red)} = (1-0.8) \times 0.5 = 0.1$$

which is different than the a priori value. If we switch the label of B to green (with probability 0.5) we find that

$$\text{Prob(B is green)} = 0.8 \times 0.5 = 0.4$$

which is the a priori probability for that particular color configuration. It is possible to have a number of models for checking both the consistency of the labeling and the correction rule. In general, such methods use probabilities of co-occurrence of interpretations. Let us assume that for all i and m, P_{im} (as defined in (6.1)) is some specified function F_{im} which depends on all the other P_{jn}. Let L denote an interpretation of all the regions. A relaxation process is defined as follows: starting with an arbitrary initial labeling L^0, we define the labeling at the kth stage by the equation

$$P_{im}^{k+1} = F_{im}(L^k) \quad . \tag{6.6}$$

We define the probability vector $\underline{P}_i$ as having components P_{im} for all m. Note that

$$\sum_m P_{im} = 1 \quad .$$

Probability vectors occupy always a compact subspace as shown in Fig.6.5. If F maps probability vectors into probability vectors then it maps a compact set into itself. If it is also continuous, then according to Brouwer's theorem [6.17] it must have a fixed point. In other words there will exist a vector $\underline{P}_i$ which will be mapped by F onto itself. Then the relaxation process will converge provided the fixed point is stable, i.e., the linearization of F there has eigenvalues not greater than 1 in absolute value. We define

$$P_{im,jn} = \text{Prob}(R_i \text{ has label } m | R_j \text{ has label } n) \quad . \tag{6.7}$$

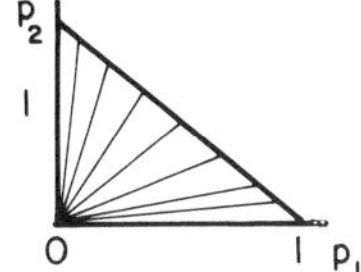

Fig. 6.5 Illustration of the compactness of the subspace by probability vectors

Note that $P_{im,in}$ is trivially 1 if n = m and zero otherwise. These conditional probabilities reflect compatibility of interpretations but only in a rather local sense and they cannot implement constraints like that of Fig.6.3. We define here the operator F by the equation:

$$P_{im}^{k+1} = \sum_j c_{ij} \left[\sum_n P_{im,jn} P_{jn}^k \right] \tag{6.8}$$

where k is the number of iterations and the coefficients c_{ij} satisfy

$$\sum_j c_{ij} = 1 \quad \text{for all } i \quad . \tag{6.9}$$

This constraint guarantees that (6.8) maps probability vectors into probability vectors as can be verified by summing its left hand side with respect to m. Eq. (6.8) requires some special attention. If R is the number of regions and L the number of possible labels, then we can define the RL-dimensional vector $\underline{Q}$ which consists of a concatenation of the vectors $\underline{P}_i$. $\underline{Q}$ contains all the labeling information about the picture. Let

B_{ij} denote the L × L matrix whose entries are $P_{im,jn}$. This is the matrix of co-occurrence probabilities for the labels of the regions i and j. If i = j then B_{ii} is an identity matrix. It is also obvious that for all i and j B_{ij} is a stochastic matrix, i.e., the sum of the elements in each column is equal to one [6.17]. Let Z denote the RL × RL matrix which has the B matrices as blocks, each multiplied by c_{ij}, as shown in Table 6.1. Then (6.8) can be written in a compact form as

$$\underline{Q}^{k+1} = Z\underline{Q}^{k} \quad . \tag{6.10}$$

Table 6.1 Definition of the Z matrix of (6.10)

$$Z = \begin{pmatrix} I & B_{12} & B_{13} & \cdots\cdots & B_{1R} \\ B_{21} & I & B_{23} & \cdots\cdots & B_{2R} \\ \cdots & \cdots & \cdots & \cdots\cdots & \cdots \\ \cdots & \cdots & \cdots & \cdots\cdots & \cdots \\ B_{R1} & B_{R2} & B_{R3} & \cdots\cdots & I \end{pmatrix}$$

Eq. (6.9) implies that Z is also a stochastic matrix. It can be shown that the eigenvalues of a stochastic matrix are all less than or equal to one in absolute value and one is always an eigenvalue [6.17]. The relaxation process multiplies the original probability vector by a power of Z so that as the number of iterations grows the result tends to a linear combination of the eigenvectors corresponding to the eigenvalues which equal one. If there is only one such eigenvector, then the result will be independent of the initial conditions and we will end up with an interpretation independent of the intrinsic labels. This is undesirable in most cases and it points to a serious defect of relaxation methods. Modifications of the exact form of (6.8) are not particularly helpful, as we shall see in Section 6.6. The remedy to these problems can be seen if we view (6.10) as a *low-pass filter*. $\underline{Q}^k$ is the input, and $\underline{Q}^{k+1}$ the output signal. It is well-known from elementary filter theory that the repeated passage of a signal through a filter results in loss of information. In the case of a moving average filter the signal is reduced to its mean value, which usually is zero. Therefore, if we let the relaxation method converge, it is likely that we will lose most information. If Z is seen as a transfer function of a "first order" filter, then it might be desirable to try Z^2, or Z^3, as higher order filters. From this viewpoint, the choice of the number of iterations in the relaxation method is very important.

Next, we discuss briefly a special case, where the matrix B_{ij} $(i \neq j) = B$, i.e., it does not depend on i and j. This produces a simplified form of (6.10). If we also assume that c_{ij} equals identically 1/R, then we can write the relaxation equation in terms of the vectors $\underline{P}$ as

$$\underline{P}_i^{k+1} = \frac{1}{R}\left[\underline{P}_i^k + B \sum_{j \neq i} \underline{P}_j^k\right] \quad . \tag{6.11}$$

Let

$$\underline{D}_i^k = \underline{P}_i^k - \underline{P}_{i-1}^k \quad .$$

Then we find that

$$\underline{D}_i^{k+1} = \frac{1}{R}(I-B)\underline{D}_i^k \quad . \tag{6.12}$$

In other words, the equations for the differences become uncoupled. Eq. (6.12) will have a nonzero fixed point if and only if the matrix I-B has R as an eigenvalue, which is equivalent to having 1-R as an eigenvalue of B. Since B is a stochastic matrix, this cannot happen for $R > 2$. Therefore $\underline{D}$ must be zero. This means that the probabilities for the final labeling will be the same for each region. Eq.(6.11) can then be replaced by

$$\underline{P}^{k+1} = \frac{I + (R-1)B}{R} \underline{P}^k \quad . \tag{6.13}$$

In this case the final result will correspond to a linear combination of eigenvectors with eigenvalue 1 of the matrix multiplying $\underline{P}^n$.

6.5 Examples of the Application of Relaxation Methods

A simple illustration of the successful application of (6.8) or (6.10) can be made in terms of a generalization of the trivial example given in the beginning of the previous section. Suppose that we know that a picture consists of alternating red and green stripes arranged in a ring as shown in Fig. 6.6. If 1 is the label value denoting green and 2 the one denoting red, then we may write the co-occurrence probability as

$$P_{im,jn} = \frac{1}{2}[1 + (-1)^{m+n+j-i}] \quad . \tag{6.14}$$

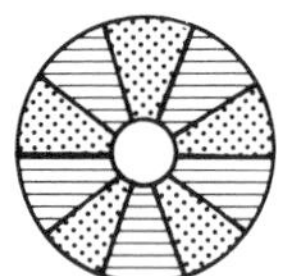

Fig. 6.6 Segmentation for the first example of Section 6.5. The two types of regions are marked by parallel lines and by dots

It is one if the two regions have the same color and the difference of their indices is even, or if they have different color and the difference is odd. Let c_{ij} be 1/3 if $j = i$ or $j = i \pm 1$ and zero otherwise. The quantity in brackets in (6.8) can be readily found to be

$$\frac{1}{2}\,(1+(-1)^{m+1+j-i})P_{j1} + \frac{1}{2}\,(1+(-1)^{m+2+j-i})P_{j2} \tag{6.15}$$

or

$$\frac{1}{2}\,[1 + (-1)^{m+j-i}] - (-1)^{m+j-i}P_{j1} \tag{6.16}$$

where we have used the fact that $P_{j1} + P_{j2} = 1$. For $m = 1$, this equals P_{i1}, if $j = i$ and $1 - P_{j1}$ if $j = i \pm 1$. Finally, we find, after multiplication by c_{ij} and addition, that the new values of the P_{i1} are given by

$$P_{i1}^{k+1} = \frac{1}{3}\,[2 - P_{i-1,1}^{k} + P_{i1}^{k} - P_{i+1,1}^{k}] \quad . \tag{6.17}$$

Let x_i denote a fixed point of the above equation. Then the final probabilities must satisfy the relation

$$x_i = \frac{1}{3}\,[2 - x_{i-1} + x_i - x_{i+1}] \tag{6.18}$$

or

$$x_i = 1 - \frac{1}{2}\,(x_{i-1}+x_{i+1}) \quad . \tag{6.19}$$

This equation has as a general solution

$$x_i = \frac{1}{2} + (-1)^i\,(vi+u) \tag{6.20}$$

where v and u are determined from the labels of the first two regions. If both are zero then all the final probabilities will be 1/2, equal to the a priori probabilities. v must be zero; otherwise the x's will not represent probabilities. Then we find that the probability that a region is green (label 1) alternates between 1/2 + u and 1/2 - u. In this case u may reflect the initial labeling. Some of the salient properties of relaxation schemes can be seen from a computer simulation which was carried out for this example. For a total of ten stripes (as in Fig.6.6) two adjacent ones were assigned probabilities of green of 0.8 and 0.2 and all the others 0.5. This corresponds to a picture processing case where the interpretation of a few regions is very clear and we want to use them as "anchor" for the interpretation of the remaining ones. Then 100 iterations were carried out. The final probabilities alternated between 0.56 and 0.44. The test was repeated with an initial assignment for four stripes of probabilities 0.95, 0.05, 0.75 and 0.25. The final answer was 0.64 and 0.36. The results are summarized in Table 6.2. The following conclusions are pertinent: The final answer reflects the intrinsic labels in more than one way. Not only the more likely color of each region is determined, but also the confidence is different, depending on the extent of our initial knowledge. In both cases, after 20 iterations the probabilities were quite close to their final value. The final values have been reached within 0.0005 after 50 iterations. This shows a very slow convergence near the solution. This example also illustrates a major property of the relaxation process. It is seen as a propagation process which starts at the regions which have been labeled with high confidence and progressively increases the labeling confidence of the other regions.

We describe next a less simple example, assuming that Fig.6.7 represents the result of a segmentation. There are eight possible interpretations:

1) A triangle floating above a plane.
2) A triangular hole in a plane.
3-5) A triangular flap folded upwards (joined at one of three possible sides).
6-8) A triangular flap folded downwards (joined at one of three possible sides).

Fig. 6.7 Segmentation for the second example of Section 6.5

Table 6.2 Probabilities that a stripe is green during a relaxation procedure

Iterations			
0	10	20	50
0.800000	0.587969	0.567124	0.560120
0.200000	0.412031	0.432876	0.439880
0.500000	0.577122	0.564402	0.560074
0.500000	0.440202	0.440000	0.440000
0.500000	0.542753	0.555598	0.559926
0.500000	0.467642	0.447123	0.440120
0.500000	0.532358	0.552877	0.559880
0.500000	0.457247	0.444402	0.440074
0.500000	0.559798	0.560000	0.560000
0.500000	0.422878	0.435598	0.439926

Iterations			
0	10	20	50
0.950000	0.681785	0.650685	0.640180
0.050000	0.303777	0.345646	0.359759
0.750000	0.688991	0.652540	0.640211
0.250000	0.336996	0.354064	0.359900
0.500000	0.628398	0.637065	0.639951
0.500000	0.401632	0.370685	0.360180
0.500000	0.584164	0.625647	0.639759
0.500000	0.408906	0.372539	0.360211
0.500000	0.616662	0.634064	0.639900
0.500000	0.348689	0.357065	0.359951

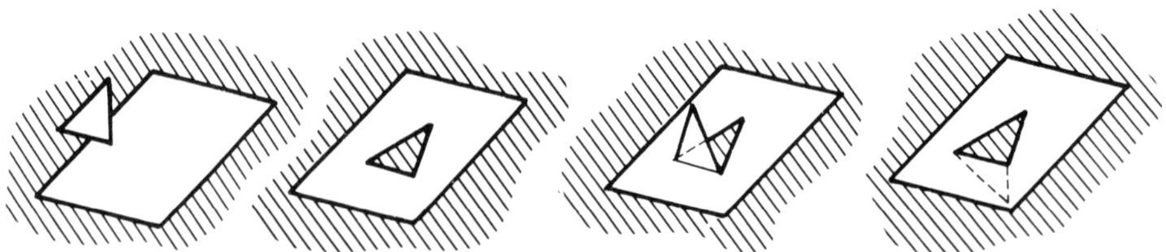

Fig. 6.8 Possible interpretations for the segmentation of Fig.6.7

These possibilities are shown in Fig.6.8. In this case the three edges are the regions to be labeled. There are four possibilities. Convex (1), concave (2), above background (3) and below background (4). An edge can have any of these labels but for a pair there are only six possibilities:

Label	Meaning
33	Vertex above background
44	Vertex below background
32	Folding above
23	Folding above
14	Folding below
41	Folding below

The eight overall interpretations shown in Fig.6.8 are

333	444	323	332
233	414	441	144

On this basis we may assign a priori probabilities for each pair: Thus 33 has a priori probability 1/4 and the probability that an edge has a label 3 given that the previous had also 3, is 2/3. Altogether we have for $j = i \pm 1$:

$$
\begin{aligned}
P_{i3,j3} &= 2/3 \\
P_{i3,j2} &= 1 \\
P_{i4,j4} &= 2/3 \\
P_{i4,j1} &= 1 \\
P_{i2,j3} &= 1/3 \\
P_{i1,j4} &= 1/3 \\
&\text{zero otherwise}
\end{aligned}
$$

Then the B matrix is

$$
B = \begin{pmatrix} 0 & 0 & 0 & 1/3 \\ 0 & 0 & 1/3 & 0 \\ 0 & 1 & 2/3 & 0 \\ 1 & 0 & 0 & 2/3 \end{pmatrix}
$$

In this case the matrix of (6.13) turns out to have two double eigenvalues: 1 and 1/9. The eigenvectors corresponding to the first have the form

$$\begin{pmatrix} a \\ .25-a \\ .75-3a \\ 3a \end{pmatrix}$$

In other words, the more likely labels are 3 and 4 with all the edges having the same label. Thus the triangle floating above or the triangular hole are more likely than the folding flap. Here the only effect of the intrinsic labels is expressed through the undetermined constant a. Under no circumstances will the final labeling contain a "fold" as a likely label.

6.6 Nonlinear Relaxation Techniques

These have been proposed [6.17-19,23] as a means of achieving labelings which depend on the initial conditions. They have been used in a number of cases with interesting results [6.18,19] but their properties have not been thoroughly investigated as yet. Contrary to early claims, the results are usually independent from the initial conditions, unless only a few iterations are performed. This has been the case with the examples discussed in the literature. Because of slow convergence the process was terminated "prematurely". In retrospect, this might have been an optimal strategy. In this section we show certain simple examples where solutions independent from the initial conditions are found, and then explain why this should be the most common case. The modification of (6.8) starts by replacing the conditional probabilities with the respective correlation functions. The correlation of two events A and B is defined as

$$\begin{aligned} \mathrm{cor}(A\&B) = {} & [\mathrm{Prob}(A\&B) - \mathrm{Prob}(A) \times \mathrm{Prob}(B)] \times \\ & [\mathrm{Prob}(A)\mathrm{Prob}(B)\ (1-\mathrm{Prob}(A))\ (1-\mathrm{Prob}(B))]^{-1/2}\ . \end{aligned} \tag{6.21}$$

This function has the property that is zero if A and B are independent, it is 1 if A implies B and B implies A and -1 if A and B can never co-occur. Then (6.8) can be written as

$$P_{im}^{k+1} = \sum_j c_{ij} \left[\sum_n R_{im,jn}\ P_{jn}^k\right] \tag{6.22}$$

where $R_{im,jn}$ is the correlation between the events "region i has label m" and "region j has label n". However, this equation does not map probability vectors into probability vectors because R is not a stochastic matrix anymore. A convergent relaxation scheme which still uses the correlation matrix is given by the following set of equations. First we define

$$Q_{im}^{k} = \sum_{j} c_{ij} \left[\sum_{n} R_{im,jn} P_{jn}^{k}\right] \quad . \tag{6.23}$$

Then we set

$$T_{i}^{k} = \sum_{n} P_{in}^{k} \, [1 + Q_{in}^{k}] \quad . \tag{6.24}$$

Finally

$$P_{im}^{k+1} = \frac{P_{im}^{k} \, [1 + Q_{im}^{k}]}{T_{i}^{k}} \quad . \tag{6.25}$$

It has been shown that this relaxation is convergent [6.40], although this is not a very interesting result, if we view (6.25) as a filtering process. Nonlinear relaxation schemes have been used with good results for line and curve enhancement and other scenes analysis problems [6.18]. We shall describe some of their applications in curve matching in Chapter 8. The following simple examples illustrate the possibility that in many cases they give solutions independent of the initial conditions, or depending on them in a very limited way.

Consider a situation where the labeling of each region is independent from that of its neighbors. This is a trivial, but certainly a legitimate case. Then

$$R_{im,jn} = 0 \quad \text{if} \quad i \neq j \quad , \tag{6.26a}$$

$$R_{im,in} = -1 \quad \text{if} \quad m \neq n \quad , \tag{6.26b}$$

$$R_{im,im} = 1 \quad . \tag{6.26c}$$

Then (6.23) becomes

$$Q_{im}^{k} = c_{ii} \left[P_{im}^{k} - \sum_{n \neq m} P_{in}^{k}\right] \quad . \tag{6.27}$$

The sum of the probabilities over all possible labels for a given region is 1 and therefore (6.27) becomes

$$Q^k_{im} = c_{ii}\,[2P^k_{im} - 1] \quad . \tag{6.28}$$

Then (6.24) is simplified into

$$T^k_i = 1 - c_{ii} + 2c_{ii} \sum_n [P^k_{in}]^2 \quad . \tag{6.29}$$

Finally,

$$P^{k+1}_{im} = \frac{P^k_{im}\,[1 - c_{ii} + 2c_{ii}\,P^k_{im}]}{1 - c_{ii} + c_{ii} \sum_n [P^k_{in}]^2} \quad . \tag{6.30}$$

The assumption of independent labels implies that the original labels should not be modified during the relaxation procedure, since the information about their neighbors is irrelevant. This will not be the case with (6.30) unless one of the following conditions holds: 1) $c_{ii} = 0$, or 2) each region has only one possible label (i.e., P_m is zero for all m, except for one value, for which it equals 1). The last case is of no interest; therefore, one must require that $c_{ii} = 0$. If we do not make that assumption, then not only the probability of each label is changed during relaxation, but the result, to which the process converges, is virtually independent of the initial assignments. This can be seen as follows: Assume that there are only two possible labels B and W, and let, for simplicity, b^k_i denote P^k_{iB}. Then $P^k_{iW} = 1 - b^k_i$. In this case (6.30) becomes

$$b^{k+1}_i = \frac{b^k_i\,[1 - c_{ii} + 2c_{ii}\,b^k_i]}{1 - c_{ii} + c_{ii}\,\{[b^k_i]^2 + [1 - b^k_i]^2\}} \quad . \tag{6.31}$$

This equation has three fixed points. 0, 0.5 and 1. 0.5 is unstable and if b^0_i exceeds it, the final answer is 1, while if b^0_i is less than 0.5, the final answer is 0. Although the solution *does* depend on the initial probabilities, it does so in a rather extreme way, in a case when the initial values should not have been modified at all. In this case linear relaxing shows actually a better behavior. It is easy to verify that (6.8) reduces into

$$P_{im}^{k+1} = P_{im} + c_{ii}\,(P_{im}^{k} - P_{im}) \quad , \tag{6.32}$$

where P_{im} is the a priori probability that region i has label m. Note that in the case of nonlinear relaxation, a small perturbation around the value 0.5 produces widely different answers. This behavior cannot be remedied in all cases by taking $c_{ii} = 0$. We demonstrate this by analyzing a second example. We consider a scene consisting of only two regions, each with only two possible labels. Furthermore, let

$$R_{1B,2B} = R_{1W,2W} = h \quad , \tag{6.33a}$$

$$R_{1W,2B} = R_{1B,2W} = -h \quad . \tag{6.33b}$$

Then we find, in a manner similar to the one used in the first example,

$$Q_1^k = h\,[2b_2^k - 1] \quad , \tag{6.34}$$

and

$$b_1^{k+1} = \frac{b_1^k\,[1 + h(2b_2^k - 1)]}{1 + h(2b_2^k - 1)\,(2b_1^k - 1)} \quad . \tag{6.35}$$

The equation for b_2 can be obtained from the above by interchanging the indices 1 and 2. If h is different from zero, then the stationary points of these two equations are (0,0), (0,1), (1,0), (1,1) and (0.5,0.5). Note that these values do not depend at all on h. The "region of attraction" of each

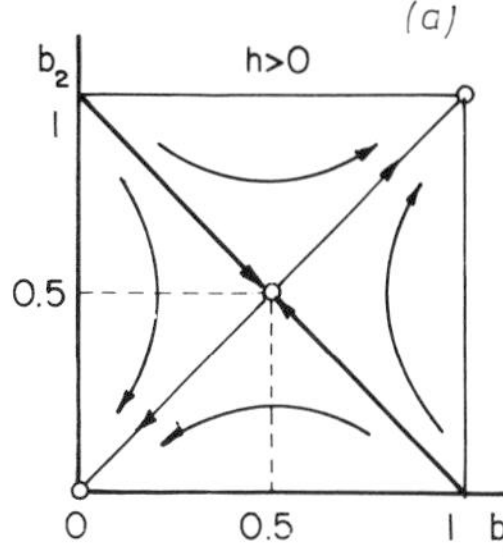

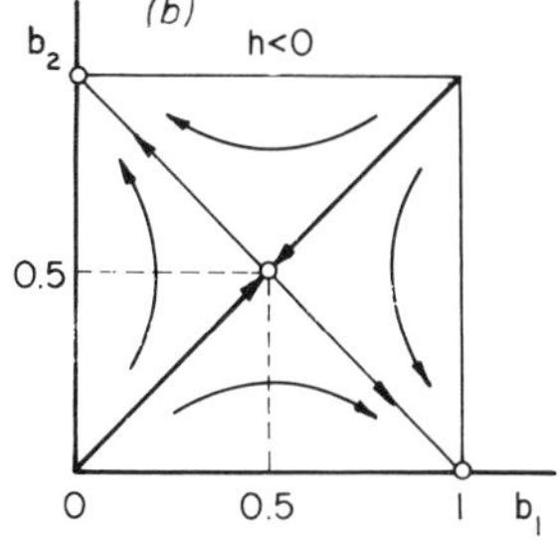

Fig. 6.9a and b Effect of the initial conditions on the final answers for the nonlinear relaxation in the case of two regions with two possible labels. a) For positive h the method converges to (1,1) or (0,0). b) For negative h the method converges to (1,0) or (0,1). In both cases (0.5,0.5) is a saddle point

one of these points was studied through numerical calculations for a variety of values of h and initial conditions. If h is positive, and if $b_1^0 + b_2^0$ exceed 1, the relaxation converges to (1,1). If this sum is less than 1, the process converges to (0,0). (0.5,0.5) is a solution only when the sum $b_1^0 + b_2^0$ equals 1. Note the rather undesirable property that (0.51,0.51) will go into (1,1), (0.49,0.49) into (0,0) and (0.51,0.49) into (0.5,0.5), *regardless of the value of h,* as long as h is positive. If h is negative, then the relaxation converges to either of (1,0) or (0,1) depending on the difference of the initial probabilities. The relaxation converges to (0.5,0.5) only when they are equal. Thus (0.5,0.5) is a "saddle point" [6.41]. Fig.6.9 illustrates these results. This behavior is typical of nonlinear filters. When a signal is passed repeatedly through such a filter, the result is substantially the same as in the case of a linear filter, except that there might be more than one "trivial" answer. If one performs only a small number of iterations of (6.35), then the answer depends very much on the initial conditions, and the value of h. It is also biased according to the a priori semantic information.

7. Analytical Description of Region Boundaries and Curves

7.1 Introduction

Our discussion up to now has dealt with determining regions with "uniform" properties in a picture and tracing their boundaries. The next step is to describe the shape of such regions. This may either be the end product of our process or an intermediate result in a scene analysis program. The former is often the case in the recognition of characters (including numerals, Chinese characters, etc.), waveforms, chromosomes, cells, and machine parts. For this reason shape discrimination is discussed, at least implicitly, in most papers dealing with the above subjects and the size of shape related literature is indeed immense.

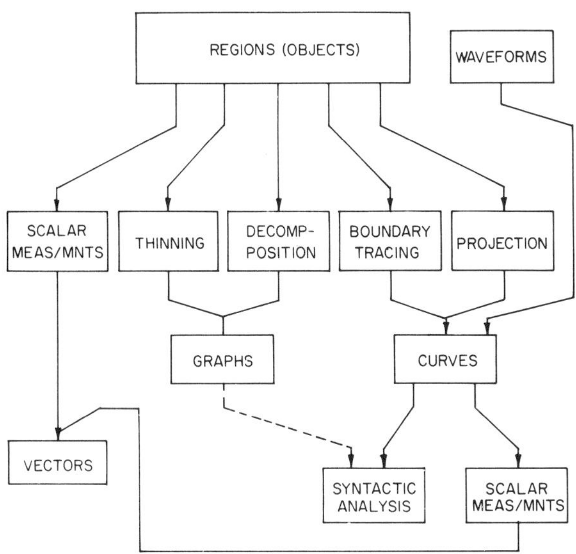

Fig. 7.1 Illustration of the applicability of various methodologies for shape recognition

There are a few basic ways to describe the shape of regions. Fig.7.1 presents a summary of the relevant methodologies. One approach is to perform directly a number of scalar measurements and thus obtain a *feature vector*. The ratio of the square of perimeter length to the area of a region is one feature which has been popular in shape studies. Methods of this type are rather simple to implement, but their disadvantages tend to limit their applicability. We discuss some of them briefly in Chapter 9. A second approach is to reduce the plane region to a *graph*, i.e., a thin line drawing which reflects the original shape. This can be done either directly by *thinning*, or indirectly by *decomposition* into simpler components. The graph describes the relative positions of regions of "simple" shape which together form a region of "complex" shape. We discuss such methods in Chapter 9. Finally, we may attempt to transform the region into a continuous plane curve. The boundary of a region is a natural choice for such a curve. Another set of curves can be obtained by *projections*. We have discussed the derivation of boundaries in the previous chapter and we will present the derivation of projections in the next section. In either case the pattern recognition problem has been reduced to that of the description of the shape of a curve. We shall devote this and the next chapter to an examination of *curve* and *boundary analysis* techniques. There are many methods which fall into this category and one can distinguish between those which scan the boundary points according to a local sequence and those which "skip across" boundary points. Usually, sequential boundary scanning algorithms require time linearly proportional to the number of boundary points while the "skipping across" type may require time proportional to their square. Typical examples of the former are the parsing of the boundary according to a simple grammar, e.g., [7.1] and the evaluation of a single coefficient of the Fourier Transform, e.g., [7.2]. An example of the latter is parsing according to context sensitive grammars as well as certain algebraic implementations of decomposition techniques. The shape of curves can be analyzed either by *scalar transform* or by *space domain* techniques. As far as subsequent processing is concerned scalar transforms are most appropriate as input to classical statistical pattern recognizers while space domain techniques are most appropriate for producing input to syntactic and/or structural pattern classifiers [7.3-9]. The study of the shape of curves is of interest not only as a means for studying the shape of regions but also as a goal in itself. In a number of applications a picture may be expressed not through regions but through edges and other one-dimensional forms. A very important set of applications deals with *waveforms*. Typical examples are electrocardiograms, speech and seismic waveforms. In some cases these can be studied through their spectrum, but in others a space domain analysis is necessary. Speech represents a complex case where a combination of both types of techniques is required.

The various methodologies can be classified according to many criteria in addition to those stated above. For example, we may distinguish between *information preserving* and *information nonpreserving* techniques depending on whether it is possible to reconstruct the picture from the shape descriptors or not. The distinction is fuzzy because some techniques allow only imperfect reconstruction. Furthermore, any pattern recognition encoding must perform some information reduction. We will resolve this problem by examining whether there is a set of parameters under which a given technique can give a replica of the original picture which is arbitrarily close to it. Thus the ratio of the square of the perimeter to the area [7.10] does not allow reconstruction under any circumstances, except for such trivial cases when the general shape is known and simple (e.g., if it is a rectangle or a regular polygon). On the other hand, a Fourier expansion allows that, provided that sufficient coefficients have been evaluated. In essence we distinguish between schemes where the loss of information can be controlled and those where it cannot. The terms *normative* and *generative* have also been suggested for those two types [7.11]. However, we prefer the present terminology for two reasons: 1) It is more descriptive and 2) the term *generative* should best be reserved for methods where the *physical process generating the shape* is taken into account for the design of descriptors. This approach has been emphasized by GRENANDER in the context of pattern synthesis [7.7] as well as in many theoretical biology studies, e.g., [7.12]. It should be pointed out that many of the publications on shape have dealt with information nonpreserving techniques. In particular, they emphasize properties like symmetry, elongation, and angularity [7.10,13-17]. Such properties give very useful information for the shape of simple objects but not for complicated ones. The description of the latter type must often be made in terms of local characteristics. In this chapter we shall focus our attention on methods which produce compact descriptions of curves without resorting to semantic or high level information. There are basically two ways to achieve this goal: Fourier Transforms and piecewise polynomial (usually polygonal) approximations. In the next chapter we discuss syntactic techniques for both boundaries and waveforms. A number of authors deemphasize the process of description and emphasize the comparison or matching of curves [7.18-24]. They have used in this context a variety of techniques, some based on approximation theory, others syntactic, and others based on heuristics. The emphasis on comparison has certain merits in view of the results of Section 2.4. On the other hand, information preserving descriptions should be quite adequate for comparisons.

While discussing the various shape description techniques we shall use as illustration their performance on a common data base, a set of handwritten numerals. These were originally digitized from handprinted FORTRAN sheets by Dr. J.H. Munson of the Stanford Research Institute and are available from IEEE which lists them as Data Base No. 1.1.2.

7.2 Projections

Let V be an object with optical transparency V(x,y,z) which is illuminated along, say, the z axis. Then its image on the x-y plane will have brightness f(x,y) given by the following equation

$$f(x,y) = \int V(x,y,z)dz \tag{7.1}$$

where the integration takes place along the volume of V. A typical practical case of such a *projection* is a radiograph. One can also have projections in the plane which will correspond to illuminations of objects along a cross-section. Mathematically a plane projection is defined in cartesian coordinates as

$$p(x) = \int f(x,y)dy \quad . \tag{7.2}$$

In this way functions of two variables may be transformed into functions of a single variable and plane regions into plane curves.

Such projections are only one of many techniques related to integral geometry, which have been proposed by various authors [7.25-37]: The object is intersected by a number of chords at different directions and locations and the length of the intersection is used as a shape descriptor. In one approach the choice of the chords may be at random and length statistics can be used as features. However, this method suffers from certain major analytical difficulties [7.27]. PAVLIDIS [7.26] used "cartesian" projections of the type defined by (7.2), with certain modifications, for the description of the shape of typewritten characters [7.20]. Similar projections have been used widely with a variety of names, including signatures [7.37], belt patterns [7.34], and stereological intercepts [7.33]. RUTOVITZ has used radial chords all passing through a common point to describe the shape of chromosomes [7.28]. KLINGER and his co-workers [7.29,30] have also used a similar technique. The term "polar projections" may be used to describe both methods. Projections of any of the above types can be used in one of two ways: Without any further processing they may be considered as a feature vector or a "profile" of the object and used in statistical pattern recognition. On the other hand, they may be processed in a structural way as waveforms to reveal salient features of the original object. Thus a stroke along one of the main directions (in the cartesian approach) or passing through the center (in the polar approach) will yield well-defined peaks.

We should mention that one of their major applications in the field of picture processing has to do, not with shape, but with *reconstruction* of cross-sections of the human body in what is called *computerized tomography*. This is based on the fact that it is possible to determine f(x,y) from its projections along a sufficiently large number of directions. Indeed, let

$$y = Ax + h \tag{7.3}$$

be a family of lines. Then a one parameter family of projections is given by

$$p(A,h) = \int f(x,Ax+h)dx \quad . \tag{7.4}$$

The Fourier Transform (FT) of p(A,h) is

$$P^*(A,u) = \int p(A,h)\, e^{-i\frac{2\pi hu}{L}} dh \tag{7.5}$$

where L is the length of a square domain of integration. Substituting (7.4) into (7.5) and interchanging the order of integration yields,

$$P^*(A,u) = \int [\int f(x,Ax+h)\, \exp(-i\,\frac{2\pi hu}{L})\, dh]dx \quad . \tag{7.6}$$

Replacing h by y-Ax we obtain

$$P^*(A,u) = \int [\int f(x,y)\, \exp(-i\,\frac{2\pi(yu-xAu)}{L})dy]dx \quad . \tag{7.7}$$

But the right hand side of this equation is the two-dimensional FT of f(x,y) F*(u,w) evaluated along the complex plane line

$$w = -Au \quad . \tag{7.8}$$

Therefore, by evaluating projections along different angles and taking their one-dimensional FT's we obtain the two-dimensional FT of f(x,y). Thus projections are indeed an information preserving technique, if enough of them are evaluated.

If only a small number of them is available, then we have a significant loss of information. Fig.7.2 shows a set of regions which have different shape but identical projections along the x and y axes. It is possible to characterize binary pictures which can be reconstructed from two such projections.

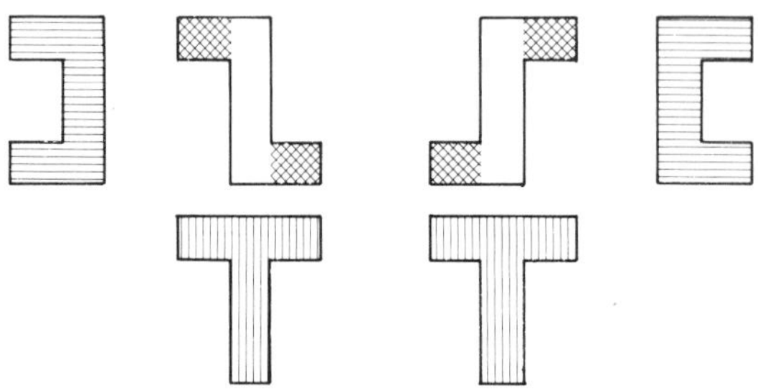

Fig. 7.2 Illustration of projections and of their nonuniqueness. Both the left and the right figure have the same projections in the x and y directions

Definition 7.1: A binary matrix f(x,y) has a *switching component* if there exist indices x_1,x_2,y_1,y_2 such that

$$f(x_1,y_1) = f(x_2,y_2) = 1 - f(x_1,y_2) = 1 - f(x_2,y_1) \quad . \tag{7.9}$$

The crosshatched parts of Fig.7.2 correspond to such a component. CHANG [7.38] has shown that only pictures without switching components can be reconstructed from their projections along the x-y axes. Unfortunately such pictures are rather rare and many rather simple shapes result in ambiguities. Thus the method of cartesian projections is best suited for the extraction of major features like strokes along one of the axes. Polar projections tend to be more robust, provided that an *appropriate* center has been chosen. Otherwise they can give little information about shape (Fig.7.3). RUTOVITZ [7.28] has

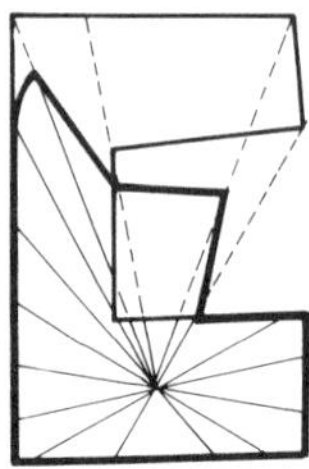

Fig. 7.3 Illustration of polar projection. The resulting contour is indicated by a heavy line

used certain figures of merit for choosing among a number of directions the one which is most appropriate for projections. A discussion of the use of a small number of projections for reconstruction is outside our scope, and we refer the reader to the papers by CHANG, HERMAN, MERSEREAU, KASHYAP, WEE and others [7.38-45].

One way to reduce the ambiguity of the description by projections in the case of binary pictures is to stop the integration given by (7.2) when a boundary is seen. In particular, let us assume a square integration region of size $L \times L$ with R being the region where $f(x,y) = 1$ and let $y(x_0)_1$, $y(x_0)_2, \ldots y(x_0)_m$ be the points where a line parallel to the y axis, intersecting the x axis at x_0, intersects the boundary of R (see Fig.7.4). We may assume without loss of generality that $y(x_0)_1$ represents a crossing from 0 to 1 along increasing y's.

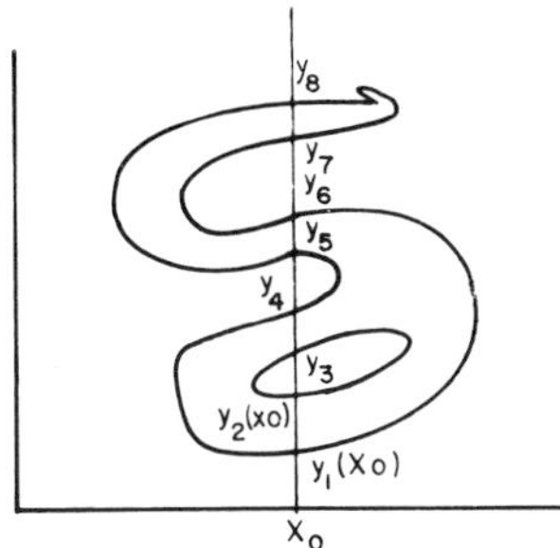

Fig. 7.4 Illustration of the choice of the bounds for partial projections

Definition 7.2: The kth projection of R is given by

$$p_k(x) = y(x)_{k+1} - y(x)_k \quad . \tag{7.10}$$

Fig. 7.5 shows an example of such projections compared to those obtained from (7.2). Information about strokes and the existence of holes is far more evident when the projections are evaluated according to (7.10).

Fig. 7.5 Projections according to (7.10) (left) and (7.2) (right)

In any case projections represent an encoding of a region into a family of plane curves or waveforms, and they can be treated by any of the techniques discussed in the remainder of this chapter and in the next one.

7.3 Boundary Scalar Transform Techniques

These involve mostly the Fourier transform (FT) of the boundary which can be expressed in terms of tangent angle versus arc length, or as complex function $bx(t) + j\, by(t)$ where $bx(t)$ and $by(t)$ denote a parametric representation of the boundary coordinates. The first approach has been used by BRILL [7.46], ZAHN and ROSKIES [7.2], BENNET and MacDONALD [7.47], and others. The second has been used by GRANLUND [7.48,49], RICHARDS and HEMAMI [7.50], PERSOON and FU [7.51], and others. We review first the ZAHN and ROSKIES formulation. Let ϕ_k be the rotation of the tangent to a boundary at the kth point in comparison to the direction of the tangent at an initial point $bx(t_0)$, $by(t_0)$. Also let ℓ_k be the arc length between these two points. These quantities are illustrated in Fig.7.6 and can be defined formally as following:

$$\ell_k = \sum_{i=1}^{k} \sqrt{[x(t_i) - x(t_{i-1})]^2 + [y(t_i) - y(t_{i-1})]^2} \quad k = 1,2,\ldots,N+1 \quad , \tag{7.11}$$

$$\phi_k = \tan^{-1} \frac{y(t_{k+1}) - y(t_k)}{x(t_{k+1}) - x(t_k)} - \tan^{-1} \frac{y(t_1) - y(t_0)}{x(t_1) - x(t_0)} \quad k = 1,2,\ldots,N+1 \quad . \tag{7.12}$$

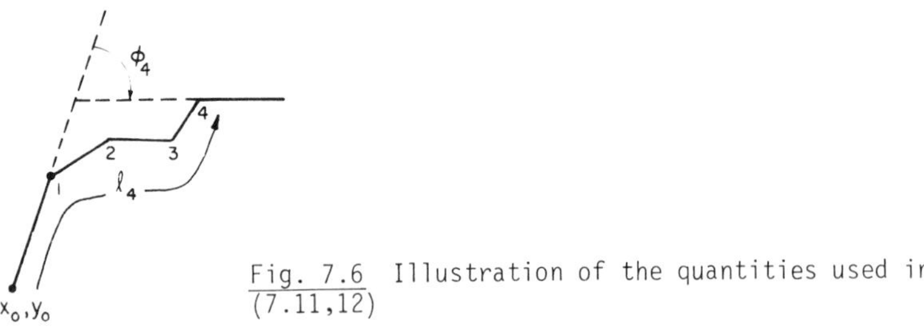

Fig. 7.6 Illustration of the quantities used in (7.11,12)

Note that ϕ_0 equals zero and ϕ_{N+1} equals -2π and that, given the function ϕ_k versus ℓ_k, one can reconstruct the boundary. This function can be normalized and be made to depend on a parameter t ranging from 0 to 2π by defining

$$a(t_k) = \phi_k + t_k \quad , \tag{7.13}$$

where

$$t_k = (2\pi/L)\ell_k \quad . \tag{7.14}$$

L is the total length so that $a(0) = a(2\pi) = 0$.

If the data points form a regular polygon then $\ell_k = k\ell_0$ where ℓ_0 is the side of the polygon and $\phi_k = -2\pi k/N$. Then (7.14) above yields $t_k = 2\pi k/N$ and therefore a(t) is identically zero. By carrying this argument to the limit ($N \to \infty$) we find that the same is true for a circle. It is easy to show that for a linear interpolation of boundary points a(t) is linear between vertices so that its overall form is that of a sawtooth wave with negative jumps corresponding to convex angles and positive jumps to concave angles. For a regular polygon, the jumps equal $2\pi/N$. Figs. 7.7,8 show a(t) for a square and an L-shaped object, respectively. The size of a jump is always proportional to the size of the angle at that point.

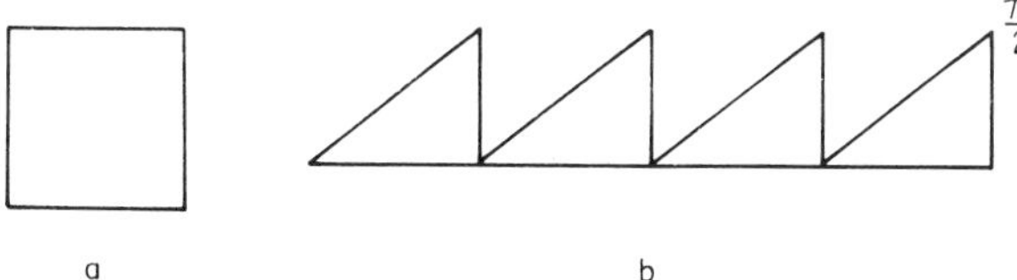

Fig. 7.7a,b Plot for a square a) of a(t) b)

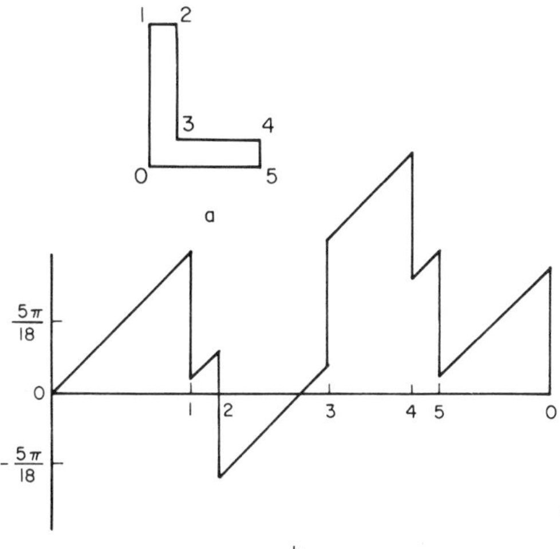

Fig. 7.8a,b Plot for an L-shaped object a) of a(t) b)

An inspection of Fig.7.8 reveals that for a figure with two "arms" we can expect a strong second harmonic in the FT of a(t). In general, strokes or lobes extending from the main body of an object produce peaks in a(t) which, if repeated, cause a high component at a frequency of the FT roughly corresponding to their number. Therefore, the coefficients of the FT of a(t) or similar functions can be used for shape description, if the counting of such elements is important for that purpose. A set of complex shape descriptors will be given by the equation

$$S_n = \frac{1}{2\pi} \int_0^{2\pi} a(t)\, e^{-jnt} dt \quad . \tag{7.15}$$

In practice a contour is given by a set of discrete points, in which case the discrete Fourier transform of $a(t_k)$ must be used. It is given in terms of real coefficients by [7.2]

$$A_0 = -\pi - \left(\frac{1}{L}\right) \sum_{k=1}^{N+1} \ell_k(\phi_k - \phi_{k-1}) \quad , \tag{7.16a}$$

$$A_n = -\left(\frac{1}{N\pi}\right) \sum_{k=1}^{N+1} (\phi_k - \phi_{k-1}) \sin(2\pi n \ell_k / L) \quad , \tag{7.16b}$$

$$B_n = -\left(\frac{1}{N\pi}\right) \sum_{k=1}^{N+1} (\phi_k - \phi_{k-1}) \cos(2\pi n \ell_k / L) \quad , \tag{7.16c}$$

so that

$$a(t) = A_0 + \sum_{n=1}^{N+1} [A_n \cos(nt) + B_n \sin(nt)] \quad . \tag{7.17}$$

In the formalism proposed by GRANLUND [7.49] and developed by PERSOON and FU [7.51] the shape descriptors are

$$T_n = \frac{1}{L} \int_0^{L} b(t)\, e^{-j\frac{2\pi n}{L}t} dt \quad , \tag{7.18}$$

where b(t) is the complex function bx(t) + j by(t). The length of the curve from an original point can serve as the parameter t but this is neither essential nor desirable for many applications. Under this formalism the FT of a circle has a zeroth order harmonic equal to the coordinate of its center and a first harmonic which is real and equal to its radius. All other harmonics are zero. One major difference between this equation and (7.15) is that the former produces only N/2 distinct descriptors ($S_{(N/2)+1} = S_0, \ldots, S_N = S_{(N/2)}$, etc.) while the latter requires N of them for a complete description because b(t) is a complex function. If the length of the curve is used as the parameter t, then the derivative of b(t) with respect to t has as modulus

$$\left|\frac{db}{dt}\right| = \sqrt{\left(\frac{dbx}{dt}\right)^2 + \left(\frac{dby}{dt}\right)^2} = 1 \quad , \tag{7.19}$$

because $dt = \sqrt{dbx^2 + dby^2}$. This means that the coefficients T_n are not independent and therefore there is redundancy in the description. Let T'_n denote the Fourier transform of b'(t) (derivative with respect to t) and let c* denote the complex conjugate of a complex number c. By a well-known property of Fourier transforms we have

$$T'_n = j\,\frac{2\pi n}{L}\,T_n \quad ,$$

while (7.19) implies that

$$|b'(t)|^2 = [b'(t)]\,[b'(t)^*] = 1 \quad .$$

Therefore

$$\sum_{n=0}^{n=N} \frac{T_n T^*_n}{\left(\frac{2\pi n}{L}\right)^2} = \sum_{n=0}^{n=N} T'_n T'^*_n \quad . \tag{7.20}$$

If N equals the total number of sample points, then the second sum equals 1 and this gives the constraint for the T_n's.

7.4 Properties and Applications of Fourier Shape Descriptors

The major advantage of the descriptors S_n and T_n is that it is very easy to write programs for finding them, and that they are backed by a well-developed theory, that of Fourier transforms. Their major disadvantage is that, of all transform techniques, the difficulty in describing local information is greatest [7.53]. Also, they can distinguish among symmetric curves only on the basis of the phase of the descriptors, which cannot be computed reliably in many cases. Thus the descriptors of the contours of a "2" and "5" are virtually identical. Nevertheless, the methodology can be used successfully for shape description provided that certain precautions are taken. We describe next the properties of each particular formulation.

I) *The descriptors* S_n*:* The function a(t) almost always has discontinuities, and therefore it is expected that the size of S_n would decrease very slowly with n. Furthermore, the property of curve closure is not preserved if one attempts a reconstruction of the boundary from a subset of the S_n's. Fig. 7.9 illustrates the reconstruction of a curve using the first ten harmonics only. In general, a given sequence of complex numbers can always be interpreted as the FT of a curve but this will not usually be closed. There is no known characterization for closure. The following are sufficient conditions proven by ZAHN and ROSKIES [7.2].

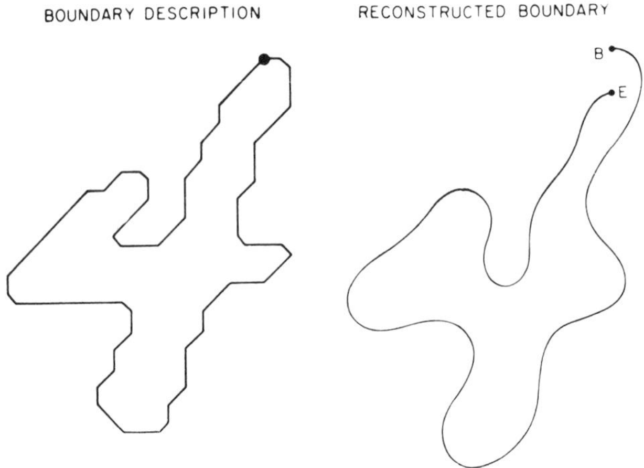

Fig. 7.9a,b Partial reconstruction of boundaries through Fourier descriptors. a) Original boundary. b) Reconstruction. (Reproduced from [7.2])

Theorem 7.1: A set of complex numbers S_n is the FT of a closed curve if either of the following two conditions holds: 1) S_1 is a zero of the first Bessel function $J_1(x)$ and $S_n = 0$ for $n \geq 2$. 2) $S_n = 0$ for all $n \neq 0 \pmod{k}$ for $k \geq 2$.

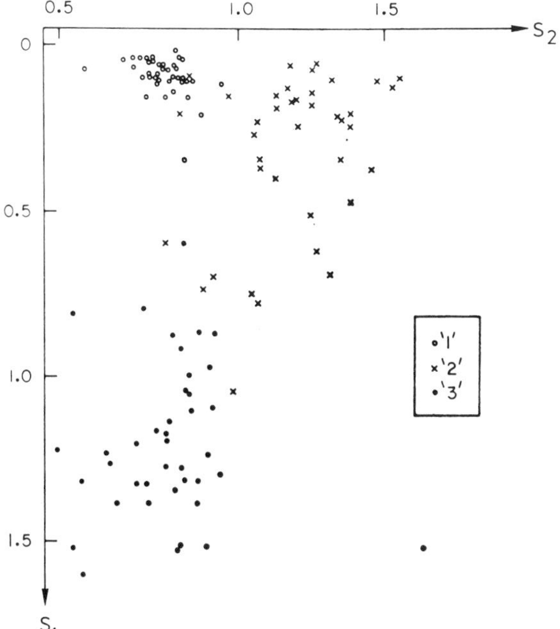

Fig. 7.10 Clustering of hand-printed characters in the two-dimensional space of the lowest order harmonic amplitudes S_1 and S_2. (Reproduced from [7.2])

This approach should be applied with great caution on sparsely quantized data, since it cannot distinguish between, say, a square and a triangle, given only by their vertices. (Both result in $a(t_k)$ identically zero). Fig.7.10 shows a plot in terms of the moduli of S_1 and S_2 of the images of hand-printed numerals from IEEE Data Base 1.2.2. One can detect a reasonably good separation of the three classes, in spite of the use of only two measurements. If one adds more numerals then the separation is lost because the classes overlap heavily. This, of course, can be remedied by using more harmonics.

II) The descriptors T_n: These are expected to decrease faster than S_n as functions of n because b(t) is usually a continuous function. Also, they have the property that the inverse transform over a subset of T_n always produces closed curves. PERSOON and FU [7.51] describe the use of such descriptors for the recognition of both handwritten numerals and machine parts. In both cases the input is of high contrast so that segmentation is achieved easily through thresholding. Then the boundary is traced and the Fourier descriptors are obtained according to a discrete version of (7.18). Each set is normalized for scaling, rotation and starting point by setting $T_0 = 0$ and multiplying all other coefficients S_n by the complex constant $se^{j(\phi+na)}$. The parameters s, ϕ and a are chosen such that S_1 and S_{-1} become pure imaginary numbers and their sum has module equal to 1. The motivation for this choice is discussed in Section 9.2. Then the following real valued measurements are defined:

$$x_1 = |S_1 - S_{-1}|, \; x_2 = \mathrm{Re}\{S_2\}, \; x_3 = \mathrm{Im}\{S_2\} \quad ,$$

$$x_4 = \mathrm{Re}\{S_{-2}\}, \; x_5 = \mathrm{Im}\{S_{-2}\}, \; x_6 = \mathrm{Re}\{S_3\}, \quad \text{etc.}$$

Classification is performed through a nearest neighbor rule using: a) a Euclidean distance for 29 measurements of the type defined above; b) a curve similarity measure given by

$$\sum_{n=-M}^{n=M} |S_n^1 - se^{j(na+\phi)}S_n^2| \quad . \tag{7.21}$$

The first measure gave a recognition rate of about 85% on 500 handwritten numerals from the IEEE Data Base 1.2.2. The second measure had a success rate of about 90%. In both cases a large proportion of the errors was caused by confusion of "8"s as "1"s. This is due to the fact that the internal boundaries (holes) are never examined and the "dents" in the external boundary can be quite insignificant, as shown in Fig.7.11.

Fig. 7.11 Illustration of the difficulty of distinguishing between an "1" and an "8" on the basis of the shape of their outside boundary

YOUNG and his co-workers [7.11] have proposed another way of using the coefficients of a Fourier expansion of the boundary. They observe that the elastic energy of a thin beam, having the shape of the boundary of an object, is given by the formula

$$E = \int_0^L |K(\ell)|^2 d\ell \quad , \tag{7.22}$$

where $K(\ell)$ is the curvature as a function of length ℓ. It can be shown that this is proportional to the second derivative of $-a(t)$ defined in the previous section. Using Parseval's theorem [7.52], we can express E as a sum of squares of the descriptors S_n. It is obvious that the use of E as a shape descriptor will not convey as much information as the use of the Fourier descriptors themselves.

7.5 Curve and Boundary Descriptions in the Space Domain

These treat the points of a curve, and in particular a region boundary, directly and in a strictly local fashion. The earliest among them are the syntactic descriptions of LEDLEY [7.1] and those based on the Freeman chain code [7.54-56]. Extensive studies on the subject have been made by FU [7.4,57-59]. PAVLIDIS has suggested that before the application of such techniques a preprocessing of the data through functional approximation should be performed [7.8,60]. DAVIS has used hierarchical curve fitting for the description of contours and, in particular, for detecting corners and sides [7.61].

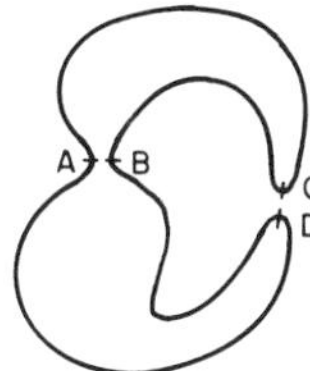

Fig. 7.12 Points A and B are neighbors but they are located far apart in a boundary encoding. The same is true about points C and D

The main disadvantage of boundary encodings is that points which are geometrically close together can be encoded quite far apart in the string. In the example of Fig.7.12, there is no simple way to describe the neck AB or the gap CD through the boundary string. However, they have many advantages, including fast algorithms for their analysis, small storage requirements and the availability of well-developed general methodologies such as the theory of formal languages. These seem quite promising because they attempt to reproduce the descriptions of human observers.

We describe first the simplest technique of all, the Freeman chain code. Assuming a rectangular grid, we define eight basic directions as shown in Fig.7.13a. At its original inception the code was derived from the quantization of line drawings. This is shown in Fig.7.13b. Each segment of the curve C which falls within one of the squares is approximated by one of the eight directions. The result is shown in Fig.7.13c and can be expressed as a string of numbers representing the basic directions: 4444570767077.

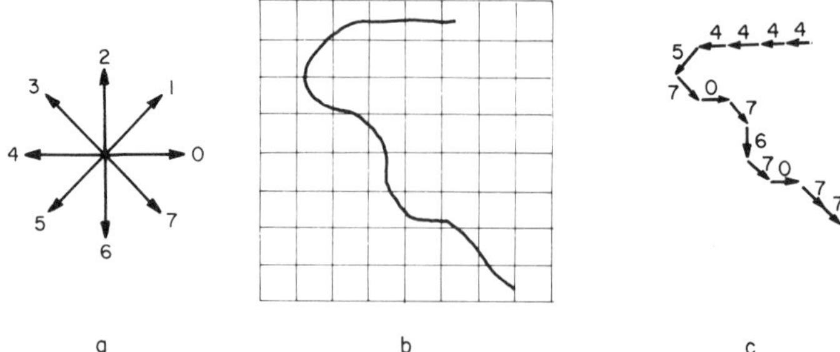

Fig. 7.13a-c Definition of the Freeman chain code. a) Principal directions. b) Curve plotted over a grid. c) Encoding of the curve in b)

Such encodings can be obtained from other representations as well, including descriptions of boundaries as lists of (x,y) coordinates, as shown in Chapter 5. If the coordinates of two adjacent points do not differ by more than one, then the encoding is straightforward. For example, the vector (15,32), (16,33) will be mapped to a "1". If only one of the coordinates is different in a pair, a sequence of repeated symbols is produced. For example, the vector (8,30), (8,34) will be mapped into 2222. Other cases require more attention. One could draw the vector between the two points and then use the original form of encoding. Or one may define a set of mappings of coordinate pairs into chain code depending on the slope of the joining line. It is obvious that at most two principal directions will appear in such an encoding. Thus a line forming a 60 degree angle will be encoded as a sequence of 1's and 2's. In any case the derivation of the chain code will be fast and straightforward.

A somewhat higher level encoding for boundaries is that according to arcs of (approximately) constant curvature proposed by LEDLEY [7.1]. The boundary is searched for segments where the curvature remains constant, and these are mapped into a finite set of symbols. Thus "a" may stand for a convex arc of high curvature, "b" for a straight line, "c" for a concave arc of high curvature, etc. This encoding has been used for chromosomes, but it is applicable to arbitrary boundaries. It can be derived either directly from the boundary data or from a chain code. Since it does not depend on orientation, it does not have some of the disadvantages of the chain code, but at the same time it is not convenient for checking for corners of given size and related features. It shares with the chain code the encoding of the boundary into a string with symbols from a fixed "alphabet".

A generalization of the above schemes is to encode a boundary into a sequence of arbitrary curves using the methodology of functional approximation discussed in Chapter 2. In all these cases, the result is a representation of the form

$$V = v_1, v_2, \dots v_n$$

where v_i may be an element of a chain code [7.54,55], an arc of constant curvature [7.1], a side of a polygonal approximation [7.60,62], a quadratic arc [7.1,18,20,63-65], etc. Techniques using functional approximation have the advantage of eliminating much of the noise, but the results are not easily quantized and therefore the string V may not be described in terms of a finite alphabet. A major difficulty in their application is the segmentation of the boundary into parts which will be approximated by a single curve. We shall classify these methods according to the criterion they use to solve this problem. In one class the boundary is searched for the longest arc where an approximation by a line or a conic will result in a sufficiently small error. Then the process is repeated until all the boundary points have been examined. These techniques resemble very much *region growing* and can be described as merging schemes. Others proceed to subdivide large arcs into smaller ones until a sufficiently small error of approximation is achieved. Either of these methods may be combined with a breakpoint adjustment algorithm of the type described in Section 2.12. A third category involves the use of the tangent versus arc length functions discussed in Section 7.2. Fig.7.14b shows a plot of the angle of the tangent ϕ versus the length ℓ for the curve shown in Fig.7.14a. One can see that segments which are close to straight lines map into horizontal lines, circular arcs into lines of fixed slope (representing the rate of change of ϕ as a function of arc length) and sharp corners into discontinuities. In this way the breakpoints can be found as discontinuities or sharp changes in slope. This is still a segmentation problem, although it may be somewhat easier than the original. This method has been used by PERKINS [7.66] as part of an object identification program. Finally it is possible to change the problem drastically, from one of curve segmentation to one of curve intersection. This is achieved by a method based on the Hough transformation, which has been described by DUDA and HART [7.69]. Let x_i, y_i $(i = 1, \dots N)$ be a set of points on the plane. For each point we can create a curve in the r-θ plane with the equation:

$$r = x_i \cos(\theta) + y_i \sin(\theta) \quad .$$

It can be shown that points which are collinear correspond to curves passing through the same point. However, finding the intersection of trigonometric curves is a nontrivial problem and does not simplify the original question in any substantial way. Therefore, it is necessary to attack the curve segmentation problem directly. We shall devote the rest of this chapter to a discussion of various approaches to the problem and the use of syntactic methodology in conjunction with these approaches.

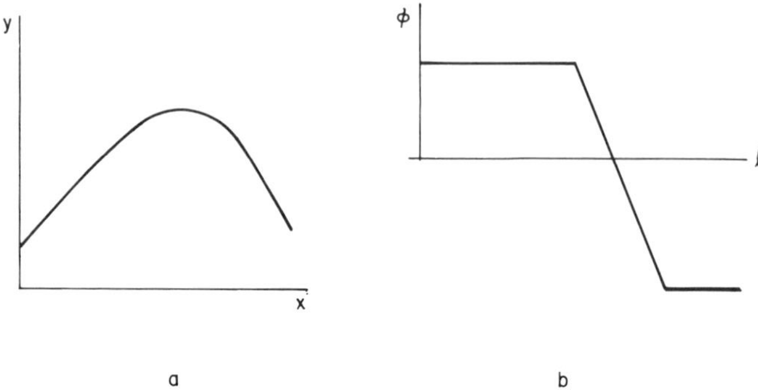

Fig. 7.14a,b Transformation from the x-y plane to the ϕ-ℓ plane

7.6 The Importance of Curvature and Corners

A review of the vast literature on shape uncovers a great diversity of approaches which might lead one to think that there is no unified approach to shape. However, a closer examination reveals that this is not the case. One common factor is that curvature maxima, and measures of curvature in general, play an important role in most shape analysis algorithms. We have already mentioned the work of LEDLEY, who has used boundary segments of constant curvature for primitives [7.1]. Strokes and lobes are also associated with regions of high curvature, and therefore the latter express themselves through the coefficients of the Fourier Transform. Similar conclusions are obtained on the basis of bending energy [7.11]. Most of the techniques dealing with the interior of regions or their encoding into graphs place significant emphasis on "intrusions" and "protrusions", both locations of high curvature (negative or positive). High curvature is reflected by steep slopes, or even discontinuities, in the ϕ versus length curve. The prominent role of curvature is hardly surprising, since some of the earliest theories of vision have stated that curvature maxima are important in shape perception [7.68,69].

It is probably true that if the outlines of objects were noise-free, then a direct evaluation of curvature would go a long way in determining their shape. However, in the presence of noise one may have to distinguish between "essential" and "inessential" curvature maxima. A number of algorithms have been suggested for finding the essential curvature maxima, e.g., [7.70]. Probably the more general among them are those based on functional approximation, e.g., [7.71]. Closely related to curvature as shape descriptor is the concept of the *corner* which is defined as a point of infinite curvature in the case of continuous curves [7.72]. The situation is not quite as clear for discrete data. It is probably best to define a corner as a point where it is necessary to switch description of the curve in terms of smooth curves. The latter may be defined as lines or quadratic arcs. There is a remarkable result from the theory of splines, due to McCLURE [7.73], which has bearing on these questions.

Theorem 7.2: Let f(t) be a function to be approximated by a spline with variable knots while minimizing the integral square error. If k is the order of the polynomials forming the spline and n the number of its knots, then the asymptotic distribution (as n tends to infinity) of the knots follows the 2/(2k+1) power of the $(k+1)^{th}$ derivative of f(t).

For continuous piecewise linear approximations, where the error is evaluated along the normal to the curve, the asymptotic distribution follows the *curvature* [7.74]. At first, the result may not seem very interesting, since one has to go to an infinite number of segments before placing the knots at curvature maxima. However, computational experience indicates that, even for a small number of knots, their distribution follows pretty much what one would call essential curvature maxima [7.62]. Part of the reason for this property is that when the number of knots is increased new ones are placed between the old ones whose position remains more or less fixed [7.62]. Furthermore, we have seen in Section 2.10 that if no continuity constraints are imposed, then the integral square error is minimized when knots are placed either near curvature maxima (with continuity there resulting as a bonus of the optimal location), or near points of inflection (curvature zeros) with the approximation being symmetric around the curve.

A formal proof of Theorem 7.2 is beyond our scope, but we may give an informal justification for it. For simplicity, we consider only approximations where the error norm is taken along a coordinate axis. If a function f(t) with continuous derivatives up to $(n+1)^{th}$ order is approximated by an nth order polynomial over an interval [a,b], then the maximum absolute pointwise error of approximation (i.e., the E_∞ norm) will be given by

$$\max \{|f(t) - p_n(t)| \; a \le t \le b\} = \frac{|b-a|^{n+1}}{(n+1)\, 2^{2n+1}} |f^{(n+1)}(z)| \qquad (7.23)$$

where z is some point in the interval [a,b]. The derivation of this expression is straightforward and it can be found in most texts on numerical analysis or approximation [7.82-84]. It is also intuitively reasonable. An nth order polynomial has a zero $(n+1)^{th}$ derivative so that the size of the respective derivative of f(t) should reflect the error. What is not obvious from (7.23) is the location of z. Fig.7.15 illustrates the situation for a linear approximation (n=1). In a) the maximum of f"(t) occurs near the middle of [a,b] while in b) it occurs at an end. The error norm in the latter case is much smaller. Thus z usually refers to a location near the "middle" of the interval of approximation. This suggests that in piecewise approximations it is desirable to have breakpoints near maxima of $f^{(n+1)}(t)$.

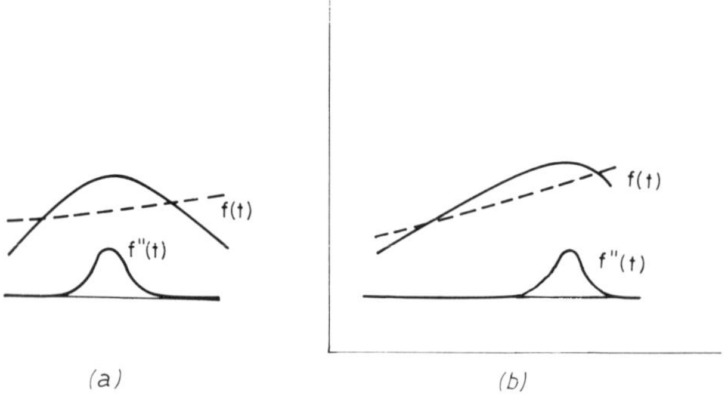

Fig. 7.15a,b In both pictures the maximum of the second derivative is the same, but the one on the right has an approximation by a straight line with a smaller error. This is due to the location of the maximum of f"(t) near the end of the interval

Thus piecewise linear approximations with variable knots offer a technique for locating "essential" maxima of curvature and therefore should have certain merits for shape analysis. Indeed this has been recognized by many investigators independently of the arguments based on the theory of splines [7.69,76-81]. It is rather obvious that higher order approximations would also be desirable, but their evaluation is quite expensive computationally [7.18].

There is one more problem. Although it is true that any essential curvature maximum is likely to be a location of a breakpoint, the converse is not true, since there are cases where breakpoints are not placed near curvature maxima. A typical example is a polygonal approximation of a circle. Because the curvature is constant the knots will be uniformly distributed and the resulting polygon will be regular. The exact placement of the knots depends on the initial conditions. Therefore if we limit our attention to the results of the approximation we may have difficulty distinguishing very dissimilar objects, like the noisy square and the circle of Fig.7.16. For a given tolerance for the E_2 error norm the approximating polygon will be a square in both cases. In the first case, the corners are "real", but not in the second. One way around the problem is to examine how sharply the minimum of the error norm depends on the chosen location of corners. Such a dependence will be very steep in the case of the square, but not in the case of the circle.

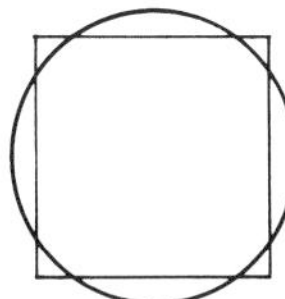

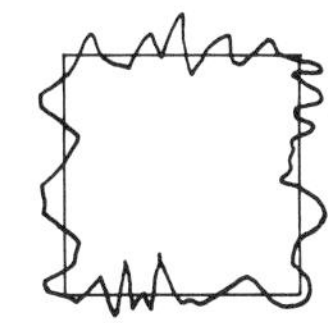

Fig. 7.16 A noise-free circle and a noisy square have identical approximations and with the same value of the integral square error

Mathematically this is manifested through the matrix of the second derivatives of the error norm with respect to the location of the breakpoints. If the minimum is "steep", then the matrix has significant diagonal dominance and a large determinant. Analytical expressions for these derivatives are given by (2.71). They depend significantly on the pointwise error and its first derivative and therefore are of limited value when the data are noisy. We shall return to this question in a later section after we describe certain algorithms for obtaining polygonal approximations.

If the data are not particularly noisy, then it is possible to evaluate the curvature through the angle formed by vectors connecting a point with its neighbors. Algorithm 7.1 performs this task. Fig.7.17 illustrates its operation for M1 = 1 and M2 = 4. The quality of the results depends significantly on the proper choice of these parameters. ROSENFELD and JOHNSTON [7.70] used M1 = 1 and M2 a fraction of N, e.g., N/10. This makes the computational requirements of the algorithm proportional to N^2. DAVIS [7.75] has used M1 = M2 = 5 or 10.

Algorithm 7.1: Estimation of the locations of curvature maxima

Input: List of boundary points bx(i), by(i), i = 1,2,...N. Neighborhood bounds M1 and M2.

Output: Indices of curvature maxima $i_1, i_2, \ldots i_n$.

Steps:

1. For i = 1 to N do block 11.

    Begin block 11;

    1. For k = M1 to M2 do block 12.

        Begin block 12;

        1. Evaluate the angle ϕ_{ik} formed by the vectors connecting the point bx(i), by(i) with bx(i-k), by(i-k) and with bx(i+k), by(i+k). (The indices i-k, i+k are computed modulo N).

        End block 12;

    2. Find the minimum of ϕ_{ik}, k = M1,M1+1,...M2. Let it be ϕ_{i0}.

    End block 11.

2. Determine the curvature maxima as corresponding to the local minima of ϕ_{i0}.

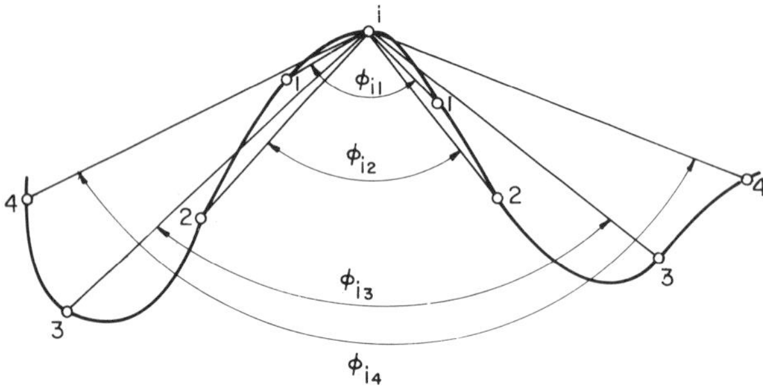

Fig. 7.17 Illustration of a simple algorithm for evaluating the curvature. Here the minimum is ϕ_{i2}

7.7 Algorithms for Polygonal Approximations: *Merging Schemes*

Polygonal approximations have been popular because of the relative simplicity of line fitting algorithms. As we pointed out in Section 7.5 they represented in essence a segmentation, since the number of segments, or their location, are not known in advance. Therefore, one can adapt the methodology of Chapter 4 toward this goal. A review of the literature reveals both merging and splitting algorithms. We shall discuss merging schemes here and cover the others in the next two sections. Merging algorithms proceed in general in a linear scan evaluating a uniformity predicate as they go along. When this is false a new segment is started. One of the most important special cases includes the algorithms for finding minimum perimeter polygons. These have been proposed by SKLANSKY [7.80] and have been developed by him and his co-workers [7.81,85] and by MONTANARI [7.77]. There exist various versions, but they can all be summarized as follows:

Each point of the boundary lies in one cell of the picture grid. Let e be its side. The union of these cells forms a strip as shown in Fig.7.18a. We can now visualize a physical model consisting of two walls corresponding to the outside and inside boundaries of the strip and a rubber band placed in the gap between them. The rubber band will then take the shape shown in Fig.7.18b, one which minimizes its length, with the resulting polygon approximating the original boundary with maximum pointwise error less than e. The method could be generalized by using other neighborhoods, besides square grid cells, but then the shape taken by the rubber band will not always be a polygon. This will be the case only when the neighborhoods are themselves polygonal. This brings out a main feature of this type of approximation. It minimizes the length while keeping the pointwise error within the range of the maximum quantization error. We proceed now to describe a method for computing it. Starting from an initial point we search for the longest line segment which connects one point from each of a series of cells. Then the process is repeated by using for a starting point the next boundary point. This process is incorporated in Algorithm 7.2.

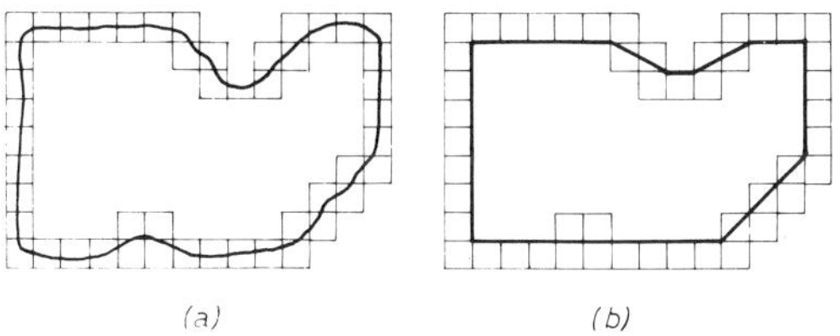

Fig. 7.18a,b Definition of the minimum perimeter polygon. In a) the solid line is the boundary of a region. In b) the solid line represents the minimum perimeter polygon

Algorithm 7.2: Minimum perimeter polygon

Input: Boundary points bx(i), by(i), i = 1,2...N.

Output: Number of vertices n and coordinates of the vertices px(i), py(i), i = 1,2,...n of the minimum perimeter polygon.

Steps:

1. Search for a convex vertex. Let i_0 be its index.
2. Set k = i_0 and n = 1.
3. While k is positive do block 31.

   Begin block 31;

   1. For i = k, k + 1,... (modulo N) do block 32.

      Begin block 32;

      1. Find a pair of lines which are tangent to the outside and inside boundaries of the strip of squares, starting from the square centered at bx(i), by(i) and ending at the square centered at bx(k), by(k). Let them be denoted by LE and LI, with LE touching the outside boundary and LI the inside (Fig.7.19). If i = k + 1 define lines LE0 and LI0 equal to LE and LI respectively.
      2. If i > k + 1 compare LE to LE0. If it lies outside of it set LE0 equal to LE. Also compare LI to LI0 and replace LI0 by LI if the latter lies inside LI0.
      3. If LE0 and LI0 cross each other (Fig.7.19) exit from the loop.
      4. If i = i_0 set k = -1 and exit from the loop.

      End block 32;

   2. If k > 0, increment n, define a polygon vertex at previous end of LE0 or LI0 and set k = i. (Fig.7.19)

   End block 31.

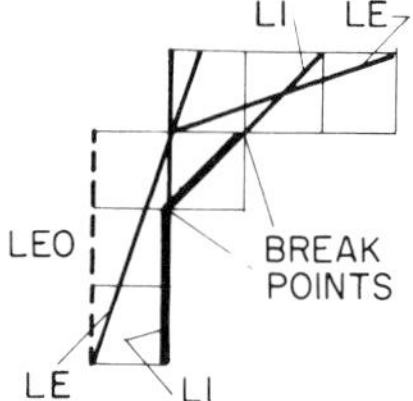

Fig. 7.19 Illustration of the quantities used in Algorithm 7.2

This algorithm could be generalized in the context of smoothing splines proposed by REINSCH [7.86,87]. This can be seen best in terms of the rubber band paradigm. One could place a thin beam between the two barriers which would take a shape minimizing its elastic energy. This approximation will give minimum length while maintaining continuous first and second derivatives. Similar generalizations can be obtained in terms of the splines under tension proposed by CLINE [7.88]. However, none of these problems has been investigated systematically and they remain open questions.

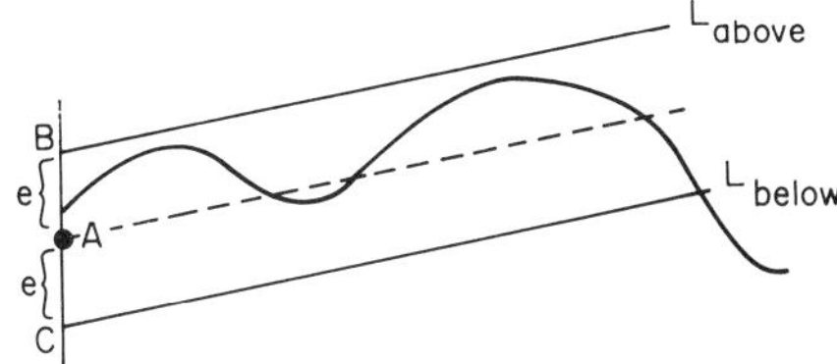

Fig. 7.20 Illustration of the quantities used in Algorithm 7.3

Algorithm 7.3: Polygonal approximation by linear scan

Input: Set of points f(i), i = 1,2...N. Parameter e. Initial point A (possibly f(0).

Output: Breakpoints z(j), u(j) j = 1,2...n. (z is the index of the breakpoint and u its abscissa).

Steps:

1. Set i_s = 1, j = 0.
2. While i_s is less than N do block 21.
   Begin block 21;
   1. Set B = A + e, C = A - e.
   2. Do block 31 for i = i_s to N.
      Begin block 31;
      1. Find the lines L_B and L_C joining B and C with f(i). If i = i_s + 1 define the lines L_{above} and L_{below} to be equal to L_B and L_C. Else do block 32.
         Begin block 32;
         1. If line L_B is above L_{above} replace L_{above} by L_B.
         2. If line L_C is below L_{below} replace L_{below} by L_C.
         3. If the angle between lines L_{above} and L_{below} is positive exit from blocks 32 and 31.

         End block 32;

      End block 31;
   3. Increment j and set z(j) = i - 1. Set u(j) at the midpoint of lines L_{above} and L_{below}. Set i_s = i.

   End block 21.

A suboptimal fast algorithm for continuous uniform approximations, which is closely related to the above, has been proposed by TOMEK [7.89] in the case of waveforms. Let e be the maximum allowable error. For a given point A, through which an approximating line must pass, one can define two points B and C at a distance e from A (Fig.7.20). Then the algorithm searches for the longest segment where the curve is contained between two parallel tangents starting from B and C.

The algorithm requires linear time because the check of the position of the pairs of lines can be made by looking at only one point each time. It is also suboptimal, as indicated by the counterexample of Fig.7.21. Its performance can be improved, but only at a significant increase of the computational cost [7.89]. Fig.7.22 shows the resulting improvement. For many cases the results may be satisfactory, even though suboptimal, as seen from the example of Fig.7.23.

A merging algorithm using the integral square error per segment as a criterion can be readily derived on the basis of the equations given in Section 2.3. If H is an upper bound for that error, then substituting (2.21) into (2.26) yields the following inequality as a condition for the uniformity predicate to be true.

$$\overline{f'f} - (B\bar{f})'(BB')^{-1}(B\bar{f}) < H \quad . \tag{7.24}$$

Most of the quantities appearing in the above equation can be evaluated quite simply when two intervals are merged. In particular, we observe that merging two intervals, 1 and 2, corresponds to concatenating the vectors $\bar{f}_1$ and $\bar{f}_2$ to form the vector $\bar{f}$ for the new interval. For scalar and matrix products this implies the addition of the quantities for each of the original intervals and in particular the following updating formulas.

$$\overline{f'f} = \overline{f'_1 f_1} + \overline{f'_2 f_2} \ . \tag{7.25}$$

$$B\bar{f} = B_1\bar{f}_1 + B_2\bar{f}_2 \tag{7.26}$$

$$BB' = B_1B'_1 + B_2B'_2 \quad . \tag{7.27}$$

Therefore, there is no loss in efficiency in evaluating these quantities when it is done by subintervals rather than a whole interval. If the sample points are uniformly spaced, then the matrix BB' does not depend on the individual

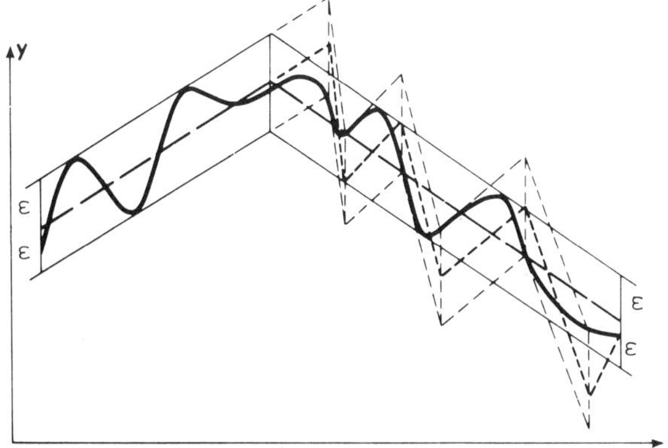

Fig. 7.21 Suboptimality of Algorithm 7.3. The function to be approximated is shown in heavy lines. Although there is an approximation with only two segments the algorithm finds seven of them. (Reproduced from [7.89])

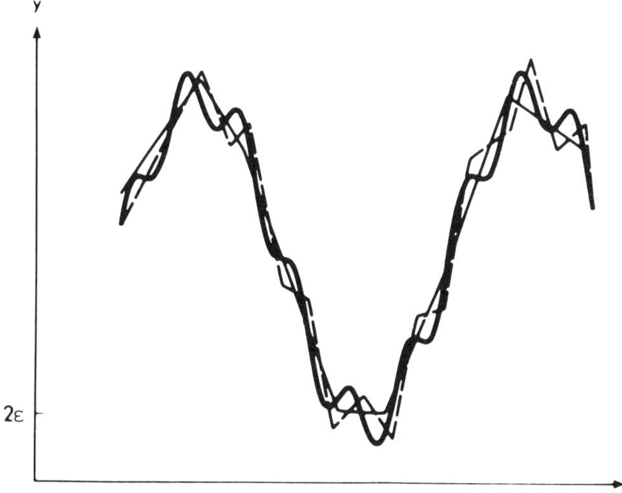

Fig. 7.22 Improvement (broken line) in the results of Algorithm 7.3 produced by an exhaustive search (solid line). The original curve is shown by a heavy line. (Reproduced from [7.89])

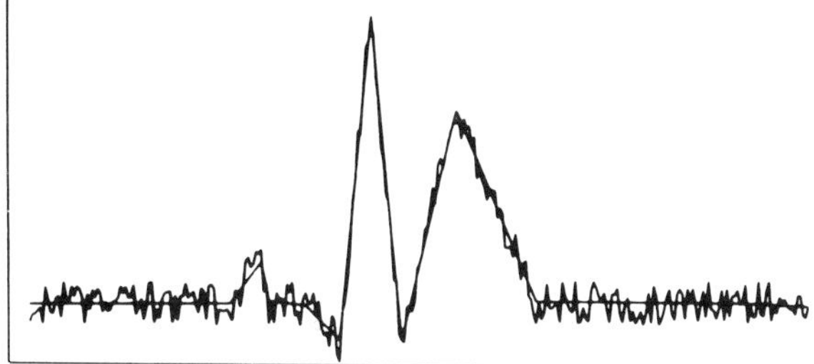

Fig. 7.23 An example of approximation by Algorithm 7.3. (Reproduced from [7.89])

data points but only on the interval length. In most cases it can be inverted formally to yield closed formulas for the evaluation of the LHS of (7.24). On the other hand, if the data points are not uniformly spaced, the inversion of the matrix BB' must be performed at each merge and this represents the major cost of the method. An alternative to this computation is offered by the *running orthogonalization* technique proposed by RICE [7.90]. There a new orthogonal basis is found for each new interval and therefore BB' reduces to the identity matrix. It turns out that the computational cost of the orthogonalization when a single point is added to an interval is less than that of the matrix inversion, although not by a large factor. Assuming a priori inversion the effort for the evaluation of (7.24) will be proportional to m^2, representing only the matrix multiplications. If the merging process proceeds point by point, then the total effort of this algorithm for an interval of N points will be

$$T_m = (pm^2 + qm)N \tag{7.28}$$

for some coefficients of proportionality p and q. The linear term reflects the cost of updating given by (7.25-27) and some of the vector operations in (7.24). If a uniform approximation is used for each interval, then the analysis of Section 2.5 shows that there is no simple updating formula and the points of each interval must be examined at each merge. This leads to a computational cost proportional to N^2 which is far above that of (7.28) since the ratio N/m^2 can easily be of the order of 50 or 100.

Fig. 7.24 Disadvantages of linear scan approximations a) as compared to one where breakpoint adjustment has been made b)

Merging algorithms guarantee that the minimum number of segments will be found, but they suffer from certain disadvantages. One is the "overshooting" of critical points as shown in Fig.7.24. This can be remedied by using the breakpoints found as input to an adjustment algorithm of the type described in Section 2.12. Another is the difficulty of the use of global criteria. Consider the example of Fig.7.25. If we insist that the maximum error per segment be under a given value, then any choice which will introduce a breakpoint in C will also introduce one around F. It may even be possible to introduce more than one breakpoint between E and A without introducing one in C. However, from the viewpoint of shape analysis the point C has far more significance than those between E and A. If the uniformity predicate requires that the integral square error over the *whole* boundary is below a certain bound then no breakpoints will be introduced between E and A, since they will not result in decrease of the total error. A simple merging algorithm cannot handle such a criterion and one must allow for approximations over the whole interval where merging occurs in an iterative fashion, in a manner similar to the one used for the picture segmentation discussed in Section 5.4. The computational cost will still be proportional to that given by (7.28), but there will be a greater overhead because of the need for an appropriate data structure.

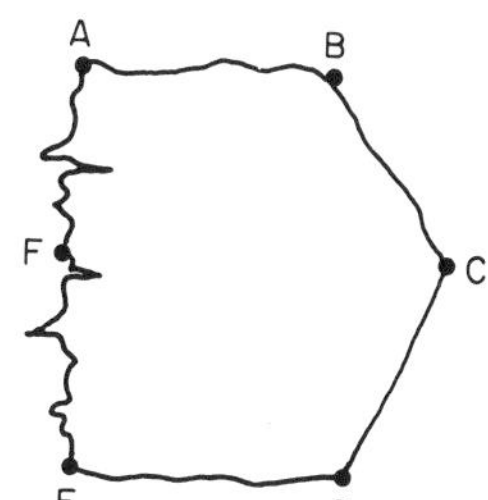

Fig. 7.25 An algorithm minimizing the error per interval will never give a single interval for AE unless it also gives one for BD. Minimizing the total error will result in merging AF and FE because this will cause no increase in the total norm. This will not be the case if BC and CD are merged

7.8 Algorithms for Polygonal Approximations: *Splitting and Mixed Schemes*

Splitting algorithms proceed usually with bisections. Segments are divided in two as long as a uniformity predicate is false. As a rule they perform fewer checks of the uniformity predicate but during each split it is necessary to reevaluate $\overline{f'f}$ and $\overline{Bf}$ for one of the intervals. Let S be the number of splits and let N_s be the total number of points where a reevaluation of these products has been necessary. Then the time of computation will be given by

$$T_s = umN_s + 2(vm^2 + wm)S \tag{7.29}$$

for parameters u,v and w. In the extreme case when one starts with the whole interval and proceeds to split down to intervals of length K the number of splits will be approximately $S = \log_2(N/K)$ while

$$N_s = \frac{N}{2} + 2(\frac{N}{4}) + \ldots + 2^{S-1}(\frac{N}{2^S}) = \frac{NS}{2} \qquad (7.30)$$

and

$$T_s = \frac{um}{2}N \log_2(\frac{N}{K}) + 2(vm^2+wm) \log_2(\frac{N}{K}) \quad . \qquad (7.31)$$

If K is very small, then a splitting method can have substantially greater requirements than a merging method. A simple splitting algorithm which has been used widely is Algorithm 7.4 [7.69,70].

Algorithm 7.4: Polygonal approximation of curve by splits

Input: List of boundary points bx(i), by(i), i = 1,...N with duplication of first point as bx(N+1), by(N+1). Tolerance e_{max}.

Output: List of vertices vx(i), vy(i), i = 1,...n.

Steps:

1. Put the index of the last point, N + 1 in lists OPEN and CLOSED. Put 1 in list OPEN.
2. While OPEN is not empty do block 11.

   Begin block 11;

   1. Let i_1 be the last element of OPEN and i_2 the last element of CLOSED. Fit a line segment on the part of the boundary between i_1 and i_2.
   2. Let i_m be a point where the maximum pointwise error occurs in that approximation. If that error exceeds e_{max}, then place i_m in OPEN. Else place i_1 in CLOSED.

   End block 11;
3. Output the points whose indices are in CLOSED as breakpoints.

Fig. 7.26a shows its application for N = 13. The thin lines denote the approximations between the indices marking them. The content of the lists CLOSED and OPEN and the operation of the algorithm are shown in Table 7.1.

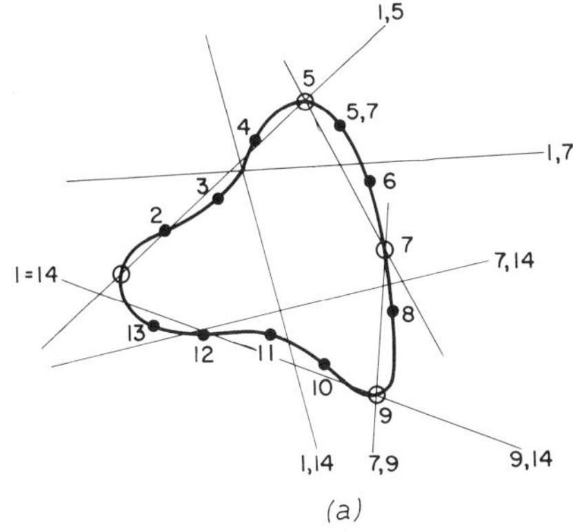

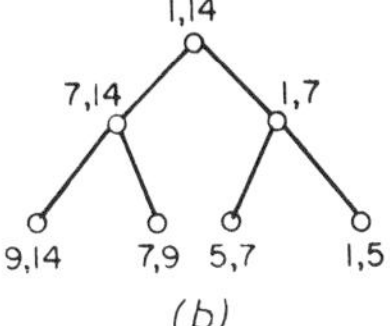

Fig. 7.26a,b Operation of split-only algorithm (7.4) while finding a polygonal approximation to a closed curve. a) Boundary and approximating lines. b) Tree denoting the sequence of approximations

Table 7.1 Illustration of the operation of Algorithm 7.4

CLOSED	OPEN	i_1	i_2	i_m	
1,14	1	1	14	7	
1,14	1,7	7	14	9	
1,14	1,7,9	9	14	11	($e<e_{max}$)
1,14,9	1,7	7	9	8	-
1,14,9,7	1	1	7	5	
1,14,9,7	1,5	5	7	6	-
1,14,9,7,5	1	1	5	3	-

The output would yield the following segments: (1,5),(5,7), (7,9) and (9,14). 1 and 14 represent the same point. The operation can be described through a binary tree: the root corresponds to the whole boundary. The children of each node correspond to the subintervals. Leaves correspond to final intervals. The tree for the example of Fig.7.26a is shown in Fig.7.26b. The algorithm traverses the tree in a depth first fashion. Intervals corresponding to leftmost branches are traversed repeatedly. If the tree is balanced, then one can show that the computational effort will be indeed given by (7.31). If it is very imbalanced towards the left, then the effort will be proportional to $(N/K)^2$, while if the imbalance is to the right the effort will be proportional to N/K. In such a case, the algorithm would operate pretty much like a linear scan algorithm. We also note that the results suffer from the type of nonoptimality indicated in Fig.7.24. However, a breakpoint adjustment algorithm would require quite a few iterations to move one such point from 9 to, say, 11 and from 7 to 9.

If one used a combination of a merging and a splitting algorithm, then the intervals (5,7) and (7,9) could have been merged and the interval (9,14) could be split to keep the number of breakpoints constant, if this were desirable. This observation leads to split-and-merge algorithms where the interval is initially divided into a number of segments n, which can be either split or merged. If Q is the number of merges and S the number of splits the total computation time will be given by

$$T_{sm} = (pm^2+qm)\ (n+Q) + umN_s + 2(vm^2+wm)S \quad . \tag{7.32}$$

Usually n is much smaller than N. If Q and S are comparable to n, then the split-and-merge method will be the fastest among the three. A good initialization is one which tries to minimize splits, since these are more expensive than merges. This can be achieved if the whole interval is divided uniformly into about twice the most likely number of segments. Such a division makes unlikely the occurrence of a large number of splits which would impose computational requirements of the order of $N \log_2 N$. They will be required only near intervals of rapid change in the form of the curve. An algorithm implementing this idea will be presented in the next section. Our previous discussion shows that merging algorithms give the minimum number of segments if the uniformity predicate is evaluated on each single interval independently of the others while splitting algorithms do not do so. The following theorem gives a criterion for the optimality of split-and-merge schemes.

Theorem 7.3: The number of segments resulting from a split-and-merge procedure, which evaluates the uniformity predicate on each subinterval, is less than or equal to $2n_0-1$, where n_0 is the minimum number possible. That bound can be reached.

Proof: Let $x_1,x_2,\dots x_{n-1}$ be the dividing points of the split-and-merge procedure and $y_1,y_2,\dots y_{n_0-1}$ those of the optimal segmentation. Because intervals are merged if the uniformity predicate is satisfied on their union we cannot have

$$(x_{i-1},x_{i+1}] \subset (y_j,y_{j+1}]$$

for any i and j. If $n = 2n_0$, then at least one such occurrence could be seen.

Therefore n is strictly less than $2n_0$. On the other hand, consider the case illustrated in Fig.7.27 where

$$x_1 < y_1 < x_2 < x_3 < y_2 < x_4 < x_5 < y_3 < \ldots$$

Each interval of the optimal segmentation contains completely one and parts of two others of the nonoptimal segmentation. This yields $n = 2n_0 - 1$. Q.E.D.

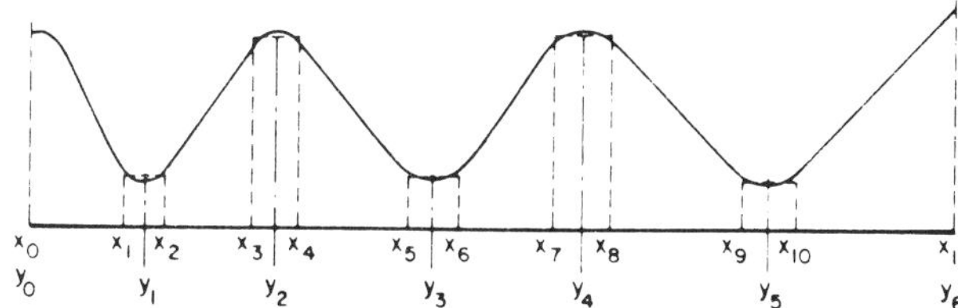

Fig. 7.27 Illustration of a "legal" segmentation (x_i, i = 1,2,...11) which is far from the optimal (y_i, i = 1,2,...6). (Reproduced from [7.93])

The breakpoint arrangement where this large deviation from optimality occurs is rather intricate and unlikely to occur in practice. Computational experience shows that n never exceeds n_0 by more than 20% [7.62]. These results are valid only for approximations without continuity constraints. For constrained approximations a merge algorithm may not give the minimum number of segments as shown in Fig.7.21.

7.9 A Split-and-Merge Algorithm for Polygonal Approximations

We will describe here in detail an algorithm integrating the split-and-merge procedure with the joint adjustment schemes of Section 2.12. We have seen in the previous section that the split-and-merge scheme is generally faster than the pure merge or pure split schemes, especially if a reasonable estimate of the number of segments n exists. Also, other schemes can be obtained as special cases. We ignore continuity constraints, since one is likely to get a continuous approximation without imposing them.

In many cases it is desirable to calculate the error norm by considering as error the distance between a point and the approximating curve rather than the difference between coordinates along an axis as in Chapter 2. This may cause some difficulties for higher order approximations but it is fairly straightforward for linear ones. Using the notation of Fig.7.28, we have for the equation of a straight line

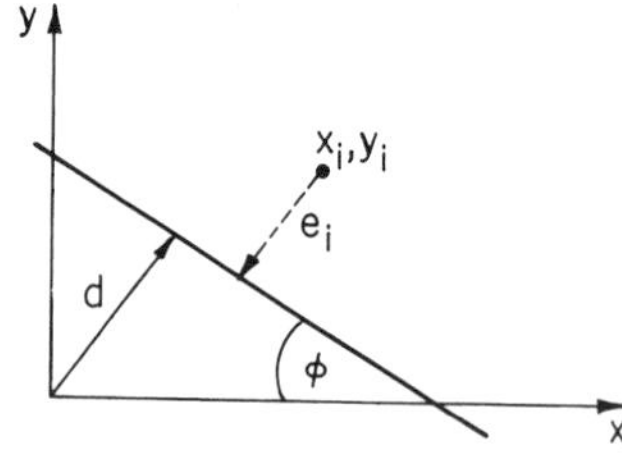

Fig. 7.28 Definition of terms used in (7.33)

$$\sin\phi x + \cos\phi y = d \quad , \tag{7.33a}$$

and for the distance of a point from it

$$e_i = |\sin\phi x_i + \cos\phi y_i - d| \quad . \tag{7.33b}$$

If the integral square error is used as a norm then an analysis similar to that of Section 2.3 shows that the error norm is minimized when ϕ and d are chosen as follows:

$$\sin 2\phi \, (V_{xx} - V_{yy}) + 2 \cos 2\phi \, V_{xy} = 0 \quad , \tag{7.34}$$

$$d = \sin\phi \, V_x + \cos\phi \, V_y \quad , \tag{7.35}$$

where

$$V_x = \frac{1}{N} \sum_{i=1}^{N} x_i \quad , \tag{7.36a}$$

$$V_y = \frac{1}{N} \sum_{i=1}^{N} y_i \quad , \tag{7.36b}$$

$$V_{xx} = \sum_{i=1}^{N} (x_i - V_x)^2 \quad , \tag{7.36c}$$

$$V_{yy} = \sum_{i=1}^{N} (y_i - V_y)^2 \quad , \tag{7.36d}$$

$$V_{xy} = \sum_{i=1}^{N} (x_i - V_x) (y_i - V_y) \quad . \tag{7.36e}$$

N is the number of points $\{x_i, y_i\}$ to be approximated. For the choice of (7.34) and (7.35) the error norm is given by

$$E_2 = \sin^2\phi \; V_{xx} + \cos^2\phi \; V_{yy} + \sin 2\phi \; V_{xy} \quad , \tag{7.37}$$

or as the smaller root of the quadratic equation

$$Z^2 + (V_{xx}+V_{yy})Z + V_{xx}V_{yy} - V_{xy}^2 = 0 \quad . \tag{7.38}$$

Eq.(7.35) shows also that the approximating line passes through the "center of gravity" of the points. In effect, it is a principal axis of inertia.

Algorithm 7.5 has as its goal to minimize E_2 over all segments and make sure it is less than an upper bound E_{max}. The symbol E_i is used to denote the error norm on the ith segment, and we define

$$E = \sum_{i=1}^{n} E_i \quad . \tag{7.39}$$

We assume that an initial segmentation for n segments is given.

Algorithm 7.5: Split-and-merge approximation of a curve

Input: Boundary points bx(i) and by(i), i = 1,2,...N. Initial segmentation x_i, i = 1,2...n given as a linked list. (Notation: $N(x_i)$ denotes the point after x_i in BL, while $P(x_i)$ denotes the point previous to x_i in BL).

Output: Final segmentation x_i.

Steps:

1. Set s = true, m = true, r = true.
2. Do block 21 while s or m or r is true.
    Begin block 21;
    1. If s = true then do block 22.
        Begin block 22;
        1. s = false.
        2. If $E < E_{max}$ then do nothing; else find the segment with the maximum E_i, split it into two segments and set s = true.
        End block 22;
    2. If (m = true or (s = true and n > 1)) then do block 23.

Begin block 23;

1. m = false.
2. For i = 1 to n - 1 by 1 evaluate the error norms F_i which would have occurred if the ith and $(i+1)^{th}$ intervals were merged.
3. For i = 1 to n - 1 by 1 evaluate $G_i = E - (E_i+E_{i+1}) + F_i$.
4. Sort the $G_{i's}$ in decreasing order and place their indices in a stack S.
5. Do block 24 while S is not empty and, if j is its first element, $G_j < E_{max}$

   Begin block 24;

   1. Remove the first element of S.
   2. Merge the jth and $(j+1)^{th}$ intervals (Note that this is now a trivial operation).
   3. m = true.
   4. Update the elements of S by $G_i = G_i + F_j - (E_j+E_{j+1})$.

   End block 24;

End block 23;

3. If r = true then do block 25 (modification of Algorithm 2.4).

Begin block 25;

1. r = false.
2. For k = 1,2 do block 26.

   Begin block 26;

   1. For i = k to n - 1 by 2 do block 27.

      Begin block 27;

      1. Evaluate the error norms over the intervals $(x_{i-1},N(x_i)]$, $(N(x_i), x_{i+1}]$, $(x_{i-1},P(x_i), x_{i+1}]$ and let them be F_1, F_2, F_3, F_4 respectively.
      2. If $F_1 + F_2 < F_3 + F_4$ set $z = N(x_i)$ and $W = F_1 + F_2$; else set $z = P(x_i)$ and $W = F_3 + F_4$
      3. If $W < E_i + E_{i+1}$ then set $x_i = z$, $E = E - E_i - E_{i+1} + W$ and r = true.

      End block 27;

   End block 26;

End block 25.

Algorithm 7.5 is correct because it terminates. Indeed each one of its major steps eventually terminates. Splitting stops when all segments become sufficiently small. If they consist of only 2 points each then E = 0. E is not increased by either the merging or the breakpoint adjustment (blocks 23 and 25). Thus block 22 eventually becomes inactive. Merging must stop, since,

at most, all segments will be merged into one. Once the minimum number of segments is reached, there will be no further splitting ($E < E_{max}$). Thus block 23 eventually becomes inactive. After splitting and merging has stopped, Algorithm 7.5 is equivalent to Algorithm 2.12.3 which terminates.
Fig.7.29 shows one example of application of this algorithm on a cell outline. Note that the algorithm is equally well-applicable to waveforms and Fig.7.30 shows such an example.

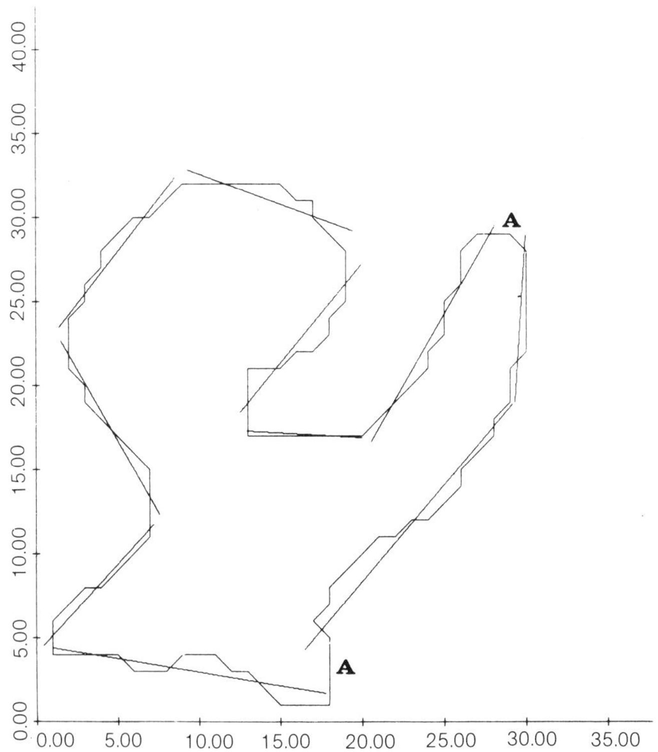

Fig. 7.29 Unconstrained piecewise linear approximation of a cell outline by Algorithm 7.5. Effective continuity is observed in all but two breakpoints (A). (Reproduced from [7.62])

The application of this algorithm in practice requires an estimate of E_{max}. This can be derived from an estimate of the maximum pointwise error e_{max}, which is usually easy to find on the basis of physical considerations. It is known from the theory of approximation that the sign of the error changes at least as many times as the number of degrees of freedom plus one and that values close to the maximum are achieved at least as many times

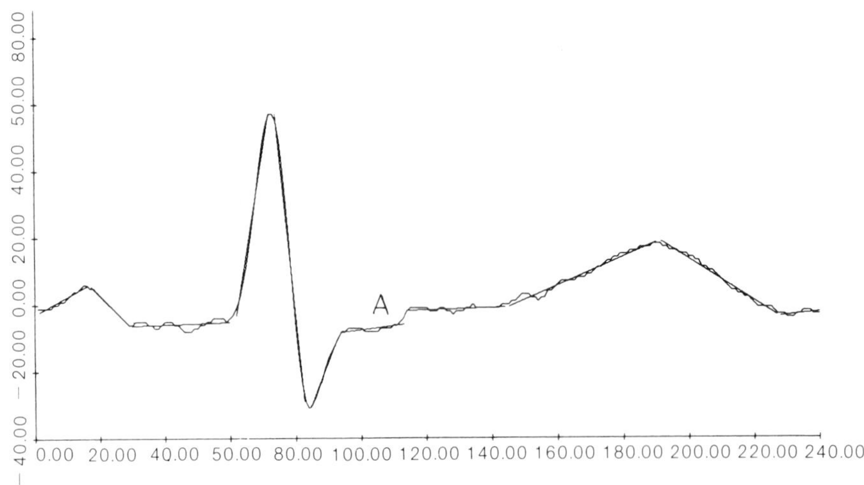

Fig. 7.30 Unconstrained piecewise linear approximation of an Electrocardiogram obtained by Algorithm 7.5. Continuity is observed in all but one breakpoint (A). (Reproduced from [7.62])

[7.82-84]. In many cases the situation shown in Fig.7.31 will be observed. A simple algebraic calculation can show that the integral square error E is related to the maximum pointwise error e by the following equation.

$$E = \frac{e^2}{3}\ell \quad , \tag{7.40}$$

where ℓ is the length of the interval. Therefore, one can use a similar formula as an estimate for E_{max} in terms of e_{max} and the boundary length. This is a rather gross estimate because of the many assumptions involved in the derivation of (7.40). It turns out this is not a serious problem because the asymptotic analysis of variable knot approximations for the linear case suggests that the number of knots is inversely proportional to the *fourth root* of the integral square error [7.73]. This dependence tends to decrease the effects of any errors in the choice of E_{max}. Our computational experience has been that one must change E_{max} by a factor of 10 before any appreciable change in the resulting approximation is seen.

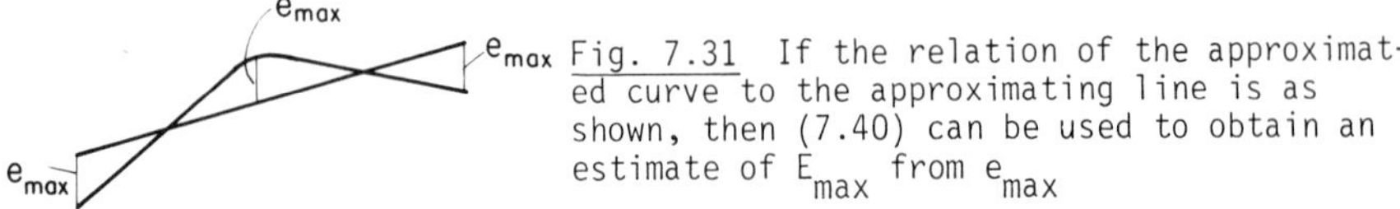

Fig. 7.31 If the relation of the approximated curve to the approximating line is as shown, then (7.40) can be used to obtain an estimate of E_{max} from e_{max}

8. Syntactic Analysis of Region Boundaries and Other Curves

8.1 Introduction

Encodings of curves as sequences of arcs are particularly suited for syntactic descriptions. If each arc is labeled by a symbol from a finite alphabet, then the curve is mapped into a string over such an alphabet and the classical theory of formal languages [8.1] is directly applicable. Much of the early work in syntactic pattern recognition has used representations based on the chain code or its variants (for a review see [8.2]). A recent example of its use can be found in the work of JARVIS [8.3]. Under this formalism each symbol corresponds to an arc of very short length and the symbol name signifies the direction of a linear segment approximating the arc (see Sec.7.5). This has the advantage of obtaining encodings very easily, but it places the burden for noise removal on the syntactic analyzer. It also requires the use of syntactic methodology for checking relatively simple geometrical properties, like length equality. These disadvantages may be overcome if we preprocess the input curves and obtain encodings in terms of symbols which represent higher order structures rather than small arc segments. Piecewise polynomial approximations offer one possibility, since they remove much of the noise and make information regarding simple properties, like length, readily available. However, they cannot be represented in terms of a finite alphabet, and, for certain applications, they may offer an encoding which is still too "elementary". In this chapter we shall describe techniques which overcome these problems and produce curve descriptions in terms of finite alphabets, but with each symbol representing a more complex part of a curve than a short arc or an arc which is nearly linear.

It turns out that such encodings must be made in general by syntactic techniques and therefore we have a *hierarchical* approach to the problem. This is not a drawback, since it often turns out that the total effort for the two levels of the syntactic analysis (for the original encoding and for the classification) is less than the effort for a syntactic analysis from "scratch". Syntactic analysis (or an equivalent technique) is necessary in the beginning because noise and the inherent variability of the data make it difficult to decide on the nature of a local feature without examining at least a few of its neighbors. We have already seen this problem in the context of scene analysis, where in its most general form it was equivalent to subgraph isomorphism. For one-dimensional data we have a significant simplification, the existence of a direction for search. Thus we may interpret the target labels as nonterminals of a grammar which has generated the current string. The grammar must be somewhat unconventional, since we do not deal with a finite alphabet and we shall show in the sequel how this can be handled. Another possibility is to use filtering or relaxation techniques of the type discussed in Chapter 6. We shall give one such example in Section 8.7. In their simplest form they seem to be far more time consuming than the syntactical analysis (see Sec.6.5) and more complex forms have not been studied properly as yet. Indeed, many context-free and all regular languages can be parsed in time which is linearly proportional to the length of the input string, without any iterations [8.4]. We demonstrate in the sequel that for a large variety of problems the syntactic analysis does not require more complex grammars and therefore filtering-relaxation, which might require many iterations, is going to be slower. A connection between filtering-relaxation and parsing techniques (especially probabilistic ones) is also likely because both label items taking into account the labeling of their neighbors [8.5].

8.2 Syntactic Analysis of Boundaries

In this section we compare the use of curve encodings using elementary descriptors to encodings using the results of functional approximations. We assume that we are given a general description of the form

$$V = v_1, v_2, \ldots, v_n \quad .$$

If the v_i's are from a finite alphabet (as in the case of the chain code), then a syntactic analysis is straightforward. If they are real numbers (or real vectors, as in the case of polygonal approximations), then syntactic analysis is still possible but it requires special techniques. We shall illustrate some of the problems involved with two simple examples, 1) the recognition of squares and 2) the recognition of "notches" in boundaries.

8.2.1 Recognition of Squares

I) *Chain code:* This is the simplest form of encoding as we saw in Section 7.5. The compactness of the resulting descriptions depends significantly on the orientation of the objects. If the square has a vertical pair of sides, it will be encoded as $6^n0^n2^n4^n$, where n is the side length in multiples of the size of the quantization grid. If it has a pair of sides which form a -60 degree angle with the horizontal, then it will be encoded as

$$(7(67)^8 7)^m\ (1(01)^8 1)^m\ (3(23)^8 3)^m\ (5(45)^8 5)^m \quad ,$$

where m is about one tenth of the side length. It is well-known from the theory of formal languages that neither set of expressions can be generated by a context-free grammar. It seems that the simplest grammar required for their recognition would be a context-free programmed grammar of the type described by FU and SWAIN [8.2,6]. If there is noise, then the chain code can become even more complicated. The same type of grammars is still sufficient but the grammars require a very large number of rules.

One possible simplification is offered by a hierarchical approach, i.e., one may attempt first to recognize straight lines. FREEMAN has suggested the following criteria which the chain code of a line must meet [8.7]:

1) At most two basic directions are present and these can differ only by unity, modulo eight.

2) One of these values always occurs singly.

3) Successive occurrences of the principal direction occurring singly are as uniformly spaced as possible.

No formal proof has been proposed for these criteria but they seem reasonable and they are certainly satisfied by the sides of the second square above. The third criterion is somewhat fuzzy, but this can be overcome, if we define straight lines through the following right linear grammar:

$$S \to S_{jk} \ /\ S_j$$

$$S_j \to S_j j \ /\ j$$

$$S_{jk} \to S_{jk} jk^i \ /\ jk^i \ /\ k /\ T_{jk} k$$

$$T_{jk} \to T_{jk} jk^i \ /\ jk^i \ /\ k$$

where j is a principal direction and the pair (j,k) represents two principal directions differing by one, modulo 8. The repetition factor i can have any value between 1 and some upper bound I. In spite of its compact description this grammar has a total of $1 + 8 + 2 \times 56 = 121$ nonterminals and $8 + (56 \times 4 + 56 \times 3) \times I$ rules. By placing an upper bound I we sacrifice certain possible values of slopes, but if we did not do that the resulting grammar would have been context sensitive. Even though this grammar can be implemented by a finite automaton, this must have a very large number of states and it is going to be quite cumbersome. The resulting acceptance of a sequence of a chain code as a line goes only partway in solving the problem of recognizing squares. One must produce a code for the direction of the line and its length, and then check for right angles and equal sides. The presence of noise can increase considerably the already large number of rules. For an additional discussion of grammars for straight lines see [8.8].

II) *Polygonal Approximations:* If the noise level is not too high, then the polygonal approximation will be indeed a four-sided polygon, with angles approximately equal to 90 degrees. In this case the problem is trivial because the line recognition has already been performed by nonsyntactic means. The final recognition algorithm need only compare the variance of the lengths of the sides to an a priori chosen threshold (usually in terms of a percentage of the average length) and check whether the size of each angle falls within an a priori given range around 90 degrees. If the amount of noise is very high, or an improper choice of parameters was made during the approximation process, then the approximating polygon may have more than four sides. In this case it will be necessary to apply first some elementary operations:

1) Merge two sides into a single side if they form an angle less than a given threshold and one of the following is true: a) The two sides are adjacent; b) the two sides are separated by a third whose length is smaller than a given percentage of the smaller of the two (see Fig.8.1).

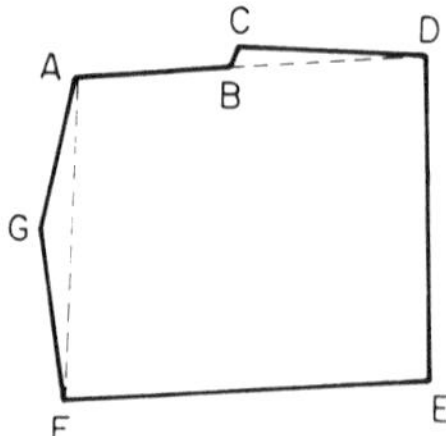

Fig. 8.1 Detection of polygons is very simple, even if the original polygonal approximation does not correspond to the visually perceived polygon. In such a case simple local rules can assure the merging of AB, BC and CD into AD and AG and GF into AF

2) Define as a corner any of the following two configurations: a) Two adjacent sides, each of which has length over a given percentage of the average length of the sides of the polygon; b) Two sides satisfying the above length condition, separated by one or two sides of length less than a given percentage of the average.

One can think of a simple right linear grammar which operates not on a finite alphabet, but on vectors $\underline{v}$ and which implements the above rules. In this simple case such a formalism would be rather presumptuous, but we shall use it in more complex situations.

8.2.2 The Recognition of Notches

These are defined as small and sharp protrusions or intrusions on the boundary.

I) The Chain Code: One may define as a sharp corner one less than or equal to 45 degrees and in this case such corners will be represented by any of the substrings 72, 74, 03, 05,... etc. However, we may impose minimal length requirements so the substrings may take the form (hijkℓm) where i, j and k, ℓ are pairs which differ by at most one modulo eight, j,k is one of the pairs listed above and h,j and ℓ,m are pairs which form a large angle. Also h,m should differ by at most one modulo eight and h should be different from j and k from m. For example, 012771 represents such a substring. Further generalizations are possible and the detection of notches can be achieved through regular expressions, although a rather large number of them may be needed.

II) Polygonal Approximations: In this case a notch may be defined as a sharp angle, less than a given threshold, with two adjacent sides having lengths within a certain range.

It is obvious that in both examples polygonal approximations offer a simpler solution and it is worthwhile looking into the reasons why this is so and also whether or not the comparison between the two methods will always yield a similar result. One problem with the chain code is that one needs a large number of nonterminals in order to reproduce expressions obtained from the same string rotated by 45 degrees. A possible simplification is to apply a transformation which yields rotation invariant representations. The following transformation accomplishes this task while preserving some rotational information through the first symbol.

$$q_1 = c_1 \quad , \tag{8.1a}$$

$$q_i = c_i - c_{i-1} \quad | \quad \text{modulo } 8 \quad i = 2,\ldots,n \quad . \qquad (8.1b)$$

In a clockwise traversal of the boundary the above transformation maps all concave angles into the indices 1,2,3 and all convex ones into 5,6,7. The index 4 should never appear on a well-formed boundary. In this way the square with a vertical pair of sides will be encoded as $60^{n-1}(20^{n-1})^3$. The one with a pair of sides forming an angle of -60 degrees with the horizontal becomes

$$7(17)^8\ 0[0(17)^8 0]^{m-1}\ \{2(17)^8 0[0(17)^8 0]^{m-1}\}^3$$

This representation can reduce the number of production rules and nonterminals listed above by replacing jk^i by 10^{i-1} or 70^{i-1}, etc. Savings by a factor between 4 and 8 are obtained, but this still leaves a large number of productions, especially when one must take into account the effects of noise.

It seems that the main difference between the two approaches is that polygonal approximations produce output corresponding to a high level structure in terms of the chain code. Thus considerable preprocessing is bypassed. Noise is reduced or eliminated by numerical rather than syntactic techniques. Furthermore, quantization is postponed until a later stage. Theoretically strings of real numbers cannot be handled by syntactical techniques but this does not pose a serious problem, since one can use very simple "syntactic-like" schemes for their analysis. We have already seen examples of such processors above.

This advantage has its price, the not insignificant preprocessing effort. It seems though that this price is not too high when nonlocal features are involved. We have seen that there exist efficient algorithms which perform the approximation in linear time as a function of the boundary length, while the parsing of grammars of high complexity requires cubic or even exponential time [8.1]. On the other hand, for local features (e.g., notches), the preprocessing may be indeed too expensive.

The basic problem with the chain code and similar encodings is that they attempt to handle length by syntactic means. For example verifying whether a string belongs to the family $a^n b^n c^n d^n$ requires a grammar more powerful than context-free. On the other hand, verifying whether a quadruple of numbers are equal requires only a finite automaton *provided that a procedure for checking equality of integers is available*. That procedure requires a pushdown stack and theoretically we have not reduced the complexity of the problem. From a practical viewpoint, however, the difference is tremendous. Since comparisons of numbers are performed by arithmetic units in modern computers, the logical complexity of the program will be that of a finite automaton, rather than the acceptor of a context sensitive language.

The remaining question is whether polygonal approximations have an advantage when the boundaries under examination do not consist of linear segments to start with. It is obvious that if general spline approximations are used they would share the advantages of piecewise linear approximations over the simple codes no matter what the shape of the original boundary is. The lack of efficient algorithms for such general approximations makes such a comparison meaningless by increasing the price of preprocessing to a prohibitive degree. Thus it is necessary to compare the efficiency of polygonal approximations for the detection of, say, arcs of constant curvature to that of chain codes. The analysis of Section 7.6 implies that such arcs will be approximated by regular polygons and a simple recognition routine could be achieved by checking the variance of both side lengths and angle sizes from their respective averages. If the length of the basic vector of the chain code is about the size of the radius of the arc, then the rotationally invariant encoding of such an arc will be 1^i. For large arcs, the representation will be $(0^k1)^i$. The presence of noise will make such strings even more complicated. Thus functional approximations in general, and polygonal approximations in particular, have distinct advantages over chain codes, whenever nonlocal features are involved.

On the positive side, encodings in a finite alphabet, like those produced by chain codes, allow the application of syntactic techniques immediately. This may be significant in an environment where software implementing compiler-compilers, regular expresssion recognizers, etc., is available. If the chain code is used strictly for the detection of local features, then it is possible to use it with reasonable results, since one does not have to go into the trouble of writing a complicated parser [8.3].

This last observation brings us to a problem, which is not peculiar to the chain code, namely, the increase in the complexity of representation resulting from an effort to describe global features, like the closing of boundaries. In the previous example the detection of a square could be achieved by simpler means if one would look only for four linear segments and four right corners. Both features can be checked with nothing more complex than a finite automaton. *If it is known a priori that the boundary is closed,* then a figure having those features could be only a square or a rectangle, and the distinction between the two can be made by comparing the lengths of two adjacent sides only.

8.3 Local Feature Detection by Syntactic Means

The discussion of the previous section suggests that considerable simplifications can occur if a) the boundary is mapped into a sequence of vectors or arcs by numerical techniques and b) only local features are examined. Such local features could then be used as input to a higher order recognizer. The peak detector developed by HOROWITZ [8.9,10] is a simple example of this philosophy. A more complex example is provided by the shape parser developed by PAVLIDIS and ALI [8.11]. Different aspects of this approach have been used by a number of authors. Examples of preprocessing by curve fitting can be found in the waveform parser by STOCKMAN et al. [8.12], while examples of local feature detection can be seen in the detection of circuit board faults by lexical analysis of chain codes proposed by JARVIS [8.3]. Such "local" grammars will result in replacing the string V by another string

$$S = s_1 s_2, \ldots, s_m$$

where s_j is a descriptor of a high order structure, e.g., stroke, lobe, concave arc, etc. It may contain a number of attributes like length of a stroke, its orientation, etc. Using the original model of LEDLEY [8.13] we may think of the V_i's as arcs of constant curvature and of the S_i's as "arms" and "concavities". In general, m will be much smaller than n. This brings out another advantage of the method. The last processing of the data dealing with their classification or final description could afford to use algorithms of very high complexity because the volume of the data will be considerably reduced.

One important feature in many applications is that of sections of the boundary consisting of two relatively smooth parts forming a sharp corner with each other and connected either directly, or by a short arc of high curvature. Authors have described these by different names, depending on the application: peaks (positive or negative) [8.8,9], protrusions or intrusions [8.14], arms [8.13], lobes [8.15], strokes [8.11,16,17], etc. We shall use the name *trusion* for such a feature and we shall describe next an automaton for its recognition.

This utilizes a procedure for detecting linear segments which will be referred to as a line detector. We assume that this is done either by nonsyntactic means, or by one of the simple schemes discussed in the previous sections. The recognizer is a finite automaton with a buffer of size at most four and uses a 'shift-reduce' parsing [8.4]. The bound on the buffer size is justified in cases where a preprocessing of the boundary has been performed. The automaton always looks at the complete contents of the buffer. We assume that a decision can be made whether a line is short (S) or long (L), depending not only on the current line but also on the contents of the buffer. The need to examine the contents of the buffer may suggest that we actually have a context sensitive parser. This is not the case because of the limit on its size. We could have constructed easily a finite automaton in the strict sense of the term to do the same tasks, but it would have a much larger number of states. Table 8.1 and Fig.8.2 describe this automaton. The operation 'shift k' means that one obtains the next k lines as the return of the line detector operating on the boundary. 'Reduce k' means that the first k elements of the buffer should be emptied and then mapped into a trusion. The 'relabel' operation consists of labeling the remaining contents of the buffer by L. The symbol # stands for end of input, while ; denotes an empty portion of the buffer. Configurations involving those symbols occur only at the beginning and the end of the parsing.

Table 8.1 Trusion parser

Buffer Contents	Action
LL;;	reduce 2 & shift 1
LSL;	reduce 3 & shift 2
LSSL	reduce 4 & shift 3
LSSS	reduce 2, relabel & shift 1
LSS#	reduce 3 & stop
LS##	reduce 2 & stop
L###	stop
####	stop

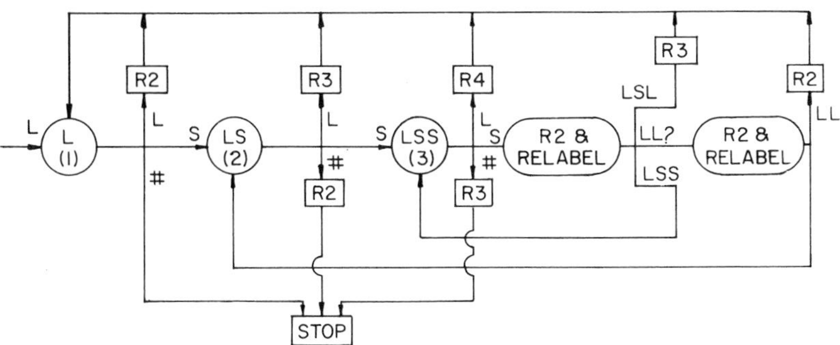

Fig. 8.2 State transition diagram of the automaton of Table 8.1

Table 8.2 Implementation of trusion parser

State	Action	New state
0	Shift	1
1	Shift	1a
1a	If L reduce	1
	If S shift	2
2	Shift	2a
2a	If L reduce	1
	If S shift	3
3	Shift	3a
3a	If L reduce	1
	If S reduce (1)	4
4	Backspace by 2	1

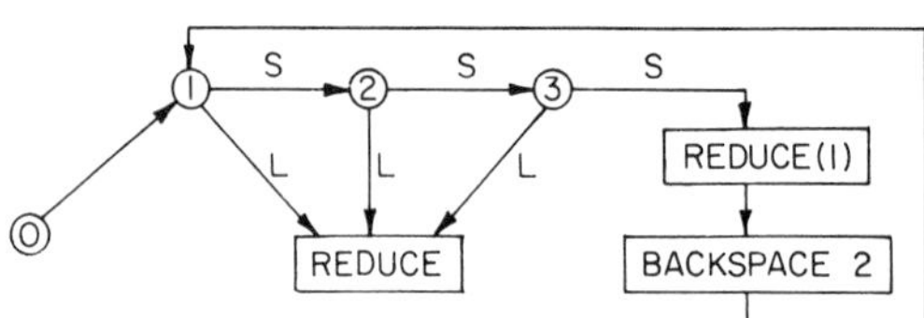

Fig. 8.3 State transition diagram of the automaton of Table 8.2

A somewhat different configuration, which is however equivalent to the above, is shown in Table 8.2 and Fig.8.3. It uses states explicitly and the operation 'shift' has only one argument, while the operation 'reduce' applies to all the contents of the buffer; 'reduce(1)' applies only to the first two entries of the buffer. This automaton is implemented by Algorithm 8.1, where a 'shift' is replaced by a recursive call to itself. This calls the line detector and, depending on the state, examines the length of its return.

Algorithm 8.1: Parser for trusion

Input: A subset of the array V. Application dependent parameters specifying the criteria for judging lines short or long. A starting index "first", denoting the starting element on the array V; and an initial "state". (The latter is 0 when the procedure is first called by the main algorithm).

Output: Labeling of the vertices as belonging to a trusion and creation of respective entries for the string S.

Steps:

1. Call the line detector. If no line is found, then *return*. Else set "first" equal to the next index after the last one returned by the line detector. 'Switch': Perform the following steps for the respective values of "state".
   "state": - 0 - 1 - 2 - 3
   step: - 2 - 3 - 6 - 9
2. ("state" = 0) Set "state" = 1; call trusion; then *return*.
3. (state = 1. This means that two lines have been detected): If the second line is smaller than the first and its length is less than a given minimum then do step 4. Else do step 5.
4. (Treat the line as short) Set "state" = 2; call trusion; then *return*.
5. A trusion has been found. Call 'reduce'; set "state" = 1 and call trusion; then *return*.
6. ("state" = 2. A third line has been found separated from the first by a short one). If the third line is shorter than the first, and its length is less than a given minimum then do step 7. Else do step 8.
7. (New line is short). Set "state" = 3; call trusion; then *return*.
8. A trusion has been found. Call 'reduce'; set "state" = 1 and call trusion; then *return*.
9. ("state" = 3; Four lines have been found with the two middle ones considered as short ones.) If the fourth line exceeds in length the previous two then do step 10. Else do step 11.
10. A trusion has been found. Call 'reduce'; set "state" = 1 and call trusion; then *return*.
11. A change of scale seems to have occurred. It is possible that the first and second lines form a trusion while the third and fourth are part of another nonterminal. Call 'reduce' for the first two. Set "first" equal to one after the last index of the second line. Set "state" = 1 and call trusion; then *return*.

Algorithm 8.1 detects only pairs of lines which form a significant angle. The 'reduce' procedure may incorporate parts which examine semantic information. In particular, depending on the size of the angle formed by the two lines, the trusion may be further specified as a corner, a stroke, a protrusion, an intrusion, etc. If this algorithm is used in connection with a detector for lines and arcs (more precisely, conics) then the string S will provide such a compact description.

8.4 Parsing of Noisy Boundaries

The above methodology is strictly deterministic and as it stands gives only "yes" or "no" answers regarding the existence of boundary features. For example, a stroke is detected when two lines in succession are seen which have significant length in comparison to the average and form a sharp angle. If the angle is above a certain size, then the two lines are said to form a corner. This classification is obviously unreliable near the critical angle values. A more realistic approach would be to introduce a probability measure over the parameters which affect the classification and instead of deciding that a feature is a stroke or corner we would estimate the probability of its being one or the other. Fig.8.4 shows a possible choice of a probability density function. Such functions could be defined for all decisions made by the preprocessors and the parsers described in the last two sections. We shall postpone until later a discussion about the choice of either of these measures. We will study first the implications of such a choice in the analysis of the shape of curves.

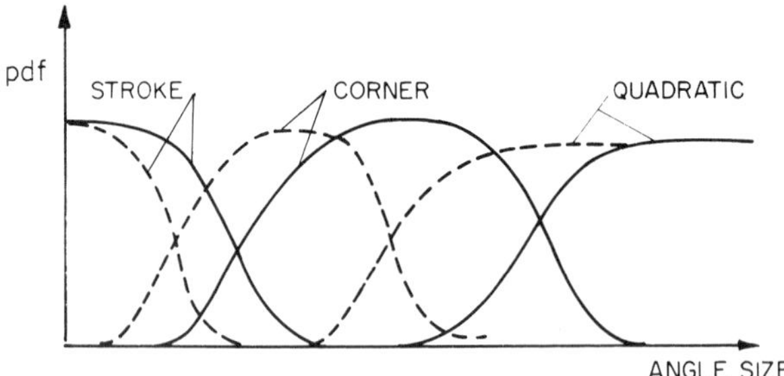

Fig. 8.4 Probability density functions that a pair of sides are part of a stroke, corner or conic (quadratic), plotted as functions of the angle size. Their value also depends on the size of the sides. Full lines correspond to large size and broken lines to small size

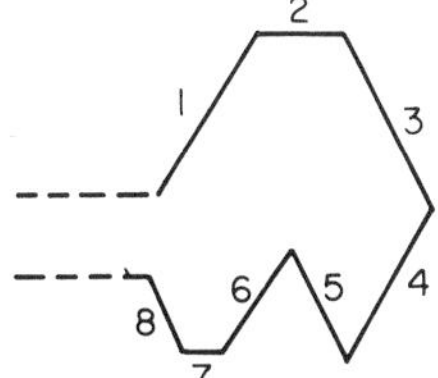

Fig. 8.5 Configuration for the parsing example of Section 8.4

It is obvious that under these conditions each part of the boundary will have multiple interpretations. We introduce the following notation: A stroke will be denoted by the symbol "|", a corner by "<", a conic by "^". "+" will stand for convex and "-" for concave. Using the probability densities of Fig.8.4 we have for the example of Fig.8.5 a probability of 0.7 that the first three segments form a stroke, 0.8 that they form two corners and 0.4 that they are part of a conic. Each one of these choices affects the subsequent parsing. If we assume a stroke, then we may proceed to find the remaining segments forming three strokes with respective probabilities 0.8, 0.8, and 0.7 and final output +|2+|6-|6+|6, or that they form corners with probabilities 0.8, 0.7, 0.6 and 0.5 for a final output +|2+<6-<6+<7+<5. Of course combinations of the latter configurations are possible. If we assume two corners the same combinations are possible. If we proceed with the assumption that 1, 2 and 3 are part of a conic, then the fourth segment may also be part of it and the final output will be +^1-|6+<7+<5. At this point the possibility that 6, 7 and 8 might be parts of a conic could be considered to give as final output +^1|6^6. It may turn out that the last configuration is the most likely one and it would have been missed if we kept at each step the most likely choice only. These observations suggest the following strategies.

When a new part of the boundary is examined, a set of multiple decisions is made and each one of them is pursued further. Thus we form a *decision tree* which is equivalent to parsing according to a *nondeterministic automaton*. In particular we may proceed along certain parts of the curve with both the line and the conic detectors. The final decision will be made on the basis of the most likely outcome for the complete boundary. In general the decision tree may be quite large so that it is desirable to prune it and avoid following very unlikely decision paths. This could be done either by a branch and bound method or by a heuristic.

Here we will describe a rather simple algorithm implementing these ideas. First, we point out that the different parsers have basically similar structure and they differ only in the value of certain parameters. Thus we have a single program, executed a number of times for different parameter values. The parsing algorithm deals only with substrings of the input consisting of successsive vertices of the same sign and contained in a stack C which is then scanned a number of times with the following goals. First, a check is made to determine whether or not pairs of vertices which are far apart along the boundary are geometrically close. This might mean that this part of the boundary has come from a "broken loop". An alternative geometrical configuration having a closed loop is produced and both V-strings are parsed. First trusions with high confidence level are detected, and the corresponding vertices are removed from further consideration. A second pass is used to detect conics and then a third to detect trusions with lower confidence level. If any conics have been found, the one with the lowest confidence level is eliminated (provided that level is less than a threshold) and the third pass is repeated. The confidence levels of the two parses are then compared and the one with the highest is kept. Additional parses are performed if there was an indication of a broken loop or very small trusions had been detected. The one with the highest confidence level is then chosen as the final one. These procedures are implemented in Algorithm 8.2.

The following notations have been used.

NEGLENG: If a side has size less that this is considered as noise.

NEGANG, ADDANG: Angle tolerances while testing for collinearity.

The output of this parser is a compact representation of the object as a sequence of descriptors, each consisting of 7 characters. The meaning of the characters and their use will be discussed in Section 8.6.

8.5 Regular Expressions

Regular expressions are a convenient notation for defining sets of strings which are accepted by a finite automaton [8.18]. The discussion of the last two sections suggests that many syntactic pattern recognition problems can be reduced to this form. For this reason we digress briefly to introduce the subject properly and establish certain notational conventions which will be used in the rest of the book.

Formally a regular set of strings is a set containing a finite set and which is closed under the operations of union, concatenation and closure [8.18]. What this means in practical terms is that a finite automaton can recognize, among others, classes of strings which are characterized in one or more of the following ways: each string contains a finite number of given

Algorithm 8.2: Boundary parser

Input: Array V; Various parameters depending on the application. (See text.) A starting index determined by the preprocessor.

Output: A description of the boundary in terms of QUADS, STROKES, CORNERS etc.

Steps:

1. Set "mask" to the sign of the current angle (initially a convex one).
2. Form a stack C of indices of vertices of the same sign as "mask". Do not include an index if the corresponding side has length less than NEGLENG.
3. If "reparse" is less than 9, check if the vectors placed in the stack C seem to have come from a broken loop. This is determined by a heuristic technique. If they do set "reparse" = 10.
4. Initialization: "mark" = 1.
5. Parse according to the rule for TRUS using COLANG = 0; Since "mark" = 1 this also imposes tight limits on BREAK.
6. Apply the QUAD detector on the vertices in C which have not been already labeled as belonging to TRUS. (i.e., mark a series of sides and vertices as representing a conic according to the rules described in the text).
7. "mark" = 0 (this relaxes the bounds on BREAK).
8. Set "comp" = 0.
9. Parse the sides in C not already labeled by QUAD according to the rule for TRUS using COLANG = ADDANG + NEGANG.
10. If no TRUS was found: Repeat parse according to the rule for TRUS tightening the condition for collinearity, in particular setting COLANG = NEGANG.
11. If "comp" = 0 and if any QUADs have been found in C and if the confidence level of any of them is less than CONF, eliminate the QUAD with the lowest confidence level, set "comp" = 1 and go to step 9. Otherwise go to step 13.
12. If "comp" = 1 compare the confidence level of the two parses and keep the results of the parsing which yields the higher value.
13. If all the vectors have been examined, rearrange the tokens so that the starting point is at the upper left corner and *output* the string.
14. Then: If reparse > 0 close gap or eliminate stroke as needed, set reparse = 0, and go to step 1.

finite substrings (e.g., the set of all integer whose decimal notation contains the digit 3 and the sequence of digits 45); each string contains one of a set of substrings (e.g., integers containing the sequence of digits 36 or 47). If we assume special symbols denoting the beginning and the end of a string, then the above definition includes as a special case strings which start or end (or both) with given substrings.

Such specifications can be expressed conveniently through the following notations: a dot (.) stands for any symbol; a star (*) denotes any number of repetition of the previous symbol (including no occurrences at all), so that ".*" denotes any sequence; a plus (+) has the same meaning as a star but it requires at least one occurrence; square brackets ([]) denote the union of the enclosed symbols (thus [abc] matches a, b, or c); the slash (/) separates subexpressions whithin brackets (thus [ab/cd] stands for ab or cd); finally, ":" stands for the start of a string and "#" for its end.

In this way the two examples mentioned above can be characterized through the expressions 3.*45 or 45.*3, the first and [36/47] the second. Also [345]0 + [12] stands for all integers having a 3 or a 4 or a 5 followed by any number of zeros and either a 1 or a 2. If the + was a *, then our interpretation would have been the same except that "followed" would have been replaced by "possibly followed". All numbers ending in 2 are described by the expression 2#, while all even integers by [02468]#.

In the case of the chain code we may define a vertical spike with sides of length at least three by the regular expression

[07]+[12][12]+[27/16/17][67]+[67][10]+ .

Figure 8.6 shows examples of spikes described by the expression. Note that we cannot demand that the sides be of equal length, since that would require a pushdown automaton for recognition.

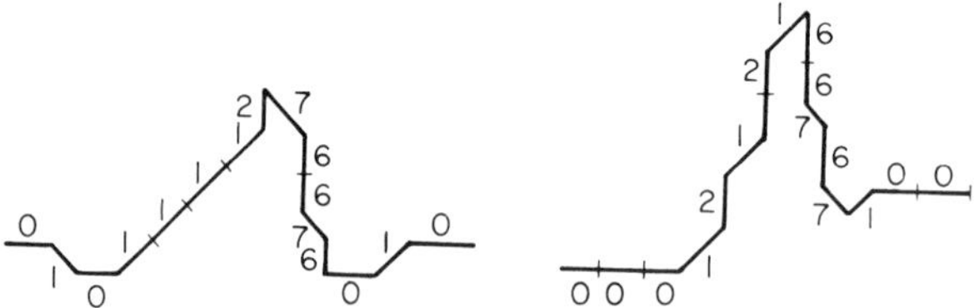

Fig. 8.6 Illustrations of strokes which are members of the set defined by the regular expression [07]+[12][12]+[27/16/17][67]+[67][10]+

8.6 A Compact Boundary Description

We shall describe here the form of the output of the parser developed in Section 8.4 and discuss some of its applications. The output is of such form that classes of shapes can be described easily through regular expressions. Each "entity" of the boundary is described by 7 characters. Trusions are classified as strokes or corners depending on the sharpness of the angle formed by their sides. The meaning of the characters is shown in Table 8.3. These data give a fairly complete description of the arc. For example, the descriptor +<3rhgL represents a large, sharp, convex corner facing NW located at top left of the object. Fig.8.8 shows a typical example of an encoding.

Table 8.3 Description of the output of the boundary parser

<table>
<tr><th>Char</th><th>Possible values</th><th>Explanation</th></tr>
<tr><td>1</td><td>+,-</td><td>+ means convex, - concave</td></tr>
<tr><td>2</td><td>|,<,^</td><td>| = stroke, < = corner, ^= quadratic arc (or conic).</td></tr>
<tr><td>3</td><td>0-7</td><td>Orientation of the bisectrix of an arc, according to one of the principal directions shown in Fig.7.13a.</td></tr>
<tr><td>4</td><td>p,q,r,s,t,u,V</td><td>This is the measure of the external angle between the first and last side of an arc. They are quantized in intervals of 45 degrees, except V which stands for any external angle greater than 270 degrees.</td></tr>
<tr><td>5</td><td>h,n,m,ℓ</td><td>This indicates the vertical location of the arc in terms of quartiles of a frame (see Fig.8.7). This assumes the definition of a frame for the object. If it is the only one in the picture and covers most of its area, then this might be the picture frame. Otherwise the frame may consist of a rectangle circumscribed to the object.</td></tr>
<tr><td>6</td><td>f,c,g</td><td>The frame is divided horizontally into three equal regions: left (f), center (c), right (g). See Fig.8.7.</td></tr>
<tr><td>7</td><td>L,M,S,N</td><td>This indicates the length of the arc as a function of given parameters and average segment length of the object. The notation used is Large (L), Middle (M), Small (S), and Negligible (N).</td></tr>
</table>

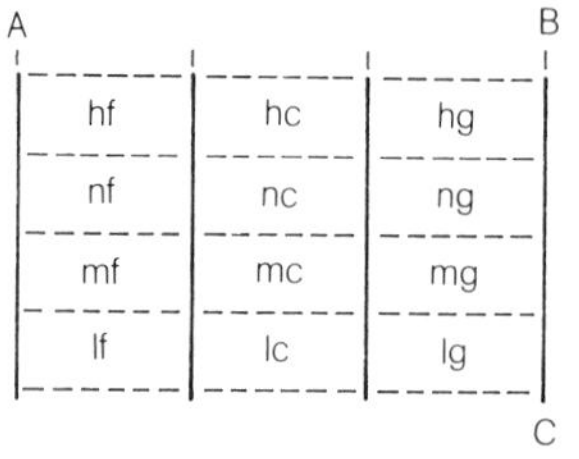

A		B
hf	hc	hg
nf	nc	ng
mf	mc	mg
lf	lc	lg
		C

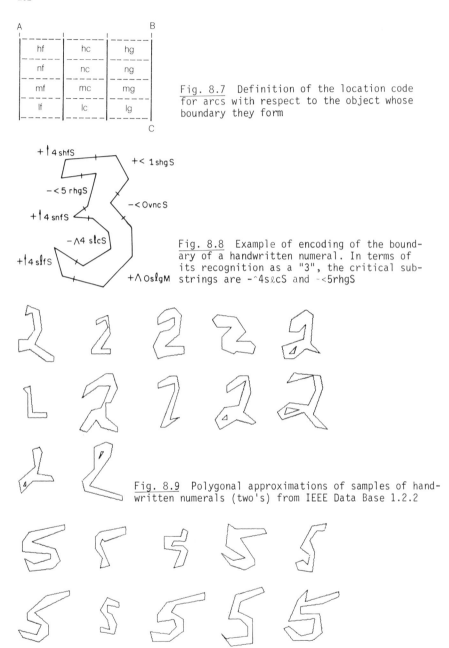

Fig. 8.7 Definition of the location code for arcs with respect to the object whose boundary they form

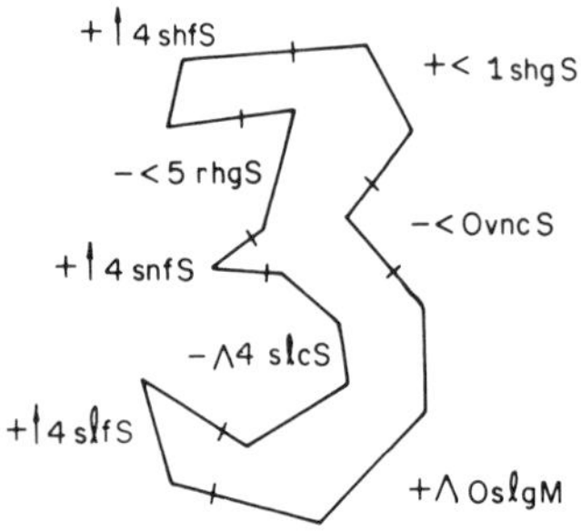

Fig. 8.8 Example of encoding of the boundary of a handwritten numeral. In terms of its recognition as a "3", the critical substrings are -∧4sℓcS and -<5rhgS

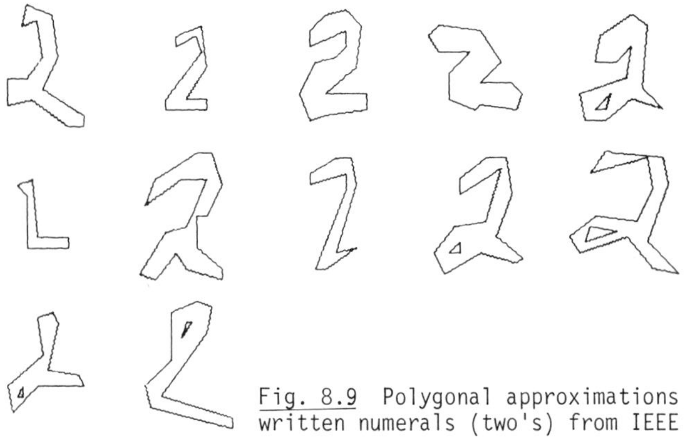

Fig. 8.9 Polygonal approximations of samples of handwritten numerals (two's) from IEEE Data Base 1.2.2

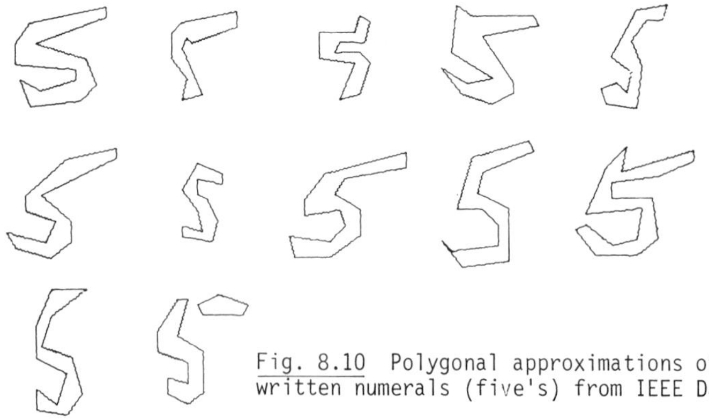

Fig. 8.10 Polygonal approximations of samples of handwritten numerals (five's) from IEEE Data Base 1.2.2

An illustration of the utility of these results is offered by their application in the recognition of handwritten numerals [8.19]. The data used in this work was a set of digitized numerals, originally taken from FORTRAN coding sheets and forming part of IEEE Data Base 1.2.2. They are of mixed quality as one can see from the examples of Figs.8.9 and 8.10. 480 of them were used as a design set and after a polygonal approximation of their contours were encoded in strings of the descriptors shown above. It was found that the majority of the strings produced from various examples of a single numeral were virtually identical. Furthermore, the strings correspond to an intuitive description of the numeral, and therefore it was relatively easy to characterize each class in terms of regular expressions. For example, it was found that many samples of the numeral "3" in the design set could be represented as (-[345].[ℓm][gc].*-[345].[hn]) & NOT(+|0.1g) (see Fig. 8.8). This string can be verbalized as follows:

> "The boundary has a concave arc facing W located in the right (or middle) lower-half of the object, followed eventually by another concave arc facing W in the top-half of the object. In addition, the lower right of the object does not have a stroke facing E."

This description is what one is likely to use if asked for a generic description of "3". In addition to the above two other regular expressions were found, which also characterized many "3"s. The union of these three representations can then serve as a classifier for "3". Table 8.4 gives an additional illustration by listing the strings representing the outside contours of ten samples from each of the numerals "5", "6" and "7". The five numbers separated by slashes have the following meaning:

1) Identification of region or object.
2) Class membership (used for the design set).
3) Number of boundaries for the region (i.e., number of holes plus one. This entry is the same for all boundaries produced from the same region).
4) Reparse index.
5) Number of segments of the polygonal approximation.

Under those conditions it is possible to design the recognizer interactively by using a standard library routine for recognizing regular expressions. In the present case this was part of the UNIX operating system run on a DEC PDP 11/45. However, it did not include all the symbols listed in the previous sections and therefore expressions tended to be more cumbersome than necessary. Those missing were the + and / operators. Such classifiers were derived for all the numerals and are given elsewhere [8.19]. Here we list only the expressions for 5, 6, and 7 in Table 8.5. Since handwritten numerals differ

Table 8.4 Encodings of handwritten numerals 5, 6 and 7

```
  5/5/1/ 0/14: +<3ghcS +|0shgS -|0sncS +^7smcM +|4sℓfS -|4smcS +<5rmfS
 15/5/1/ 0/11: +<4snfM +|0shgM -<0rnfS +^7tℓcM +|4sℓfS -|4smcS
 25/5/1/ 0/14: +<3qhfS +|0shgM -|0snfS +^7uℓcM +|3smfS -|4smcS +<5rmfS
 35/5/1/ 0/13: +<3qhcM +|0shgS -^0sncM +|0sℓgM +|4sℓfS -|4sℓcS +<5qmfS
 55/5/1/ 0/14: +<3qhcM +|0shgM -^0sncS +^0sℓcS +|4sℓfS -|4smcS +<5rmfS
 65/5/1/ 0/15: +<3qhcM +|0shgS -<7rhcM +^7rℓcS +|3sℓfS -^4tmfS +<5rmfS
 85/5/1/ 0/12: +<1rhcS -<1rhcS +|0shgM -<7qncM +^6sℓfM +<3rmfS
 -|3smfS +<4rnfS
 95/5/1/ 0/13: +<3rhfS -<2phfS +|0shgM -<7rncS +^7sℓcM +|3smfS
 -|4smcS +<5qnfS
105/5/1/ 0/14: +<3qhfS +|0shgM -<7rhcS +^7sℓcM +|3smfS -|4smcM +<4rnfS
115/5/1/ 0/13: +<3qhfM +|0shgM -|0rnfS +<7rℓgM +|4sℓfS -|4smcS +<5rmfS

  6/6/2/ 0/10: +|1shgM -<1rmcM +^7VℓcL
 16/6/2/ 0/11: +|1shgM -|1smfM +^6VmcL
 26/6/2/ 0/ 8: +|2shcM -<1rmcM +^7VℓcL
 56/6/2/ 0/ 8: +|1shgM -<0rmcM +^6VℓcL
 66/6/2/ 0/10: +|1shcM -|1sℓfM +^7VℓcL
 76/6/2/ 0/ 9: +|2shgM -<1rncM +^7VℓcL
 86/6/1/ 0/11: +|2shgM -<1rmcM +<1qmgS +<7rℓgM +<5rℓfM
 96/6/2/ 0/ 9: +|1shcM -|1smcS +^7VmcL
106/6/2/ 0/10: +|1shcM -|1smfM +^7VmcL
126/6/1/ 0/10: +|1shgS -<1rmcM +^6VmcL

  7/7/1/ 0/ 8: +|4shfM +<1rhgL +|5sℓfM -<5rhcM
 17/7/1/ 0/ 7: +|5shfM +<1rhgM +|6sℓfL -|5shgM
 27/7/1/ 0/ 9: +<3rhfM +<1qhgM +|6sℓgL -|6shcM +|6sncS
 37/7/1/ 0/11: +<3rhfS +<1rhgM +|6sℓcM -|5shcM +|6shfN
 47/7/1  0/ 7: +|4shfM +<1rhgL +|5sℓfL -<5rhcM
 57/7/1/ 0/12: +<3qhfS +^1rhgM +|5sℓfM -|6shcM +|6snfS
 67/7/1/ 0/ 8: +|5shfS +<1rhgM +|5sℓfL -|5shgM
 87/7/1/ 0/ 7: +|4shfM +<1rhgL +|6sℓcL -<5rhcM
 97/7/1/ 0/ 8: +|4shfM +<1rhgL +|5sℓfL -<5rhcM
107/7/1/ 0/ 8: +|4shfM +<1rhgL +|6sℓcL -<5rhgM
```

widely among authors, we needed more than one regular expression for each class. Fig.8.11 shows the three prototypes for the numeral "seven". The middle character has a different topology than the other two. The expressions for the other two characters could be merged if a more powerful program for checking regular expressions were used. The recognition rates achieved were significantly higher than those obtained by other techniques on the same data base [7.51,8.30] In particular, we were able to achieve an error rate of 1.46% and a rejection rate of 1.04% on the design set of 480 characters. We checked our results on a testing set of 840 digits and had an error rate of 3.57% and rejection rate of 3.45%. Thus, we had an overall error plus rejection rate of 5.37% on the total set of 1320 characters.

Table 8.5 Regular expressions for recognition of numerals 5, 6 and 7

```
   "5" = t51 U t52 U t53
  t51 = (+|[012].h[gc]. -.[70].[hn].. +.[706].[ℓm].. +...... -.[2345].[ℓm]...) &
   NOT(-.[345].* +.* -.[345])
  t52 = (/./[12]/.* +.[701][rst]hg. -.[70][pqrst][hn].* +.[4567].ℓ.* -.[345].[ℓm])
   & NOT(-.* +.* -.* +.* -)
  t53 = (+|[012].h[gc]. -.[70].[hn].. -.[01].... +.[706].[ℓm].. +......
-.[234].[ℓm]) &
   NOT(-.[345].* -.[345])

   "6" = t61 U t62 U t63 U t64 U t65

  t61 = (: +|[012].h.. -[|<][7012]....* +^[4567]) & NOT(+^.* -..[qrstuV]) & NOT(-
.* +.* -)
  t62 = (: +^[45]V..L -.[70])
  t63 = (/./[12]/.* +|[012].h.. -.[012]) & NOT(-.* +.* -)
  t64 = (: +|[012].h.. -[|<][012].... +[^|][4567].... -<.p.f) & NOT(-.* +.* -.*
+.* -)
  t65 = (: +|[012].h.. -[|<][012].... +[^|][701].... -<[67][pq].[fc]) &
   NOT(-.* +.* -.* +.* -)

   "7" = t71 U t72 U t73

  t71 = (/./1/.* +.[0123].[hn][g][ML] +|[56].ℓ.[ML].* -.[456].[hn].[MLS]) &
   NOT(-.[0123][rstuV]..[LMS])
  t72 = (/./1/.* +.1.hg. -.[01].... +.[017]..g. -.[07].... +|6sℓ.. -.[54]....
+.[345].... -)
  t73 = /./1/.* +.[0123].[hn][g][ML] -.[701]p... +|[56].ℓ.[ML].*
-.[456].[hn].[MLS]) &
   NOT(-.[0123][rstuV]..[LMS])
```

Fig. 8.11 Three prototypes of the numeral seven. The white parts can be present or absent without affecting the defining regular expressions shown in Table 8.5

Table 8.6 Encoding of contours of printed wiring board

```
  1/0/2/ 0/16: +^2uhcL -<7pℓcS +<7qℓcS +<5rℓfS -<4pmfS
  1/0/2/ 0/ 9: -^1VmcL
  2/0/3/ 0/45: +|2shgL +|6sℓgM -|5sℓcS +^4uℓfS -<3rmgS -<5qngS
-<6qncN +|5snfS -<2qncN -<3qngS
  2/0/3/ 0/ 9: -<1qℓfM -<3qℓgM -^5thcL
  2/0/3/ 0/ 9: +<0qnfN -^4VmcL
  3/0/2/ 0/26: +^2VhgS -<7qhgM +|6sℓfM -<4phcS
  3/0/2/ 0/ 8: -<7qhfM -^3VmcL
  4/0/1/ 0/28: +|2shfM -<0pnfM +|6sℓcM -<4qmgS
  5/0/2/ 0/45: +|2shcS +^0phcS -<0pncS +|6sℓfS -<5qℓfS +|4sℓfN -<3qℓfS -^4qmcS
+<5qnfN +<3qnfN -<5rnfS +|4snfN -<3qnfS -<5qhfS +|4shfN -<3qhfS
  5/0/2/ 0/ 8: -^2VncL
  6/0/2/ 0/30: +^0uhgS -<7qhcS +<7qncS -|0rncN +<1qncS +<7qmcS
-|0smcN +<1qmcS +|6sℓfL +^3qhfS
  6/0/2/ 0/ 8: -^6VncL
  7/0/2/ 0/32: +^4VhcS -<1phcS +^0rngM -<7pℓfS +|6sℓfS -^5rhgS
  7/0/2/ 0/ 9: -^6VmcL
  8/0/1/ 0/12: +^2rhcL +|7sℓgS -^6smcM +<7qℓcS +<5rℓfM
  9/0/4/ 0/39: +^4uhfS +^1qhgS -<1qngS +|0sngN -<7qngS +|6sℓgM
-<5rngM +^4VnfS -<1qncN +<1rncN -|2sncN +<3qncN -<3rngS -^6qhcS
  9/0/4/ 0/ 9: +<4qhcS -<5rhgS -^2VmcL
  9/0/4/ 0/ 4: -|4sngL -|0shfL
  9/0/4/ 0/ 8: -^2VncL
 10/0/1/ 0/45: +|2shfS +|6sℓgL +^4pℓfS
 11/0/2/ 0/15: +^7VmcL
 11/0/2/ 0/ 8: -^6VncL
 12/0/2/ 0/13: +^0VmcL
 12/0/2/ 0/10: -^4VmcL
 13/0/2/ 0/13: +<3qhfM +^7VmcL
 13/0/2/ 0/ 8: -^2VmcL
 14/0/2/ 0/15: +^0VncL -<4pnfN
 14/0/2/ 0/ 7: -^6VncL
 15/0/2/ 0/12: +<3qhfM +^7VncL
```

Table 8.6 (continued)

```
15/0/2/ 0/ 9: +<7phcS -^3VmcL
16/0/2/ 0/14: +^0VncL
16/0/2/ 0/11: +<0rmcS -<0rmfS -^5VncL
17/0/2/ 0/13: +^0VncL
17/0/2/ 0/ 8: -^6VmcL
18/0/2/ 0/12: +^0VncL
18/0/2/ 0/ 8: -^2VmcL
19/0/2/ 0/14: +^4VmcL
19/0/2/ 0/ 8: -^6VmcL
20/0/2/ 0/19: +^5VℓfM -<2qmcM +<1rhgS +<7qngM -<7qℓcM
20/0/2/ 0/ 9: -^1VmcL
21/0/2/ 0/11: +<3qhfM +^7VmcL
21/0/2/ 0/ 9: +<6phcS -^1umcL -<5rhgS
22/0/2/ 0/14: +^2VncL +<6qℓfM
22/0/2/ 0/ 8: -^2VmcL
23/0/3/ 0/23: +<2rhcS -<1qncS +^7uℓcM +<3rmfS -^4umcS +<5rmfS +<3qhfS
-<4rhfN +|3shfS -<2qhfN
23/0/3/ 0/ 3: -|0snfL -|4sℓgL
23/0/3/ 0/ 4: -|0snfL -|4sngL
24/0/2/ 0/13: +^0VncL
24/0/2/ 0/ 8: -^6VncL
25/0/2/ 0/14: +^4VmcL -<0qhgS
25/0/2/ 0/ 8: -^5VmcL
```

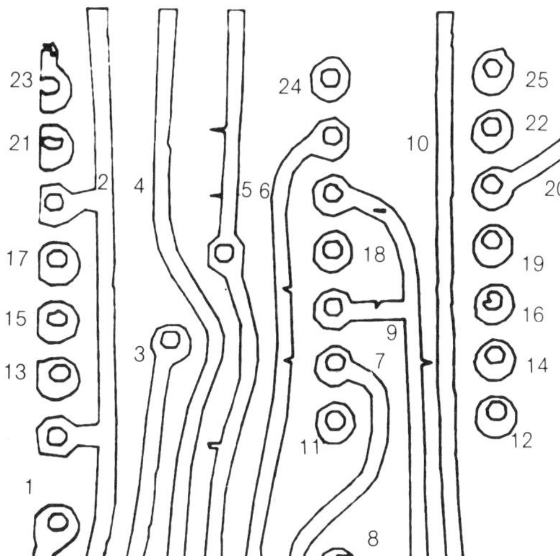

Fig. 8.12 Contours of a printed wiring board whose descriptions are given in Table 8.6. Note that the size notations in the table (L, M, S, N) are relative with respect to the size of the whole contour

Table 8.7 Encodings of white blood cell boundaries
(Each boundary can be either from a cytoplasm or a nucleus)

```
 1/0/1/ 0/10: +^1VncL -<5pℓfN
 2/0/1/ 0/17: +|2shfM -^2tmcM +^1uhgS -<0qngS +^7sℓgM -<5pmfS +<5qmfS
 3/0/1/ 0/13: +^6VmcL
 4/0/2/ 0/ 8: +^1ungL -<6pℓcS +<5rℓfM
 4/0/2/ 0/12: +^3uhfM -<1rmcS +<1qmgS -<2rℓgS +|2smgS +<0qℓgS +^6sℓgM -<5qmfS
 5/0/1/ 0/13: +^4VmcL
 6/0/2/ 0/ 6: +^6VmcL
 6/0/2/ 0/12: +^3VnfL -^1smcM +^0tmgM
 7/0/1/ 0/15: +^6VmcL -<2qhcN
 8/0/2/ 0/13: +|3snfS -<2qmcM +^1ungM -<6pmcS +<6qℓcS -<6qℓfS +<5rℓfS
 8/0/2/ 0/ 6: +^4VmcL
 9/0/1/ 0/12: +^0VmcL
10/0/2/ 0/ 8: +|3shcN +<1qhgS +^6VmcL -<3rhgS
10/0/2/ 0/15: +<2qhfS -<2qhcS +^0uhgM -<6qhcS -<0rnfS +^6VℓfM -<4pnfS +<4qhfS
11/0/1/ 0/14: +^3rnfM +^7VmgL
12/0/1/ 0/14: +^3uhfM -^2tmcM +^0VmgL -<5qmfS
42/0/1/ 0/10: +^4VmcL
43/0/1/ 0/10: +^0VncL
44/0/2/ 0/11: +^3VncL
44/0/2/ 0/ 5: +^0VmcL
45/0/1/ 0/11: +^3VmcL
46/0/1/ 0/11: +^0VmcL
47/0/1/ 0/ 9: +^4VmcL
48/0/1/ 0/ 9: +^0VncL
49/0/1/ 0/ 7: +^4VncL
50/0/2/ 0/ 9: +^3VncL
50/0/2/ 0/ 4: +|2shcL +|6sℓfL
51/0/1/ 0/ 9: +^3VncL
52/0/1/ 0/18: +^7VngM -|6shcS -<1qmfS +^6VmfM
53/0/2/ 0/ 9: +^4VncL
53/0/2/ 0/ 8: +^3VncL
54/0/1/ 0/17: +^2VhcM -|0sngN +<1qngN +^5VℓcL -|4sngS
55/0/1/ 0/16: +^4umfM -<2qhcS +^0VmgM -<6rncS
```

Note: Due to a programming error the contours of Fig.8.13 are actually mirror images of the contours seen by the analyzer. For consistency the reader should interchange 0 and 4, 1 and 5, and, 3 and 7.

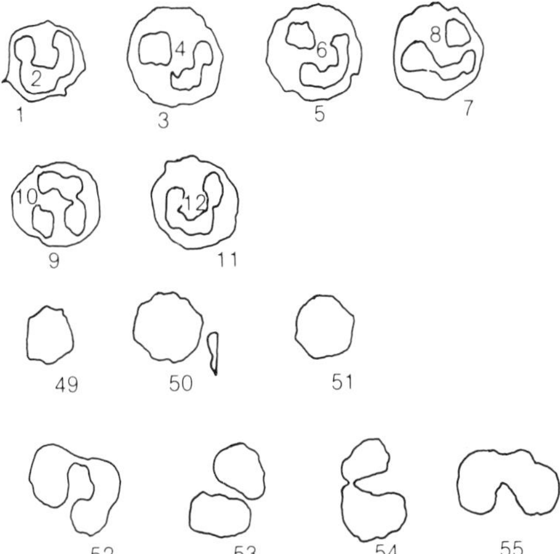

Fig. 8.13 Contours of white blood cells whose descriptions are given in Table 8.7. Contours 42-48 are not shown since they are almost identical to 49

Tables 8.6 and 8.7 show examples of encodings corresponding to the contours of the printed wiring board of Fig.8.12 and the blood cell contours of Fig. 8.13. Encodings of wiring boards can be used for two purposes: the first is description of a board which serves as model for manufacturing [8.20]; the second is detection of defects [8.3,21,22]. An inspection of Fig.8.12 and Table 8.6 reveals that defects manifested as protrusions or intrusions can be detected as strokes of "negligible" length and in particular by the regular expression "|....N" where "." stands for any character. Such expressions occur only in the representations of objects 5, 6 and 9. Note also that holes are identified by a negative sign, since they are indeed concave boundaries. This is by no means a complete diagnostic system, but it shows the power of the approach. Without any additional effort the same software which was used as a basis for recognition of handwritten numerals has produced a detector for certain faults of printed wiring boards. Similarly a comparison of Fig.8.13 and Table 8.7 shows that a faithful and compact description of the shape of the blood cells has been obtained.

8.7 Filtering and Relaxation Matching

An alternative to stochastic parsing is offered by filtering or relaxation, of the type described in Section 6.6. These techniques can be used for shape matching in the following manner, proposed by ROSENFELD and DAVIS [8.23]. Let

$$V = v_1, v_2, \ldots v_n$$

and

$$W = w_1, w_2, \ldots w_m$$

be compact representations of two curves. The v_i, w_i may be angles or sides of polygons, arcs of constant curvature, etc. Then a matching measure $M(v_i, w_j)$ can be defined in terms of the similarity between v_i and w_j. For example, M may be a weighted sum of the difference in length and direction of polygon sides. It is also possible to have W in terms of higher order structures like strokes, although this possibility has not been explored in the literature yet. A graph can then be established whose nodes correspond to pairs v_i, w_j provided that $M(v_i, w_j)$ exceeds a given threshold (if high values of M denote good matching) or is below a threshold if M is a "distance" function. By proper normalization this measure can be interpreted as a probability P_{ij}, that the "region" i has "label" j. Nodes of the graph are connected by branches labeled with the label correlation function $R_{ij,k\ell}$ defined in Section 6.6. This expresses the compatibility between the events; component i matches j and component k matches ℓ. Then a relaxation process of the type described by (6.25) can be used to determine the overall probability of matchings. Of course, it is important to keep the number of iterations small.

A search procedure may be used over this graph to find the best possible matching and in this way one can compute a probability of matching between V and W. In [8.24] DAVIS has proposed a combination of search and relaxation, and he also describes an example of application of this method to cartography. The overall procedure is given by Algorithm 8.3.

It can be shown that this algorithm is correct [8.24]. The resulting decision tree can be used in a number of ways. The path with the maximum probability may be chosen as that denoting the probability of matching between V and W. The cartographic application of this method used contours of five locations (islands and capes) which were approximated by polygons using a direct evaluation of curvature maxima (see Sec.7.6). Two sets of such approximations were obtained using different projections for the original map data and then they were matched using the above procedure. The elements used for the matching were the angles rather than the sides of the polygons [8.24].

Algorithm 8.3: String matching by relaxation

Input: Pair of strings V and W with matching and compatibility criteria.

Output: Decision tree for matching V to W.

Steps:

1. Form the graph G whose nodes correspond to pairs (v_i, w_j) labeled by $M(v_i, w_j)$ and $R_{ij,k\ell}$.
2. Perform the relaxation procedure on G.
3. Place a pointer to G in a stack S.
4. Do block 41 while the stack S is not empty.

    Begin block 41;

    1. Remove the top element of S. Let G be the graph pointed by it.
    2. While the graph G is not empty do block 42.

        Begin block 42;

        1. Choose the node P* in G which has the highest matching value. Assuming that the matching described by it is definite, remove the nodes of G which are now incompatible with this interpretation. Let G' be the new graph.
        2. Perform the relaxation procedure on G'. Place a pointer to the resulting labeled graph in S.
        3. Add a node to the decision tree corresponding to G' as labeled after the relaxation procedure. (Its father is the node corresponding to G).
        4. Remove P* and modify G according to the interpretation imposed by this removal.

        End block 42;

    End block 41;

8.8 Waveforms

Waveforms are special cases of plane curves and as such do not require any basically different methodology. In many cases they are functions of time but can be also functions of distance. The projections discussed in Section 7.2 are such an example. Picture raster lines are another [8.25]. Their analysis is, in general, simpler than that of the contours. For example, instead of strokes in a variety of directions, one has to consider only positive or negative peaks. We shall describe briefly two waveform parsing systems. The first one, proposed by HOROWITZ [8.9,10] uses as its input a polygonal approximation. The second, proposed by STOCKMAN, KANAL and KYLE [8.12] derives approximations simultaneously with the parsing. Both of these systems have used as examples of applications medical waveforms: electrocardiograms and carotid pulse waves. They are noteworthy because such waveforms have often been analyzed by purely heuristic techniques which are implemented through fairly complex and lengthy computer programs. Other interesting waveform analyzers have been proposed by ERLICH and FOITH [8.26] and by LOZANO-PEREZ [8.27].

One could also classify speech recognition as a waveform analysis problem in the following manner. Each *phoneme* can be interpreted as part of piecewise approximation in terms of impulse responses of linear filters. It could be mapped into the appropriate symbol for the sound it represents and then parsed by syntactic techniques. An example of this approach has been described by DeMORI [8.28]. The problem is far more difficult than most of the medical waveform recognition problems, since segmentation according to phonemes is much harder than segmentation according to curvature or slope. Speech waveforms are far more complex than, say, electrocardiograms and human recognition is certainly not achieved on the basis of the shape of the waveform. Research in speech recognition has often emphasized modeling of the physical properties of human speech and has created a body of literature, somewhat separate from pictorial pattern recognition. The reader is referred to the review paper by D.R. REDDY [8.29] for a discussion of speech recognition in general. For these reasons we shall limit our discussion to the two methodologies mentioned above.

In the method proposed by HOROWITZ [8.9,10] the slope s of each segment of the approximation is compared with an a priori chosen threshold STOL and a "slope string" is generated in the following way.

If $s > \text{STOL}$ place the symbol / in the string.
If $s < -\text{STOL}$ place the symbol ∖ in the string.
If $|s| \le \text{STOL}$ place the symbol 0 in the string.

In this way the segments of the approximation are mapped into a finite alphabet. In addition a "baseline string" is constructed by comparing the amplitude y of the waveform approximation at the start of a segment with another, a priori chosen tolerance BTOL.

If $y > \text{BTOL}$ place the symbol A in the string.
If $y < \text{BTOL}$ place the symbol - in the string.
If $|y| \le \text{BTOL}$ place the symbol 0 in the string.

Only the slope string is parsed with the baseline string used for semantic information. Recognition of positive and negative peaks can be achieved through regular expressions. Using the notation of Section 8.5 we have

/+0*\+ for a positive peak and
\+0*/+ for a negative peak

provided that no pair 00 occurs in the baseline string for segments corresponding to a peak. Figs.8.14,15 show examples of application of this method to the detection of the peaks in an electrocardiogram.

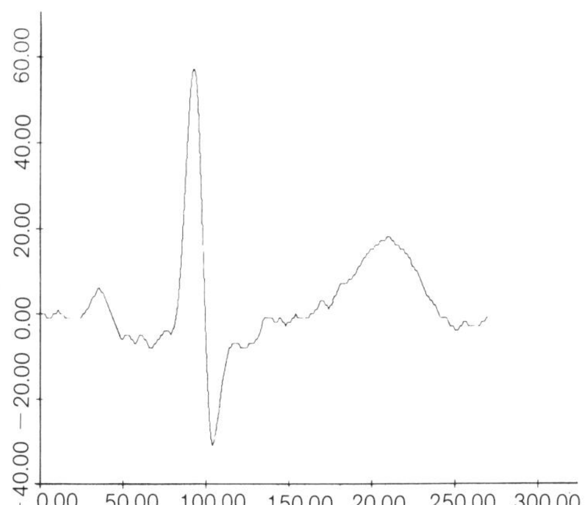

Fig. 8.14 Digitized waveform of an electrocardiogram. (Reproduced from [8.9])

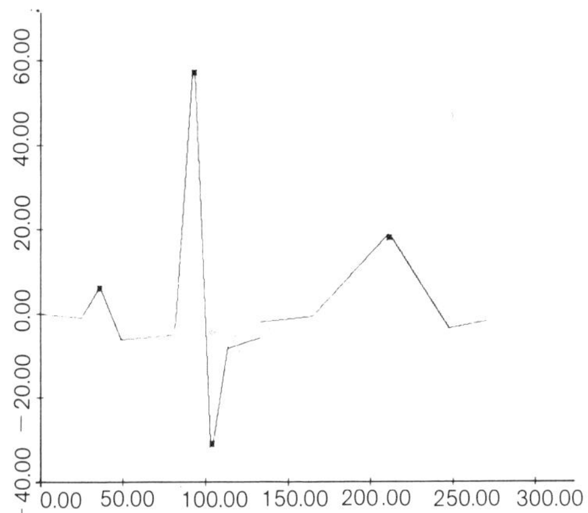

Fig. 8.15 Peaks marked on the polygonal approximation of the waveform of Fig. 8.14. (Reproduced from [8.9])

The system proposed by STOCKMAN et al. [8.12] attempts functional approximation by a pure merging scheme into either lines or parabolas. These are in turn mapped into the set of symbols shown in Table 8.8.

Table 8.8 Notation used in waveform parser

Symbol	Interpretation
u	Upslope: Long line with large positive slope.
P	Medium length line with large positive slope.
N	Medium length line with large negative slope.
p	Medium length line with positive slope.
n	Medium length line with negative slope.
t	Trailing edge: Long line of medium negative slope.
h	Horizontal line (approximately).
c	Cap: High curvature top of convex parabola.
k	Cap with very high curvature.
cc	Low curvature bottom of concave parabola.
cv	Same as cc but with higher curvature.
r	Right half of parabola
ℓ	Left half of parabola

Fig.8.16 shows the segmentation of a carotid pulse wave in terms of these primitives. Up to this point this system is not very different from those

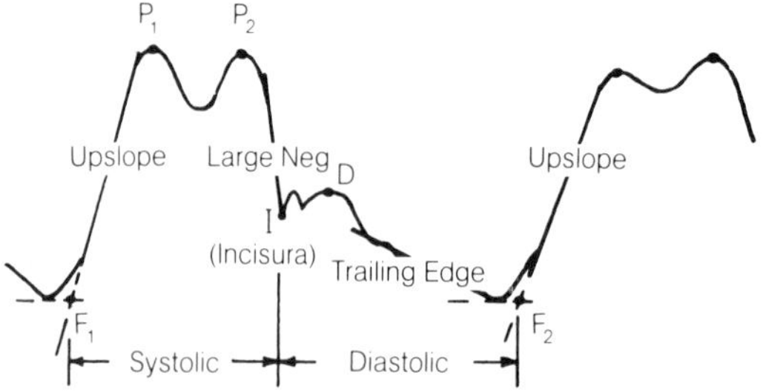

Fig. 8.16 Labeling of arcs of a cartoid pulse waveform. (Reproduced from [8.12])

discussed earlier in this chapter. However, the authors propose that the functional approximation not be performed a priori but during a top down parsing, according to the grammar generating the waveform in question. This certainly reduces the risks of overcommitment to a representation, but it entails an increase in computational costs.

9. Shape Description by Region Analysis

9.1 Introduction

One approach to shape analysis is to perform certain measurements directly on a region or object. Quantities like width, elongation, ratio of perimeter square over area, etc., have all been used as shape descriptors. In general, these convey only gross information and they are inadequate for subtler distinctions, like separating a printed "f" from a "t". An alternative approach is to check the occurrence of certain simple configurations on the input picture. The two characters "f" and "t" could be distinguished from others by the occurrence of a short arc and from each other by the location and orientation of that arc. This "mask matching" may be generalized to the evaluation of weighted integrals over the whole picture. A rigorous way of doing this is offered by the method of moments which is described in the next section.

The description of the shape of complicated objects cannot be done in terms of such scalar measures unless some "simplifying" transformation is used first. Starting with Section 9.3 we describe ways by which an object is transformed into a labeled graph, so that its shape can be expressed through properties of that graph. Such a transformation can be performed in one of two basic ways. The first is *thinning*, where the object, a plane set, is reduced into a line drawing (*a skeleton*) which can then be treated as a graph. The second is *decomposition* where the object is expressed as a union of simpler shapes and is represented by an adjacency or intersection graph of its components.

Thinning techniques are particularly appropriate for applications in which the original data are linelike and in particular where human perception of a shape is in terms of lines or strokes. Such examples include bubble chamber or spark chamber pictures (studied by SHAW [9.1]) and fingerprints (studied by MOAYER and FU [9.2]).

Decomposition techniques do not suffer from this limitation and are applicable to any type of regions. For thin regions their results are in close agreement with those obtained by thinning algorithms. The earliest discussion of such techniques in the literature can be found in the work of FRISHKOPF and HARMON [9.3] and of EDEN [9.4] where cursive script is decomposed into strokes. The extrema of a character in the X and Y directions were used as break points in the first case while Eden's paper describes a generative method.

Most of the subsequent schemes have emphasized the concepts of convexity and concavity and have assumed polygonal approximations of the original object. The reasons for this preference are many. One possible definition of a convex object is that of one having no points of negative curvature along its boundary. Thus, given the importance of curvature in shape perception it is natural to place special emphasis on convex objects as prototypes of simplicity. The many desirable mathematical properties of convex sets [9.5-7] are another factor. Generally speaking, the recognition of the shape of convex objects is much easier than that of arbitrary objects, and there exist a number of techniques applicable only to this class. Many of the simple shape descriptors give far more meaningful results on convex sets than on nonconvex. This is true for measures of elongation, symmetry, etc., even though they can be defined on arbitrary sets.

One possible decomposition is into primary convex subsets (PCS) and this is described in Sections 9.5 and 9.6. A second technique uses for dividing lines of the polygon those connecting certain pairs of concave vertices. The primitive elements are either convex sets or *spirals*, which are defined as polygons which have all their concave vertices adjacent to each other. This is described in Sections 9.7 and 9.8.

The results of the thinning and of decomposition have a number of desirable features.

1) They are translation and rotation invariant and insensitive to registration. Rotation invariance can be controlled through the description of the juxtaposition relations in the final graph. The insensitivity to registration is important for many practical applications including optical page readers, mail sorters, cell counters, etc.

2) To a large extent they are size invariant. Problems may occur only when some of the objects in a picture are so small as to be of the same order of magnitude as what is considered noise for others.

3) They produce usually "anthropomorphic" descriptions, and therefore they can be quite useful for feature extraction.

4) They produce data structures which are particularly appropriate for syntactic or structural pattern recognition. This is not unexpected, since the methodology of decomposition is itself structural.

The only disadvantage of decomposition schemes is that the programs implementing them tend to be quite complex. Such complexity does not necessarily imply slow processing, but it may impose certain difficulties during research and development. Of course, this may be an unavoidable problem with any reasonable shape description scheme. After all, we are trying to imitate a very complex mechanism, the human visual and perceptual processes.

9.2 Masks and Moments

Strictly speaking, these are not structural techniques and they are reviewed here primarily for completeness. In general, a set of masks must be used in order to obtain adequate information about shape. Let $g_i(x,y)$ be the "transparency" of the ith mask. Then the integral of the product $f(x,y)g_i(x,y)$ gives a measure of the degree of matching between the mask and the picture. If both of them are binary, let 1 denote signal for the picture and transparency for the mask and 0 be background for the picture and opaqueness for the mask. Then integration can be replaced by a bitwise AND operation between f and g_i.The matching is usually performed not at a single location but the mask is shifted all over the picture. Let g_i^s be the mask at location s. Then a *feature* F_i is defined as

$$F_i = OR_s(f \text{ AND } g_i^s) \quad . \tag{9.1}$$

Masks of this type have been studied by a number of authors and a detailed review of this approach can be found in [9.8]. Masks of a slightly different kind have been used in some of the commercially available systems for OCR. They can be implemented very easily using shift registers [9.9]. Figure 9.1 shows one set of masks used in the IBM 1975 optical page reader in order to separate T's from I's. Each box represents an individual mask. Those marked by an O output an OR function of their bits, while those marked by A output an AND function. Bits are marked by 1 if the output of the box will be one when they are matched with black pixels, and by 0 if the output will be one when they are matched with blank pixels. All such sets of masks are not information preserving so that there is no guarantee that two very dissimilar figures will not yield the same feature vector for a given set of masks. When the objects to be recognized have limited variations in shape (as it is the case with typewritten or machine printed characters), then it is possible to find a relatively small (less than 100) set of masks which perform the separation.

A set of information preserving masks can be obtained through the method of moments [9.10-15] which are defined as follows:

$$M_{uv} = \int f(x,y)x^u y^v \, dxdy \quad . \tag{9.2}$$

In this case $g_{uv}(x,y) = x^u y^v$. The concept has originated in mechanics, and it can be shown that the sequence of moments for u,v = 0,1,2... is indeed information preserving [9.12]. If f(x,y) is binary, then the moments convey shape related information. We note that M_{00} is the area of the region R where f(x,y) equals 1, while M_{10} and M_{01} are the coordinates of its center of gravity multiplied by its area. In order to obtain features which are location invariant we introduce the *normalized moments*,

$$m_{uv} = \int f(x,y)(x-X)^u (y-Y)^v \, dxdy \quad , \tag{9.3}$$

where

$$X = \frac{M_{10}}{M_{00}} \quad \text{and} \quad Y = \frac{M_{01}}{M_{00}} \quad . \tag{9.4}$$

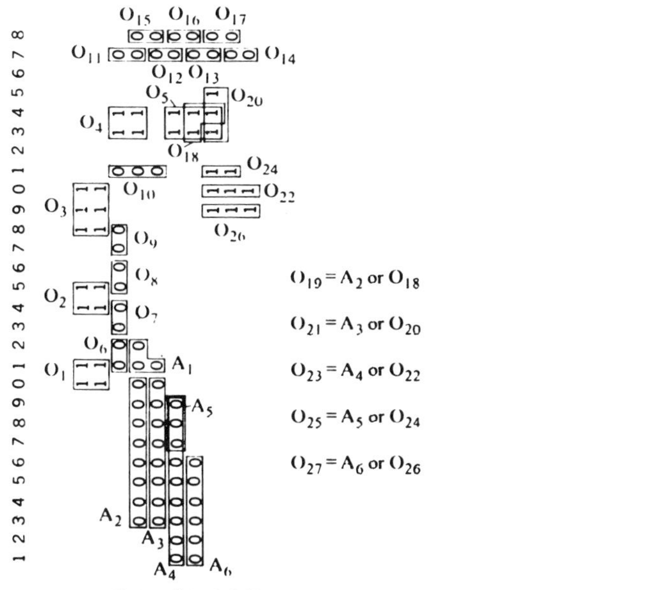

Fig. 9.1a Arrangement of a set of masks of the IBM Optical Page Reader 1975. O and A denote whether the mask acts as an OR or AND function

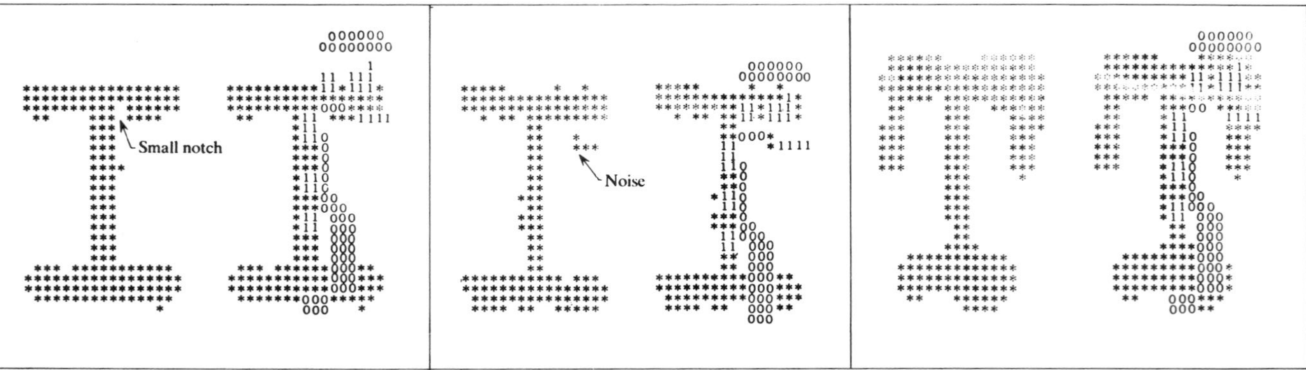

Fig. 9.1b Superposition of the masks on a set of characters. (The particular examples chosen illustrate some of the difficulties of the method). (Reproduced from [9.9])

Features which are invariant under orthogonal transformations and rotation can be obtained by linear combinations of the above [9.12]. For example, the following three features fall in this category.

$$m_{20} + m_{02} \quad , \tag{9.5a}$$

$$(m_{20}-m_{02})^2 + 4m_{11}^2 \quad , \tag{9.5b}$$

$$(m_{30}-3m_{12})^2 + (3m_{21}-m_{03})^2 \quad . \tag{9.5c}$$

ALT [9.10] has proposed transformations which preserve invariance with respect to slanting, etc. Features of this kind can be programmed easily and their evaluation does not require ordering of the boundary points the way Fourier Transforms and syntactic techniques do. Instead, one must have a list of the points where R intersects lines parallel to one of the coordinate axes. Such information can be obtained easily in a number of ways, for example by a raster scan of the picture. The time required for such computations is proportional to the area of R and this, together with the need to find high order powers of x and y, makes the overall computational requirements quite substantial, in spite of the programming simplicity.

The major disadvantage of this methodology is that although the first few moments convey significant information for simple objects, they fail to do so for more complicated ones. Thus they have found limited applications as "total" descriptors. SMITH and WRIGHT [9.14] have used them for ship identification from aerial photographs and recently DUDANI, BREEDING and McGHEE [9.15] for aircraft identification. In both cases the method was tested on relatively small data bases. On the other hand, moments can be quite valuable as supplements to other recognition techniques. For example, they can be used to normalize data before other measurements are taken [9.15]. It can be shown that there always exists a linear transformation which can transform R into a region where the three second order moments (m_{20}, m_{02}, and m_{11}) have given values. CASEY [9.16] proposed the use of the following values

$$m_{20} = m_{02} = k; \quad m_{11} = 0 \quad ; \tag{9.6}$$

for some given arbitrary constant k. This transformation has the effect of making the horizontal width of R approximately equal to its vertical width and also placing R in a more or less upright position. Figure 9.2 shows a transformation of numerals through such a normalization. One can see that the "1"s have been severely distorted, but they are still quite distinct from the other digits. Moments can also be used as features for the simple components resulting from the decomposition algorithms discussed in Sections 9.5-9.8.

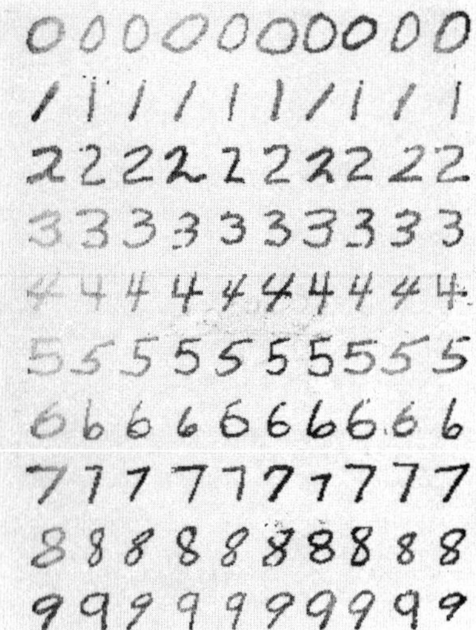

Fig. 9.2 Numerals before a) and after b) normalization by moments [9.16]. Note the significant distortion of the "1"s

Another set of information preserving masks is given by the two-dimensional Fourier transform of f(x,y). The coefficients of the transform convey shape information but their computation is quite expensive. Many of the heuristic measures used for shape can be expressed as masks, in the sense that they evaluate integrals over the area of the object.

9.3 Thinning Algorithms and the Medial Axis Transformation

Most thinning algorithms operate by removing points from the boundary until a set which coincides with its boundary (i.e., has thickness 1 or 2) is found.

It turns out that thinning can also be performed in terms of the Fourier descriptors of the boundary of a region. Algorithm 9.1 is a very simple thinning algorithm.

Algorithm 9.1: Simple Thinning

Input: Plane region R.

Output: Thin region Q.

Notation: IB(P) = Inside boundary of set P. C(P) = Points in IB(P) whose only neighbors are in IB(P) or the complement of P. These sets are shown in Fig.9.3.

Steps:

1. NEWSET = R; OLDSET = ∅;
2. While (OLDSET ≠ NEWSET) do steps 3 and 4;
    3. OLDSET = NEWSET;
    4. NEWSET = Union of C(OLDSET) and OLDSET-IB(OLDSET);

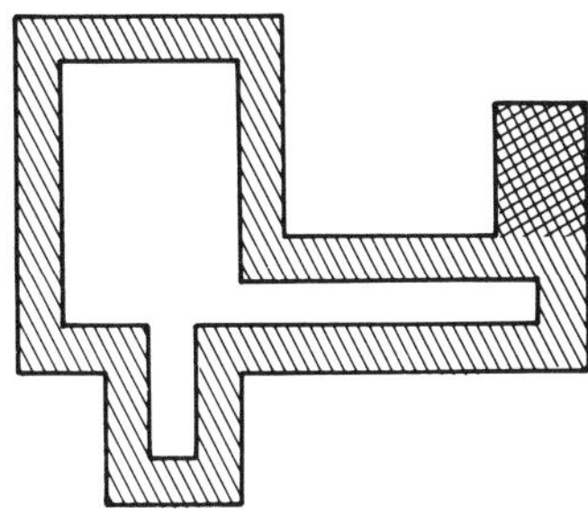

Fig. 9.3 Illustration of the sets IB(P) (lightly shaded) and C(P) (heavily shaded)

-1	-1	-1	-1	-1	-1						
-1	-2	-2	-2	-2	-1						
-1	-2	3	3	-2	-1					1	1
-2	-2	3	3	-2	-1					1	1
-2	-2	3	3	-2	-1					1	1
-1	-2	3	3	-2	-1	-1	-1	-1	-1	-1	-1
-1	-2	-2	-2	-2	2	2	2	2	2	2	-1
-1	-1	-1	2	-1	-1	-1	-1	-1	-1	-1	-1
		-1	2	-1							
		-1	2	-1							
		-1	-1	-1							

Fig. 9.4 Demonstration of thinning by Algoritm 9.1. The number of each point denotes the iteration during which it was examined. The minus sign marks points which are removed

It will terminate when IB(OLDSET) equals C(OLDSET), i.e., when all the points of the OLDSET are boundary points. Figure 9.4 shows a simple example of its application when an 8-point neighborhood is used. The time for each execution if proportional to the picture size times the neighborhood size. It has one disadvantage: It may result in disconnected components. In some cases this may may be desirable since such components would correspond to lobes as shown in Fig.9.5. If a connected "skeleton" is desired, then it must be modified as shown in Algorithm 9.2.

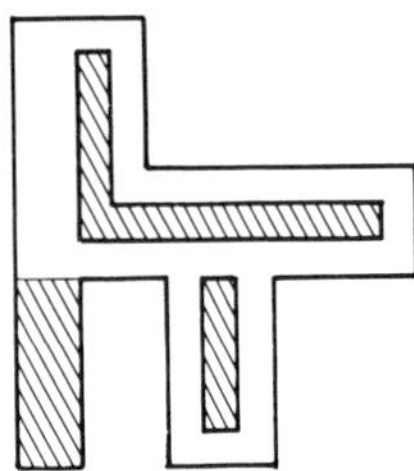

Fig. 9.5 The shaded parts denote the results of the thinning process. Most "lobes" give rise to disconnected components

---

Algorithm 9.2: Modified Thinning

Input - Output - Notation: As in Algorithm 9.1. Also OB(P) = Outside boundary of set P.

Steps:

1. NEWSET = R; OLDSET = $\emptyset$;
2. While (OLDSET $\neq$ NEWSET) do steps 3 and 4;
   3. OLDSET = NEWSET;
   4. NEWSET = Union of C(OLDSET) and (OLDSET-IB(OLDSET)) and (Intersection of OB(C(OLDSET)) and OLDSET);

The last set produces exactly the necessary connections of the components. Figure 9.6 shows examples of its application. Regions of width two can be further reduced by removing all points which have both their E_1P and E_2P neighbors in the set, unless this would change the connectivity of the set. A number of simpler thinning algorithms have been proposed which are applicable under certain restricted conditions. For example, in the case of fingerprint analysis it is not necessary to find the center of the regions, and thick lines may be replaced simply by one of their edges. An automaton performing the thinning in this case has been described by MOAYER and FU [9.2].

The medial axis transformation (MAT), proposed by BLUM, is another thinning algorithm and it is also one of the earliest and probably the most widely studied systematic technique for shape description [9.17-24]. The MAT of a plane figure is defined as follows:

-1	-1	-1	-1	-1	-1							
-1	-2	-2	-2	-2	-1							
-1	-2	3	3	-2	-1						1	1
-1	-2	3	3	-2	-1						1	1
-1	-2	3	3	-2	-1						1	1
-1	-2	3	3	-2	-1	-1	-1	-1	-1	-1	+1	+1
-1	-2	-2	+2	2	2	2	2	2	2	2	2	-1
-1	-1	-1	2	-1	-1	-1	-1	-1	-1	-1	-1	-1
		-1	2	-1								
		-1	2	-1								
		-1	-1	-1								

Fig. 9.6 Demonstration of thinning by Algorithm 9.2. Notation as in Fig. 9.4, except that the plus sign marks points belonging to the intersection of OB(C(P)) and P, where P is the current set

Definition 9.1: For each point X of a set R find its closest neighbors on the boundary B(R). (There always exists at least one). If X has more than one such neighbor, then it is said to belong to the medial axis of R [9.17].

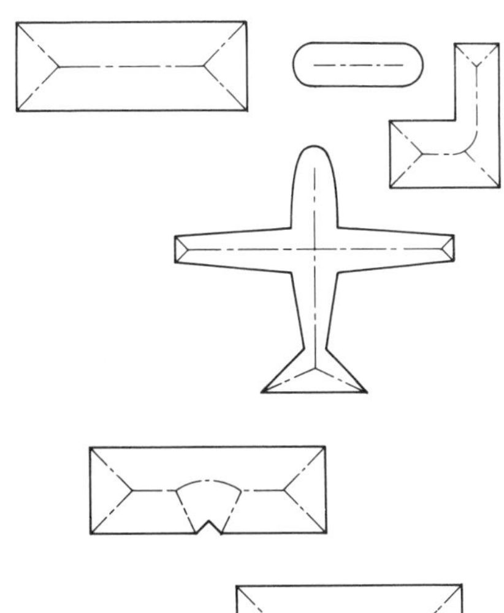

Fig. 9.7 Examples of the medial axis (denoted by —·—·—). The last two figures illustrate the effects of noise

Figure 9.7 shows a few simple examples. The line drawing may be labeled with the distance of each of its points from the boundary, and this allows the reconstruction of the original figure as an envelope of circles centered on that *skeleton*. It is easy to verify certain simple results: The skeleton of a circle is a single point, its center; that of an ellipse, a linear segment, its focal axis between the foci. The skeleton of a polygon consists only of linear segments and parabolic arcs. If the polygon is convex, it consists only of linear segments. If the region is simply connected (i.e., without holes) the skeleton is a tree (in the graph theoretic sense).

The skeleton may be used to derive information about the shape of the original figure. However, except for some rather gross properties (e.g., elongation [9.19]), the process of doing so is by no means straightforward. The computation of the skeleton can be quite time consuming [9.19] and very sensitive to noise as can be seen by comparing the first and last two of the drawings in Fig.9.7. These are problems which are shared by other thinning algorithms as well. One way around them is to perform first a *polygonal approximation* of the original contour. This can certainly remove noise and also allows a relatively fast computation of the skeleton [9.22]. Of course, obtaining such an approximation is a nontrivial task and it can also be quite sufficient in itself for shape description as we have seen in the previous chapter. In some cases the simple smoothing Algorithm 4.2 might be adequate. Another way for reducing the effects of noise is offered by a generalization of the MAT proposed by BLUM and NAGEL [9.25].

Definition 9.2: For each point X of a set R find a circle with center at X which is tangent to the boundary of R and does not intersect any parts of it. This will be called the *touching circle* of X. (It is obviously unique). Let r be a given real number. Then the *r-symmetric axis* of R (abbreviated r-SA) is defined as the locus of all points X having a touching circle with radius greater than r and which has at least two contact points with the boundary.

If r = 0 then the 0-symmetric axis is the same as the medial axis. Fig. 9.8 shows some examples of symmetric axes with finite radius. The effects of noise have been reduced but not eliminated.

PERSOON and FU [9.26] have proposed a method for finding skeletons, which is based on the Fourier descriptors T_n, described in Sections 7.2 and 7.3. Let

$$s(t) = sx(t) + jsy(t) \quad , \tag{9.7}$$

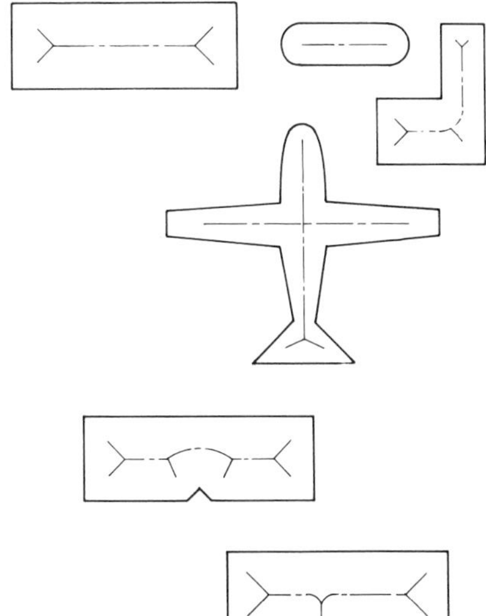

Fig. 9.8 Examples of the r-symmetric axis. The effects of noise have been reduced but not eliminated

be a parametric representation of a curve S with t representing arc length. This may generate another curve B with parametric representation b(t) given by the following equation.

$$b(t) = s(t) + js'(t)w(t) \quad , \tag{9.8}$$

where s'(t) is the derivative of s(t) with respect to t and w(t) a real, positive function. The curve B is a displacement of S by a distance w(t) along the direction of the normal to S, as shown in Fig.9.9. In the first example S is a line with equations

$$sx(t) = \cos(P)t \quad , \quad sy(t) = \sin(P)t \quad ,$$

and B has equations

$$bx(t) = \cos(P)t + w(t)\sin(P) \quad , by(t) = \sin(P)t + w(t)\cos(P) \quad .$$

In the second example

$$sx(t) = R\cos(t/R) \quad , \quad sy(t) = R\sin(t/R) \quad ,$$

and

$$bx(t) = (R-w(t)) \cos(t/R) \quad , \quad sy(t) = (R-w(t)) \sin(t/R) \quad .$$

In both cases curves for variable and constant w(t) have been drawn. In the third example S has discontinuities in its derivative and B is not a "well-formed" curve. One can show that if w(t) is continuous and less than the radius of curvature of S at each point, then B will be a continuous curve. However, it may still cross upon itself as shown in the last example of Fig. 9.9.

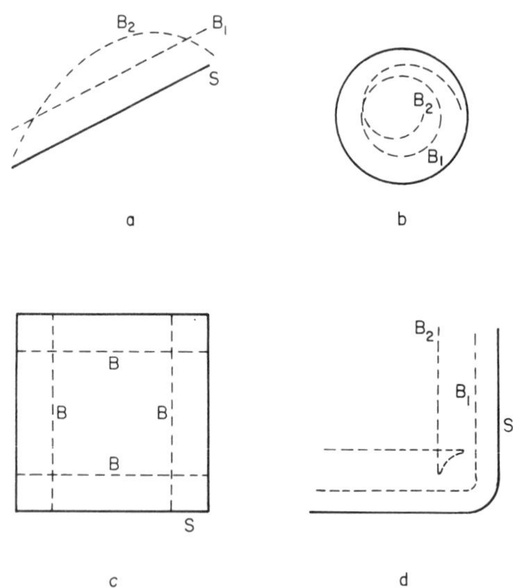

Fig. 9.9a-d Sets of S (solid line) and B curves (broken line) as defined by (9.7,8). a) and b): B_1 is for w(t) = const., while B_2 is for variable w(t). c) w(t) = const. d) The value of w(t) is smaller for B_1 than for B_2

The direction of the displacement depends on the direction of traversal of S. If S is traversed twice, then B consists of two parts as shown in the first two drawings of Fig.9.10. If w(t) is a periodic function with w(0) = w(L) = 0, where L is the length of S, then the B curve resulting from a double traversal of S will consist of a single part because the displacements at the beginning and end of S will be zero. Examples of this form are shown in the last three drawings of Fig.9.10. In this case S resembles a skeleton of B and one can reverse the process by starting with B and attempting to find a curve S related to it by (9.8). If B is the boundary of a region with constant thickness $2w_0$, then taking the Fourier transform of both sides of (9.8) we obtain

$$T_n = U_n\ (1-\frac{2\pi n}{L}w_0) \quad , \tag{9.9}$$

$$T_{-n} = U_n\ (1+\frac{2\pi n}{L}w_0) \quad , \tag{9.10}$$

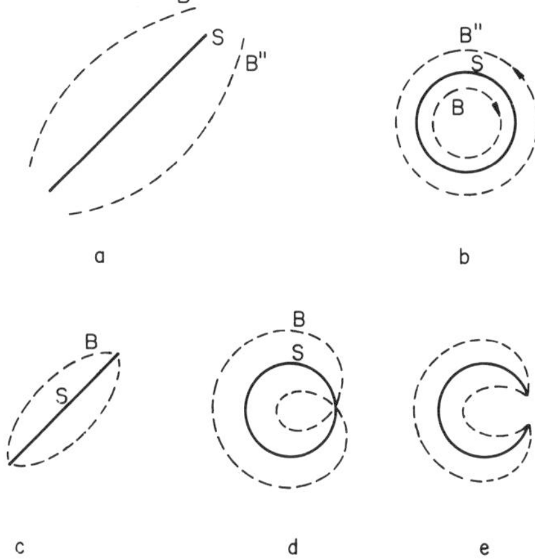

Fig. 9.10a-e B curves produced from multiple traversals of S. When w(t) has a period equal to the length of S, then the resulting curves consist of one piece

where T_n and U_n denote the Fourier transforms of b(t) and s(t), respectively. This ignores actually two small segments of the boundary marked by X in Fig. 9.11. A practical difficulty in its application is that the proper starting point for the parametrization of B is not immediately obvious. This problem can be solved by observing that for small values of w_0, T_n and T_{-n} have approximately the same phase angle. Moving the start of the parametrization by s on a closed curve has simply the effect of multiplying all Fourier coefficients by the quantity $e^{-j(2\pi n/L)s}$. Therefore, for given T_n and T_{-n} a quantity s can be found so that

$$\text{phase}[T_n e^{j(2\pi n/L)(s/2)}] = \text{phase}[T_{-n} e^{-j(2\pi n/L)(s/2)}] \quad . \tag{9.11}$$

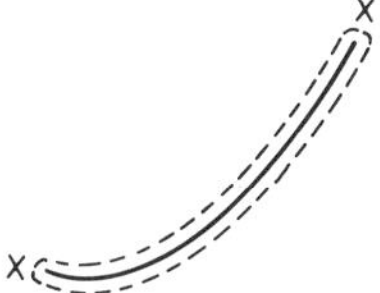

Fig. 9.11 The S curve as a "skeleton" of the B curve. The two small arcs marked by X are ignored

These normalized coefficients can be replaced in either of the two equations (9.9) and (9.10) which can then be solved easily with respect to U_n, and the inverse Fourier transform can be used to find the form of S. Although the method can be applied formally to any contour, its results will be meaningful only if the assumptions on small width are valid. This is illustrated in Fig.9.12 [9.26] where the skeletons found for the "3" and the "5" are indeed the correct ones while that for the "9" is not.

Fig. 9.12 Examples of "skeletons" of numerals obtained by the Fourier Descriptors T_n and U_n. (Reproduced from [9.26])

In conclusion, we may state that thinning algorithms are applicable when the original figure is of a more or less linear structure. For other situations examination of the boundary or decomposition techniques seems more appropriate.

9.4 Forming Graphs and Trees out of Skeletons and Thin Line Images

The results of a thinning algorithm are not graphs, but they can be put in that form without too much trouble. In particular, for the case of the symmetric axis we have:

Definition 9.3: 1) A discrete contact of a touching circle is a set of contiguous contact points (see Fig.9.13). 2) If an axis point has two discrete contacts it is called a *normal point*. 3) If an axis point has one discrete contact it is called an *end point*. A point which is not part of a symmetric axis but is the limit of a sequence of normal points will also be an end point. 4) An axis point with more than two discrete contacts will be called a *branch point*.

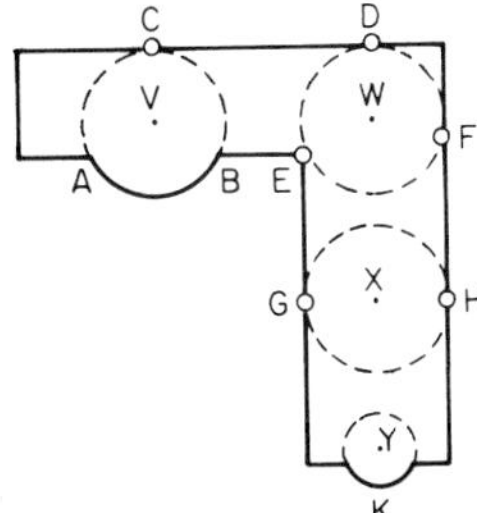

Fig. 9.13 Illustration of Definition 9.3: X and V are normal points. Y an end point and W a branch point

It turns out that end and branch points are always isolated, and therefore they qualify as nodes of a graph. Two nodes will be connected if there is a sequence of normal points between them. It can also be shown that each curvature maximum corresponds to a node of degree one of the MAT graph, and therefore it plays a central role in determining its form. The results of other thinning algorithms can be put in this form if points with at most one direct neighbor are identified as end points, those with exactly two neighbors as normal points, and those with more as branch points. However, it is not true any more that branch points are isolated and some additional criteria may have to be used to generate nodes out of them. The structure of the resulting graph reflects the shape of the original object in a number of ways, provided that the object was indeed of linelike shape. The branches of the graph correspond usually to strokes or lobes. Sharp changes in the boundary direction will cause similar changes in the corresponding branches (Fig.9.14) but this is not always true, especially if the object is not linelike. Nodes of degree one correspond to points of high curvature, typically ends of strokes. Other nodes correspond to points where a number of strokes are congruent.

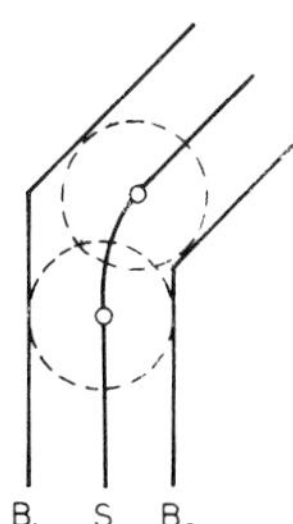

Fig. 9.14 "Bending" of the symmetric axis due to large changes in direction

In many cases when the original images consist mostly of thin lines it is possible to do a graph encoding without going explicitly through the process of finding a skeleton. A scanning of the picture line by line can reveal narrow segments and in this way detect thin lines which are roughly orthogonal to the direction of the scan. For such lines the LAG provides an immediate graph encoding. If a picture has many thin lines in one direction only, then this method is sufficient for encoding into a graph, provided that one or two preliminary scans are made to detect the desired direction.

Algorithm 9.3: Transformation of a LAG into a Tree.

Input: Line adjacency Graph. Path length L corresponding to a tree node.

Output: Tree where each node has four fields: Identifying label, pointer to the preceding node (B-field), pointer to the next node (C-field) and pointers to adjacent "black" regions (S-field).

Steps:

1. Set up an initial tree node with label "." and set its B-field to null.
2. Scan the LAG in a left to right, top to bottom order. If an unmarked node R is found set F = 1 and do block 11. (This block is a recursive procedure TREESET with arguments a starting node S (R for the first call) and a flag F which indicates whether a new tree (F=1) or a subtree (F=0) is formed).

   Begin block 11: Procedure TREESET;

   1. If F = 1 set V = "." If F = 0 V = null. (Initially V is the tree parent of the starting node). Else V = P.
   2. F = 2 (Thus only at the start of execution of TREESET F can be 0 or 1).
   3. If there is a path of length L starting from S and consisting of leftmost children only, then set up a tree node P whose B-field points to V and set up the C-field of V to point to P. Its symbol is chosen by a semantic subroutine according to the shape of the arc corresponding to the path in the LAG. All nodes of the LAG which lie on that path are marked as visited. If there is no such path go to step 5.
   4. If a node in that path has two children (branching point), let R" be the rightmost child. Call TREESET with R" as a starting node and F = 0. Upon return set up a tree node Q_1 with symbol "X", linked through its S-field to the first tree node generated by R". Its B-field should point to P and the C-field of P should point to Q_1.
   5. If any of the nodes in the path has a second parent R', in addition to the one from R (a merging point) do block 12.

Begin block 12;

1. Proceed upwards from R' until a node K is found, which either has no parent in the LAG or whose parent in the LAG has two children.
2. If K is a node with no parents
   then call TREESET with F = 0 and using K as the first node. Upon return create a tree node Q_1 with symbol "*" linked through its S-field to the last tree node generated by K. Its B-field should point to P and the C-field of P should point to Q_1.
   else do block 13.

   Begin block 13; (K's parent in the LAG has two children and therefore it corresponds to a branching point.)
   1. Replace the symbol "X" of the tree node corresponding to the branching point by "-".
   2. Set up tree nodes Q_1 and Q_2, both with symbol "-". Q_1 is a successor of P with S-field pointing to Q_2 and Q_2 is a successor of the last tree node in the right branch starting from K with S-field pointing to Q_1.

   End block 13;

End block 12;

6. Set R to be the leftmost child of the last node in the LAG which generated the tree node P. If there is no such node *return*. Else go to step 1.
7. If the last node of the LAG visited has a child *return* (merge from right). Else set up a tree node with symbol "#" and *return*. (A short path is found).

End block 11: Procedure TREESET;

3. Examine the generators of all tree nodes with B-field "." (Roots of trees). If any two of the generators have the same first coordinate and successive second coordinates (e.g., (4,6) and (4,7)), pair the respective tree nodes and place them in an array A.
4. Remove all duplicates entries of A.
5. For each pair in A, say P and Q, do block 14.

   Begin block 14;
   1. Set up a tree node K with symbol "L" and B-field and S-field both pointing to P and C-field pointing to Q.
   2. Change the B-field of Q to point to K.
   3. Change the S-field of P to point to K.

   End block 14;

This approach has been followed by MOAYER and FU [9.2] in the analysis of fingerprints. The LAG can be further compacted by establishing a new graph where the nodes correspond to arcs of a given length and are linked to nodes representing the previous and following arcs as well as nodes representing neighboring arcs. By using different types of links one can assure that the resulting graph is a tree. This restriction has certain advantages in subsequent processing by syntactic techniques. We present here a generalization of their algorithm in terms of a line adjacency graph. Paths of the LAG are mapped into tree nodes and the LAG nodes of such a path will be called the *generators* of the respective tree node. Tree nodes are also generated without corresponding paths in order to describe congruence of other paths. We assume that no node in that graph has more than two parents or more than two children. Figure 9.15 shows a tree produced from a thin-line region. Lateral branches correspond to links via the S-field.

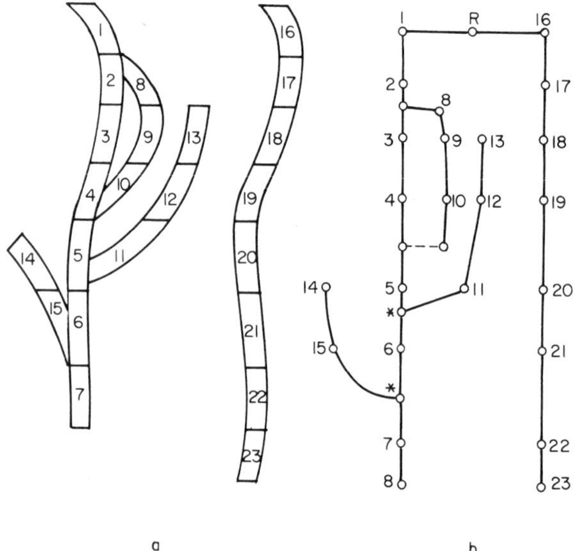

Fig. 9.15 A thin line picture a) and the tree b) produced by the application of Algorithm 9.3. The numbers mark corresponding parts of the picture and the tree

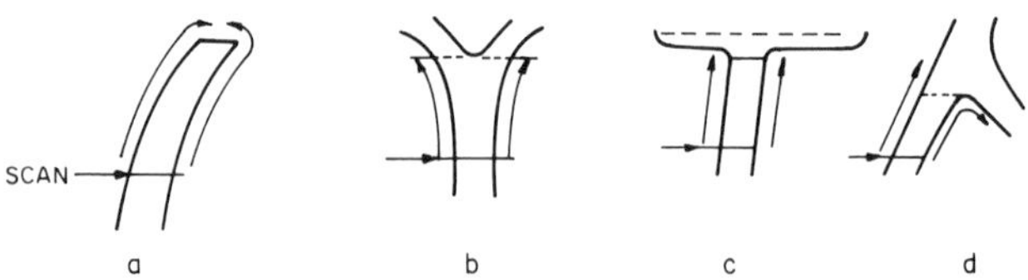

Fig. 9.16 Combination of scans and boundary tracings according to STALLINGS' method [9.27,28]

A somewhat related approach has been used by STALLINGS [9.27,28] in the analysis of Chinese characters. A line-by-line scan is performed until a narrow segment is found. Then both sides of the boundary are traced, until one of these events happens: 1) The two tracers meet. This signifies the tip of a stroke (Fig.9.16a). 2) "White" points appear between the tracers. This signifies a fork (Fig.9.16b). 3) There is a significant increase in the length of the strip between the two tracers. This signifies an intersection of strokes (Fig.9.16c). 4) One of the tracers reverses direction. This signifies an inverted fork (Fig.9.16d). Forks and intersections correspond to nodes of the graph. After the operation of all the tracers is completed, sequences of their endpoints are scanned as shown in Fig.9.17 and labeled appropriately to indicate which "strokes" meet at each node. The resulting graph is then labeled according to the direction of its branches and other criteria.

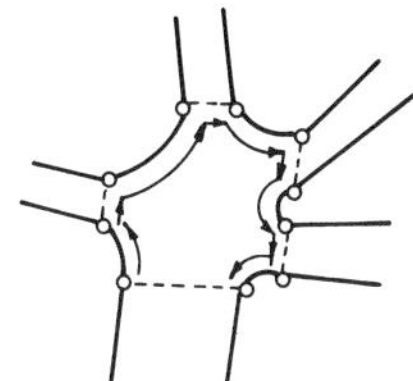

Fig. 9.17 Definition of nodes in the graph produced from a picture according to STALLINGS [9.27,28]

The above three techniques show that graphs obtained from the encoding of pictorial data can carry many labels. This is also true for graphs obtained from the segmentation of pictures (Chap.3) as well as the decomposition techniques discussed in Sections 9.5-8. It is useful to introduce a simple concept, that of a *label stack* in order to describe such labels. A given entity can have more than one label, and these can be organized in a stack where each label occupies a level. For example, each region in a picture may be given five labels: two coordinates of its center of gravity, area, ratio of area over boundary length square, and color. They can be placed in a label stack in the above order. We may assume that this set of labels gives all the available information about the regions. If we remove the top two labels from the stack, the remaining ones give location invariant information. By ignoring the top three we achieve location and size invariance, etc. Another example is provided by a classification tree. This produces a classification key which can be thought of as a stack of labels. The more generic descriptors are placed in the bottom of the stack. This is in effect an encoding of a classification tree into a string. Obviously, we can have *stack-labeled graphs* with stacks of labels assigned to either their branches, or nodes, or both. Such graphs can be used directly for shape description.

An example of the direct use of graphs can be found in the work of E.T. LEE [9.29], where the length of the arms and the angles between arms of a thinned image of chromosome have been used for shape description.

9.5 Decomposition into Primary Convex Subsets

Decomposition techniques are prime examples of structural methodologies and are based on the assumption that shape perception is a hierarchical process [9.30-32]. The first step in their study is to define what we shall use as the simplest forms of shape, namely the *shape primitives*. One possibility is to use convex sets as those of the simplest shape form, and we shall devote this and the next section to this approach. Given this assumption we are faced with two major tasks. One is the decomposition of complex shapes into simpler ones. The other is the further analysis of the primitive shapes. Both tasks can be facilitated if we limit our attention to polygons. Expressing a polygon as a finite union of its convex subsets is a problem without a unique solution. For the poloygon of Fig.9.18 we have the following representations, among others.

(ABFG) U (HDEG)
(ABCH) U (HCEG) U (CDE)
(ABCH) U (KJML) U (HDEG)   etc.

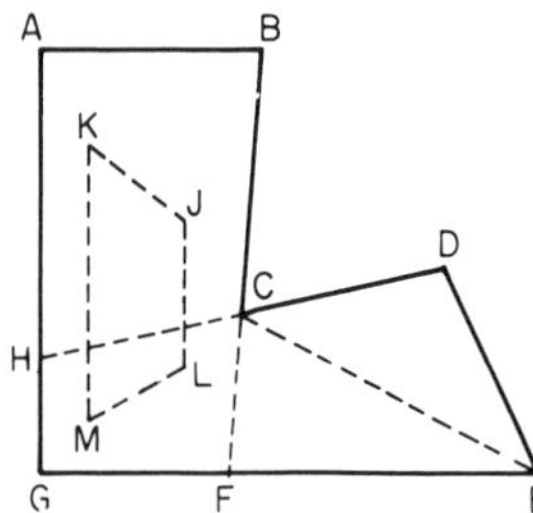

Fig. 9.18 Expression of a polygon as a union of some of its convex subsets

Thus we must impose some additional restrictions. Without any loss of generality we consider only *oriented polygons* whose sides have been assigned a direction in a clockwise manner in the outside boundary and counterclockwise in the interior (Fig.9.19). We introduce the following definitions:

Definition 9.4: A basic halfplane of an oriented polygon P is a halfplane defined by the right side of the extension of a directed polygon side (Fig. 9.19).

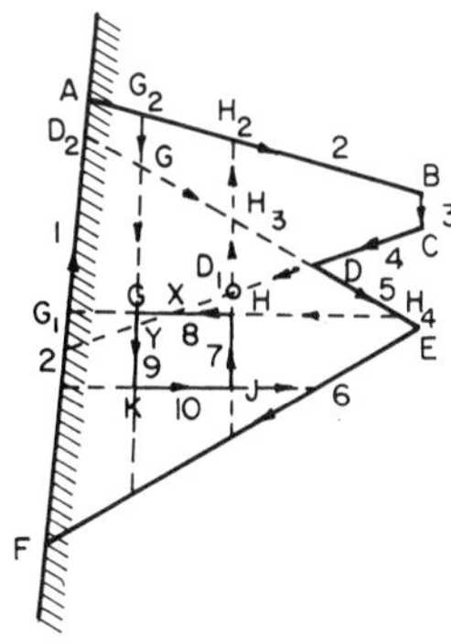

Fig. 9.19 An oriented polygon, with one basic halfplane shown by shading. Numbers mark basic halfplanes (and sides), letters mark polygon vertices and the other nodes of the fundamental graph

Definition 9.5: A Q-subset of an oriented polygon P is the intersection of some of its basic halfplanes, provided that it is contained in P.

In Fig.9.18 the polygons (ABFG), (HDEG) and (HCFG) are Q-subsets while (KJLM) and (CDE) are not. In Fig. 9.19 (AH_2HG_1) is not a Q-subset (among others) while (D_1H_2BCD) is. A trivial consequence of the definitions is that.

Proposition 9.1: A Q-subset is always a convex polygon, and it requires at least three basic halfplanes for its definition.

Definition 9.6: The *fundamental graph* of an oriented polygon is the directed graph formed by the extensions of its sides, provided such extensions do not go outside the polygon. A *convex circuit* of such a graph is a circuit where the directed angle between any two successive branches is less than or equal to 180 degrees.

In Fig.9.19 the legal extensions are shown by broken lines. The line XYZ is not a legal extension. $D_2DXG_1D_2$ is a convex circuit; $D_2H_3H_2BCDXG_1D_2$ is not.

Proposition 9.2: A Q-subset is equivalent to a convex circuit of the fundamental graph.

Definition 9.7: The *formative list* of a Q-subset A of P is the list of the indices of the basic halfplanes of P which are required to form A and only those. The *exclusion list* of A is the list of the indices of those halfplanes which if added to the above intersection would change the form of A.

For example, in Fig.9.19 the Q-subset ($D_2DXG_1D_2$) has the formative list {1,4,5,8} and the exclusion list {7,9}. We can now form a partially ordered sequence of Q-subsets as following. We start with an empty exclusion list and then form successive lists by adding one, two, three, etc., halfplanes. This structure can be expressed as a tree (*Q-tree*) whose nodes correspond to Q-subsets. Fig.9.20 shows an example. Note that successors of nodes corresponding to unbound sets are not given. Also the addition to the exclusion list of a halfplane which does not appear in the formative list does not modify the corresponding polygon. All subsequent sets must be unbounded because their formative lists contain at most two halfplanes.

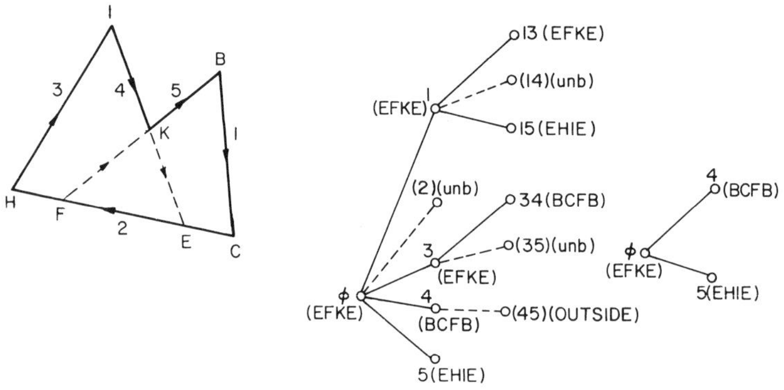

Fig. 9.20 A polygon, its Q-tree, and its reduced Q-tree

Note that the tree has been "trimmed" so that each exclusion list label appears only once (e.g., 51 is not shown because it is equivalent to 15). The tree can be further trimmed by removing all leaves which are the same as a node in the previous level. This is easy to verify by checking the formative lists. The leaves of the reduced Q-tree have the property that they are convex subsets of the polygon formed as intersections by the smallest possible number of halfplanes. They are in a sense maximal Q-subsets. One may also distinguish minimal Q-subsets as elements of the reduced Q-tree which have no nonempty predecessors. Thus we have:

Definition 9.8: A *primary (convex) subset* of an (oriented) polygon P is a set corresponding to a leaf of its reduced Q-tree while a *nucleus* of an (oriented) polygon P is a Q-subset which has no nonempty predecessors.

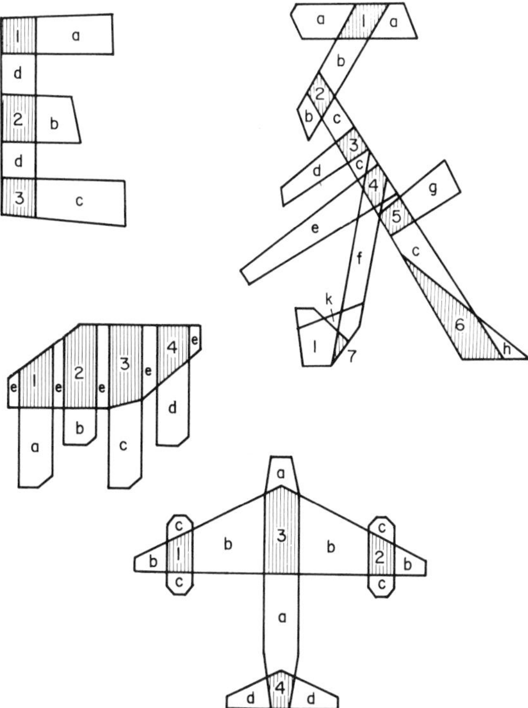

Fig. 9.21 Decomposition into primary subsets (marked by letters) and nuclei (shaded and marked by numbers) of the polygonal outlines of some common objects. The one on the top right is the Chinese ideogram for "pig"

Figure 9.21 shows the primary subsets (labeled by lower case letters) and the nuclei (shaded and numbered) for a number of polygons approximating the outlines of common objects. One can see that these decompositions have very much an intuitive appeal and at the same time can be derived in a straightforward formal way. It is also obvious that their form is independent of the indexing of the sides of the polygon. Not surprisingly, primary subsets form a cover for a polygon. Indeed

Theorem 9.1: The union of the primary subsets of P equals P.

Proof: Since primary subsets are Q-subsets by Definition 9.5 their union does not contain any points not in P. On the other hand, every point x of P belongs to some intersection Y of its basic halfplanes (at least three of them). If Y is not a subset of P it must be so because there is at least one side of P between x and one of the vertices of Y. But then the basic halfplane defined by that side may be added to the intersection and so forth until Y becomes a subset of P. The latter must be either a primary subset or a subset of one, and therefore every point of P belongs to a primary subset. Q.E.D.

Computationally it is not easy to find the primary subsets as basic halfplane intersections. On the other hand, we have the following obvious result.

Proposition 9.3: A *nucleus* corresponds to an *elementary circuit* of the fundamental graph while a *primary subset* corresponds to a convex circuit which cannot be extended without going outside the polygon.

Finding the circuits of a directed planar graph is not a very difficult problem, especially if we have an estimate of their number.

Proposition 9.4: A nonconvex polygon P has at most as many primary subsets as twice the number of its concave angles. This bound can be reached.

Proof: By the definition of Q-subsets a primary subset must have in its formative list at least one basic halfplane corresponding to a concave angle. Otherwise it would contain points not in P. On the other hand, two primary subsets cannot have formative lists which differ only on the basic halfplanes contributed by convex angles. Indeed the intersection of P with the (common) halfplanes contributed by the concave angles must be a convex set (if it were not it would contradict the convexity of the primary subsets). But then this set would coincide with the two primary subsets. Hence each primary subset can be uniquely identified with one side of at least one concave angle. This completes the proof for the bound because each concave angle can have at most two distinct sides. Figure 9.20 shows an example where the bound is reached. Q.E.D.

Proposition 9.5: A polygon has a fundamental graph with at most n(n-3) convex circuits.

Proof: A polygon with n vertices can have at most n/2 of them concave and therefore can have at most n primary subsets. Since each subset has 3 sides the reduced Q-tree has at most (n-3) levels. A tree with n leaves and (n-3) levels can have at most n(n-3) nodes. Thus a polygon can have at most n(n-3) Q-subsets. Because of Proposition 9.2 we have completed the proof. Q.E.D.

Note that the fundamental graph can have at most n(n-1)/2 nodes so that we are faced with a situation where the number of circuits to be examined is comparable to the number of nodes. Thus it is quite feasible computationally to find the primary convex subsets of a given polygon. SHAMOS [9.33,34] has proposed recently a number of efficient algorithms for performing geometrical operations by computer, and it is likely that they could be used to develop fast algorithms for finding the primary subsets.

Unfortunately, primary subsets have also a number of disadvantages and do not always produce results which agree with our intuition. Small boundary details can produce primary sets of significant area (Fig.9.22). The requirement of convex decomposition can be too strict, since it does not allow one to use as primitives simple shapes like the minisque of Fig.9.23. This, in effect, excludes slightly curved strokes which are met often in cursive script.

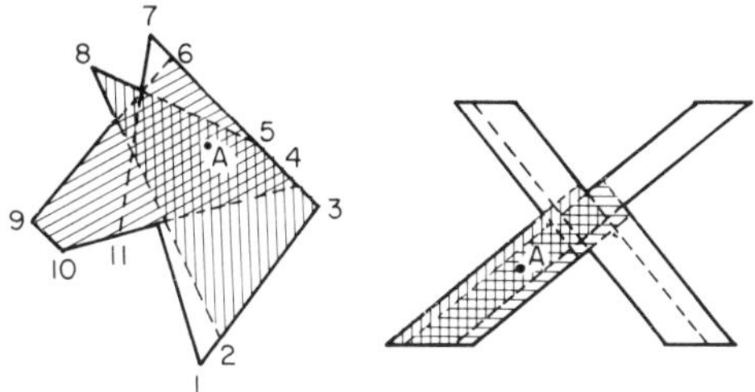

Fig. 9.22a,b Redundancy introduced by primary subsets. a) Point A belongs to five PCS: (4,6,9,10,4), (4,7,11,4), (2,3,5,8,2) etc. (The reader may try to identify the other two). b) Point A belongs to three PCS. PCS are identified by common vertex labeling and/or shading

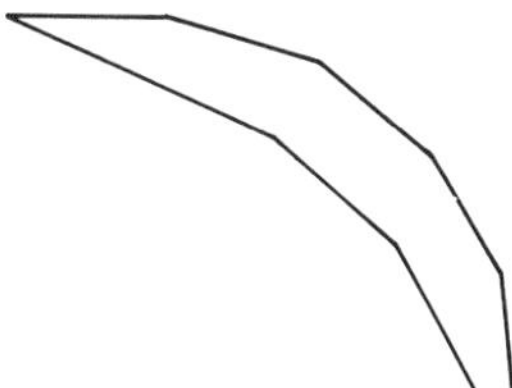

Fig. 9.23 A "simple" shape requiring decomposition

It is not too surprising that a certain relationship exists between the MAT and the PCS. Indeed, let us define as *primary branches* those branches of the MAT graph which connect nodes of degree 2 or greater at both ends. Then, for many shapes, there is a one-to-one correspondence between primary branches and primary convex subsets.

9.6 Primary Graphs

In order to use the decomposition into primary convex subsets for shape description, it is necessary to establish appropriate data structures. These can be graphs with nodes corresponding to primary subsets and branches connecting intersecting nodes. It is easy to see that such a representation fails to distinguish among substantially different shapes (Fig.9.24a,b). On the other hand, the introduction of nodes corresponding to nuclei removes some of the difficulties (Fig.9.24c). Thus we define [9.31,32]:

Definition 9.9: The *primary graph* of a polygon P is a labeled bigraph (a bipartite graph) whose nodes correspond to the primary subsets (labeled P) and to the nuclei (labeled N) and nodes of different labels corresponding to intersecting sets are connected.

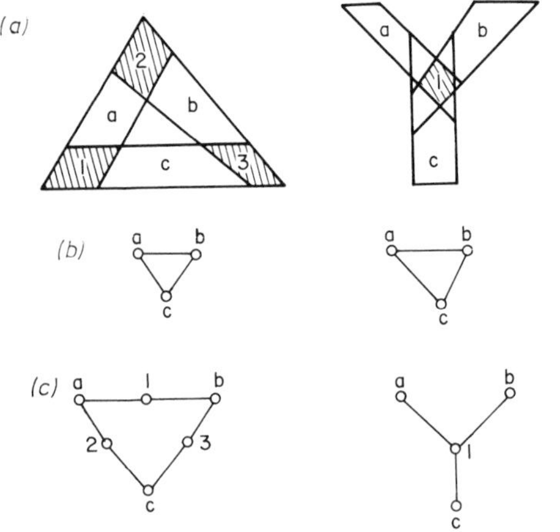

Fig. 9.24a-c. Illustration of the need to use nuclei in describing a polygon by a graph

Figure 9.25 shows examples of primary graphs corresponding to the decompositions of Fig.9.21. We can label nodes of primary graphs as follows:

1) Kind (P or N)
2) Number of vertices
3) Area
4) Direction of major axis of inertia
5) Coordinates of center of gravity

Note that a description involving only labels 1-4 is translation invariant. Labels 1-3 are also rotation invariant and labels 1-2 also size invariant. The controlled introduction of invariance under certain types of transformations is a major advantage of such representations. An important set of labels for primary graphs involves the formative and exclusion list. F_N, E_N, F_P, E_P denote these lists for a nucleus and a primary set. Then we can define two quantities.

$$S(P,N) = |F_P \cap F_N| \tag{9.12a}$$

$$T(P,N) = |E_P \cap F_N| \quad . \tag{9.12b}$$

Note that by definition

$$E_P \cap E_N = E_N \quad .$$

Each branch then can be labeled by these quantities. T(P,N) seems to be the more important of the two. Figure 9.26 repeats the graphs of Fig.9.25 with multiple branches denoting the value of T(P,N). Examining these labels we can distinguish among three fundamental types of intersection among primary subsets: L, T and X (Fig.9.27). This is based on the following simple results.

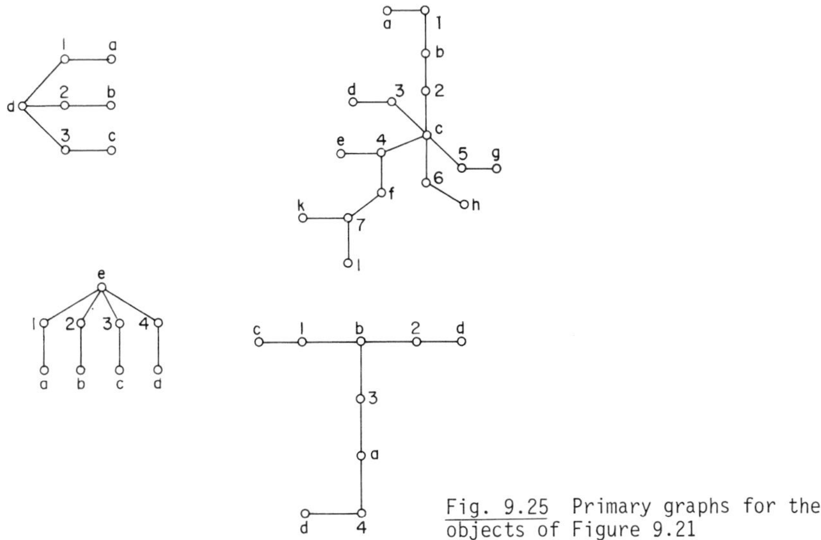

Fig. 9.25 Primary graphs for the objects of Figure 9.21

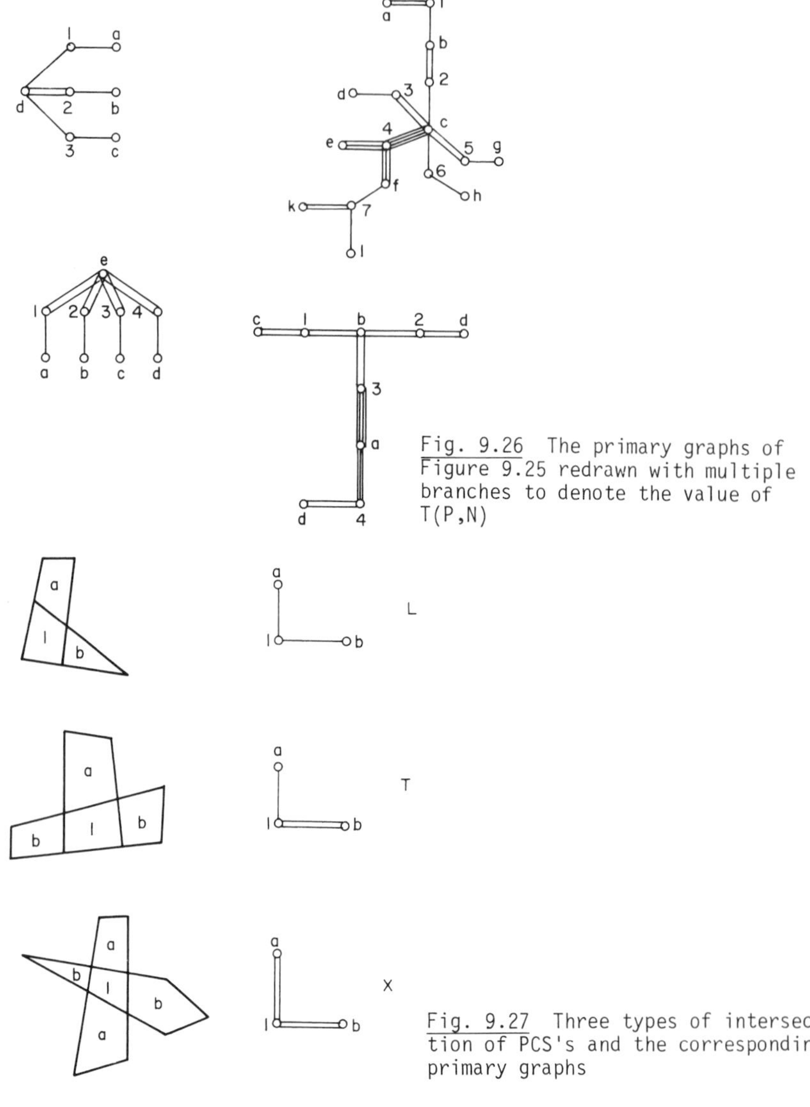

Fig. 9.26 The primary graphs of Figure 9.25 redrawn with multiple branches to denote the value of T(P,N)

Fig. 9.27 Three types of intersection of PCS's and the corresponding primary graphs

Proposition 9.6: If a nucleus is common to k primary subsets $P_1, P_2, \ldots P_k$ then

$$\sum_{j=1}^{k} S(P_i, N) \geq |F_N| \quad . \tag{9.13}$$

Proposition 9.7: Always

$$S(P,N) + T(P,N) = |F_N| \quad . \tag{9.14}$$

We can see now that an X-type configuration is characterized by any of the following (equivalent) relations:

$$S(P_1,N) + S(P_2,N) = |F_N| \tag{9.15a}$$

$$T(P_1,N) + T(P_2,N) = |F_N| \tag{9.15b}$$

$$S(P_1,N) = T(P_2,N) \tag{9.15c}$$

$$S(P_2,N) = T(P_1,N) \tag{9.15d}$$

An L or T-type configuration is characterized by

$$S(P_1,N) + S(P_2,N) > |F_N| \tag{9.16a}$$

$$T(P_1,N) + T(P_2,N) < |F_N| \quad . \tag{9.16b}$$

Furthermore, an L-type configuration has the property that

$$T(P_1,N) = T(P_2,N) = 1 \tag{9.17}$$

Algorithm 9.4 can distinguish among types of intersections.

Algorithm 9.4: Classification of Intersections of Primary Sets.

Steps:

If ($T(P_1,N) = 1$) then do block 11;

Block 11: If $T(P_2,N) = 1$ then return (L); else return (T)

else do block 12.

Block 12: If $T(P_1,N) + T(P_2,N) < |F \text{ sub } N|$ then return (T); else return (X).

9.7 Decomposition at Concave Angles

In order to eliminate some of the disadvantages of the decomposition into primary convex subsets it is necessary to expand the class of primitives. We may allow as primitives nonconvex sets provided that their boundary can be divided into two contiguous arcs where the curvature does not change sign.

A minisque has this property so it can now be admitted as a primitive element. The most complex figure satisfying this condition is obviously a winding spiral. This leads us to a fast method which examines only the boundary of a polygon. The subsequent analysis follows closely the work of FENG and PAVLIDIS [9.35-37]. We define a *concave arc* to be a sequence of concave vertices uninterrupted by convex vertices. If a is used to denote a convex corner and b a concave corner then the *angular characteristic* of the polygon P_n is defined as

$$AC(P_n) = x_1 x_2 \dots x_n \quad ,$$

where x_i equals a or b. Without loss of generality we may assume that $x_1 = a$ always. Then a sequence of b's, a *b-string* will correspond to a concave arc. A convex polygon has no b-strings while polygons with exactly one b-string (concave arc) are shown in Fig.9.28. We shall call such polygons *spirals*. Formally, we have:

Definition 9.10: A simply connected polygon P_n is *decomposable* if its angular characteristic $AC(P_n)$ contains at least two b-strings.

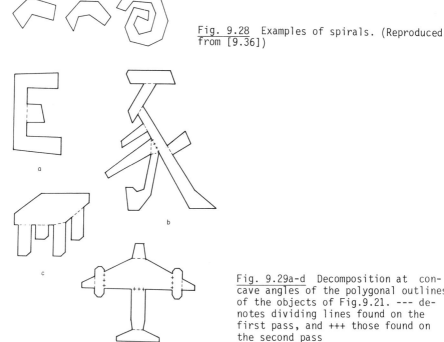

Fig. 9.28 Examples of spirals. (Reproduced from [9.36])

Fig. 9.29a-d Decomposition at concave angles of the polygonal outlines of the objects of Fig.9.21. --- denotes dividing lines found on the first pass, and +++ those found on the second pass

This definition implies that if a polygon is convex or a spiral, then it is nondecomposable. Such a decomposition can map a picture into a graph by having nodes correspond to components and branches linking nodes if the respective components share a boundary. Figure 9.29 illustrates this approach applied to the same objects as those used in Fig.9.21 for decomposition into PCS's. The dotted lines in the figure are the dividing lines. We shall describe next a decomposition procedure which uses as dividing lines those joining vertices belonging to adjacent concave arcs; first for polygons without holes (simply connected) and later for polygons with holes. The scheme is recursive and the term "nondecomposable element" will refer to a subset which is of simple form and will not be processed any more at a given step. It may well be analyzed further in subsequent steps. The term *baseline* will refer to the line dividing two components. When a line joining two concave vertices from different arcs is found, it is a candidate for a baseline provided that it satisfies the following two criteria: 1) The line must not lie totally outside the polygon (Fig.9.30a), and 2) The line must not intersect the boundary of the polygon (Fig.9.30b). The first condition can be checked in a number of ways. The fastest method is one based on the measurement of the oriented angles shown in Fig.9.31. The concave angle w between the original sides is greater than the angle θ between the line BB' and either of the sides when BB' lies within the polygon, while the opposite is true if BB' is outside.

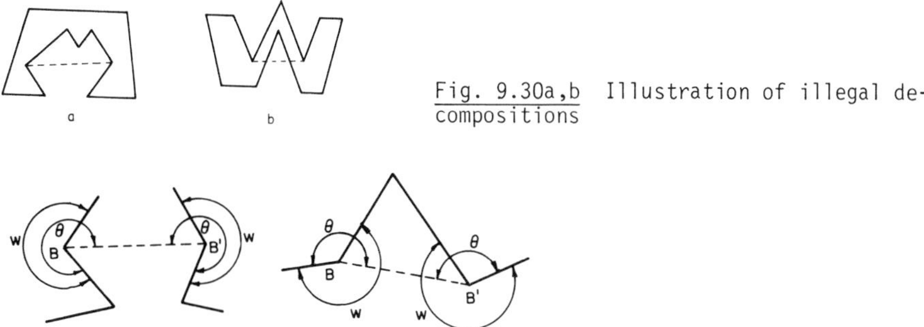

Fig. 9.30a,b Illustration of illegal decompositions

Fig. 9.31 Comparison of the angles θ and w shows whether BB' lies inside the polygon

The second condition can be verified on the basis of the following formula. Let (x_1,y_1), (x_2,y_2) and (x_3,y_3), (x_4,y_4) be the endpoints of a pair of segments. Define four quantities:

$$S_1 = \text{sign}\,[y_1(x_3-x_4) - x_1(y_3-y_4) - (y_4x_3-x_4y_3)] \quad ,$$

$$S_2 = \text{sign}\,[y_2(x_3-x_4) - x_2(y_3-y_4) - (y_4x_3-x_4y_3)] \quad ,$$

$$S_3 = \text{sign}\,[y_3(x_1-x_2) - x_3(y_1-y_2) - (y_2x_1-x_2y_1)] \quad ,$$

$$S_4 = \text{sign}\,[y_4(x_1-x_2) - x_4(y_1-y_2) - (y_2x_1-x_2y_1)] \quad .$$

It can be shown that the two segments will intersect as shown in Fig.9.32 if and only if S_1 and S_2 have opposite signs and the same is also true for S_3 and S_4. Thus, one must check the sign of at most four quantities to verify that that two linear segments do not intersect.

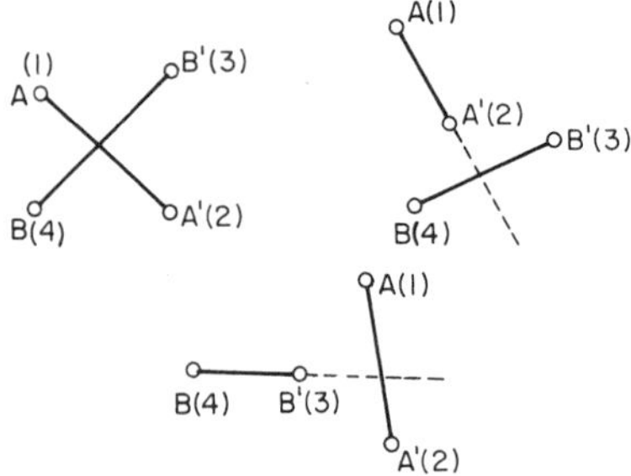

Fig. 9.32 Checks of the relative location of two linear segments

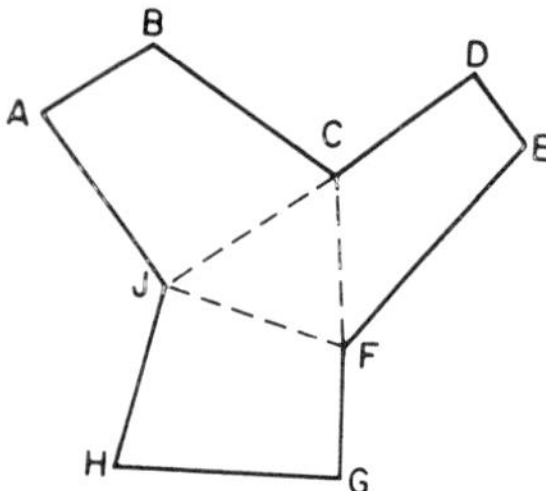

Fig. 9.33 Nonuniqueness of representation by polygons obtained from decomposition at concave angles. (Reproduced from [9.37])

In general, the decomposition will not be unique because there may be more than one legal dividing line between the vertices of two successive concave arcs. This ambiguity may be removed by choosing the shortest among such lines. However, one more source of nonuniqueness remains if we remove subpolygons as they are found. For example, the polygon of Fig.9.33 can have either of the following three representations:

(ABCDEFJA) and (JFGHJ) ,
(ABCFGHJA) and (CDEFC) ,
(ABCJA) and (HJCDEFGH) .

This ambiguity may be removed if we find all legal dividing lines and then proceed with the decomposition in an order independent criterion, for example, in order of the length of the dividing lines starting with the shortest. It is easy to verify on the basis of elementary geometrical considerations that no legal dividing lines ever cross each other, and therefore such a procedure will not encounter any impasses. We have formally.

Proposition 9.8: No dividing lines cross each other.

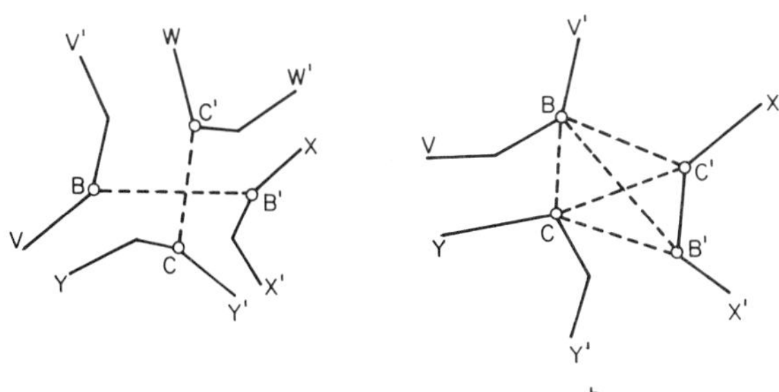

Fig. 9.34a,b Drawings used in the proof of Proposition 9.8

Proof: Suppose they do (Fig.9.34a). This means that arcs vv' and xx' correspond to successive b-strings, and therefore there must be at least a pair of endpoints which are joined by convex angles. Hence either ww' or yy' must coincide with one of them (Fig.9.34b). It is well-known that the sum of the diagonals of quadrangle exceeds the sum of the lengths of each of the pairs of opposite sides. Thus in Fig.9.34b we have:

$$(BB') + (CC') > (BC') + (CB') \quad . \tag{9.18}$$

Because of the minimum length of legal dividing lines we must have

$$(CC') \leq (CB') \quad \text{and} \quad (BB') \leq (BC') \quad . \tag{9.19}$$

But according to (9.18) it is not possible for both of these inequalities to be true. This contradiction resulted because we assumed that the configuration of Fig.9.34b is possible. Therefore, no dividing lines may cross.

Q.E.D.

Algorithm 9.5: Decomposition at Concave Angles

Input: Ordered list of the corners of simply connected polygon P.

Output: Description of nondecomposable subpolygons and their adjacency relations.

Arrays: i(*) starting vertex of concave arcs, j(*) last vertex of concave arcs, L(x,y) length of line joining vertices x and y, I(X) vertex where baseline between X^{th} and $X + 1^{th}$ starts, J(X) vertex where previous baseline ends, M(X) length of previous baseline.

Functions: INSIDE (x,y) returns true if line x,y lies inside the polygon, INTERSECT (x,y) returns true if line (x,y) intersects the polygon.

Steps:

```
1. Find Angular Characteristic of P, rearrange (if necessary) vertices so
   that the first one is convex and fill arrays i(*) and j(*).
2. Do block 21 while m > 1.
     Begin block 21;
     1. For k = 1 to m do block 22;
          Begin block 22;
          1. Set I(k) = 0, J(k) = 0, M(k) = maximum;
          2. For x = i(k) to j(k) do block 23;
               Begin block 23;
               For y = i(k+1) to j(k+1) do block 24;
                    Begin block 24;
                    1. If {L(x,y) < M(k)} & {INSIDE(x,y)} & {INTERSECT(x,y)} then
                            I(k) = x, J(k) = y, M(k) = L(x,y)
     End blocks 24, 23, 22;
     2. Sort M(k) in increasing order and let r(*) be the permutation mapping
     the new ordering onto the original.
     3. Set a = 0.
     4. For k = 1 to m do block 41 while I[r(k)] > 0.
          Begin block 41;
          1. Set a = a + 1, b = I[r(k)], c = J[r(k)].
          2. Define the polygon P(a) by the vertices b, b+1,...c-1,c.
          3. Establish the adjacency of P(a) and P.
          4. Modify P by replacing vertices b+1,b+2,...c-1 by the linear seg-
             ment joining b and c.
          End block 41;
     5. Inspect all vertices of P and redefine its Angular Characteristic.
     End block 21;
```

These concepts are implemented by Algorithm 9.5. The following result from elementary geometry (see also [9.35]) guarantees that the algorithm will indeed terminate.

Proposition 9.9: If a polygon has at least two concave angles which do not share any sides, then there exists a pair of such angles which can be joined by a legal dividing line.

In this way we know that as long as m exceeds 1 at least one decomposition will be performed and therefore the number of vertices will decrease by at least one. Because their initial number is finite the algorithm will eventually terminate.

9.8 Further Decomposition and Shape Description

In certain cases it might be necessary to further decompose a spiral into convex subsets. This can be performed easily by the Algorithm 9.6. Fig.9.35 shows the dividing lines used by it. It can be easily shown that no two bisectrices intersect inside the polygon and therefore the above decomposition

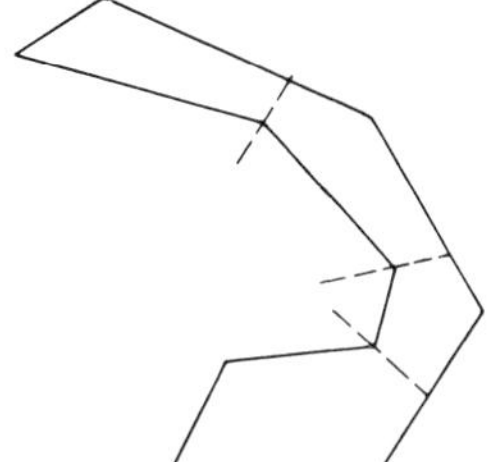

Fig. 9.35 Decomposition of a spiral according to Algorithm 9.6. (Reproduced from [9.37])

Algorithm 9.6: Decomposition of Spirals into Convex Subsets

Input: Ordered list of vertices of spiral S.

Output: Description of Convex subsets of the spiral.

Steps:

1. For each concave corner find the bisectrix.
2. For each bisectrix find the first point of intersection with the boundary of the polygon.
3. Use the segments of the bisectrices lying inside the polygon as dividing lines.

---

is well-defined. It is also obvious that the resulting polygons are convex. Therefore, the description of the shape of a spiral can be reduced to that of a sequence of convex sets together with the sequence of the sizes of the original concave angles. Of course subsets of this description may be used in the same manner as in Section 9.6. The description of the shape of convex polygons is much more tractable than the general shape description problem. For one thing, one may define for them concepts like width, elongation, etc., [9.6,19]. For another, it is possible to produce some rather simple grammars which will generate exactly all convex polygons [9.38].

Up to this point we have ignored the case of polygons with holes. Such polygons can be decomposed by one of three general approaches.

Approach 1:

I) For each polygon which is the boundary of a hole find a vertex which is closest to one of the external boundary. Then the pair of these vertices is joined by a dividing line and two additional "pseudovertices" are created as shown in Fig.9.36. This step will yield a simply connected polygon.

II) Apply the Main Decomposition Algorithm.

III) Establish the adjacency relation among all pairs of components which share a pair of pseudovertices (A-B and B-C in Fig.9.36).

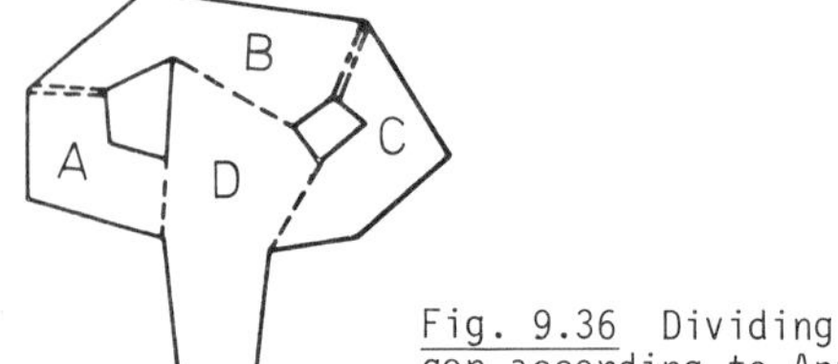

Fig. 9.36 Dividing lines of a multiply connected polygon according to Approach 1. (Reproduced from [9.37])

Approach 2:

I) Match pairs of vertices on different boundaries if their distance is below a threshold. Join such vertices by dividing lines obtaining, *possibly*, a simply connected polygon.

II) As in Approach 1.

III) As in Approach 1.

This method works well when the picture is composed primarily of strokes because in such a case it is easy to find pairs of vertices which are close to each other. For example, the Chinese character "the eye" can be decomposed as shown in Fig.9.37.

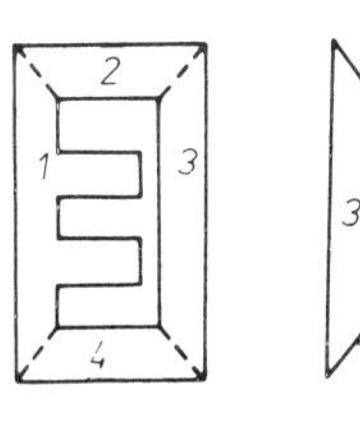

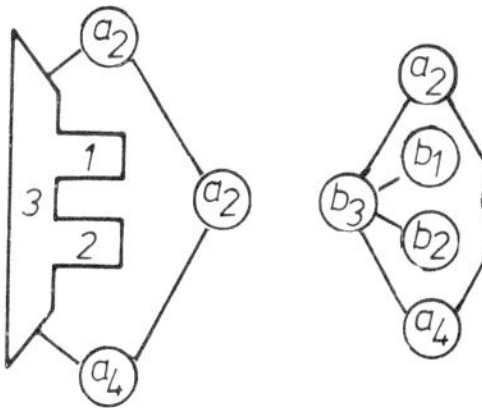

Fig. 9.37 Dividing lines of a multiply connected polygon according to Approach 2. (Reproduced from [9.37])

Approach 3:

I) Proceed with the Main Decomposition Algorithm as though there were no holes.

II) Describe the holes as independent simply connected regions.

III) Generate positional relations between holes and components.

This approach is applicable when the holes are expected to fall within primitive components and do not play a major part in the description of the shape except, possibly, by their occurrence.

The Main Decomposition Algorithm and Approach 1 have been implemented in FORTRAN IV and run on an IBM 360-91 computer at Princeton University. They were tested on handwritten numerals and on pictures of chromosomes and Chinese characters. In the first case the data were stored as binary 24 × 24 matrices, while in the last two cases a 64 × 64 grid was used with 7 bits per pixel. The results of the processing are shown in Figs.9.38 and 9.39 in the following manner: a) is the original picture presented via an overprinting routine; b), c) and d) are CALCOMP plots showing the boundaries obtained by thresholding, the polygonal approximations obtained by a split-and-merge algorithm (see Sec.7.9) and the results of the application of Decomposition Algorithm 9.5; e) shows the resulting adjacency graphs with the following notation: C stands for a convex set, S for a spiral and T for a T-type set. The latter are polygons with two concave arcs which have been "excused" from further decomposition. Figures 9.40 and 9.41 show the application of these algorithms to handwritten numerals. They are all CALCOMP plots showing the polygonal approximation with the vertices sequentially numbered. Figure 9.40 shows four simply connected polygons with the dividing lines indicated by broken lines. Figure 9.41 shows two examples of multiply connected polygons corresponding to the numerals 6 and 8. The heavy continuous lines indicate the dividing lines obtained by Approach 1. It is worthwhile noticing the resulting renumbering of the vertices. Due to a minor "bug" in the plotting program the numbers for the "split" vertices are

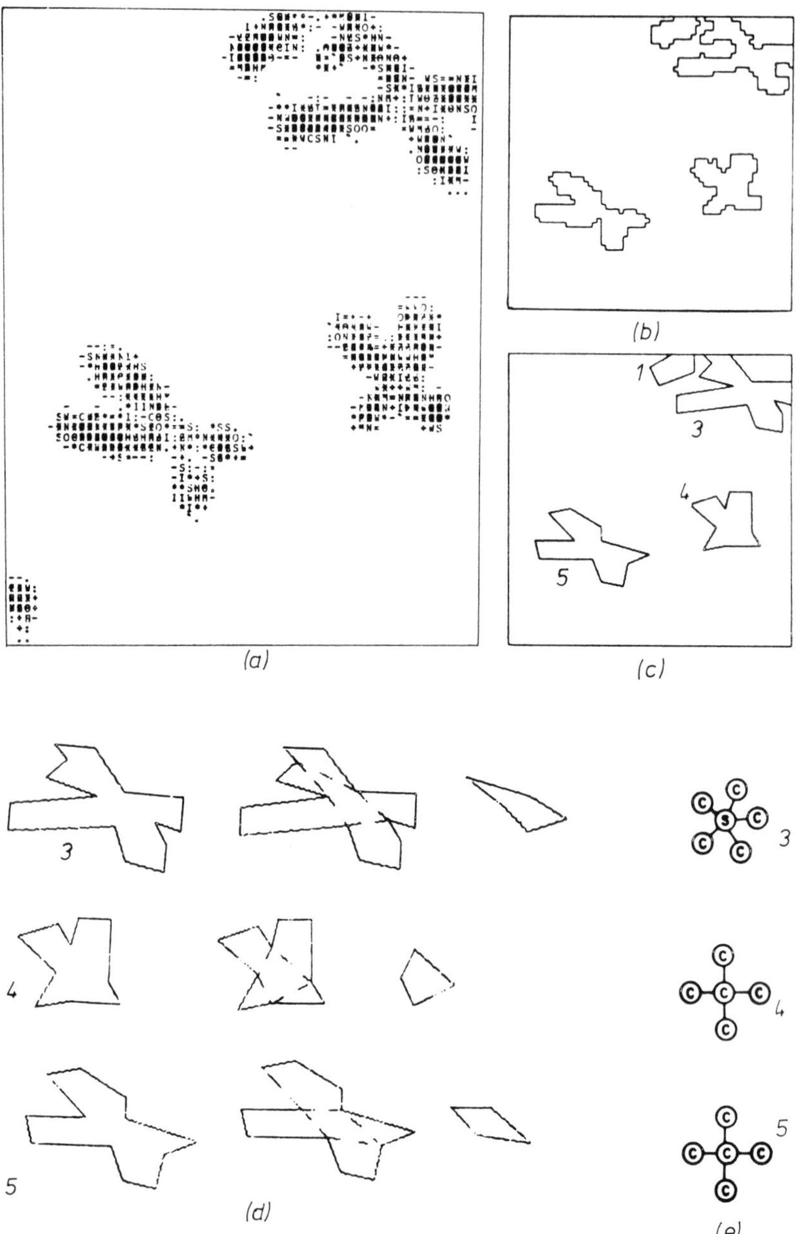

Fig. 9.38 (a) Grey scale picture of chromosomes reproduced by overprinting. (b) Traced outlines after thresholding of (a). (c) Polygonal approximation of boundaries of (b). (d) Decomposition at concave angles of three of the chromosomes in (c). (e) Graphs representing the decompositions in (d). (Reproduced from [9.37])

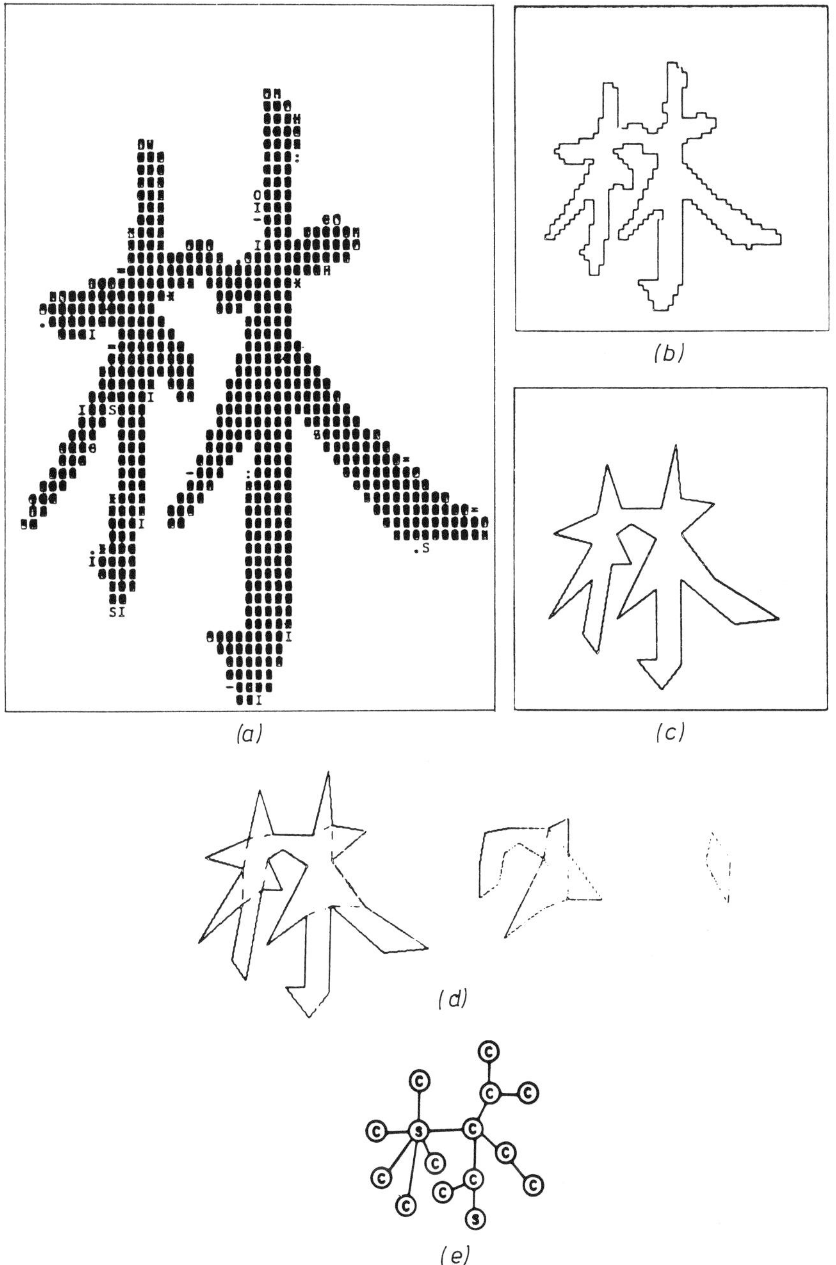

Fig. 9.39 (a) Grey scale picture of the Chinese character for "forest" reproduced by overprinting. (b) Traced outlines after thresholding of (a). (c) Polygonal approximation of boundaries of (b). (d) Decomposition at concave angles of the polygon in (c). (e) Graph representing the decomposition in (d). (Reproduced from [9.37])

plotted one on top of the other and some sophisticated human pattern recognition is needed to tell them apart. (Of course the internal representation is the correct one).

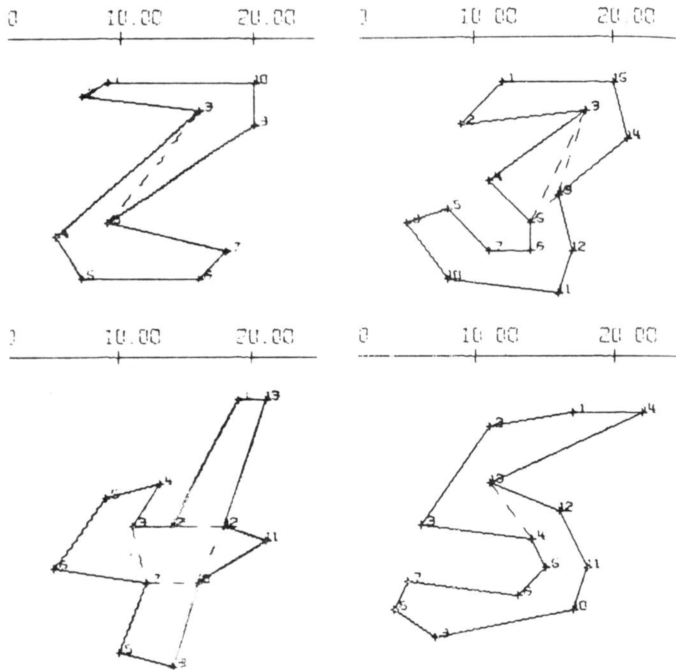

Fig. 9.40 Examples of decomposition at concave angles of certain simply connected numerals. (Reproduced from [9.37])

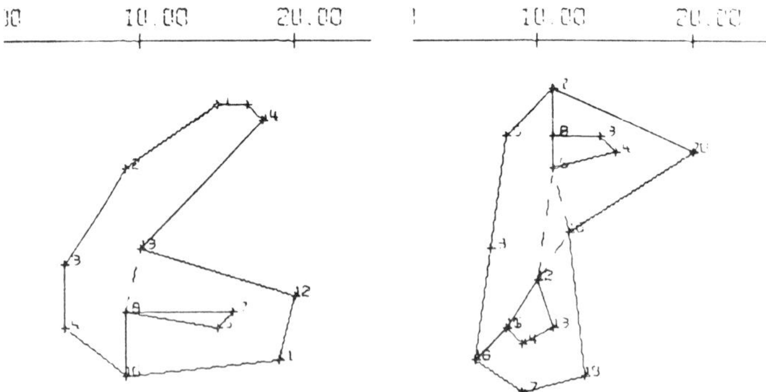

Fig. 9.41 Examples of decomposition at concave angles of certain multiply connected numerals. (Reproduced from [9.37])

It is obvious that the decomposition algorithms are able to analyze quite complex shapes although their results do not always correspond to human intuition. For example, the numeral 2 (in Fig.9.40) is decomposed into two "boomerang" type components rather than three strokes. This can be rectified during spiral decomposition into convex sets when the possibility of merging such sets is examined. It is also possible to see the relation between these features and those derived on the basis of empirical considerations for all types of data considered: chromosomes, Chinese characters, and handwritten numerals. Recently, the method was used for the analysis of crystals in titanium alloy photomicrographs [9.39]. The results of the decomposition can be used to construct a stack-labeled adjacency graph by labeling branches with the number of common corners. In Fig.9.42 full lines are used to denote branches with label 2 or more and broken lines for branches labeled with 1. The resulting graphs could be used for further syntactic description.

Decomposition is still an open research subject, and there is a need for methods, which produce results in agreement with human intuition, and which are computationally feasible.

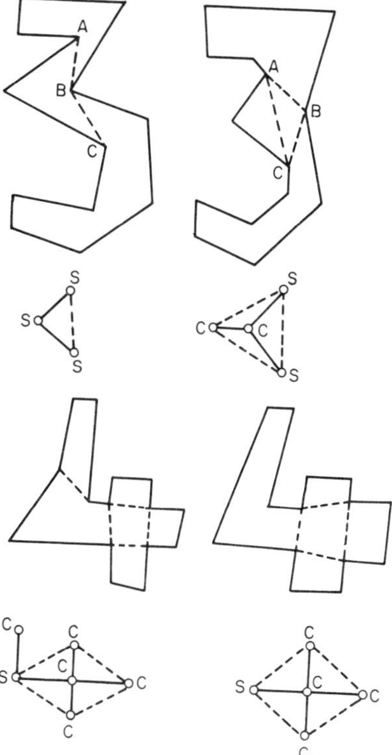

Fig. 9.42 Decomposition of numerals at concave angles and the corresponding graphs

10. Classification, Description and Syntactic Analysis

10.1 Introduction

By this time we have seen how a picture (or a waveform) can be transformed into a vector (e.g., one whose components are the Fourier descriptors), a string of symbols (e.g., the chain code), or a graph (e.g., the RAG). We are faced now with the problems of *description* and/or *classification*. Description requires that a text in a natural language, or a language which can be translated easily into such, be produced which contains all relevant information about a picture. Classification requires the assignment of a picture (or parts of it) to one of a finite number of classes. In many cases the two processes overlap. For example, in order to describe a picture of a room we may have to classify first the various objects in it. Conversely, a number of classification techniques are based on descriptions, as it was shown to be the case with the examples of Section 8.6. One may even go as far as to state that structural pattern recognition is a sequence of alternating classifications and descriptions: A pixel is classified as belonging to one of several regions. These regions provide a rudimentary description of the picture. Parts of each region are classified as belonging to its boundary or to some of its simpler components. Then a region may be described through its parts, or its boundary may be described as a sequence of arcs, etc.

The classification problem is also closely connected to that of *inference* or *learning*. In a typical pattern recognition situation there is no formal description of the classes but rather one is given a set of examples from each class and is required to infer the class definitions from them. There are even cases where the class to which each example belongs is not known. The latter is not a well-defined problem unless one imposes some form of a similarity measure among objects. Then we have the *clustering* problem.

The difficulty of classification, description and learning (as well as clustering) varies enormously with the form of the mathematical structure representing the original pictorial data. Classification, learning and clustering have been studied thoroughly for the case of vectors and there is a substantial literature on the subject [10.1-12]. Vectors are not very helpful for description unless the features have well-defined physical meaning. The case of strings represents the next degree of difficulty. For them the problem of description is, as a rule, relatively easy because syntactic descriptions of the type discussed in Section 8.6 are readily transformed into descriptions in terms of natural languages. Classification can be performed by defining for each class a grammar (or an automaton) and then assigning a string to the class whose grammar can generate it. This is a relatively straightforward procedure through parsing or the recognition of regular expressions [10.13,14]. On the other hand, the inference and clustering problems are very difficult for strings, due to the lack of well-defined similarity measures for them [10.13,15]. All three (or four) problems are fairly difficult for graphs unless one proceeds to map them into strings or vectors. On the other hand graphs offer a natural way of encoding pictorial data because they are inherently two-dimensional structures. In this chapter we shall review the methodologies for strings and vectors only briefly, and we shall center our attention on graphs. In spite of the difficulty of the general problem, the situation is not without hope for the following reason. Because graphs (or in some cases strings) offer "natural" descriptions of pictures, it is sometimes straightforward to infer classifiers by heuristic techniques and in other cases the automatic analysis may be helped by interaction with the experimenter.

Graphs occur in a number of ways. We have seen in Chapter 5 the region adjacency graphs and other related to them and in Chapter 9 the graphs obtained from thinning and decomposition. These are all labeled graphs and they offer a compact description of the pictorial data. They can be processed in a number of ways: If the goal is classification then a set of measurements can be performed on them to produce a feature vector. In scene analysis the major goal is description, and then it is necessary to translate graphs into sentences of a natural language. This leads into the development of *graph languages* and *graph grammars*. If a graph grammar were available, then a given graph could be parsed according to it and the resulting parsing tree could be used for the generation of a sentence in a natural language describing the graph, and through it the original picture. Such a parse can also be used for classification in the manner mentioned above for strings. Measurements which can be performed on graphs are of two types. One is graph theoretic properties: maximum degree of the nodes, connectivity, number of branches etc. The other is information about the labels of the graph which often may be descriptors or the regions corresponding to some of the nodes of the graph. For example, the number of spiral components in the examples of Section 9.8, maximum elongation of any of the components, etc.

10.2 Statistical Pattern Classification for Vectors

Classification techniques for vectors represent one of the best studied subjects in pattern recognition. This is particularly true about statistical methods which are the subject of a number of books [10.1-11]. For this reason we will treat them here very briefly and refer the reader to the literature. If the object has been mapped into a vector $\underline{x}$ (of dimension d), then one is interested in the probability $p(i|\underline{x})$ that the object belongs to class i. This probability can be estimated by the Bayes formula, if a set of objects with known classification is available. This allows the direct estimation of the probability of observing $\underline{x}$ given that the object belongs to class i, $p(\underline{x}|i)$. If p(i) is the a priori probability of class i we have:

$$p(i|\underline{x}) = \frac{p(x|i)p(i)}{\sum_k p(\underline{x}|k)p(k)} \quad . \tag{10.1}$$

In general $\underline{x}$ is a vector of rather high dimensions, and it is not feasible to estimate the above probabilities in a tabular form. Instead some functional form is assumed for them. Then the problem becomes one of estimating a finite number of parameters. For example, we may assume that we have Gaussian distributions and that

$$p(\underline{x}|i) = \frac{1}{\sqrt{(2\pi)^d |Q_i|}} \exp\left[-\frac{1}{2}(\underline{x}-\underline{m}_i)'Q_i^{-1}(\underline{x}-\underline{m}_i)\right] \quad , \tag{10.2}$$

where Q_i is the covariance matrix for the ith class and $\underline{m}_i$ the mean for the class. In many cases, the classification decision is made on the basis of a maximum likelihood criterion, i.e., we decide that the object belongs to the ith class if

$$p(i|\underline{x}) > p(j|\underline{x}) \qquad j \neq i \quad . \tag{10.3}$$

Obviously we may compare monotonic functions of the probabilities rather than the probabilities themselves to get the same results. Thus we may omit the common denominator and compare only the products $p(\underline{x}|i)p(i)$. In the Gaussian case we may also take the logarithm and obtain the following *discriminant function*:

$$g_i(\underline{x}) = -\frac{1}{2}(\underline{x}-\underline{m}_i)'Q_i^{-1}(\underline{x}-\underline{m}_i) + \frac{1}{2}\log[|Q_i|] + \log[p(i)] \quad . \tag{10.4}$$

Terms which do not depend on i have been omitted. In general a discriminant function is defined as a function of i and $\underline{x}$ whose value is maximized when $\underline{x}$ belongs to class i. If the dependence on $\underline{x}$ is linear, then it is called a linear discriminant function. This will be the case in (10.4) if Q_i is independent of i, i.e., all classes have the same covariance matrix Q. Then (10.4) is simplified into

$$h_i(\underline{x}) = \underline{m}'Q\underline{x} + \underline{m}'\underline{m} + \log[p(i)] \quad , \tag{10.5}$$

by keeping only terms which depend on the class. Linear discriminant functions may also be justified in cases where the above assumptions do not hold,

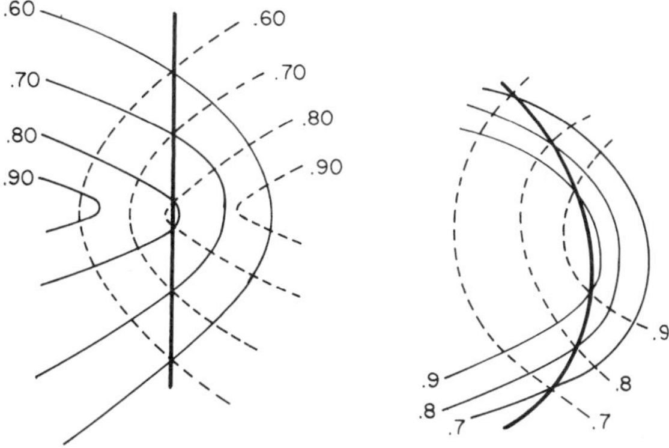

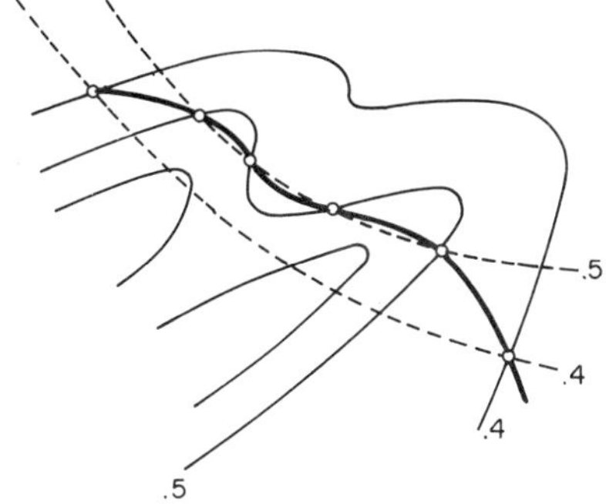

Fig. 10.1 Probability density contours shown in solid line for one class and in broken line for the other. The heavy lines denote optimal separating lines

provided that the vectors representing each class form tight clusters which are far apart from each other. Figure 10.1 illustrates this for the case of two features. The close curves enclose regions where the measurement lies with the noted probability if the objects belong to the respective class. In Fig.10.1a these are plotted for the Gaussian case with equal covariance matrices. The locus of the intersections of similarly labeled contours is the dividing curve between classes, in this case a straight line. In Fig.10.1b the separating curve is a quadratic, but it can be approximated by a straight line with very little worsening in performance. This is also true for the rather "exotic" example of Fig.10.1c. Additional motivations for the use of linear discriminant functions can be found in the literature [10.1-11].

If one adds a "dummy" feature equal always to 1, then a linear discriminant function can be written in homogeneous form as

$$g_i(\underline{x}) = \underline{w}'_i\underline{x} \quad . \tag{10.6}$$

There is a simple iterative procedure which permits one to find the vectors $\underline{w}_i$ from given samples of vectors from each class X_i. It is listed as Algorithm 10.1, and it can be shown that it always terminates, if a set of vectors exists with the property:

$$\underline{w}'_i\underline{x} > \underline{w}'_j\underline{x} \quad \text{for all} \quad j \neq i \quad \text{if } \underline{x}\varepsilon X_i \quad . \tag{10.7}$$

If no such set exists the procedure does not terminate. It is possible to find estimates for the maximum number of iterations and thus convert the procedure into a correct algorithm.

The coefficient c is usually chosen equal to 1, unless there is some specific reason to choose another value. It can be shown that the expected number of iterations depends only on the initial choice of $\underline{w}_i$'s and the spread of the vectors within each class in comparison to the distance between classes [10.4].

One of the problems associated with this, and related techniques, is the possibility of spurious separation. We shall discuss this problem for the case of two classes. In this case, instead of two vectors $\underline{w}_1$ and $\underline{w}_2$ we may look for their difference $\underline{w} = \underline{w}_1 - \underline{w}_2$, which will result in having $\underline{w}'_i\underline{x}$ positive if $\underline{x}\varepsilon X_1$ and negative otherwise. Let N be the total number of samples. Then, successful classification requires that N linear inequalities be satisfied. On the other hand, we have d degrees of freedom in choosing the vector $\underline{w}$. If d exceeds or equals N, then the problem will have always a solution (except for certain degenerate cases). Such a solution implies no clustering of the vectors from each class, and furthermore it will be found no matter how poor the selection of features has been. It can be shown that even for N = 2d there is a 50% probability of spurious classification [10.1,4]. Therefore, one should always choose N equal to at least 3 or 4 times d.

Algorithm 10.1

Input: Sets of vectors X_i, i = 1,2,...C, where C is the number of classes. A constant c.

Output: Vectors $\underline{w}_i$, i = 1,2,...C.

Steps:

1. Initialize: Choose a value for all $\underline{w}_i$'s. Set flag F = 1. Choose estimated of maximum number of passes P. Set count of passes p = 0.
2. While (F=1 and p<P) do block 11.

    Begin block 11;

    1. Increment p and set F = 0.
    2. For all $\underline{x}$ belonging to $\bigcup_{i=1}^{C} X_i$ do block 12.

        Begin block 12;

        1. Evaluate the scalar products $\underline{w}_i\underline{x}$ for i = 1,2,...C.
        2. Let j be the index for which $\underline{w}_j\underline{x}$ achieves its maximum value and let $\underline{x}\varepsilon X_k$. If j ≠ k do block 13. Else do nothing.

            Begin block 13;

            1. Replace $\underline{w}_j$ by $\underline{w}_j + c\underline{x}$.
            2. Replace $\underline{w}_k$ by $\underline{w}_k - c\underline{x}$.
            3. Set F = 1.

            End block 13;

        End block 12;

    End block 11;

10.3 Pattern Classification for Strings

Pictorial data can be encoded in strings in many ways. We have seen in Chapters 7 and 8 how this can be done by boundary tracings. If the elements of the strings come from a finite set (e.g., the eight numbers used by the chain code), then the theory of formal languages can be used for the purpose of pattern recognition. We have already seen the simplest case in Section 8.6, where a finite automaton performs that operation. In general, we can have C grammars, $G_1, G_2, \ldots G_C$, each accepting only the strings from one of C classes. The time required for parsing depends significantly on the complexity of the grammar. For regular and for many context free grammars, it is linearly proportional to the length of the string and, therefore, of the same order as the computation of scalar products described in Section 10.2. It can be an exponential function of the length for context sensitive grammars. Therefore, the method is attractive only when the grammars involved are of low order in the hierarchy of languages [10.13,16,17]. We have demonstrated in Chapter 8 that the proper preprocessing of the data can result in significant reduction in the complexity of the grammars required for recognition.

A major problem in the application of grammatical techniques is the *inference* of the grammars from a finite set of samples. In its simplest form, the problem can be expressed as following: Let S_1 and S_2 be two finite, disjoint sets of strings. We want to find a grammar which generates all the strings in S_1 and none of the strings in S_2, or an automaton which accepts all the strings in S_1 and none of the strings in S_2. (The two formulations are equivalent [10.13,15,16]). The problem has always a trivial solution, since it is a straightforward process to find a finite automaton, which accepts all the strings from a finite set and none of the strings from another finite set, provided the two sets are disjoint. Such an automaton may have an enormous number of states and be quite impractical to use. A desirable modification of the problem is to require that the automaton have the minimum number of states possible. This is not a well-defined problem, unless one restricts the optimization over specific classes of automata only. In any case, the inference problem in the presence of the optimization condition seems to be of a very high degree of complexity [10.13,15]. Many of the algorithms described in the literature use heuristics in order to simplify the inference procedure [10.15]. A complete treatment of the subject of grammatical inference is beyond the scope of this work, but it is worth pointing out a major reason for its difficulty. The inference of separating surfaces, in the case of vectors, made extensive use of the distance or the angle between vectors. Thus one could always tell whether two vectors $\underline{x}_1$ and $\underline{x}_2$ were close to each other. There are no such measures for strings. Most of the classical string distances, which have been used in communication theory (e.g., Hamming distance) are not meaningful in the context of pattern recognition. For a further treatment of the subject the reader is referred to [10.13]. In practice, grammatical inference can be performed in an interactive way by having a human observer postulate grammars, and then modify them until the two sets of strings are separated.

From a practical viewpoint it is more meaningful to ask not whether a string has been generated by a given grammar, but what is the probability that this has been the case. Therefore, it is necessary to deal with stochastic grammars. The parsing of such grammars is not fundamentally different than the parsing of non-stochastic ones. In the latter case a number of derivation paths are created as one proceeds along the length of the string. Eventually all but one of them are eliminated. In the case of stochastic grammars the paths are assigned probabilities and at the end of the process there will usually be more than one left. Then the probabilities are compared according to a maximum likelihood criterion and one of them is chosen. A complete discussion of this approach can be found in the work of FU and his students [10.13,18-20]. In addition to maximum likelihood, Bayesian statistics have been considered and the analysis includes both stochastic languages and non-stochastic languages with substitution, insertion and deletion errors.

10.4 Tree Grammars

Tree grammars have received special attention in the context of pattern recognition for a number of reasons: 1) Trees represent the next level of generalization from strings, and it is advisable to investigate their properties first before proceeding with more complex graphs. 2) The recognizer of a regular tree grammar is a tree automaton (which is a straightforward extension of a finite automaton) even though the leaves of the tree generated by the grammar form a context-free language [10.21]. 3) The inference of tree grammars is comparatively simpler [10.22]. 4) As we shall see in Sections 10.5-9, trees are, in effect, one of the only two classes of graphs which can be handled efficiently by syntactic techniques. Tree grammars were first considered in the context of automata theory by BRAINERD [10.21], ROUNDS [10.23] and THATCHER [10.24]. FU and his students [10.25-31] developed various types of such grammars for pictorial data. Additional studies on tree grammars have been carried out by GONZALES and THOMASON [10.32]. The use of certain special conventions enables tree grammars to generate graphs of higher connectivity than trees.

Pictures can be mapped into trees in a number of ways. One is through a thinning process of the type described in Section 9.3. Another is by creating a spanning tree from a graph. In its simplest form this method operates as follows. Let G be the picture grid as described in Chapter 3. This forms a graph with pixels as nodes and branches connecting neighbors (or only direct neighbors). All nodes belonging to a given region can be now considered as a subgraph G_i. The region can be then be represented by a spanning tree of G_i. The method is straightforward, but the resulting trees preserve shape properties only to a rather limited degree. More complex versions of this method can use either the RAG or the adjacency graphs resulting from the decomposition algorithms of Chapter 9. In this case one can attempt to find maximum weight spanning trees (see Sec.3.3). Such weights can be introduced in the RAG in terms of the length and other properties of the boundary between two regions (see Sec.6.3). This particular approach has not been exploited yet in any significant way and represents an open area for research. FU and his associates have described a number of techniques, utilizing both grid and region information, which encode satellite pictures into trees (and arbitrary graphs as well) [10.26,27].

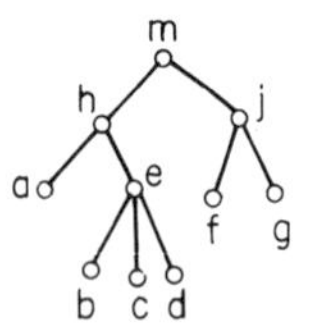

Fig. 10.2 Tree

We proceed now with the description of tree grammars and observe first that a tree can be mapped trivially on a string, by using parentheses. The tree of Fig.10.2, for example, can be described by the string m{h[ae(bcd)]j(fg)} where the labels of all the nodes were present, or by the string {[a(bcd)](fg)} which contains the labels of the leaves only. If we use [) to denote a nonterminal node, then the following rules will generate all strings which represent trees.

$$[\rightarrow [[) \qquad [\rightarrow (n \quad .$$

For binary trees we may use a simpler notation and in particular

$$N \rightarrow (NnN) \qquad N \rightarrow (Nn)$$

to denote either of the two productions shown in Fig.10.3. Such descriptions are not convenient for all problems, though. BRAINERD [10.21] used the following formalism for trees (originally due to GORN [10.33]): Let N^+ be the set of positive integers. Then one can form a set of strings U recursively by the rules: If $i \in N^+$ then $i \in U$. If $a \in U$ then $a.i \in U$ where $i \in N^+$. In other words the strings of U consists of positive integers separated by ".". Figure 10.4a shows how the set U represents a tree, generally referred to as the universal tree. A partial ordering is established on U by defining $a \leq b$ if and only if there exists an $x \in U$, such that $a.x = b$, i.e., a is an ancestor of b under the terminology of Section 3.2.

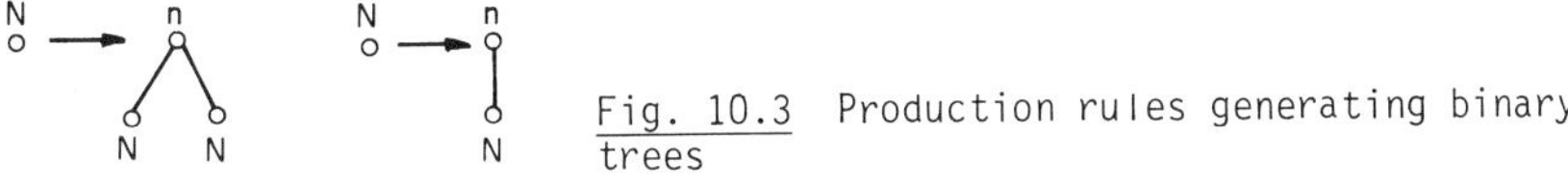

Fig. 10.3 Production rules generating binary trees

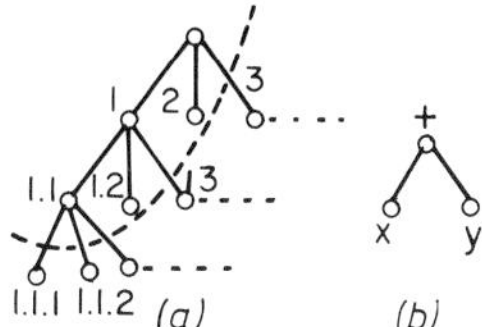

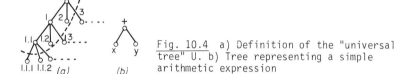

Fig. 10.4 a) Definition of the "universal tree" U. b) Tree representing a simple arithmetic expression

Definition 10.1: A *tree domain* D is defined as a connected finite subset of U, containing the root 0 and no node at any level without containing the nodes to its left. More precisely, if it satisfies the following conditions: $b \in D$ and $a < b$ implies $a \in D$, and $a.j \in D$ and $i < j$ $(i,j \in N^+)$ implies $a.i \in D$. (The broken line in Fig.10.4a delimits a tree domain.)

Definition 10.2: A *ranked* (or *stratified*) alphabet $< A,r >$ is an alphabet A with a function r mapping the elements of A into the set of nonnegative integers N.

Definition 10.3: A *tree over a ranked alphabet* is a mapping m() from a tree domain D into a ranked alphabet $< A,r >$, such that if $a \in D$, then

$$r(m(a)) = \max\{\, i \mid a.i \in D \,\} \quad . \tag{10.8}$$

What the combination of functions r() and m() does, is to assign a position in the tree for an element of A. In particular, the rank of a label at the node of a tree must equal the number of branches leaving the node. For example: Let A = {x,y,+}, r(x) = r(y) = 0, and r(+) = 2. m(0) = +, m(1) = x and m(2) = y are then legal assignments and the corresponding tree is shown in Fig.10.4b. This notation makes convenient the introduction of tree grammars.

Definition 10.4: A *regular tree grammar* over a ranked alphabet of terminal symbols V_T is a quadruple

$$G = \{V, r', P, S\} \tag{10.9}$$

where r' is an extension of r over the union V of terminals and nonterminals, P is a set of production rules, and S is a set of starting trees.

The following example shows a tree grammar which generates a rectangular grid [10.22].

Nonterminals: S, A, B.

Terminals: a (horizontal vector of unit length), b (vertical vector of unit length, # (marker of lower left corner).

Ranking function: r(a) = {2,1,0}, r(b) = {2,1,0}, r(#) = 2.

Rules:

$S \to A/^{\#}\backslash B$

$A \to A/^{a}\backslash B$

$A \to a$

$B \to A/^{b}\backslash B$

$B \to b$

Starting tree: S.

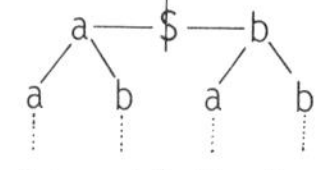

Fig. 10.5 Rectangular grid and its tree representation

Figure 10.5 shows a grid generated by this grammar and the corresponding tree. MOAYER and FU [10.26,27] have used tree grammars for the automatic recognition of *fingerprints*. A fingerprint sample consists of an aggregation of curves, some of them splitting into two. Each specimen is digitized with 192 × 192 resolution and then it is divided into a matrix of sixteen 48 × 48 windows. Each window is classified separately and the overall fingerprint classification is made on the basis of these decisions. We discussed in Section 9.4 how the digitized windows are mapped into trees. The trees contain nodes describing both elements of ridges and relative positions (left or right). The following grammar generates a set of parallel ridges.

> Terminals: L (left), R (right), t. The latter stands for any one of four symbols denoting ridge direction. The rank of all of them can be either 1 or 2.
>
> Nonterminals: S1, T1.
>
> Rules:
>
> S1 → L --.-- R / L --. / .-- R
>
> R → L --R--T1 / T1--R--R / T1
>
> L → L --L--T1 / T1--L--R / T1
>
> T1 → L --t--T1 / T1--t--R / t--T1 / t

A production rule allowing for branching can be added to the above to produce windows with such ridges.

T3 → T1--X--T1 .

In this case X has rank 2. Figure 10.6 shows a grammar generating windows with two branching ridges, one sudden ending, and a set of simple continuous ridges, while Fig.10.7 shows a digitized sample of the type described

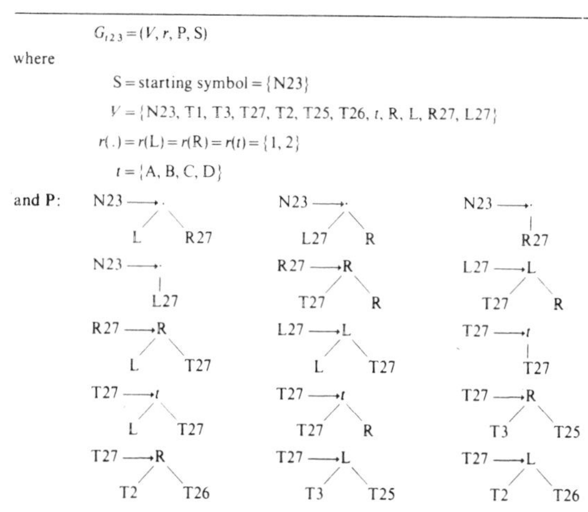

Fig. 10.6 Tree grammar generating fingerprints. (Reproduced from [10.27])

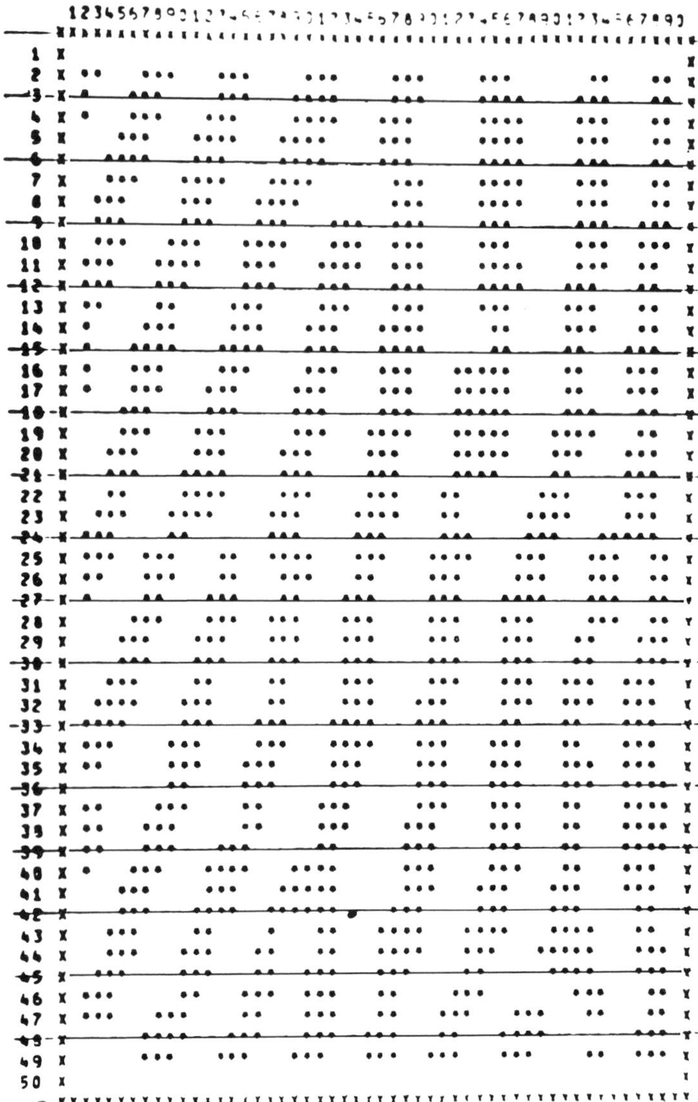

Fig. 10.7 Digitized sample from a fingerprint generated by the grammar of Fig.10.6 (Reproduced from [10.26])

by such a grammar. A total of 193 such grammars were inferred on the basis of a training sample of fingerprints. An unknown window will be accepted in general by one of the grammars. For each window a directional code is found: 0 (135 degrees with the horizontal), 1 (horizontal), 2 (45 degrees) and

3 (vertical). For a group of four windows a base 4 number can be used to denote their directions, starting from the lower right and proceeding clockwise. Then a pyramidal data structure, of the type discussed in Chapters 4 and 5, may guide the overall classification of the fingerprint.

Tree grammars have been used in the interpretation of satellite images where they attempt to label a scene by considering consistencies of labels allowed by the rules of the grammar. See [10.22,28,29] for more details.

10.5 Graph Languages and Graph Grammars

Graphs offer a very general structure for the encoding of pictorial data and this has motivated a large amount of work in graph grammars and languages, which has appeared under a number of names. The term picture languages is often used to denote what is, in effect, graph languages. The first papers on two-dimensional grammars were published in 1964 by KIRSCH [10.34] and NARASIMHAN [10.35]. One of the first systematic studies was carried out by SHAW [10.36,37], who investigated what he called Picture Description Languages. This was followed by the Web Grammars proposed by PFALTZ and ROSENFELD [10.38,39] and by the Plex Languages studied by FEDER [10.40]. DACEY [10.41], SCHWEBEL [10.42], and CLOWES [10.43] also described various models of two-dimensional languages. Research in the theory of graph grammars has been carried out by MONTANARI [10.44], PAVLIDIS [10.45,46], MYLOPOULOS [10.47,48], ABE et al. [10.49] and COOK [10.50]. The related topics of array or matrix grammars and grammars with coordinates have been investigated by ANDERSON [10.51,52], ROSENFELD and MILGRAM [10.53,54], SIROMONEY et al. [10.55], and OTA [10.56]. A special symposium was held in 1972 on the relation between picture and graphics languages [10.57]. WATANABE [10.58] has described a graph language for chemical structures. A complete treatment of the various models is beyond our scope. In any case, most of them are closely related (in spite of different terminology), and their restrictions to certain important special cases give identical results (e.g., for context-free grammars).

In any discussion of this subject, one must first distinguish between what may be called *genuine graph grammars* and *graph-generating-string grammars*. The former use rewriting rules which apply directly to graphs and are typified by the web grammars. The latter proceed by establishing a mapping between graphs and strings, and then use string rewriting rules. SHAW'S work belongs to this class. The development of rewriting rules for graphs presupposes the establishment of nontrivial insertion rules. In the case of string grammars, when a nonterminal is replaced by a string the insertion process is trivial. For example the rule A → aAb applied to the string acaABab produces the new string acaaAbBab. In the case of graphs a nonterminal will be characterized by its position on the plane rather than on the line and its replacement must be embedded in a structure which has no well-defined start and end, and where elements may be connected to each other by more than two points. A major difference among the various models that have been studied in the literature is the way in which they handle the embedding problem in the rewriting rules. The two definitions given next are motivated by this problem.

Definition 10.5: An mth order structure is an entity which is connected to the rest of the graph by m nodes. A second order structure will also be called a *branch structure* and a first order structure a *node structure*.

Definition 10.6: A mth order graph grammar is one where all the nonterminal structures are of order at most m.

These definitions provide a rather general model, of which many particular studies are special cases. If one insists on producing only graphs as members of the language, then structures of order greater than two must be nonterminals. In order to clarify some of these concepts, we present a simple example, that of a grammar which generates exactly all *wheels*, i.e., graphs where all but one of the nodes lie on a circuit and the extra node is connected to all the others (see Fig.10.8a). The grammar has only one nonterminal, a third order structure T with three attachment points, labeled 1, 2, 3. The starting configuration is S, consisting of three structures connected in the following manner: All points 3 are joined together and each point 1 is joined with a point labeled 2 in a cyclical manner (see Fig.10.8b). The first rewriting rule is: Replace $T(1_i,2_i,3_i)$ by $T(1_j,2_j,3_j)$ and $T(1_k,2_k,3_k)$ with connections $[1_i,1_j]$, $[2_i,2_k]$,$[3_i,3_j]$, $[3_i,3_k]$, $[2_j,1_k]$. (See Fig.10.8c). The labeling of the attachment points is necessary so that one can specify the way the structures are connected. The second and final rewriting rule is: Replace T(1,2,3) by a graph with nodes (1,2,3) and branches (1,2) and (2,3) (Fig.10.8d). Formally the grammar appears to be context-free and one could even find a linear grammar to generate the same class of graphs.

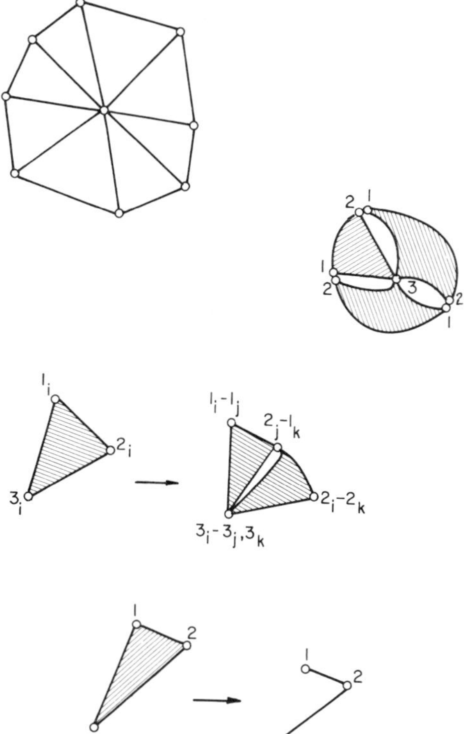

Fig. 10.8 Description of a third order grammar generating all wheels

One could achieve the same result with the string grammar: $S \rightarrow TTT$, $T \rightarrow TT$, $T \rightarrow t$, where T will be interpreted as a branch labeled as nonterminal, and t as a branch labeled as terminal. The final step of the mapping of the string into a graph would be expressed by the nongrammatical rule "connect all nodes to a (new) central node". One can see a major difference between the two approaches. The first grammar can be easily generalized or modified to produce other classes of graphs, but the second cannot because the mapping rule depends strongly on the family of graphs to be generated. It is possible to define more general mapping rules but this still imposes restrictions on the class of graphs which can be generated.

10.6 First Order Graph Grammars

First order grammars are those where the nonterminal structure have only one attachment point. Such structures can be seen as nodes which are labeled as nonterminals and we may say that such grammars use only *node rewriting rules*. A typical example is the grammar generating all trees, which is given next.

Nonterminal N:
Terminals: n (node) and b (branch).
Starting symbol: N.
Rules:
$N_i \rightarrow N_i bN \ / \ n$

i.e., a nonterminal node can be replaced by itself and a branch with a new nonterminal node attached to it, or by a terminal node. Since one never links two already existing nodes by a branch, a graph generated by this grammar cannot have any circuits. Furthermore, it will be connected and therefore it will be a tree. Conversely any tree can be parsed according to the grammar by labeling all its nodes by N, and then replacing branches of the form NbN by N. Thus the grammar generates indeed all trees and only trees. A small modification of the rules results in a more interesting case, a grammar generating all binary trees:

$$N_i \rightarrow n_i nN \ / \ Nbn_i bN \ / \ n \quad .$$

Both grammars have only one nonterminal at the left hand side of their rules and therefore they can be called justifiably context-free. A first order context sensitive grammar could include rules which attach subgraphs simultaneously to more than one nonterminal nodes. In particular, we could have a rule of the form,

$$N_1 \ N_2 \rightarrow N_1 bN_2$$

which allows the connection of any pair of such nodes by a branch. In this way one can generate graphs of arbitrary complexity. Such grammars were studied first by PFALTZ and ROSENFELD [10.38] under the name *web grammars*.

It is well-known from the theory of formal languages that the parsing of context sensitive string grammars is a very difficult process which typically requires exponential time as a function of string length. The parsing of graphs is expected to be at least as difficult as that of strings (a string is after all a degenerate graph) and for this reason context sensitive grammars cannot be of much practical interest in pattern recognition. Therefore we shall restrict our attention in the sequel to grammars of no greater complexity than context free. It turns out that first order context free graph grammars (CFGG) cannot generate many interesting classes of graphs besides trees. The reason is that each time a rewriting rule is applied, a cutnode is generated, the node where the attachment is made. The only way that one can have loops is to include them in the right hand side of a rule. Since there is only a finite number of rules there can be only a finite number of subgraphs with loops which can appear in a graph generated by a first order context free graph grammar. This leads us to the following theorem.

Theorem 10.1: A necessary condition for the existence of a first order CFGG generating a class of graphs S is that there will be a finite set of graphs B, such that all blocks found in any graph in S are members of B.

Corollary 10.1: A necessary condition for the existence of a first order CFGG generating a class of graphs S is that there will be a number k such that all blocks of any member of S will have fewer than k nodes.

These conditions are not sufficient because there may be other specifications on S in addition to those having to do with connectivity. For example, the class of all *perfectly balanced* binary trees is defined as consisting of all binary trees where all the leaves are equidistant from the root and each node has exactly two children. The number of leaves in such a tree will always be a power of 2. The leaves can be mapped trivially into a string, and if there were a CFGG producing this class of graphs, then it could be made to produce all strings whose number of symbols is a power of 2. It can be shown easily (e.g., by using the "pumping" lemma [10.16]), that such a language cannot be generated by a context free grammar, and therefore there can be no CFGG producing the class of all perfectly balanced binary trees.

Trees are graphs which can described rather easily as strings (see Sec. 10.4, also [10.59]) and this suggests the possibility of string grammars for their generation. We introduce here a subset of the Picture Description Grammar (PDG) proposed by SHAW [10.36,37] which accomplishes this task. The alphabet of this grammar consists of two types of elements: Branch images having a head (h) and a tail (t) and denoted by letters of the roman alphabet; and operations denoted by the special symbols +, x, - and /. The first three are binary and the last unary having the effect of head/tail reversal. The binary operations have the following meanings (see also Fig. 10.9a):

1) $a + b$ join $h(a)$ to $t(b)$; $h(a+b) = h(b)$; $t(a+b) = t(a)$.

2) $a \times b$ join $t(a)$ to $t(b)$; $t(a\times b) = t(a) = t(b)$; $h(a\times b) = h(b)$.

3) $a - b$ join $h(a)$ to $h(b)$; $h(a-b) = h(a) = h(b)$; $t(a-b) = t(a)$.

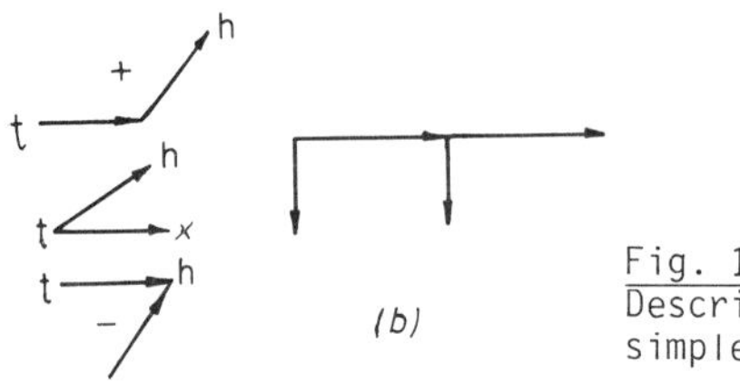

Fig. 10.9 Operations of the Picture Description Grammar [10.36,37] and a simple graph generated by it

Once these conventions are established, one can describe a given graph in terms of a string language. For example, the graph of Fig.10.9b can be expressed as $(b\times b) + (b\times b)$. In order to determine the class of graphs which can be described in such a way, we observe that all the binary operations result in the introduction of cutnodes. Loops can be introduced only if some of the terminals are replaced by graphs having them. Therefore such grammars will have at most the generative power of the first order CFGG. If we exclude the trivial introduction of loops, they can produce at most trees. We shall show next that any tree can be expressed in terms of the operations defined above, and therefore, it can be produced by such a grammar. Let a,b,c,...k denote a set of leaves which are all the children of a node m. Let n be the parent of m. Assume that the leaves are ordered from left to right with "a" being the leftmost. (See Fig.10.10a). Then the branches descending from m can be described as {..[(am-bm) - cm] -..-km} which assumes originally tails at the leaves and heads at m. The expression itself has a tail at a and a head at m. The branch mn (tail at m, head at n) can now be added with the + operation resulting in the string {..[(am-bm) - cm] -..-km} + (mn) which has a tail at a and a head at n. If m was the leftmost child of n then we have a configuration similar to the one we started with. By applying recursively these operations we can encode the whole tree in a string with the tail corresponding to the leftmost leaf and the head to the root. For example, the tree of Fig.10.10b is encoded as

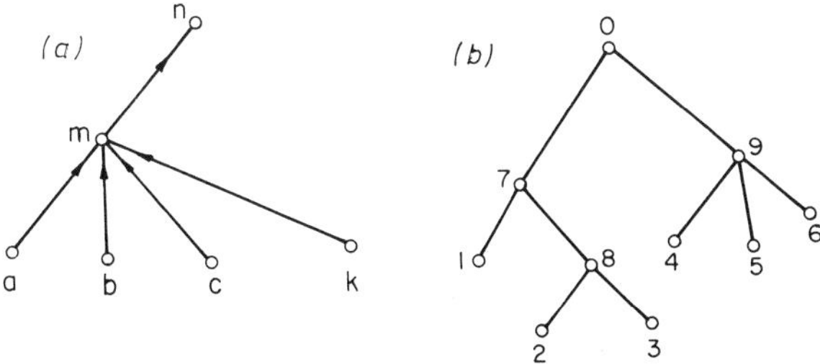

Fig. 10.10 Illustrations of the use of PDG's for tree description

{17 - [(28-38) + 87]} + 70 - {[(49-59) - 69] + 90} .

An equivalent encoding is obtained if the second node of each branch is omitted:

{1 - [(2-3) + 8]} + 7 - {[(4-5) - 6] + 9} .

We note that the encoding into strings has its price. The order by which operations are applied is very important, and we need two types of rewriting rules (involving the + and - operations) rather than one as before. On the other hand, we may conclude that the mapping of graphs into strings has resulted in no loss of generative power, since CFGG produce (in essence) only trees.

10.7 Second Order Graph Grammars

The nonterminals of such grammars can have one or two attachment points. Thus a 2nd order graph grammar can have both node and branch rewriting rules [10.45]. The following simple example generates all *series-parallel networks* (SPN).

Nonterminal: B.
Terminals: n (node) and b (branch).
Starting symbol: N.
Rules:
(1)B(2) → (1)BnB(2) / (1)B(2) (1)B(2) / (1)b(2)

where the numbers in parentheses denote attachment points. It is possible to simplify the notation by omitting the explicit notation of the attachment points and introducing a star (*) operator which denotes the "parallel" connection of 2 branches, i.e., B*B stands for (1)B(2) (1)B(2). In this way the graph grammar takes the appearance of a string grammar. The star operator has also been used in the PDL with formal definition:

4) a*b join h(a) to h(b) and t(a) to t(b) .

A grammar of this type can produce all SPNs if the following rules are used:

$B \rightarrow B*B \quad B \rightarrow B+B' \quad B \rightarrow b$.

It turns out that this is about all that such grammars can produce, in addition, of course, to trees. In order to show that, we need a formal characterization of SPNs.

Definition 10.7: A series-parallel network (SPN) is a graph with two nodes A and B (its ports) with all other nodes lying on a path between A and B and where all such paths have the following property. Let u and w be two of them and let x and y be node disjoint subpaths of u and w, respectively. Then there are no branches joining any of the nodes in x to any of the nodes in y and this is true for all possible u, w, x, and y.

Definition 10.8: A class of graphs C is defined recursively as follows:

a) All trees are in C.

b) All SPN's are in C.

c) If a graph is in C, then attaching to one of its nodes a tree results in a graph also in C.

d) If a graph G is in C, then replacing one of its branches by a SPN results in a graph also in C.

We shall show now that a PDG with the four given rules cannot produce any graphs which are not in C. The essential part of the proof is that the production rules cannot introduce any "crossbranches" in the paths between the head and the tail. We shall use induction on the number of productions. It is obviously true that the first application of any of the four productions cannot introduce such a branch. Suppose this is true for k productions and let G and F be two graphs produced this way with t(G) connected to the tail of the starting symbol S and h(F) connected to the h(S). The paths between t(G+F) and h(G+F) are unions of the paths between t(G) and h(G) and t(F) and h(F), all of them joining at h(G). Thus no branches between nodes in disjoint parts of the paths have been introduced. The same is true about the graphs resulting from the operations x and -. The graph G*F has as paths between its head and tail all those which were in G and F, and no connections have been introduced between any nodes in the paths, except for the joining of their first and last nodes. Therefore, we have proven the following.

Theorem 10.2: If a graph is produced by a PDG with rules (1-4), then it belongs to the class C for some choice of a pair of its nodes for head and tail.

There is a certain difficulty in using this result in order to check whether a given graph has been produced by a PDL. We may have to search for a pair of nodes such that the graph can be reduced to a SPN with these nodes as ports. An alternative characterization is given by the following theorem.

Theorem 10.3: A graph G can be produced by the PDG with rules (1-4) if and only if the following is true. Let A and B be a pair of nodes in G such that there are more than two node disjoint paths between A and B. Then for all such pairs there are no branches between any nodes of two different paths.

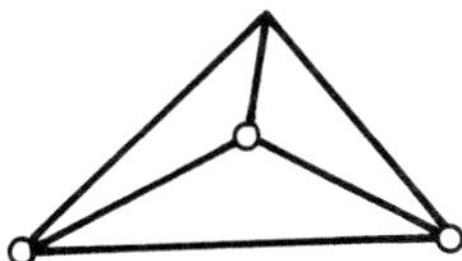

Fig. 10.11 The complete graph with four nodes (K_4)

Proof: a) Necessity. Fig.10.11 shows a graph, K_4, where this condition is violated. One can verify by exhaustive search that there is no pair of nodes for which this graph is a SP network. b) Sufficiency. The statement of the theorem allows for crossconnections between at most one pair of paths between two nodes. Let A and B be the nodes which are ends of the path and X and Y a pair where there is a crossconnection. Assume that there is only one such branch. Then X and Y are connected by three disjoint paths and therefore there can be no crossconnections between those paths by hypothesis. Therefore, by choosing X and Y as ports the graph becomes a SPN. Suppose now that the paths between A and B have two crossconnections, X-Y and U-V. Then by choosing X-Y as ports the path XUVY satisfies the requirements of the definition of SPN's. Q.E.D.

This limitation on the type of graphs produced by the PDG's carries to some extent to the general second order CFGG's since the restriction imposed by the choice of head and tail is implicit in the choice of an initial branch structure. Graphs with higher connectivity can be produced only by their explicit introduction in the rewriting rules. The following theorem is a parallel to theorem 10.1.

Theorem 10.4: A necessary condition for the existence of a second order CFGG generating a given class of graphs, S, is that there exists a number k such that any graph in S can be reduced to a graph in C by the combination of any of the following operations: a) Replace by one branch a subgraph with fewer than k nodes connected to the rest of the graph by two nodes; b) eliminate any subgraph with fewer than k nodes connected to the rest of the graph by one node.

Note that if the initial graph is not in C, the reduction process will end as the trivial graph consisting of a single node. The condition is not sufficient for the reasons stated in the previous section. There are a number of results which are direct corollaries of the above theorem and we list some of them below.

Corollary 10.2: If a graph is generated by a second order CFGG then its connectivity is either less than 3 or does not exceed that of the initial graph.

Corollary 10.3: If a set of graphs S is generated by a second order CFGG then its members have either connectivity less than 3 or they are homeomorphic to one of a finite number of graphs.

Corollary 10.4: The following sets of graphs cannot be generated by a second order CFGG.

a) all graphs;

b) all complete graphs;

c) all graphs with connectivity greater than some given number j;

d) all planar graphs.

In summary we may state that only "weakly" connected graphs can be generated by context free graph grammars. We give some specific examples of such classes in the next section. SHAW [10.36,37] has used some additional rules in order to increase the power of the PDL. These were, in essence, semantic rules allowing the overlaying of branches. These features increase the complexity of the parsing (a terminal branch may have been produced twice). There have been no quantitative studies of the parsing complexity of such grammars, but it is certain to be higher than that of grammars where each terminal is produced only once.

10.8 Examples of Graphs Generated by CFGG's

One nontrivial class of graphs which can be generated by a CFGG is that of outerplanar graphs. Such graphs have always connectivity less than 3.

Theorem 10.5: The following grammar H generates exactly all outerplanar graphs:

Nonterminals: B, N.
Terminals: b, n.
Initial symbol: S.
Rules:
S → N / (1)NBNBNB(1)
(1)N → (1)NBN / (1)n
B → BNB / b*BNB / b

where the symbol (1) identifies attachment points.

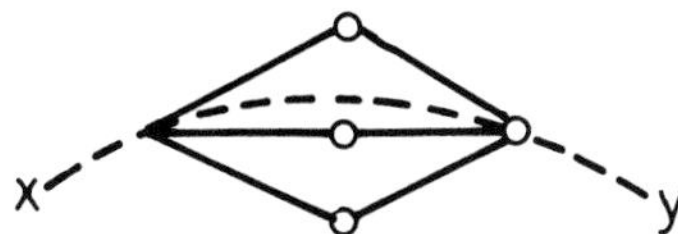

Fig. 10.12 The graph $K_{2,3}$, which, like K_4, cannot occur as a subgraph of outerplanar graphs

Proof: Outerplanar graphs are characterized by not containing homeomorphisms of K_4 and $K_{2,3}$ except { K_4-one branch } [10.60] (Figs.10.11 and 10.12 show these graphs). It can be readily verified that none of these graphs can be produced by H and neither can their homeomorphisms. It remains to verify that they cannot be formed as subgraphs by the application of the rules. This can be excluded because the application of a rule leads to a 2-separ able graph. K_4 is 3-connected and therefore cannot be part of both components;

$K_{2,3}$ can only if divided by a line xy (Fig.10.12). This can be excluded because the only way to produce "parallel" structures is through rule B → b*BNB. Thus H cannot generate any non-outerplanar graphs.

To show that H can produce all outerplanar graphs we proceed as follows. Let G be such a graph and let T', T", ... be subgraphs of it which are trees and are connected to the rest of the graph by their root. Since H contains G_3 the inverse application of the corresponding production rules will result in "collapsing" the trees to their roots.

Let G' be a subgraph "between" two cutnodes P and Q which does not contain any cutnodes. Thus there will be a branch connecting P and Q. G' is also outerplanar. Removing the branch $\overline{PQ}$ results in more cutnodes in the remaining branches of the graph (if this were not the case it would mean the existence of three independent paths between P and Q which contradicts outerplanarity). One can proceed until he finds subgraphs which consist only of chains of nodes and branches. If the path between two nodes involves more than one node, these can be "collapsed" into one by the inverse application of the rule B → BNB. Such a path now, together with the original branch between the two nodes, can be collapsed into a single branch by the inverse application of the rule B → b*BNB. One can thus proceed backwards until the whole graph is reduced to a triangle which is the RHS of a rule. Q.E.D.

10.9 Linear Graph Grammars (LGG)

These are special cases of CFGG's and they are defined in the same way with the additional constraint that there will be only one nonterminal in the RHS of each production rule [10.45]. The following LGG generates all the homeomorphisms of a given graph G.

Nonterminal: B.
Terminals: b and n.
Starting symbol: G with all branches labeled by B.
Rules:
B → Bnb / b

A more interesting example is given by the LGG which generates cycle graphs with branches labeled by one of two colors, and with all branches having the same color being contiguous. (See Fig.10.13).

Nonterminals: B, C, D, E.
Terminals: n (node), r (red branch), g (green branch).

Fig. 10.13 Example of cycle graph

Starting symbol: S.

Rules:

$S \rightarrow (1)rnBnrn(1)$ / $(1)gnCngn(1)$

$B \rightarrow r$ / rnB / D $\quad$ $C \rightarrow g$ / gnC / E

$D \rightarrow g$ / gnD $\quad$ $E \rightarrow r$ / rnE

The starting graphs are two cycle graphs: One has two red branches and one labeled B, and the other two green branches and one labeled C. B can generate a "string" of red branches and then, by changing into D, a string of green branches. Similarly, C can produce green branches followed by a string of red ones, generated by E.

Not too surprisingly, LGG's can produce only graphs which have no more structure than that imposed by the starting graph. This is so because the rewriting rule is, in effect, one dimensional. A formal characterization is offered by the following theorem.

Theorem 10.6: A set of graphs S is generated by a 2^d order LGG if and only if there exists a number k such that any cutnode of the graph or any pair of adjacent cutnodes separate the graph into components such that not more than two of them have more than k nodes.

Proof: Let k be the maximum of nodes or node structures in the RHS of the RR's of the grammar. Suppose now that a graph has been generated which contains a nonterminal node structure M. Such a graph will have in general more than k nodes but it will not contain any other nonterminals by definition. Let us denote this graph by G'. There are two types of rules which can be applied: $N \rightarrow Ng$ or $N \rightarrow nG$ where g denotes a graph without any nonterminals (and hence with at most k nodes) and G a graph with exactly one terminal (node or branch structure) different than M. The last type of rule must be applied at least once. Let m be the resulting node from M. It is obvious that m will be a cutnode separating the graph into subgraphs G', G" (which is G plus any graphs generated from its nonterminal structure) and $g_1, g_2, \ldots, g_n$. Since the latter have at most k nodes, there will be at most two subgraphs with more than k nodes, G' and G". Q.E.D.

A similar argument can be repeated for the case when the nonterminal structure in G' is a branch structure. Thus all nonterminals result in cutnodes (or pairs of adjacent cutnodes). Suppose now that m is an interior cutnode on the RHS of a rule. The graph in the RHS of the rule will be connected to the rest of the graph by two cut sets resulting from nonterminal structures. Figure 10.14 illustrates this situation. The graph inside the dotted lines is the RHS of the rule. Then it is obvious that $G'_1 \cup G_2$ and $G''_2 \cup G_2$ will be the only components which can have more than k nodes. A similar argument holds for an interior part of adjacent cutnodes. Thus if a graph is generated by an LGG it has the properties mentioned in the statement of the theorem.

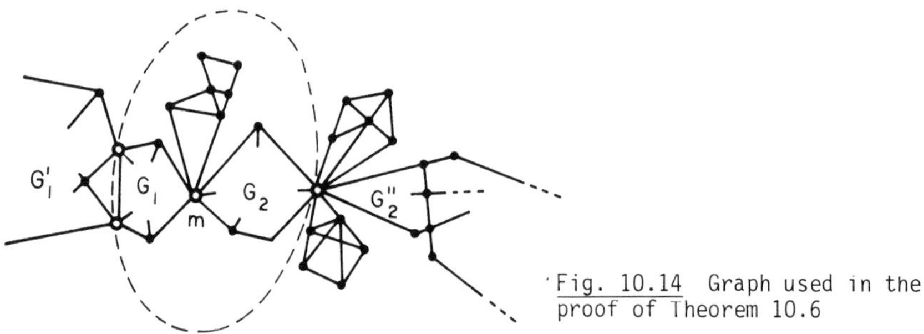

Fig. 10.14 Graph used in the proof of Theorem 10.6

Conversely, suppose that there exists a set of graphs with these properties for some number k. Consider now a linear grammar which contains all rules whose RHS contains not more than k nodes. Then we can write a generating tree for any given graph by considering all its cutnodes (and pairs of adjacent cutnodes) as nonterminals at some stage.

Corollary 10.5: The set of all trees cannot be generated by an LGG.

Note that although the theorem was proved for 2^d order LGG's, it is obvious that the last result will be valid for arbitrary order.

Corollary 10.6: The set of all strings over a finite alphabet can be generated by a LGG.

References

Chapter 1

1.1 P.H.Lindsay, D.A.Norman: *Human Information Processing* (Academic Press, New York 1972)
1.2 L.S.Frischkopf, L.D.Harmon: Proceedings of the Symposium on Information Theory, ed. by C.Cherry (Butterworth, London 1961) pp. 300-316
1.3 M.Eden: IRE Trans. Inform., Theory IT-8, 160-166 (1962)
1.4 R.Narasimhan: Inform. Control 7, 151 (1964)
1.5 R.S.Ledley: Science 146, 216-223 (1964)
1.6 A.C.Shaw: Inform. Control 14, 9-52 (1969)
1.7 K.S.Fu: *Syntactic Methods in Pattern Recognition* (Academic Press, New York, 1974)
1.8 T.Pavlidis: *Frontiers of Pattern Recognition*, ed. by S.Watanabe (Academic Press, New York 1972) pp. 421-451
1.9 M.Luckiesh: *Visual Illusions* (Dover, New York 1966)

Chapter 2

2.1 J.R.Rice: *The Approximation of Functions*, Vol.I, 1964; Vol.II, 1969 (Addison-Wesley, Reading 1964,1969)
2.2 E.Isaacson, H.B.Keller: *Analysis of Numerical Methods* (Wiley, New York 1966)
2.3 P.J.Davis: *Interpolation and Approximation* (Random House, Blaisdell, New York 1963)
2.4 G.Meinardus: Approximation of Functions: *Theory and Numerical Methods*, (Springer, Berlin, Heidelberg, New York 1967)
2.5 G.Dahlquist, A.Bjork: *Numerical Methods* (Prentice Hall, New York 1974)
2.6 W.B.Davenport,Jr., W.L.Root: *Random Signals and Noise* (McGraw-Hill, New York 1958)
2.7 C.W.Helstrom: *Statistical Theory of Signal Detection* (Pergamon Press, Oxford 1968)
2.8 F.R.Gantmacher: *The Theory of Matrices*, Vol.I (Chelsea, 1959) pp.231 -239
2.9 J.Raviv, D.N.Streeter: *Linear Methods for Biological Data Processing* (IBM Res. Rep. RC-1577 1965)
2.10 S.Watanabe: *Trans. Fourth Prague Confer. Information Theory* (1965)
2.11 K.Fukanaga, W.Koontz: IEEE Trans. C-19, 311-318 (1970)
2.12 K.Fukanaga: *Introduction to Statistical Pattern Recognition* (Academic Press, New York 1972)
2.13 G.S.Fang, T.Pavlidis: IEEE Trans. IT-18, 631-636 (1972)
2.14 R.M.Haralick, N.Griswold, N.Kattiyakulwanich: SPIE 66, 144-159 (1975)
2.15 G.E.Lowitz: Proc. 3rd Intern. Joint Conf. Pattern Recognition (Coronado, Calif. Nov. 8-11, 1976) pp. 673-677
2.16 G.Nagy: IEEE Proc. 56, 836-862 (1968)
2.17 Y.T.Chen, K.S.Fu: Inform. Control, 12, 395-414 (1970)

2.18 P.Rabinowitz: SIAM Rev. 10, 121-159 (1968)
2.19 R.E.Esch, W.L.Eastman: *Computational Methods for Best Approximation*, Tech. Report SEG-TR-67-30 (Sperry Rand Research Center 1967)
2.20 S.I.Gass: *Linear Programming*, 2nd ed. (McGraw-Hill, New York 1964)
2.21 M.J.D.Powell: In *Methods of Numerical Approximation*, ed. by D.C. Handscomb (Pergamon Press, Oxford 1966) Chap. 7, pp. 73-81
2.22 D.Braess: Numer. Math. 17, 357-366 (1971)
2.23 I.J.Schoenberg: Quart. Appl. Math. 4, 45-99 (Part A); 112-141 (Part B) (1946)
2.24 J.H.Ahlberg, E.N.Nilson, J.L.Walsh: *The Theory of Splines and Their Applications* (Academic Press, New York 1967)
2.25 I.J.Schoenberg (ed.): *Approximations with Special Emphasis on Spline Functions* (Academic Press, New York 1969)
2.26 T.N.E.Greville: *Theory and Applications of Spline Functions* (Academic Press, New York 1969)
2.27 M.H.Schultz: *Spline Analysis* (Prentice Hall, New York 1973)
2.28 C.deBoor: J. Approx. Theory 6, 50-62 (1972)
2.29 G.Birkhoff, C.R.deBoor: In *Approximation of Functions*, ed. by H.L. Garabedian (Elsevier Publishing Co., Amsterdam 1965) pp. 164-190
2.30 G.Birkhoff: In *Approximations with Special Emphasis on Spline Functions*, ed. by I.J.Schoenberg (Academic Press, New York 1969) pp. 185-221
2.31 G.Birkhoff: J. Math. Analysis and Applic. 42, 474-484 (1973)
2.32 A.R.Forrest: CGIP 1, 341-359 (1972)
2.33 T.Pavlidis: IEEE Trans. C-23, 689-697 (1973)
2.34 T.Pavlidis: IEEE Trans. C-24, 98-102 (1975)
2.35 T.Pavlidis, A.Maika: J. Approx. Theory 12, 61-69 (1974)
2.36 J.Vandewalle: IEEE Trans. C-24, 843-846 (1975)

Chapter 3

3.1 J.Sklansky: Pattern Recognition 2, 3-10 (1970)
3.2 J.Sklansky, D.F.Kibler: IEEE Trans. SMC-6, 637-647 (1976)
3.3 A.T.Fam: Proc. 3rd Intern. Joint Conf. Pattern Recognition (Coronado, Calif. Nov. 8-11, 1976) pp. 193-197
3.4 A.Rosenfeld: JACM 17, 146-160 (1970)
3.5 J.P.Mylopoulos, T.Pavlidis: JACM 18, 239-246 (1971)
3.6 J.P.Mylopoulos, T.Pavlidis: JACM 18, 247-254 (1971)
3.7 F.Harary: *Graph Theory* (Addison-Wesley, Reading 1969)
3.8 O.Ore: *Graphs and their Uses* (Random House, New York 1963)
3.9 C.L.Liu: *Introduction to Combinatorial Mathematics* (McGraw-Hill, New York 1968)
3.10 D.E.Knuth: *Fundamental Algorithms*, 1 (Addison-Wesley, Reading 1968)
3.11 W.Hacken, K.Appel: (Reported in Amer. Math. Society Meeting, 1977)
3.12 A.V.Aho, J.E.Hopcroft, J.D.Ullman: *The Design and Analysis of Computer Algorithms* (Addison-Wesley, Reading 1974)
3.13 C.T. Zahn: IEEE Trans. C-20, 68-86 (1971)
3.14 B.L. Bullock: *Pattern Recognition and Artificial Intelligence*, ed. by C.H. Chen (Academic Press, New York 1976) pp. 61-85
3.15 D.J. Burr, R.T. Chien: Proc. 3rd Intern. Joint Conf. Pattern Recognition (Coronado, Cailf. Nov. 8-11, 1976) pp. 519-523
3.16 K. Steiglitz: *An Introduction to Discrete Systems* (Wiley, New York 1974)
3.17 M.R. Garey, D.S. Johnson, R.E. Tarjan: SIAM J. of Computing 5, 704-714 (1976)
3.18 J.L. Kelly: *General Topology* (Van Nostrand, New York 1955)
3.19 B. Brons: CGIP 3, 48-62 (1974)
3.20 J.P. Mylopoulos: On the Definition and Recognition of Patterns in Discrete Space, Ph. D. Thesis (Dept. of Electr. Engin. Princeton University, 1970)

3.21 J. Mylopoulos: CGIP 1, 308-316 (1972)
3.22 S. Yokoi, J. Toriwaki, T. Fukumura: CGIP 4, 63-73 (1975)
3.23 M.J.E. Golay: IEEE Trans. C-18 733-740 (1969)
3.24 C.T. Zahn: 2nd Inter. Joint Conf. on Pattern Recognition (Copenhagen, August 1974) pp. 136-140
3.25 D. McClure: personal communication
3.26 G. Tourlakis, J. Mylopoulos: JACM 20, 439-455 (1973)
3.27 H.Y. Feng, T. Pavlidis: IEEE Trans. CAS-22, 427-439 (1975)

Chapter 4

4.1 P.H. Lindsay, D.A. Norman: *Human Information Processing* (Academic Press, New York 1972)
4.2 J.P. Strong, III, A. Rosenfeld: CACM 4, 237-246 (1973)
4.3 C.A. Harlow, S.A. Eisenbeis: IEEE Trans. C-22, 678-689 (1973)
4.4 S.L. Horowitz, T. Pavlidis: Journal of the ACM 23, 368-388 (1976)
4.5 S.L. Horowitz, T. Pavlidis: Proc. Conf. Comp. Graphics, Pattern Recognition and Data Structure (Los Angeles 1975) pp. 125-129
4.6 T.Pavlidis: CGIP 1, 360-372 (1972)
4.7 H.Y.Feng, T.Pavlidis: IEEE Trans. CAS-22, 427-439 (1975)
4.8 M.D.Kelly: In *Machine Intelligence*, 6 (Edinburgh Univ. Press, Edinburgh 1971)
4.9 A.Klinger: In *Optimizing Methods in Statistics*, ed. by J.S. Rustagi (Academic Press, New York 1971) pp. 303-337
4.10 L.Uhr: IEEE Trans. 21, 758-768 (1972)
4.11 R.A.Kirsch: In *Graph Languages*, ed. by F.Nake, A.Rosenfeld (North-Holland, Amsterdam 1972) pp. 1-19
4.12 E.M.Riseman, A.R.Hanson: Techn. report 74C-1 Dept. of Comp. Inform. Sci., Univ. Mass. (1974)
4.13 S.Tanimoto, T.Pavlidis: CGIP 4, 104-113 (1975)
4.14 S.Tanimoto: CGIP 5, 333-352 (1976)
4.15 A.Klinger, C.R.Dyer: CGIP 5, 68-105 (1976)
4.16 A.Hanson, E.M.Riseman, P.Nagin: Proc. 3rd Milwaukee Symp. On Automatic Computation And Control (1975) pp. 407-417
4.17 M.D. Levine, J. Leement: Proc. 3rd Intern. Joint Cof. Pattern Recognition (Coronado, Calif. Nov. 8-11, 1976) pp. 494-498
4.18 S.W. Zucker: CGIP 5, 382-399 (1976)
4.19 C.R. Brice, C.L. Fennema: Artificial Intelligence Journal 1, 205-226 (1970)
4.20 R.Bajcsy: CGIP 2, 118-130 (1973)
4.21 J.A.Feldman, Y.Yakimovsky: Artificial Intelligence Journal 5, 349-371 (1974)
4.22 J.N.Gupta, P.A.Wintz: IEEE Trans CAS-22, 351-362 (1975)
4.23 F.Holdermann, H.Kazmierczak: CGIP 1, 66-80 (1972)
4.24 T.Pavlidis: CGIP 1, 360-372 (1972)
4.25 H.Y.Feng, T.Pavlidis: IEEE Trans. CAS-22, 427-439 (1975)
4.26 D.Ernst, D.Bargel, F.Holdermann: Proc. 3rd Intern. Joint Conf. Pattern Recognition (Coronado, Calif. Nov. 8-11, 1976) pp. 679-683
4.27 C.Somerville, J.L.Mundy: Proc. 3rd Intern. Joint Conf. Pattern Recognition (Coronado, Calif. Nov. 8-11, 1976) pp. 745-748
4.28 E.U.Ramer: IEEE Trans. CAS-22, 363-374 (1975)
4.29 M.L.Baird: Proc. 3rd Intern. Joint Conf. Pattern Recognition (Coronado, Calif. Nov. 8-11, 1976) pp. 3-7
4.30 L.Mero, T.Vamos: Proc. 3rd Intern. Joint Conf. Pattern Recognition (Coronado, Calif. Nov. 8-11, 1976) pp. 31-36
4.31 W.A.Perkins: Proc. 3rd Intern. Joint Conf. Pattern Recognition (Coronado, Calif. Nov. 8-11, 1976) pp. 739-744

4.32 R.M.Haralick, I.Dinstein: IEEE Trans CAS-22, 440-450 (1975)
4.33 T.V.Robertson, P.H.Swain, K.S.Fu: TR-EE 73-26, Purdue University, 1973
4.34 T.Pavlidis, S.L.Horowitz: IEEE Trans. C-23, 860-870 (1974)
4.35 T.Pavlidis: ACM Trans. on Mathematical Software 2, 305-321 (1976)
4.36 R.N.Nagel, A.Rosenfeld: Proc. 1st Intern. Joint Conf. Pattern Recognition (1973) pp. 59-66
4.37 M.R.Bartz: IBM J. Res. Dev. 12, 354-360 (1968)
4.38 M.Nagao, S.Hashimoto, T.Sakai: Proc. 1st Intern. Joint Conf. Pattern Recognition (1973) pp. 499-503
4.39 R.Ohlander: *Analysis of natural scenes*. Ph.D. dissertation, Dept. of Computer Sci., Carnegie-Mellon Univ. (April 1975)
4.40 M.L.Baird, M.D.Kelly: CGIP 3, 1-22 (1974)
4.41 R.O.Duda, P.E.Hart: *Pattern Classification and Scene Analysis* (Wiley, New York 1973)
4.42 M.Hueckel: JACM 18, 113-125 (1971)
4.43 M.Hueckel: JACM 20, 634-647 (1973)
4.44 Y.Yakimovsky: JACM 23, 599-618 (1976)
4.45 B.L.Bullock: In *Pattern Recognition and Artificial Intelligence*, ed. by C.H.Chen (Academic Press, New York 1976) pp. 61-85
4.46 L.S.Davis: CGIP 4, 248-270 (1975)
4.47 H.Enomoto, T.Katayama: Proc. 3rd Intern. Joint Conf. Pattern Recognition (Coronado, Calif. Nov. 8-11, 1976) pp. 811-815
4.48 E.Persoon: CGIP 4, 425-446 (1976)
4.49 T.Pavlidis, S.Tanimoto: Proc. Conf. Comp. Graphics, Pattern Recognition and Data Structure (Los Angeles 1975) pp. 201-203

Chapter 5

5.1 S.L.Horowitz, T.Pavlidis: JACM 23, 368-388 (1976)
5.2 J.K.Hawkins: In *Picture Processing and Psychopictorics*, ed. by B.S. Lipkin and A.Rosenfeld (Academic Press, New York 1970) pp. 347-368
5.3 J.S.Weszka, C.R.Dyer, A.Rosenfeld: IEEE Trans. SMC-6, 269-285 (1976)
5.4 R.W.Conners, C.A.Harlow: Tech. Report IAL-4-76 (Univ. of Missouri, Columbia, 1976)
5.5 T.Pavlidis, S.Tanimoto: Proc. Conf. Comp. Graphics, Pattern Recognition and Data Structure (Los Angeles 1975) pp. 201-203
5.6 J.A.Feldman, Y.Yakimovsky: Artificial Intelligence Journal 5, 349-371 (1974)
5.7 R.Bajcsy, M.Tavakoli: IEEE Trans. CAS-22, 463-474 (1975)
5.8 J.M.Tenenbaum, H.G.Barrow: Proc. 3rd Intern. Joint Conf. Pattern Recognition (Coronado, Calif. Nov. 8-11, 1976) pp. 504-513
5.9 B.Julesz: IRE Trans. IT-8, 84-92 (1962)
5.10 R.M.Haralick, K.Shanmugan, I.Dinstein: IEEE Trans. SMC-3, 610-621 (1973)
5.11 M.M.Galloway: CGIP 4, 172-179 (1975)
5.12 R.Bajcsy: CGIP 2, 118-130 (1973)
5.13 R.P.Kruger, W.B.Thompson, A.F.Turner: IEEE Trans. SMC-4, 40-49 (1974)
5.14 N.J.Pressman: *Optical Texture Analysis for Automatic Cytology and Histology: A Markovian Approach, Ph.D. Thesis*. Univ. of Pennsylvania. Available as Tech. Report UCRL-52155, Lawrence Livermore Laboratory, Livermore, Calif. (Oct. 1976)
5.15 R.M.Haralick: In *Digital Picture Analysis*, ed. by A.Rosenfeld, Topics in Applied Physics, Vol. 11 (Springer, Berlin, Heidelberg, New York 1976) pp. 5-63
5.16 B.H.McCormick, S.N.Jayamurthy: Int. J. Comp. Inform. Sci. 3, 329-343 (1974)
5.17 S.W.Zucker: CGIP 5, 190-202 (1976)

5.18 S.D.Shapiro: Proc. 3rd Intern. Joint Conf. Pattern Recognition (Coronado, Calif. Nov. 8-11, 1976) pp. 205-207
5.19 H.Tamura, S.Mori, T.Yamawaki: Proc. 3rd Intern. Joint Conf. Pattern Recognition (Coronado, Calif. Nov. 8-11, 1976) pp. 273-277
5.20 J.F.O'Callaghan: Proc. 3rd Intern. Joint Conf. Pattern Recognition (Coronado, Calif. Nov. 8-11, 1976) pp. 294-298
5.21 J.T.Tou, D.B.Kao, Y.S.Chang: Proc. 3rd Intern. Joint Conf. Pattern Recognition (Coronado, Calif. Nov. 8-11, 1976) pp. 590-590p
5.22 S.L.Tanimoto, T.Pavlidis: CACM 20, 223-229 (1977)
5.23 H.Y.Feng, T.Pavlidis: CGIP 2, 103-117 (Oct. 1973)
5.24 B.Moayer, K.S.Fu: IEEE Trans. C-25, 262-274 (1976)
5.25 D.E.Knuth: *Fundamental Algorithms*, 1 (Addison-Wesley, Reading 1968)
5.26 T.Pavlidis: CGIP 1, 360-372 (1972)
5.27 H.Y.Feng, T.Pavlidis: IEEE Trans. CAS-22, 427-439 (1975)

Chapter 6

6.1 A.Guzman: Proc. Fall Joint Comput. Conf. 33, 291-304 (1968)
6.2 H.G.Barrow, A.P.Ambler, R.M.Burstall: In *Frontiers of Pattern Recognition*, ed. by S.Watanabe (Academic Press, New York 1972) pp. 1-29
6.3 Y.Yakimovsky, J.Feldman: Proc. 3rd Int. Joint Conf. Artificial Intelligence (Stanford Aug. 1973) pp. 580-588
6.4 R.Nevatia, T.O.Binford: Proc. 3rd Int. Joint Conf. Artificial Intelligence (Stanford Aug. 1973) pp. 641-647
6.5 W.A.Perkins, T.O.Binford: CGIP 2, 355-376 (1973)
6.6 M.Nagao, S.Hashimoto, T.Sakai: CGIP 2, 272-280 (1973)
6.7 J.M.Tenenbaum: CGIP 2, 308-320 (1973)
6.8 J.A.Feldman, Y.Yakimovsky: Artificial Intelligence Journal 5, 349-371 (1974)
6.9 M.Aiello, C.Lami, U.Montanari: CGIP 3, 225-235 (1974)
6.10 R.Bajcsy, M.Tavakoli: IEEE Trans. CAS-22, 463-474 (1975)
6.11 J.M.Tenenbaum, H.G.Barrow: Proc. 3rd Intern. Joint Conf. Pattern Recognition (Coronado, Calif. Nov. 8-11, 1976) pp. 504-513
6.12 T.D.Garvey: Proc. 3rd Intern. Joint Conf. Pattern Recognition (Coronado, Calif. Nov. 8-11, 1976) pp. 567-575
6.13 T.Sakai, T.Kanade, Y.Ohta: Proc. 3rd Intern. Joint Conf. Pattern Recognition (Coronado, Calif. Nov. 8-11, 1976) pp. 581-585
6.14 C.A.Harlow, S.A.Eisenbeis: IEEE Trans. C-22, 678-689 (1973)
6.15 C.A.Harlow, S.J.Dywer III, G.Lodwick: In *Digital Picture Analysis*, ed. by A.Rosenfeld, Topics in Applied Physics, Vol. 11 (Springer, Berlin, Heidelberg, New York 1976) pp. 65-150
6.16 D.Waltz: In *Applied Computation Theory*, ed. by T.Yeh (Prentice Hall, New York 1976) pp. 468-529
6.17 A.Rosenfeld, R.A.Hummel, S.W.Zucker: IEEE Trans. SMC-6, 420-433 (1976)
6.18 S.W.Zucker: Proc. 3rd Intern. Joint Conf. Pattern Recognition (Coronado, Calif. Nov. 8-11, 1976) pp. 852-861
6.19 S.W.Zucker, R.A.Hummel, A.Rosenfeld: IEEE Trans. C-26, 394-403 (1977)
6.20 J.E.Hopcroft, J.D.Ullman: *Formal Languages and Their Relation to Automata* (Addison-Wesley, Reading 1969)
6.21 J.M.Brayer, P.H.Swain, K.S.Fu: In *Syntactic Pattern Recognition, Applications*, ed. by K.S.Fu (Springer, New York, Heidelberg, Berlin 1977) pp. 215-242
6.22 J.Keng, K.S.Fu: Proc. Symp. Current Math. Problems in Image Science (Monterey, Calif. Nov. 1976)
6.23 S.W.Zucker: *Production Schemes with Feedback*, Tech. Report No. 77-2 (McGill Univ., Febr. 1977)
6.24 D.Nitzan, A.E.Brain, R.O.Duda: IEEE Proc. 65, 206-220 (1977)

6.25 M.R.Garey, D.S.Johnson, R.E.Tarjan: SIAM J. of Computing 5, 704-714 (1976)
6.26 J.R.Ullmann: JACM 23, 31-42 (1976)
6.27 M.O.Rabin: Proc. IFIPS 615-619 (1974)
6.28 R.Ford,Jr., D.R.Fulkerson: *Flows in Networks*, (Princeton Univ. Press, Princeton 1962)
6.29 S.L.Tanimoto, T.Pavlidis: CACM 20, 223-229 (1977)
6.30 S.Tanimoto: In Proc. IEEE Dec. Control Conf. (Clearwater, Florida Dec. 1976)
6.31 N.Badler: 2nd Intern. Joint Conf. Pattern Recognition (Copenhagen, August 1974) pp. 157-161
6.32 L.Uhr: Proc. 3rd Intern. Joint Conf. Pattern Recognition (Coronado, Calif. Nov. 8-11, 1976) pp. 287-293
6.33 J.K.Aggarval, R.O.Duda: IEEE Trans. C-24, 966-976 (1975)
6.34 C.R.Brice, C.L.Fennema: Artificial Intelligence Journal 1, 205-226 (1970)
6.35 Y.Yakimovsky: JACM 23, 599-618 (1976)
6.36 K.S.Fu: *Sequential Methods in Pattern Recognition and Machine Learning* (Academic Press, New York 1968)
6.37 D.Marr: *On the purpose of low level vision*, MIT-Art. Intel. Tech. Report 324 (1974)
6.38 E.C.Freuder: In *Pattern Recognition and Artificial Intelligence*, ed. by C.H.Chen (Academic Press, New York 1976) pp. 248-256
6.39 B.L.Bullock: In *Pattern Recognition and Artificial Intelligence*, ed. by C.H.Chen (Academic Press, New York 1976) pp. 61-85
6.40 S.W.Zucker, E.V.Krisnamurthy, R.L.Haar: Tech. Report TR-477, Univ. of Mayland, August 1976
6.41 E.A.Coddington, N.Levinson: *Theory of Ordinary Differential Equations* (McGraw-Hill, New York 1955)

Chapter 7

7.1 R.S.Ledley: Science 146, 216-223 (1964)
7.2 C.T.Zahn, R.Z.Roskies: IEEE Trans. C-21, 269-281 (1972)
7.3 K.S.Fu, P.H.Swain: *Software Engineering*, Vol. 2, ed. by J.Tou (Academic Press, New York 1971) pp. 155-182
7.4 K.S.Fu: *Syntactic Methods in Pattern Recognition* (Academic Press, New York 1974)
7.5 K.S.Fu (ed.): *Syntactic Pattern Recognition, Applications* (Springer, Berlin, Heidelberg, New York 1977)
7.6 U.Grenander: Quarterly of Applied Mathematics 27, 1-55 (1969)
7.7 U.Grenander: *Pattern Synthesis: Lectures in Pattern Theory Vol. 1* (Springer, Berlin, Heidelberg, New York 1976)
7.8 T.Pavlidis: *Software Engineering*, Vol. 2, ed. by J.Tou (Academic Press, New York 1971) pp. 203-225
7.9 T.Pavlidis: Pattern Recognition 4, 5-17 (1972)
7.10 J.W.Bacus, E.E.Gose: IEEE Trans. SMC-2, 513-526 (1974)
7.11 I.T.Young, J.E.Walker, J.E.Bowie: Inform. Control 25, 357-370 (1974)
7.12 S.Løvtrup, B.Vonsydow: Bull. Math. Biophys. 36, 567-575 (1974)
7.13 L.Kaufman et al.: Final Report Contract AF19 (628)-5830 (Sperry Rand Research Center Sudbury, Mass. Sept. 1967)
7.14 P.A.Kolers: *Picture Processing and Psychopictorics*, ed. by B.S.Lipkin, A.Rosenfeld (Academic Press, New York 1970) pp. 181-202
7.15 D.J.Landridge: *Frontiers of Pattern Recognition*, ed. by S.Watanabe (Academic Press, New York 1972) pp. 347-365
7.16 B.Rosenberg: CGIP 1, 193-200 (1972)
7.17 J.F.O'Callaghan: CGIP 3, 300-312 (1972)

7.18 D.B.Cooper: In *Pattern Recognition and Artificial Intelligence*, ed. by C.H.Chen (Academic Press, New York 1976) pp. 145-163
7.19 L.D.Harmon, W.F.Hunt: Proc. 3rd Intern. Joint Conf. Pattern Recognition (Coronado, Calif. Nov. 8-11, 1976) pp. 183-188
7.20 N.Yalabik, D.B.Cooper: Proc. 3rd Intern. Joint Conf. Pattern Recognition (Coronado, Calif. Nov. 8-11, 1976) pp. 350-354
7.21 L.S.Davis, A.Rosenfeld: Proc. 3rd Intern. Joint Conf. Pattern Recognition (Coronado, Calif. Nov. 8-11, 1976) pp. 591-597
7.22 L.G.Shapiro: Proc. 3rd Intern. Joint Conf. Pattern Recognition (Coronado, Calif. Nov. 8-11, 1976) pp. 759-763
7.23 K.Rao, K.Balck: Proc. 3rd Intern. Joint Conf. Pattern Recognition (Coronado, Calif. Nov. 8-11, 1976) pp. 778-782
7.24 A.Rosenfeld, J.S.Weszka: Computer 9, 28-38 (1976)
7.25 R.J.Spinrad: Inform. Control 8, 124-142 (1965)
7.26 T.Pavlidis: Inform. Control 14, 526-537 (1968)
7.27 E.Wong, J.A.Steppe: *Methodologies of Pattern Recognition*, ed. by S. Watanabe (Academic Press, New York 1969) pp. 535-546
7.28 D.Rutovitz: In *Machine Intelligence* 5, 435-462 (1970)
7.29 A.Klinger: CACM 14, 21-25 (1971)
7.30 A.Klinger, A.Kochman, N.Alexandridis: IEEE Trans. C-20, 1014-1022 (1971)
7.31 Y.Nakimano, K.Nakato, Y.Uchikura, A.Nakajima: Proc. 1st Intern. Joint Conf. Pattern Recognition (1973) pp. 172-178
7.32 M.Yoshida, K.Iwata, E.Yamamoto, T.Masui, Y.Kabuyama: Proc. 3rd Intern. Joint Conf. Pattern Recognition (Coronado, Calif. Nov. 8-11, 1976) pp. 645-649
7.33 K.Preston: In *Digital Picture Analysis*, ed. by A.Rosenfeld, Topics in Applied Physics, Vol. 11 (Springer, Berlin, Heidelberg, New York 1976) pp. 209-294
7.34 T.Fujita, M.Nakanishi, K.Miyata: Proc. 3rd Intern. Joint Conf. Pattern Recognition (Coronado, Calif. Nov. 8-11, 1976) pp. 119-121
7.35 J.H.Kulich, T.W.Challis, C.Brace, S.Christodoulakis, I.Merrit, P. Needlands: Proc. 3rd Intern. Joint Conf. Pattern Recognition (Coronado, Calif. Nov. 8-11, 1976) pp. 233-237
7.36 F.A.Groen, P.W.Verbeek, G.A.vanZee: Proc. 3rd Intern. Joint Conf. Pattern Recognition (Coronado, Calif. Nov. 8-11, 1976) pp. 547-550
7.37 S.Dywer: In *Pattern Recognition and Artificial Intelligence*, ed. by C.H.Chen (Academic Press, New York 1976)
7.38 S.K.Chang: CACM 14, 21-25 (1971)
7.39 G.T.Herman: CGIP 1, 123-144 (1972)
7.40 G.T.Herman, S.W.Rowland: CGIP 2, 151-178 (1973)
7.41 R.M.Mersereau: CGIP 2, 179-195 (1973)
7.42 R.L.Kashyap, M.C.Mittal: IEEE Trans. C-24, 915-923 (1975)
7.43 S.K.Chang, Y.R.Wang: Pattern Recognition 7, 167-176 (1975)
7.44 G.T.Herman, A.Lent: CGIP 5, 319-332 (1976)
7.45 W.G.Wee, T.T.Hsieh: IEEE Trans. SCM-6, 486-493(1976)
7.46 E.L.Brill: Presented at the 1968 WESCON Conference, Session 25
7.47 J.R.Bennet, J.S.MacDonald: IEEE Trans. C-24, 803-820 (1975)
7.48 G.H.Granlund: IEEE Trans. C-21, 195-201 (1972)
7.49 G.H.Granlund: IEEE Trans. BME-23, 182-192 (1976)
7.50 C.W.Richards,Jr., H.Hemami: IEEE Trans. SMC-4, 371-378 (1974)
7.51 E.Persoon, K.S.Fu: IEEE Trans. SMC-7, 170-179 (1977)
7.52 R.V.Churchill: *Fourier Series and Boundary Value Problems* (McGraw-Hill, New York 1941)
7.53 J.R.Rice: *The Approxiamtion of Functions* 2 (Addison-Wesley, Reading 1969)
7.54 H.Freeman: IEEE Trans. EC-10, 260-268 (1961)
7.55 H.Freeman: *Picture Processing and Psychopictorics*, ed. by B.S.Lipkin, A.Rosenfeld (Academic Press, New York 1970) pp. 241-266

7.56 G.Gallus: *Applicazioni Bio-mediche del Calcolo Elettronico* (1968) pp. 95-108
7.57 T.Huang, K.S.Fu: CGIP 1, 257-283 (1972)
7.58 P.H.Swain, K.S.Fu: Pattern Recognition 4, 83-100 (1972)
7.59 H.C.Lee, K.S.Fu: IEEE Trans. C-21, 660-666 (1972)
7.60 T.Pavlidis: Proc. 3rd Intern. Joint Conf. Pattern Recognition (Coronado, Calif. Nov. 8-11, 1976) pp. 95-99
7.61 L.S.Davis: IEEE Trans. C-26, 236-242 (1977)
7.62 T.Pavlidis, S.L.Horowitz: IEEE Trans. C-23, 860-870 (1974)
7.63 D.B.Cooper, N.Yalabik: IEEE Trans. C-25, 1020-1032 (1976)
7.64 A.Albano: Comp. Graphics and Image Proc. 3, 23-33 (1974)
7.65 H.Wechsler, J.S.Sklansky: Pattern Recognition 9, 21-30 (1977)
7.66 W.A.Perkins: Tech. Report GMR-2125, General Motors Research Laboratories, April 1976. (Summarized in Proc. 3rd Intern. Joint Conf. Pattern Recognition (Coronado, Calif. Nov. 8-11, 1976) pp. 739-744)
7.67 R.O.Duda, P.E.Hart: CACM 15, 11-15 (1972)
7.68 F.Attneave: Psychol. Rev. 61, 183-193 (1954)
7.69 R.O.Duda, P.E.Hart: *Pattern Classification and Scene Analysis* (Wiley, New York 1973)
7.70 A.Rosenfeld, E.Johnston: IEEE Trans. C-22, 874-878 (1973)
7.71 T.Pavlidis: Proc. Conf. on Computer Graphics, Pattern Recognition and Data Structure (Los Angeles, Calif. May 1975) pp. 215-219
7.72 H.Freeman, L.S.Davis: Tech. report TR-399 Univ. of Maryland (1975)
7.73 D.E.McClure: *Quarterly of Applied Mathematics* 33, 1-37 (1975)
7.74 D.E.McClure: personal communication
7.75 L.S.Davis: Proc. 1977 Pattern Recognition and Image Processing Conference, pp. 191-197
7.76 T.Kaneko, P.Mancini: Proc. 6th Annual Princeton Conf. on Information Sciences and Systems (1972) pp. 337-341
7.77 U.Montanari: CACM 13, 41-47 (1970)
7.78 T.Pavlidis: *Frontiers of Pattern Recognition*, ed. by S.Watanabe (Academic Press, New York 1972) pp. 421-451
7.79 U.Ramer: Computer Graphics and Image Processing 1, 244-256 (1972)
7.80 J.Sklansky: Pattern Recognition 2, 3-10 (1970)
7.81 J.Sklansky, R.L.Chazin, B.J.Hansen: IEEE Trans. C-21, 260-268 (1972)
7.82 P.J.Davis: *Interpolation and Approximation* (Blaisdell, New York 1963)
7.83 E.Issacson, H.B.Keller: *Analysis of Numerical Methods* (Wiley, New York 1966)
7.84 L.Fox, I.B.Parker: *Chebyshev Polynomials in Numerical Analysis* (Oxford University Press, London 1968)
7.85 J.Sklansky, D.F.Kibler: IEEE Trans. SMC-6, 637-647 (1976)
7.86 C.H.Reinsch: Numer. Math. 10, 177 (1967)
7.87 C.H.Reinsch: Numer. Math. 16, 451 (1971)
7.88 A.K.Cline: CACM 17, 218-220 (1974)
7.89 I.Tomek: IEEE Trans. C-23, 445-448 (1974)
7.90 J.R.Rice: J. Approx. Theory 4, 332-338 (1971)
7.91 A.Lotz, W.Vogt, B.Popp, M.Knedel: Comp. Biomed. Research 9, 21-30 (1976)
7.92 J.R.Ellis,Jr., M.Eden: Inform. Control 30, 169-186 (1976)
7.93 T.Pavlidis: ACM Trans. on Mathematical Software 2, 305-321 (1976)

Chapter 8

8.1 J.E.Hopcroft, J.D.Ullman: *Formal Languages and Their Relation to Automata* (Addison-Wesley, Reading 1969)
8.2 K.S.Fu: *Syntactic Methods in Pattern Recognition* (Academic Press, New York 1974)

8.3 J.F.Jarvis: Proc. 3rd Intern. Joint Conf. Pattern Recognition (Coronado, Calif. Nov. 8-11, 1976) pp. 189-192
8.4 A.V.Aho, J.D.Ullman: *The Theory of Parsing, Translation, and Compiling, Vol.I* (Parsing, Prentice Hall, New York 1972)
8.5 S.W.Zucker: *Production Systems with Feedback*, Technical Report No. 77-2, (February 1977) Dept. of Electrical Engineering, McGill University, Montreal
8.6 P.H.Swain, K.S.Fu: Pattern Recognition 4, 83-100 (1972)
8.7 H.Freeman: *Picture Processing and Psychopictorics*, ed. by B.S.Lipkin, A.Rosenfeld (Academic Press, New York 1970) pp. 241-266
8.8 B.Brons: CGIP 3, 48-62 (1974)
8.9 S.L.Horowitz: CACM 18, 281-285 (May 1975)
8.10 S.L.Horowitz: In *Syntactic Pattern Recognition, Applications*, ed. by K.S.Fu (Springer, Berlin, Heidelberg, New York 1977) pp. 31-49
8.11 T. Pavlidis, F. Ali: IEEE Trans. PAMI-1,2-9 (1979)
8.12 G.Stockman, L.Kanal, M.C.Kyle: CACM 19, 688-695 (1976)
8.13 R.S.Ledley: Science 146, 216-223 (1964)
8.14 A.Rosenfeld, J.S.Weszka: Computer 9, 28-38 (1976)
8.15 I.T.Young, J.E.Walker, J.E.Bowie: Inform. Control 25, 357-370 (1974)
8.16 W.W.Stalling: CGIP 1, 47-65 (1972)
8.17 W.W.Stalling: In *Syntactic Pattern Recognition, Applications*, ed. by K.S.Fu (Springer, Berlin, Heidelberg, New York 1977) pp. 95-123
8.18 A.V.Aho, J.E.Hopcroft, J.D.Ullman: *The Design and Analysis of Computer Algorithms* (Addison-Wesley, Reading 1974)
8.19 F.Ali, T.Pavlidis: IEEE Trans. SMC-7,537-541 (1977)
8.20 J.F.Jarvis: personal communication
8.21 C.Harlow: *Computer Graphics and Image Processing 2* (1973) 60-82
8.22 M.Ejiri, T.Uno, M.Mese, S.Ikeda: *Computer Graphics and Image Processing 2* (1973) 326-339
8.23 L.S.Davis, A.Rosenfeld: Proc. 3rd Intern. Joint Conf. Pattern Recognition (Coronado, Calif. Nov. 8-11, 1976) pp. 591-597
8.24 L.S. Davis: IEEE Trans. PAMI-1, 60-72 (1979)
8.25 M.D.Levine, J.Leemet: Pattern Recognition 7, 177-185 (1975)
8.26 R.W.Erlich, J.P.Foith: IEEE Trans. C- 25, 725-736 (1976)
8.27 T.Lozano-Perez: CGIP 6, 43-60 (1977)
8.28 R.DeMori: *Syntactic Pattern Recognition, Applications*, ed. by K.S.Fu (Springer, Berlin, Heidelberg, New York 1977) pp. 65-94
8.29 D.R.Reddy: Proc. IEEE 64, 501-531 (1976)
8.30 T.Pavlidis, F.Ali: IEEE Trans. SMC-5, 610-614 (1975)

Chapter 9

9.1 A.C.Shaw: Inform. Control 14, 453-481 (1969)
9.2 B.Moayer, K.S.Fu: IEEE Trans. C-25, 262-274 (1976)
9.3 L.S.Frischkopf, L.D.Harmon: Proc. of the Symposium on Information Theory, ed. by C.Cherry (Butterworth, London 1961) pp. 300-316
9.4 M.Eden: IRE Trans. Inform. Theory, IT-8, 160-166 (1962)
9.5 G.Ewald, G.C.Shephard: Math. Zeitschr. 91, 1-19 (1966)
9.6 F.A.Valentine: Convex Sets (McGraw-Hill, New York 1964)
9.7 D.E.McClure, R.A.Vitale: J. Math. Anal. Appl. 51, 326-358 (1975)
9.8 G.Nagy: IEEE Trans. SSC-5, 273-278 (1969)
9.9 D.R.Andrews, A.J.Atrubin, K.C.Hu: IBM J. Res. Devel. 12, 364-371 (1968)
9.10 F.L.Alt: Journal of the ACM 11, 240-258 (1962)
9.11 V.E.Guliano, P.E.Jones, G.E.Kimball, R.F.Meyer, B.A.Stein: Inform. Control 4, 332-345 (1961)
9.12 M.K.Hu: IRE Trans. Inform. Theory IT-8, 179-187 (1962)

9.13 M.J.Hannah: M. Sc. Thesis, Industrial Engin. Dept. Univ. of Missouri, Columbia (June 1971)
9.14 F.W.Smith, M.H.Wright: IEEE Trans. C-20, 1089-1095 (1971)
9.15 S.A.Dudani, K.J.Breeding, R.B.McGhee: IEEE Trans. C-26, 39-46 (1977)
9.16 R.G.Casey: IBM J. Res. Dev. 14, 91-101 (1970)
9.17 H.Blum: In *Symposium on Models for the Perception of Speech and Visual Form* (M.I.T. Press 1964)
9.18 O.Philbrick: Report No. 288, Air Force Cambridge Research Laboratories, November 1966.
9.19 A.Rosenfeld, J.L.Pfaltz: JACM 13, 471-494 (1966)
9.20 C.J.Hilditch: In *Machine Intelligence 4* (1969) pp. 403-420
9.21 J.C.Mott-Smith: In *Picture Processing and Psychopictorics*, ed. by B.S.Lipkin, A.Rosenfeld (Academic Press, New York 1970) pp. 267-283
9.22 U.Montanari: JACM 16, 534-549 (1969)
9.23 H.Blum: J. Theor. Biol. 38, 205-287 (1973)
9.24 J.S.N.Murthy, K.J.Udupa: CGIP 3, 247-259 (1974)
9.25 H.Blum, R.Nagel: Proc. 1977 Pattern Recognition and Image Processing Conference
9.26 E.Persoon, K.S.Fu: IEEE Trans. SMC-7, 170-179 (1977)
9.27 W.W.Stallings: CGIP 1, 47-65 (1972)
9.28 W.W.Stallings: In *Syntactic Pattern Recognition, Applications*, ed. by K.S.Fu (Springer, Berlin, Heidelberg, New York 1977) pp. 95-123
9.29 E.T.Lee: IEEE Trans. SMC-5, 629-632 (1975)
9.30 T.Pavlidis: Pattern Recognition 1, 165-178 (Nov. 1968)
9.31 T.Pavlidis: Pattern Recognition 4, 5-17 (1972)
9.32 T.Pavlidis: *Frontiers of Pattern Recognition*, ed. by S.Watanabe (Academic Press, New York 1972) pp. 421-451
9.33 M.I.Shamos, D.Hoey: Proc. 168th9 IEEE Symp. Found. Comp. Science, pp. 208-215 (1976)
9.34 J.L.Bentley, M.I.Siamos: Inform. Proc. Letters
9.35 F.Y.H.Feng: *Ph. D. Thesis* (Princeton University, Princeton 1974)
9.36 H.Y.Feng, T.Pavlidis: IEEE Trans. C-24, 636-650 (1975)
9.37 T.Pavlidis, H.Y.Feng: In *Syntactic Pattern Recognition, Applications*, ed. by K.S.Fu (Springer, Berlin, Heidelberg, New York 1977) pp. 125-145
9.38 T.Pavlidis: In *Graphic Languages*, ed. by F.Nake, A.Rosenfeld (North-Holland, Amsterdam 1972) pp. 210-224
9.39 F.H.Feng, M.J.Gillotte: Tech. Report 76-63, American Society for Metals, Metals Park, Ohio (1976)

Chapter 10

10.1 N.J.Nilsson: *Learning Machines* (McGraw Hill, New York 1965)
10.2 K.S.Fu: *Sequential Methods in Pattern Recognition and Machine Learning* (Academic Press, New York 1968)
10.3 J.M.Mendel, K.S.Fu: *Adaptive, Learning and Pattern Recognition Systems*, (Academic Press, New York 1970)
10.4 R.O.Duda, P.E.Hart: *Pattern Classification and Scene Analysis* (Wiley, New York 1973)
10.5 K.Fukunaga: *Introduction to Statistical Pattern Recognition* (Academic Press, New York 1972)
10.6 W.S.Meisel: *Computer-Oriented Approaches to Pattern Recognition* (Academic Press, New York 1972)
10.7 E.A.Patrick: *Foundations of Pattern Recognition* (Prentice Hall, New York 1972)
10.8 Ya.Z.Tsypkin: *Foundations of the Theory of Learning Systems* (Academic Press, New York 1973)

10.9 J.T.Tou, R.C.Gonzales: *Pattern Recognition Principles* (Addison-Wesley, Reading 1974)
10.10 T.Y.Young, T.W.Calvert: *Classification, Estimation and Pattern Recognition* (Elsevire, New York 1974)
10.11 K.S.Fu (ed.): *Digital Pattern Recognition* (Springer, Berlin, Heidelberg, New York 1976)
10.12 K.S.Fu, A.Rosenfeld: IEEE Trans. C-25, 1336-1346 (1976)
10.13 K.S.Fu: *Syntactic Methods in Pattern Recognition* (Academic Press, New York 1974)
10.14 A.V.Aho, J.E.Hopcroft, J.D.Ullman: *The Design and Analysis of Computer Algorithms* (Addison-Wesley, Reading 1974)
10.15 K.S.Fu, T.L.Booth: IEEE Trans. SMC-5, 95-111 (1975), (Part I) and pp. 409-423 (Part II)
10.16 J.E.Hopcroft, J.D.Ullman: *Formal Languages and Their Realtion to Automata* (Addison-Wesley, Reading 1969)
10.17 A.Aho, J.D.Ullman: *The Theory of Parsing, Translation and Compiling, I:* Parsing (Prentice Hall, New York 1972)
10.18 K.S.Fu: In *Frontiers of Pattern Recognition*, ed. by S.Watanabe (Academic Press, New York 1972) pp. 113-137
10.19 L.W.Fung, K.S.Fu: IEEE Trans. C-24, 662-667 (1975)
10.20 S.Y.Lu, K.S.Fu: IEEE Trans. C-26 (1977) (in press)
10.21 W.S.Brainerd: Inform. Control 14, 217-231 (1969)
10.22 K.S.Fu: In *Pattern Recognition and Artificial Intelligence*, ed. by C.H.Chen (Academic Press, New York 1976) pp. 257-291
10.23 W.C.Rounds: Proc. 10th IEEE Symp. Switch. and Automata Theory (1969) pp. 143-148
10.24 J.W.Thatcher: Proc. 10th IEEE Symp. Switch. and Automata Theory (1969) pp. 129-142
10.25 K.S.Fu, B.K.Bhargava: IEEE Trans. C-22, 1087-1099 (1973)
10.26 B.Moayer, K.S.Fu: IEEE Trans. C-25, 262-274 (1976)
10.27 B.Moayer, K.S.Fu: In *Syntactic Pattern Recognition, Applications* ed. by K.S.Fu (Springer, Berlin, Heidelberg, New York 1977) pp. 179-214
10.28 J.M.Brayer, P.H.Swain, K.S.Fu: In *Syntactic Pattern Recognition, Applications*, ed. by K.S.Fu (Springer, Berlin, Heidelberg, New York 1977) pp. 215-242
10.29 Brayer, K.S.Fu: In *Pattern Recognition and Artificial Intelligence*, ed. by C.H.Chen (Academic Press, New York 1976)
10.30 R.Y.Li, K.S.Fu: Proc. 1976 Symp. on Machine Processing of Remotely Sensed Data, pp. 2A.10-2A.16
10.31 J.Keng, K.S.Fu: Proc. Symp. Current Math. Problems in Image Science (Monterey, Calif. Nov. 1976)
10.32 R.C.Gonzales, J.J.Edwards, M.G.Thomason: Int. J. Comp. Inf. Sciences 5, 145-164 (1976)
10.33 S.Gorn: Proc. Syst. and Comp. Science Conf. (London, Ont. Canada, 1965) [Quoted by Brainerd, op.cit.].
10.34 R.A.Kirsch: IEEE Trans. EC-14, 363 (1964)
10.35 R.Narasimhan: Inf. Control 7, 151 (1964)
10.36 A.C.Shaw: Inf. Control 14, 9-52 (1969)
10.37 A.C.Shaw: JACM 17, 453-481 (1970)
10.38 A.Rosenfeld, J.L.Pfaltz: Proc. Joint International Conference on Artificial Intelligence (Washington D.C. 1969) pp. 609-619
10.39 J.L.Pfaltz: CGIP 1, 193-200 (1972)
10.40 J.Feder: Inform. Sciences 3, 225-241 (1971)
10.41 M.F.Dacey: Pattern Recognition 2, 11-31 (1970)
10.42 J.C.Schwebel: In *Graph Languages*, ed. by F.Nake, A.Rosenfeld (North-Holland 1972) pp. 195-207
10.43 M.B. Clowes: In *Graph Languages*, ed by F. Nake, A. Rosenfeld (North-Holland, Amsterdam 1972) pp. 70-82

10.44 U. Montanari: Inform. Control 16, 243-267 (1970)
10.45 T. Pavlidis: JACM 19, 11-22 (1972)
10.46 T. Pavlidis: In: *Graph Languages*, ed by F. Nake, A. Rosenfeld (North-Holland, Amsterdam 1972) pp. 210-224
10.47 J. Mylopoulos: CGIP 1, 308-316 (1972)
10.48 J. Mylopoulos: Proc. 13th IEEE Symp. Switch and Automata Theory, (1972) pp. 108-120
10.49 N.Abe, M.Mizumoto, J.Toyoda, K.Tanaka: Journal of Computer System Science 7, 37-65 (1973)
10.50 C.P.Cook: Siam J. Comput. 3, 90-99 (1974)
10.51 R.H.Anderson: *Ph.D. Thesis* (Harvard University 1968)
10.52 R.H.Anderson: In *Syntactic Pattern Recognition, Applications*, ed. by K.S.Fu (Springer, Berlin, Heidelberg, New York 1977) pp. 147-177
10.53 A.Rosenfeld: Machine Intelligence 6, 281-294 (1971)
10.54 D.L.Milgram, A.Rosenfeld: In *Graph Languages*, ed. by F.Nake, A. Rosenfeld (North-Holland, Amsterdam 1972) pp. 187-191
10.55 G.Siromoney, R.S.Siromoney, K.Krithivanasan: CGIP 1, 284-307 (1972)
10.56 P.A.Ota: Pattern Recognition 7, 61-65 (1975)
10.57 F.Nake, A.Rosenfeld (eds.): *Graph Languages* (North-Holland, Amsterdam 1972)
10.58 S.Watanabe: Proc. 3rd Intern. Joint Conf. Pattern Recognition (Coronado, Calif. Nov. 8-11, 1976) pp. 602-606
10.59 D.E.Knuth: *Fundamental Algorithms*, 1 (Addison-Wesley, Reading 1968)
10.60 F.Harary: *Graph Theory* (Addison-Wesley, Reading 1969)

Subject Index

A. H. Eschenfelder

Magnetic Bubble Technology

1980. 271 figures, 8 tables. Approx. 360 pages
(Springer Series in Solid-State Sciences, Volume 14)
ISBN 3-540-09822-4

Contents:
Introduction to Magnetic Bubbles. – Static Properties of Magnetic Bubbles. – Dynamic Properties of Magnetic Bubbles. – Basic Permalloy-Bar Bubble Devices. – Other Bubble Device Forms. – Bubble Materials. – Device Chip Fabrication. – Chip Packaging. – Applications. – Future Prospects. – References. – Subject Index.

Digital Pattern Recognition

Editor: *K. S. Fu*

1976. 54 figures, 4 tables. XI, 206 pages
(Communication and Cybernetics, Volume 10)
ISBN 3-540-07511-9

Contents:
K.S. Fu: Introduction. – *T. M. Cover, T. J. Wagner:* Topics in Statistical Pattern Recognition. – *E. Diday, J.-C. Simon:* Clustering Analysis. – *K. S. Fu:* Syntactic (Linguistic) Pattern Recognition. – *A. Rosenfeld, J. S. Weszka:* Picture Recognition. – *J. J. Wolf:* Speech Recognition and Understanding.

T. Kohonen

Associative Memory

A System-Theoretical Approach

Corrected printing. 1978. 54 figures, 7 tables. IX, 176 pages
(Communication and Cybernetics, Volume 17)
ISBN 3-540-08017-1

Contents:
Introduction. – Associative Search Methods. – Adaptive Formation of Optimal Associative Mappings. – On Biological Associative Memory.

Syntactic Pattern Recognition, Applications

Editor: *K. S. Fu*

1977. 135 figures, 19 tables. XI, 270 pages
(Communication and Cybernetics, Volume 14)
ISBN 3-540-07841-X

Contents:
K. S. Fu: Introduction to Syntactic Pattern Recognition. – *S. L. Horowitz:* Peak Recognition in Waveforms. – *J. E. Albus:* Electrocardiogram Interpretation Using a Stochastic Finite State Model. – *R. DeMori:* Syntactic Recognition of Speech Patterns. – *W. W. Stallings:* Chinese Character Recognition. – *Th. Pavlidis, H.-Y. F. Feng:* Shape Discrimination. – *R. H. Anderson:* Two-Dimensional Mathematical Notation. – *B. Moayer, K. S. Fu:* Fingerprint Classification. – *J. M. Brayer, P. H. Swain, K. S. Fu:* Modeling of Earth Resources Satellite Data. – *T. Vámos:* Industrial Objects and Machine Parts Recognition.

Springer-Verlag
Berlin
Heidelberg
New York

Digital Picture Analysis

Editor: *A. Rosenfeld*

1976. 114 figures, 47 tables. XIII, 351 pages
(Topics in Applied Physics, Volume 11)
ISBN 3-540-07579-8

Contents:
A. Rosenfeld: Introduction. – *R. M. Haralick:* Automatic Remote Sensor Image Processing. – *C. A. A. Harlow, S. J. Dwyer III., G. Lodwick:* On Radiographic Image Analysis. – *R. L. McIlwain, Jr.:* Image Processing in High Energy Physics. – *K. Preston, Jr.:* Digital Picture Analysis in Cytology. – *J. R. Ullmann:* Picture Analysis in Character Recognition.

Nonlinear Methods of Spectral Analysis

Editor: *S. Haykin*

1979. 45 figures, 2 tables. XI, 247 pages
(Topics in Applied Physics, Volume 34)
ISBN 3-540-09351-6

Contents:
S. Haykin: Introduction. – *S. Haykin, S. Kesler:* Prediction: Error Filtering and Maximum-Entropy Spectral Estimation. – *T. J. Ulrych, M. Ooe:* Autoregressive and Mixed Autoregressive-Moving Average Models and Spectra. – *E. A. Robinson:* Iterative Least-Squares Procedure for ARMA Spectral Estimation. – *J. Capon:* Maximum-Likelihood Spectral Estimation. – *R. N. McDonough:* Application of the Maximum-Likelihood Method and the Maximum-Entropy Method to Array Processing. – Subject Index.

Image Reconstruction from Projections

Implementation and Applications

Editor: *G. T. Herman*

1979. 120 figures, 10 tables. XII, 284 pages
(Topics in Applied Physics, Volume 32)
ISBN 3-540-09417-2

Contents:
G. T. Herman, R. M. Lewitt: Overview of Image Reconstruction from Projections. – *S. W. Rowland:* Computer Implementation of Image Reconstruction Formulas. – *R. N. Bracewell:* Image Reconstruction in Radio Astronomy. – *M. D. Altschuler:* Reconstruction of the Global-Scale Three-Dimensional Solar Corona. – *T. F. Budinger, G. T. Gullberg, R. H. Huesman:* Emission Computed Tomography. – *E. H. Wood, J. H. Kinsey, R. A. Robb, B. K. Gilbert, L. D. Harris, E. L. Ritman:* Applications of High Temporal Resolution, Computerized Tomography to Physiology and Medicine.

Picture Processing and Digital Filtering

Editor: *T. S. Huang*

2nd corrected and updated edition 1979.
113 figures, 7 tables. XIII, 297 pages
(Topics in Applied Physics, Volume 6)
ISBN 3-540-09339-7

Contents:
T. S. Huang: Introduction. – *H. C. Andrews:* Two-Dimensional Transforms. – *J. G. Fiasconaro:* Two-Dimensional Nonrecursive Filters. – *R. R. Read, J. L. Shanks, S. Treitel:* Two-Dimensional Recursive Filtering. – *B. R. Frieden:* Image Enhancement and Restoration. – *F. C. Billingsley:* Noise Considerations in Digital Image Processing Hardware. – *T. S. Huang:* Recent Advances in Picture Processing and Digital Filtering. – Subject Index.